Guns and Butter

CESifo Seminar Series
Edited by Hans-Werner Sinn

See ⟨http://mitpress.mit.edu⟩ for a complete list of titles in this series.

Guns and Butter

The Economic Causes and Consequences of Conflict

Edited by Gregory D. Hess

CESifo Seminar Series

The MIT Press
Cambridge, Massachusetts
London, England

For information about special quantity discounts, please email ⟨special_sales@mitpress.mit.edu⟩

This book was set in Palatino on 3B2 by Asco Typesetters, Hong Kong.
Printed and bound in the United States of America.

Library of Congress Cataloging-in-Publication Data

Guns and butter : the economic causes and consequences of conflict / edited by Gregory D. Hess.
     p.   cm.—(CESifo seminar series)
Includes bibliographical references and index.
ISBN 978-0-262-01281-2 (hbk. : alk. paper)
1. War—Economic aspects. I. Hess, Gregory D. II. CESifo.
HB195.G86   2009
303.6—dc22   2008041413

10 9 8 7 6 5 4 3 2 1

Contents

Series Foreword

This book is part of the CESifo Seminar Series. The series aims to cover topical policy issues in economics, largely from a European perspective. The books in this series are the products of the papers that were presented and the intensive debates that took place during the seminars hosted by CESifo, an international research network of renowned economists organized jointly by the Center for Economic Studies at Ludwig-Maximilians-Universität, Munich, and the Ifo Institute for Economic Research. All publications in this series have been carefully selected and refereed by members of the CESifo research network.

Contributors

S. Brock Blomberg Claremont McKenna College

Bruce Bueno de Mesquita New York University

Ethan Bueno de Mesquita University of Chicago

Steven J. Davis University of Chicago

Michelle R. Garfinkel University of California, Irvine

Edward L. Glaeser Harvard University

Gregory D. Hess Claremont McKenna College

Kai A. Konrad Social Science Research Center Berlin (WZB)

Kevin M. Murphy University of Chicago

B. Peter Rosendorff New York University

Stephen Sheppard Williams College

Stergios Skaperdas University of California, Irvine

Constantinos Syropoulos Drexel University

Robert H. Topel University of Chicago

Marijke Verpoorten Catholic University of Leuven

Guns and Butter

Introduction

Gregory D. Hess

I began my formal education at the age of five in a small school in California. The year was 1967. The president of the United States at that time was from Texas. There was a large, unpopular war going on that involved U.S. combat forces on foreign soil. Neither at that time or now was it clear whether we were involved in a civil war or a war that would fundamentally resolve historic forces that might pull the world in one direction or another.

Forty years later the world is, of course, much different. Or is it? I am no longer five years old, but I do teach at a small school in California. The United States has a president from Texas, and the results from the Iraq conflict have become, according to recent U.S. Senate and House election results and debates, a grave concern to voters. Moreover, long-suppressed intranational tensions have risen to the surface during Iraq's regime change. The result has been that national boundaries have not prevented the conflict from spilling out into neighboring states and across nonstate actors. Once more, the fundamental tug of good and evil has been widely discussed, although neither side in the conflict can agree on who is filling the roles of the "good guys" and the "bad guys." So, perhaps, the times have changed less than we like.

Thus, although every international and intranational conflict contributes to the historical record by supplying its own surprising, alarming, and even innovative details, a common set of elements prevails across such episodes. Some of these elements have escaped economists' notice for a period of time, even while political scientists have not ignored them. Accordingly, no book that investigates the causes and consequences of conflict would be complete without economists and political scientists jointly evaluating the phenomenon of conflict. It is in such a spirit that I helped to organize the CESifo conference Guns and Butter: The Economic Causes and Consequences of Conflict, held in Munich,

Germany, December 9 and 10, 2005. It goes without saying that I deeply appreciate the support of the CESifo Institute and Professor Hans Werner Sinn in making the conference and this book a reality. Indeed, Marko Koethenbuerger and Deirdre Hall were also exceptionally helpful at keeping me on task and on pitch.

This book looks at three main areas of the current work in the political economy of conflict. Part I contains several chapters that evaluate theoretical aspects of wars between nations and insecurity within nations. The chapters in Part II evaluate theoretical and empirical aspects of a type of conflict with which we are now all too familiar—terrorism. Part III comprises chapters that expand our empirical and theoretical understanding of the costs of two recent wars.

The political economy perspective is common to all these works. That is, incentives and constraints that individuals and collections of individuals face are paramount for understanding conflict decision making, even when that decision making from a 30,000-foot perspective seems to lead to a messy and largely unnecessary loss of welfare for all. In other words, as social scientists we must all come to grips with the fact that while we would all benefit if there were no war, individual and collective decision making always seems to lead us toward it—a clear prisoner's dilemma.

In addition to its functional structure, the book possesses a thematic structure based on some timeless principles that seem to underlie many historical episodes of conflict:

1. Conflict is an equilibrium phenomenon rather than an exogenous process.[1]

2. Interactions among politics, economics, and institutions affect the frequency and severity of conflicts.

3. Conflict is costly.

4. Conflict, though inevitable and inexorable, is also innovative.

Each of these tenets is reinforced and reaffirmed in the chapters in this volume.

Conflict Is an Equilibrium Phenomenon

The contributions by Bruce Bueno de Mesquita, "Paths to Peace and Prosperity" (chapter 1), Edward Glaeser, "The Political Economy of Warfare" (chapter 2), and Ethan Bueno de Mesquita, "The

Factionalization of Terror Groups" (chapter 6) demonstrate this key understanding.

Bruce Bueno de Mesquita highlights the fact that domestic politics shape foreign policy decision making and incentives via constraints and institutions. In particular, rather than taking a unidimensional, nationcentric view of conflict decision making that can differ across different regime types (e.g., democracies or nondemocracies), he delineates states with respect to two groups, the selectorate and the winning coalition. The selectorate are those who determine who participates in office holding and who stand to gain rents from a leader's being in office. The winning coalition, a subset of the selectorate, includes those whose support is necessary to keep the leader in office. Generally speaking, democracies have both large selectorates and winning coalitions, whereas nondemocracies tend to have small ones, although there is heterogeneity within each type of category.

As a clear example of the important implications of his approach to matching observed phenomena, Bueno de Mesquita points out that democracies are less likely to engage in risky conflicts because these reduce resources and hence jeopardize leaders' ability to maintain a winning coalition. By contrast, nondemocracies have small winning coalitions and selectorates, and hence privileging the elite status of their backers is more important than funding war efforts. Two fact patterns that this theory clearly matches—unlike any other formal theory that I am aware of—is that democracies don't often fight each other (it's too costly), they win a higher fraction of wars that they do fight (because they chose less risky ones), and losing wars leads to their leaders' ouster (again, because it is costly). By contrast, nondemocratic leaders are protected from foreign policy misadventures as long as they protect their small winning coalitions, so they lose wars more frequently and are more willing to engage in wars with democratic and nondemocratic governments alike (even though they are more likely to lose to democratic ones, given the observation that democracies choose less risky conflicts from their perspective). One cannot walk away from a careful reading of Bruce Bueno de Mesquita's work on conflict without fundamentally altering one's views on conflict as a theoretical or practical matter.

Glaeser's contribution provides an equally sweeping theoretical treatment of conflict with a large assortment of historical examples and compelling case studies to highlight his approach to understanding equilibrium conflict decision making. What appears to drive his effort is a desire to understand how conflict can be popular. An innovative aspect of this chapter is his investigation of how a domestic challenger's attitude toward war affects a domestic incumbent's war decision making. In particular, across a broad set of models, Glaeser helps us understand why incumbent leaders could be influenced to undertake foreign conflicts that they might not otherwise engage in if a domestic challenger prefers war. This scenario could occur if the incumbent is particularly unpopular and seeks to improve reelection chances by initiating conflict.

Ethan Bueno de Mesquita's study is described in the last section of this introduction.

Interactions among Politics, Economics, and Institutions Affect Conflict

The second main theme of the book is how economics and politics interact with one another more broadly to affect conflict. Several contributions speak directly to this: Michelle Garfinkel, Stergios Skaperdas, and Constantinos Syropoulos, "Globalization and Insecurity" (chapter 3), Kai Konrad, "Investing in Regimes with Stationary or Roving Bandits" (chapter 4), and Brock Blomberg and Peter Rosendorff, "A Gravity Model of Globalization, Democracy, and Transnational Terrorism" (chapter 5).

Blomberg and Rosendorff set forth an empirical treatment of the effects of globalization and governance (democratic versus nondemocratic) on the net supply of terrorism across countries. An important contribution here is that the authors examine the bilateral terrorism trade across pairs of countries in order to isolate amongst each pair who is the net importer or exporter of terrorism. A hopeful message (one of the few in the book) is that a more democratic world that increases trade and economic development will reduce the supply of terrorism from terrorism-producing nations. Unfortunately, as countries become richer, more open and democratic, they often become net targets of terrorism. These two forces work in opposite directions, but the authors point to reasons that policy attention should be turned toward the first one: increasing trade and economic development.

Garfinkel, Skaperdas, and Syropoulos provide a theoretical assessment of how a more open trade environment affects the likelihood of conflict within and between nations. Again, the authors point to opposing forces: a "realist" tradition sees trade as improving countries' economic welfare, which enables them to afford increased military strength; and a "classical liberal" tradition views open markets as driving better cross-cultural understanding, which makes countries less likely to engage in conflict. The authors also examine the effects of trade on countries with contested natural resources such as oil. Their key finding is that trade in a contested resource can make a country worse off because it crowds in guns to protect its rights, which can have an overall welfare-reducing effect. Since international organizations have yet to safeguard a country's resources, the competition for resources driven by globalization can lead to a rise in military spending to defend such resources. The resulting change in net welfare is then unclear: with regard to security, globalization can be both a blessing and a curse.

Finally, whereas the two prior works considered the effects of conflict and property security on trade in goods, the chapter by Kai Konrad considers the effects on trade in capital. This topic is timely because of nationalization and expropriation episodes in Eastern Europe and Latin America. With respect to the intricacies of the model, Konrad looks at a game where an individual investor in an environment of uncertain property rights must decide whether to undertake a foreign investment and then how to protect it from a "roving bandit" who has only one chance to expropriate it. Konrad compares and contrasts his results to those of papers in the literature that analyze a more dominant and ever-present "bandit" (e.g., the government). Key considerations that work to raise the importation of capital are higher-quality property rights and a lesser ability for the "bandit" to actually run the venture successfully should he expropriate it.

Conflict Is Costly

The third main theme of the book ties into the second theme by trying to establish the extent to which conflict is costly while further clarifying the cost of not fighting (or even maintaining the status quo). These topics are explored in three chapters: Stephen Sheppard, "Urban Structure in a Climate of Terror" (chapter 7), Steven Davis, Kevin Murphy and Robert Topel, "War in Iraq versus Containment" (chapter 8), and Marijke Verpoorten, "Using Household Data to Study the Economic Consequences of Violent Conflict: The Case of Rwanda" (chapter 9).

Davis, Murphy, and Topel's study is an intellectual and empirical *tour de force*. There is no denying that researchers who consider the likely cost of conflict do so against an unlikely benchmark, that is, the choice not to go to war is seldom peace. Clearly, when the United States and coalition partners agreed to invade Iraq in 2003, they did so against a backdrop that *not* to go into Iraq would also entail a great deal of expenditure. The alternative in most other studies on the cost of war, including my own (Hess 2003), is some presumed benevolent peace, with which war is to be contrasted. Simply put, Davis, Murphy, and Topel have done a great service to the profession and to public policy by detailing the reasonable expected costs of the war in Iraq versus the costs of not invading but trying to contain the Iraq regime. Even if one takes the unidimensional view that war and peace occupy opposite ends of a violence spectrum, containment falls somewhere in the middle. From a financial perspective as well, calculating the expected costs of containment is necessary.

Davis, Murphy, and Topel investigate three key issues. First, what would have been the detailed resources required to contain a hostile Iraqi government had the United States and coalition partners not intervened? Second, what were the detailed expected costs from the war in Iraq, including occupation, military fatality and injury costs, and other assistance and aid? Finally, what are the present values of these alternatives based on plausible scenarios? In addition, they also look at issues such as the cost of Iraqi lives lost and what if containment allowed for additional terrorist activity in the United States. Based on their calculations, the authors determine that the per-year cost for containment of Iraq would have been just under $18 billion. It turns out that keeping troops ready to fight is almost as expensive as having them fight. Of course, the regime could fall on its own, so there would always be some hope of regime change with containment, if only because of succession or other forms of infighting by the regime.

By contrast, the expected cost of the war in Iraq (based on what was known in 2003) depends on a myriad of factors, including the mix of ground versus air operations emphasized in the conflict, and pessimism or optimism about defeating the Iraqi forces. Further, the number of fatalities and the duration and intensity of the conflict could vary, which would clearly change the expected costs of the conflict. In painstaking detail, the authors outline seven scenarios that attempt to capture the reasonable variation of opinion that could have existed on the possible ways the war could have evolved.

Reconciling these two sets of alternatives, the authors gauge that the expected costs of the war in Iraq, viewed in an *ex ante* sense, ranged between $100 billion and $850 billion. By contrast, the present value costs of containment (including costs for containing the Iraqi regime until it ultimately fell) would have been expected to be in the $400 billion to $600 billion range. Thus, the choice of the better strategy—to contain or to go to war—is unclear *ex ante* because one does not dominate the other. What we can say is that whereas war is costly, "peace" is not cheap either, and it may not even be all that peaceful.

Sheppard's chapter is a major contribution for analyzing how demography is changed by a particular type of conflict—terrorism. The author provides theoretical and empirical work outlining the change in the urban footprint for cities around the world in response to identified patterns of terrorism. In particular, one could expect that patterns of urban development would evolve in response to physical threats, with terrorism being one type. From a historical standpoint, imagine how the architecture of a moat around a castle evolved in response to changes in threat levels. Interestingly, Sheppard finds that a doubling of terrorism incidents has a statistically and economically significant effect in reducing the development of larger cities. Development is under way in many countries that experience terrorist incidents, so this finding indicates that research on such issues would be relevant.

Whereas the previous two chapters evaluate the aggregate and urban costs of conflict, Verpoorten's study evaluates the costs of conflict from a microeconomic household standpoint. She administers best practices in the field of modern development economics in her analysis of the economic response of Rwandan households to the genocide that took place along Tutsi and Hutu fault lines in 1994.

Based on interviews, the author assembled a microdata set to evaluate how and to what extent Rwandan households offset the deleterious income shock associated with the genocide. Because Rwanda has underdeveloped financial markets, real assets such as livestock are often the best stores of wealth. Accordingly, during the genocide, livestock were a prime means for smoothing consumption over time to the extent possible. The results indicate that the material impact of the genocide was devastating in the short run. Given the disruption, the livestock market did not turn out to be a useful device to stabilize or smooth consumption. Food shortages and the general economic anarchy made the usefulness of a food supply an asset of limited though nonzero benefit. Verpoorten also uses data from a follow-up 2002 survey demonstrating that, except for imprisonment, the long-run material impact of the genocide on surviving households was not significant.

It is important to note that the work described in these chapters complements many of the new approaches to understanding the costs of conflict. By and large, these new approaches review an individual country or region in a case study and use exogenous identifying information to pinpoint how the economic effects of conflict can be quantified. These modern case studies are important for appreciating more broadly the results contained in these chapters.

For example, Davis and Weinstein (2002) evaluate how relative city size in Japan responded to bombings during World War II. Follow-up work was undertaken by Miguel and Roland (2005) for the Vietnam War. Both sets of results indicate that the costs of these types of conflicts are mostly short-run. Second, Abadie and Gardeazabal (2003) evaluate the costs of the terrorism outbreak in Basque country. Using a synthetic of regions and the short truce in the late 1990s, they estimate that the terrorism outbreak was associated with a ten percentage point drop in gross domestic product (GDP). They also investigate financial market activity and find that favorable financial market responses are associated with peace and unfavorable ones with conflict resumption. Finally, Bellows and Miguel (2006) evaluate data on institutions in Sierra Leone and find some evidence that regions in Sierra Leone that faced more violence had greater political activity and mobilization after the war.

Overall, the modern case study approach complements the cross-country (Blomberg and Rosendorff), detailed cost accounting (Davis, Murphy, and Topel), urban footprint (Sheppard), and household-level (Verpoorten) studies of the costs of conflict presented in this book. One may wonder, however, to what extent these individual case studies can be generalized, and how important are the identifying assumptions that underlie these modern case studies. Nevertheless, the chapters in this book, as well as the broader literature, point to a very large cost from conflict that society simply cannot ignore.

Conflict Is Innovative

The final theme explored in this book, namely, the innovative character of conflict, is addressed in Ethan Bueno de Mesquita, "The Factionalization of Terror Groups" (chapter 6). The author makes a novel and important contribution toward helping us understand the evolving industrial organization of terrorist groups. What is so intriguing from an academic perspective, but so worrying and disturbing from a policy perspective, is how terrorist organizations bloom and subdivide, exit and enter, agglomerate and splinter, even within a periodic episode of terrorism. The chapter examines the theoretical aspects of this fundamental policy issue. Using a spatial model in which potential splinter groups are motivated by the desire to gain adherents, Bueno de Mesquita analyzes the equilibrium behavior of what drives terrorist groups to splinter (or not), and why individuals would choose to join a terrorist group or a splinter group, or not join at all. He also traces the effect of stronger economic activity on the equilibrium reorganization of terrorist groups. This vein of research is likely to be especially fruitful because understanding the equilibrium behavior of terrorism and its organization is likely to be a defining question in the coming decades.

In sum, the chapters in this collection highlight consistent and timeless themes for understanding conflict: it is costly; its frequency depends on institutions, constraints, and economic opportunities such as level of development and opportunities for trade; and economics and conflict are interlinked. The contributors also point to additional avenues for research: a better understanding of how domestic political institutions affect foreign policy decisions; a clearer picture of the costs of conflict (as well as the true cost of not going to war) from the government, household, and urban development standpoints; the interactive effects of globalization and broader trade in goods and capital on conflict; and finally, an improved appreciation of the evolving organization of terrorist groups and the innovative character of conflict that makes it ever-morphing and potentially everlasting.

I am certain these questions will linger with readers for quite some time.

Note

1. In my own work with Athanasios Orphanides (1995; 2001), we consider such issues in trying to understand individual leader decision making and its effects on the equilibrium behavior of nations and on the general equilibrium behavior across nations.

References

Abadie, A., and J. Gardeazabal. 2003. The economic costs of conflict: A case study of the Basque country. *American Economic Review* 93: 113–132.

Bellows, J., and E. Miguel. 2006. War and institutions: New evidence from Sierra Leone. *American Economic Review* 96: 394–399.

Davis, D. R., and D. E. Weinstein. 2002. Bones, bombs and break points: The geography of economic activity. *American Economic Review* 92: 1269–1289.

Hess, G. D. 2003. The economic welfare cost of conflict: An empirical assessment. CESifo Working Paper 852. Munich: CESifo Group.

Hess, G. D., and A. Orphanides. 1995. War politics: An economic, rational voter framework. *American Economic Review* 85: 828–846.

———. 2001. War and democracy. *Journal of Political Economy* 109: 776–810.

Miguel, E., and G. Roland. 2005. The long-run impact of bombing Vietnam. ⟨http://www.econ.berkeley.edu/~groland/⟩.

I   Theories of Wars between Nations and Insecurity

1   Paths to Peace and Prosperity

Bruce Bueno de Mesquita

"The causes of conflict" is a daunting subject because we know so little and an urgent one because violent conflict has such deadly consequences. To understand conflict we must consider what motivates disputes and what expectations conflicting parties have about the expected outcome of their actions. In the end, whether guns are employed to resolve differences depends on whether those making war and peace choices believe that threatening, actually fighting, negotiating, or living with the status quo is likely to lead to the best feasible outcome. Therefore, this chapter is about both the expected results of conflict and how those results relate to decisions to participate in war.

In discussing these topics I take as my charge to reflect on what we know, how we might improve our knowledge, and what we think we know that is probably false. The latter, unfortunately, encompasses the inferences of a substantial proportion of research on international conflict. For instance, much of the literature on war initiation and participation begins without consideration of the "backward induction" from anticipated outcomes to choices over actions, thereby treating conflict-related decisions as if they were not purposeful.[1] I begin with a brief summary of a few useful background facts about war and peace intended to set aside some common misconceptions and then suggest why past ways of thinking about these issues are less likely to be informative than is the more recent political economy perspective.

Some Stylized Views of War's Causes

The question, Are rich or poor people more likely to wage war? is a useful place to begin, given current thinking in the academic and the policymaking communities. Dividing the countries of the world up annually from 1960 to 2001 according to the per capita income quartile to

Table 1.1
Income Effects on the Risk of War, 1960–2001

	Countries of the World, Income Quartile (by year)			
	Lowest	Second-Lowest	Second-Highest	Highest
No. of nonviolent engagements	1,312 (90%)	1,295 (87%)	1,396 (94%)	1,356 (91%)
No. of violent engagements	153 (10%)	192 (13%)	83 (6%)	134 (9%)

Note: Data calculations are from Bueno de Mesquita et al. (2003).

which they belong provides one quick way to evaluate whether rich or poor countries are more likely to find themselves at war. Table 1.1 reveals that about 10 percent of the lowest income quartile of countries engaged in violent disputes with other states. The comparable percentage in the next lowest quartile is 13 percent, and on average for each of the two upper quartiles, about 7 percent. So, although the difference is not very large, there is some indication that peace tends to accompany prosperity and that the misery of war is added to the burden of people who live in poverty. Of course, whether poverty causes war, or war causes poverty, is a separate and perhaps more interesting question that is beyond my scope here.

In recent years it has become fashionable to argue that certain religious groups are conflict-prone or that violent interactions follow what Huntington (1993) has called clashes of civilizations. Yet the evidence does not support these views. Careful analysis indicates that clashes of civilizations turn out not to be statistically more common today than they were before the end of the cold war (Russett, Oneal, and Cox 2000; Henderson and Tucker 2001; Chiozza 2002). Additionally, as shown in figure 1.1, although Muslim countries have enjoyed less peace than countries dominated by other religions in the last couple of decades, over a longer span of history there has been no difference in war-proneness as a function of whether a country was primarily Roman Catholic, Protestant, or Muslim, the religious groups for which data are readily available.

Similarly, as shown in table 1.2, regime type alone provides little predictive power. Military juntas are most likely to engage in war; monarchies are least likely; democracies and autocracies fall in between. Yet, an important discovery of the past few decades is that pairs of democracies are substantially less likely to wage war—although not

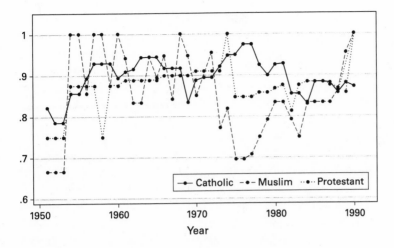

Figure 1.1
Probability of peace, by religion, 1950–1990.
Note: Figures based on author's calculations.

Table 1.2
War and Government Type, 1960–2001

	Countries of the World			
	Autocracy	Monarchy	Junta	Democracy
No. of nonviolent engagements	1,935 (88%)	239 (93%)	171 (83%)	1,898 (90%)
No. of violent engagements	267 (12%)	17 (7%)	34 (17%)	221 (10%)

Note: Data calculations are from Bueno de Mesquita et al. (2003).

less likely to engage in lesser conflicts—with each other than are other pairings of regime types. Later I explore this observation, known as the democratic peace, to illustrate how a political economy perspective differs from standard accounts of international conflict.

Some Fundamentals about Conflict

The English language has no word to refer to inter*nation*al conflict—and this is true of other languages as well—without invoking the *nation*. Indeed, for as long as war and peace have been subjects of investigation—and this takes us back at least to biblical times—the focus of research and philosophical speculation has been on what makes nations choose conflict over negotiating a resolution of their differences. I believe that this linguistic limitation—this compulsion to think in terms of nations or states—reflects a mistaken central focus in conflict research. The state is the wrong unit of analysis; states, after all, do not make war, people do. To begin a discussion of this critical issue, let me explore what we know, or think we know, about international conflict and especially issues of war and peace.

We can think of war from the perspective of states in two analytic contexts. We can examine the initiation, escalation, and termination of disputes from the perspective of the war-of-attrition model or from the viewpoint of models that see war and peace as choices over risky lotteries. In a war of attrition, the good in dispute often is indivisible, as in combat over mates in evolutionary biology. In these winner-take-all contests, one party either quits at the outset before fighting commences, or the combatants face a problem akin to an ascending price auction. When do you stop bidding if each bid incurs a sunk cost? The answer, of course, is to bid as long as the expected benefit is at least equal to the marginal expected cost. Naturally, this can lead to a war that persists until one or the other side completely depletes its resources.

In lottery models the parties face a probability of victory and of defeat, and their beliefs about those probabilities presumably change endogenously as a function of what they learn on the battlefield (Gartner 1997; Wagner 2000; Powell 2004). Suppose that state A's probability of winning a war is known to be p before fighting begins, and B's probability of victory is therefore known to be $1 - p$.[2] War costs are anticipated to equal k for each side, and A's and B's dispute is over X, with the winner getting all of X. A's utility is increasing in the proportion of X it gets if there is a negotiation, and B's utility is decreasing in the quantity of X that A gets. For computational ease, I normalize the value of X to fall between 0 and 1. A's utility for victory in war, then, is $p - k$, and B's is $1 - p - k$.

What if a prewar settlement is proposed that divides X between A and B such that A's value for the proposed settlement is x, that is, a fraction of X, and B's value for the proposed settlement is $1 - x$. Then, as shown in figure 1.2, a range of acceptable settlements exists to avoid war while satisfying both A's and B's expectations. With complete and perfect information—a very demanding condition—A accepts offers made such that $x > p - k$, and B accepts offers if $x < p + k$.

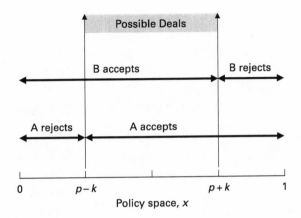

Figure 1.2
Bargaining, war, and *ex post* inefficiency.

Although the opportunity for a bargaining agreement exists, we know that many such situations become wars. This seems puzzling, much as labor strikes or lockouts or many lawsuits seem puzzling. From the perspective of the welfare of a nation-state, by which I mean the welfare of the majority of the citizenry, war is always *ex post* inefficient. That is, knowing how a war turned out, there must have existed an *ex ante*, Pareto-improving outcome, an outcome that at least could have avoided the transaction costs associated with conducting and concluding the war. As Fearon (1995) has shown, war, looked at from the perspective of states, can only arise rationally under three conditions: an asymmetry of information, a commitment problem, or a dispute over an indivisible good. These conditions may be triggered by asymmetric beliefs arising out of, for example, divisions between the rich (who may believe others share their value for efficiency) and the poor (who may believe that others share their value for equity); by commitment issues created by inherent disparities in the incentives created by different types of regimes; or by indivisible clashes between the fundamental value systems of contending civilizations. These specific potential sources of conflict, however, barely scratch the surface of possible sources of uncertainty, lack of trust, or indivisibility. Perhaps that is why these potential causes seem inadequate to account for variation in prospects of war or peace.

An asymmetry of information, of course, can mean that one or both parties miscalculate the bargaining range, and so offers are made that result in war rather than agreement. Commitment problems arise when one or the other party cannot trust the rival's statements because the rival has incentives to bluff and to renege. As Admiral Yamamoto, the architect of the attack on Pearl Harbor, was fond of observing "an efficient hawk hides his claws" (Prange 1981, 13). And indivisibility means that the contest is necessarily a winner-take-all affair so that there is no room for compromise.

The insight that war arises between states because at least one of these three conditions is in place is an important advance in knowledge. It contrasts sharply with more venerable and particularistic views, such as that a balance of power (Morgenthau 1978; Waltz 1979; Gulick 1955) or a severe imbalance of power (Organski 1958) promotes peace and stability. Yet it imposes an implicit assumption that we know to be problematic. Implicit in the claim that war is always *ex post* inefficient is the idea that the welfare of the citizenry—generally referred to as the national interest—is the same as (or at least highly correlated with) the well-being of those making war and peace choices. That is not to say that war is ever *ex post* efficient or that the factors Fearon points to are not critical, but rather to suggest that the source of uncertainty or of commitment problems may be remote from decisions about war and peace when those choices are not correlated with the national interest (Chiozza and Goemans 2004).

Why Challenge the Statecentric Perspective?

I argue throughout that a political economy perspective provides deeper insights into war and peace choices than do the standard statecentric accounts that dominate research in international affairs. Before setting out the case for the political economy perspective, however, I should briefly highlight the reasons that prompt me to seek an alternative explanation of guns and butter to the received wisdom of the field.

The standard account, so-called realism or neorealism, is dominated by the idea that uncertainty about the distribution of power and the reliability of commitments between states shapes international politics (Waltz 1979; Niou, Ordeshook, and Rose 1989). For realists, the primary subject matter concerns the balance of power and efforts by states to maximize their security as they pursue the national interest. For those who share a political economy approach, however, the central concern is with how domestic conditions help give rise to international policies so that the primary subject matter is the impact of interstate relations on the welfare of political leaders and on the welfare of the constituents whose support maintains them in office.

A common and venerable statecentric idea holds that a balance of power promotes peace and an imbalance war (Thucydides 1959; Morgenthau 1978; Waltz 1979; Elman and Elman 1997). Ideas about the balance of power and conflict permeate the thinking of influential statesmen and continue to occupy a central place in research and teaching about international conflict. Given their long and distinguished pedigree, we should not dismiss balance-of-power hypotheses lightly. Yet it now seems evident that neither careful theoretical nor rigorous empirical analysis supports a monotonic, clear, or even straightforward relationship between the distribution of power and the likelihood, intensity, or settlement of international disputes.

Kim and Morrow (1992) and Powell (1996; 1999), for instance, demonstrate that neither power balance nor power preponderance between rivals is necessary or sufficient for war and may not even probabilistically influence its likelihood. Kim and Morrow also provide extensive statistical tests that support their formally derived hypotheses and contradict balance-of-power notions. And Wittman (1979) shows that because the price at which rivals will settle a dispute changes as battlefield performance changes, establishing a military power advantage does not necessarily facilitate conflict resolution as long as demands depend endogenously on expectations regarding the probability of victory (or defeat). As the prospects of victory improve, the conditions under which the prospective victor will settle escalate to meet updated expectations and may overshoot the mark.

Indeed, as Downs and Rocke (1995) highlight, it is possible that a high probability of defeat may embolden individual leaders to take risks in war that would be unwarranted by a statecentric, balance-of-power, national-interest motivated perspective. They do so to resurrect themselves, not their state. Examples include the successful North Vietnamese Tet offensive, the unsuccessful Nazi effort in the Battle of the Bulge, or Saddam Hussein's fostering of uncertainty about whether he had weapons of mass destruction. Bueno de Mesquita and Lalman (1992), taking the Downs and Rocke resurrection hypothesis a bit further, identify and test empirically conditions under which unusually weak states, or weak actors like terrorist groups, are particularly likely to rationally initiate violence against stronger adversaries, seemingly in

contradiction of standard balance-of-power tenets. These and other political economy findings stand in contrast to realism's view that what
happens within states is irrelevant for understanding what happens
between states. These findings call for a fresh examination of international conflict from a microlevel, within-state perspective.

A Political Economy View of Conflict

War, viewed from the perspective of states is, as we have established,
always *ex post* inefficient. This, however, does not mean that war cannot or does not serve the interests of leaders. The sources of uncertainty or of commitment problems that contribute to international
disputes and to inefficiency may reside in a disconnection between the
interests of leaders and those in whose name they lead. We have only
to consider Margaret Thatcher's poor prospects of reelection as Britain's prime minister before she fought the Falklands/Malvinas War,
resulting in a successful military effort to defend British claims to that
territory. Her popularity soared following the war, a factor that may
well have been instrumental in her reelection in 1983. We can only
speculate on what the electoral consequences would have been for
Thatcher had she bought off Argentina's generals and the Falkland
shepherds rather than fighting to defend Britain's territorial claims.
Buying concessions would surely have been economically more efficient than fighting but probably would have been politically disastrous
for Thatcher.

If attention is turned to national political leaders rather than to
states, it is apparent that fundamental policy choices—even war and
peace choices—may be made without regard for citizen welfare or the
national interest. One has only to reflect on Myanmar's ruling junta,
North Korea's Kim Jong-il, or Zaire's late Mobutu Sese Seko to recog-
nize that many leaders govern for their own benefit at the cost of the
welfare of their subjects. So many nations have been beggared by their
leaders that it is difficult to see how one can maintain the fiction that
the national interest dictates even the most important foreign policy
choices.

From a political economy perspective (and in fact), leaders, not
states, make policy choices, including those concerned with the initiation, escalation, and termination of conflict. As a number of models
have shown, unencumbered leaders are predators; they engage in
kleptocracy and rent seeking rather than national welfare maximiza-

tion (Wintrobe 1990; McGuire and Olson 1996; Acemoglu and Robinson 2001; Bueno de Mesquita et al. 2003). To flesh out how these perspectives inform conflict studies and the sources of inefficiency, let me briefly elaborate on a leader-based theory of politics and conflict.

The Selectorate Perspective

The selectorate theory on which I rely assumes that leaders are instrumentally interested first in attaining and sustaining themselves in offices that confer political power (Bueno de Mesquita et al. 2003). Conditional on ensuring their political survival, leaders are then interested in some mix of personal wealth maximization and opportunities to exercise policy discretion. I leave as a matter of taste the extent to which a given leader, having ensured her or his political survival and therefore access to the resources of the state, chooses to allocate discretionary resources to the pursuit of policy goals or to a secret bank account. Either use of discretionary resources, however, is constrained so as not to jeopardize the incumbent's future hold on power.

All states can be mapped onto a two-dimensional institutional space. One dimension, the size of the selectorate (S), indicates the number of people with the prospect of entering a winning coalition and gaining access to government-provided private goods. The second dimension, the winning coalition (W), is a subset of the selectorate and reflects the number of people whose support is essential to keep an incumbent in office. While, by definition, everyone in a given society reaps the benefits of public-goods-producing policies like national security, members of the winning coalition also receive private benefits from the government. These private rewards may come in the form of preferential tax policy, preferential access to patronage or government contracts, opportunities to extort money from noncoalition members, or a host of other rent-seeking, black-market-exploiting, corruption-reinforcing opportunities, including the opportunity to extract tribute or to steal valuable goods from conquered territories.

By thinking of polities in this two-dimensional space we can escape the necessity of drawing arbitrary boundaries between governmental categories. Although, as shown in figure 1.3, all countries generally referred to as democracies tend to have large selectorates (as a proportion of total population) and large winning coalitions, there is substantial variation among them. Switzerland restricted its selectorate to exclude adult women long after other "democracies" expanded

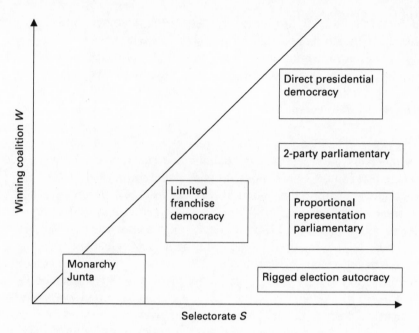

Figure 1.3
Winning coalition, selectorate, and government type.

their franchise. Britain's electoral rules allow a prime minister to lead with support from as little as 25 percent of the voters.[3] Some proportional representation systems require much less, and directly elected presidents need a simple majority in a two-candidate race. The U.S. Electoral College effectively reduces the required coalition size to something under 25 percent of the voters.

Similarly, there is great variation from junta to junta, monarchy to monarchy, and rigged-election autocracy to rigged-election autocracy. Juntas typically require a small winning coalition—a few handfuls of generals and bureaucrats—drawn from a small pool of officers and civil servants. They share with democracies that the coalition is a relatively large proportion of the selectorate, but they differ from democracies in that both institutions—the selectorate and the winning coalition—are small. Rigged-election autocracies share with juntas and monarchies a very small winning coalition, but they share with democracies a large selectorate.

Coalition size affects the relative focus of public policy. Large coalition systems encourage efficient public policy; small coalition systems promote cronyism, corruption, and graft. These differences are not engendered by different motivations. Leaders in all forms of political system seek the same thing, survival in office. Political institutions determine which types of policy allocations best allow leaders to fulfill this goal.

The types of policies induced by political institutions affect the ease with which leaders fulfill their survival objectives. In large coalition systems political survival is relatively difficult. Because most of the policy rewards are in the form of public goods, which benefit selectors whether or not they are in the winning coalition, supporters jeopardize only the small private portion of the rewards they receive if they defect from the incumbent. In contrast, in small coalition systems the private goods focus engenders a loyalty norm. When a new leader attains office, he requires the support of a winning coalition of size W drawn from S potential supporters. When W is small (and particularly when S is large), each supporter has only a relatively low probability of being included in the new coalition. Since in small W systems private goods provisions are valuable and the prospects of obtaining them under alternative leadership are relatively low (W/S), supporters in small coalition systems tend to be loyal.

Bueno de Mesquita et al. (2003) have shown that the ratio of the winning coalition to the selectorate is inversely related to the degree of loyalty given to incumbents by coalition members. The larger the ratio, the less loyalty is induced. The reason is straightforward and is pertinent to understanding how the incentives of leaders and of citizens may diverge when it comes to foreign (and domestic) policy, including choices about war participation, war outcomes, and the pursuit of peace.

It follows from the selectorate perspective that (speaking colloquially) democrats must produce effective public policies, have little discretion to wander from the interests of the voters, and are highly vulnerable to being replaced by a political rival. Autocrats produce corrupt, rent-seeking, crony-based societies; perform relatively poorly in producing effective public policies; have ample discretionary opportunities to steal or to use society as policy guinea pigs, including sometimes having good ideas that lead to economic growth while insulating them from the risk of political reform; and yet keep their jobs for a long time. As several teams of researchers have concluded, bad public policy is often good politics.

Domestic Incentives and Foreign Policy

That bad public policy is often good politics carries over in significant ways to choices that influence the risks and costs of international conflict. Inclusive, democratic leaders find it incentive-compatible to be cautious about launching policies that present a high risk of leading to their deposition. Of course, term limits may free them near the end of their tenure to behave poorly, but most of the time they must be mindful of the domestic reselection consequences of their policy choices. As Schultz (2001) has shown, the existence of an electorally motivated, legitimate opposition disciplines incumbents in democratic regimes to reject foreign policies that garner strong resistance from their political rivals. Democratic opponents resist policies when they believe there is an electoral advantage to doing so, that is, when they believe the policy will fail. Incumbents, observing or anticipating such opposition, modify the policy to avoid negative electoral consequences. Indeed, this disciplining of democratic incumbents to be cautious about foreign policies that are opposed by their rivals may well be why we so often observe nonpartisan declarations in support of major foreign policies *ex ante* but often see deep political rifts emerge *ex post* when, as sometimes happens, the chosen policy fails. This may well be exactly the pattern Americans experienced during the Vietnam War and are experiencing today regarding the war against Iraq.

These considerations within the framework of survival-oriented leaders give rise to implications about conflict participation, resolution, and outcomes that do not follow from theories of international affairs that treat states as unitary actors (Milner 1998; Powell 1994). In the discussion that follows, I highlight several of the more important such implications, especially with regard to the so-called democratic peace and with regard to foreign policy efforts at nation building.

The Democratic Peace: A Strategic Perspective

State-centric theories, like realism or liberalism, lack an explanation of the generally accepted observation that democracies tend not to fight wars with one another even though they are not especially reluctant to fight with autocratic regimes (Babst 1964; Rummel 1983; Maoz and Abdolali 1989; Russett 1993). Yet this particular apparent empirical regularity is one of the few discoveries regarding war and peace that is sufficiently widely endorsed to be considered by many as a law of international politics (Levy 1988). What is more, it is a discovery that has influenced and continues to influence the foreign policy agenda of the United States and other democratic polities at least since the presidency of Bill Clinton.

The political economy perspective provides an explanation of the democratic peace and associated empirical regularities while also cautioning against leaping too easily to the inference that since pairs of democracies tend to interact peacefully, therefore democracies have strong incentives to promote democratic reform around the world.

Democratic leaders cannot afford to pursue overly risky foreign policies because they are judged primarily in terms of how good a job they do in providing public benefits, including foreign policy benefits. Defeat in war is always costly for society and therefore for broadly accountable democratic leaders (Werner 1996; Schultz 1998; 2001; Chiozza and Goemans 2003; 2004). That is exactly one of the senses in which war is understood to be *ex post* inefficient both for leaders and democratic incumbents (Fearon 1994; 1995). Given the political costs of defeat, democrats are only prepared to become involved in wars when they believe at the outset that their chance of victory is high or when all efforts at negotiation fail (as in the period 1938–1939) (Powell 1996; 1999; Reiter and Stam 1998; 2002; Bueno de Mesquita et al. 1999; 2004).

Autocrats, by contrast, are judged on their ability to deliver private benefits to their backers. Defeat in war is often less costly politically for autocrats than it is for democrats (Chiozza and Goemans 2003; 2004). For autocrats, winning a war by spending on the war effort money that they could have used to bribe cronies jeopardizes their hold on power because their supporters have no reason to remain loyal if they are deprived of their private rewards. Autocrats, even militarily defeated autocrats, are more likely to be deposed (and executed) by disgruntled domestic backers than by an outside, victorious power. As a result, autocrats do not try nearly as hard as democrats do to win wars or to find negotiated settlements of their disputes (Dixon 1994). To the contrary, to survive in office autocrats need to be sure that they can pay their essential supporters enough so that they do not defect. For democrats, saving money to bribe backers is not nearly as politically beneficial as spending money to ensure policy success, including victory in war (Bueno de Mesquita et al. 2003).

Because democrats are selective about the circumstances under which they are prepared to fight, they almost always win the wars they initiate. In fact, democracies have won about 93 percent of the wars they initiated over the past two centuries, whereas autocrats have won only about 60 percent of the time (Reiter and Stam 2002). Allowing for the small advantage gained by striking first, autocrats basically have even odds of winning when they start a war, whereas for democrats victory is practically certain. But if two democrats are at loggerheads, then war is unlikely. Each democratic leader has similar institutionally induced incentives, including an incentive to try hard if war ensues. Each must provide policy success in order to be retained by his or her constituents. Each must believe *ex ante* that the probability of winning the war is a near certainty. The likelihood is practically naught that leaders of two rival democracies each believe at the same time about the same dispute that their prospects of victory are nearly certain. When democrats do not feel nearly certain of victory, they opt for negotiations over fighting. This way, they cut their losses and reduce the risk of deposition (Morrow 1991; Nincic 1997). Thus, the leaders of two democracies are unlikely to find that the circumstances are right for them to gamble on war rather than negotiate (Downs and Rocke 1995; Dixon 1994). Autocrats do not face the same constraints. They do not try especially hard to win most of their wars; they are prepared to fight even when the chances of victory are not exceptionally good; and they are more likely to be overthrown if they spend on the war the resources they need to bribe their cronies than if they lose the war (Bueno de Mesquita et al. 1999; 2004; Chiozza and Goemans 2004).

Exceptions to these conditions arise theoretically and empirically when at the outset an autocrat thinks that defeat means being deposed by the victor. For reasons explained later, this exception is unlikely to arise in a war with another autocracy but is likely when the rival governs a democracy. To summarize, a focus on leadership survival from a political economy perspective explains why we observe democracies fighting with autocracies; autocracies fighting with one another; democracies not fighting with each other; democracies winning most of the wars in which they engage; and democracies showing greater eagerness than autocracies to resolve disputes through negotiations.

In the political economy account of the so-called democratic peace democratic leaders are not more civic-minded (Niskanen 1997); their actions are not shaped by superior social norms or values (Maoz and Russett 1993); and they are not inherently better at fighting wars than other types of political leaders. This approach allows us to explain not only the apparently peaceful behavior of democracies but also such less attractive characteristics as the preparedness of democracies to engage in wars of colonial or imperial expansion and even the willingness of a powerful democracy to force a much weaker democracy to capitulate to its demands rather than pay the price of fighting back (Bueno de Mesquita et al. 2004).

Furthermore, conditional on having decided to fight, democrats pursue a rather different pattern of combat than do autocrats if they discover that, contrary to their initial expectation, victory does not come easily. Democrats are more likely to shift resources into the war effort because winning is crucial for their political survival; for autocrats, winning is nice but not essential. Except when they fight policy-oriented democrats, autocrats are infrequently deposed following military defeat. They are able to cut deals with tribute-seeking or resource-seeking autocratic victors that allow them to stay in office. Thus, both the decision to participate in war and the decision how to conduct the war differs markedly across the institutionally induced incentive structures of national leaders (Bueno de Mesquita et al. 2004).

Nation Building and Democratization

Looking beyond the democratic peace to other differences in foreign policy conduct that depend on the internal institutional arrangements of states reveals still other regularities that are overlooked when treating states, rather than leaders, as the central players in international affairs. For instance, we know that the timing of wars by democratic leaders is strongly influenced by the election cycle and electoral rules (Gaubatz 1999; Fordham 1998; Smith 2004), and we believe that democratic leaders are more constrained than autocrats are to carry out the threats they make because of domestic audience costs (Fearon 1994). Further, leader-oriented models suggest that even the impetus for nation building that so many associate with democratic polities can be and often is thwarted by democratic forms of governance.

Political economy models have shown that democracies are prepared to overthrow foreign rivals and restrict democratic political reform more often than are nondemocratic interveners. This is a perhaps surprising but an empirically well-supported claim. Specifically, democracies are particularly unlikely to foster meaningful democratic reform in countries they target for military intervention (Bueno de Mesquita and Downs 2005), and they help stifle the domestic impetus for democratic reform when they provide foreign economic assistance (Bueno de Mesquita and Smith 2006). They fight or assist economically to gain policy advantages and so need compliant regimes in conquered or assisted territories, regimes that will fill policy wants of the victor's domestic constituents even when doing so harms the welfare of most citizens in the vanquished state. One can get such compliance from nondemocratic leaders of small coalitions because they can trade policy for money, with that money often taking the form of foreign aid. Indeed, this pattern of aid or intervention for policy compliance has been robust across all bilateral aid relations since 1960 and across all military interventions since the end of World War II. The patterns do not differ whether one considers all OECD aid donors or just U.S. assistance, and whether one contrasts all democratic interveners to other types or separates the effects of the United States (Bueno de Mesquita and Smith 2006).

Each of these studies shares a conviction that policy decisions are strategic, taking into account expected responses by both foreign and domestic adversaries and supporters, and are designed to maximize the leader's (not the state's) welfare. Each leads to conclusions that cannot be true according to theories of international politics that treat states as undifferentiated unitary actors. As such they suggest both critical breaks from prior theorizing and critical tests to help sort out the reliability of competing perspectives.

Conclusion

By explicitly treating leaders rather than states as the relevant unit of analysis in studies of virtually every aspect of international politics, the political economy view argues that relations among nations are a product of the normal pulls and tugs of domestic affairs, taking into account the political, social, and economic constraints under which different leaders in different settings must operate. Strategic political economy models assess foreign policy guns or butter choices as equilibrium behavior induced in part by domestic institutional structures, in part by endowments like human capital and natural resources, and in part by how the exercise of leader discretion influences political survival prospects. These models see the choice of foreign policy interactions as incentive-compatible with the motivations of national leaders to maintain their personal hold on political power. Thus, stability is brought to interactions by the expectation that every decision maker chooses what he or she believes is the best available option given internal and external constraints, with options being evaluated in terms of how much they enhance or how little they diminish the decision maker's—not the state's—welfare. This perspective leads to predictions that are borne out by the evidence and yet cannot be true if a statecentric perspective is taken.

Political economy models have helped sort out the microfoundations of important choices in international affairs. They reinforce some venerable views and contradict others. It seems, therefore, that those who want to understand and advance knowledge about the political economy of conflict, about how guns and butter shape conflict resolution, should avoid falling into the trap of anthropomorphizing the state. Instead, researchers should look at the institutions, endowments, and ease with which citizens opposed to government policies can coordinate so as to understand how domestic conditions shape the incentives of political leaders to pursue guns or butter.

Notes

1. For an early and unfortunately too often overlooked exception, see Starr (1972).

2. I exclude for convenience the possibility of a draw.

3. The prime minister requires support from at least half the members of parliament to rule, and each member requires a simple majority in a two-party race (and less in a three- or more-party race), so the prime minister needs $\frac{1}{2} \times$ no. of MPs, and MPs need $\frac{1}{2} \times$ no. of voters in their district. The U.S. presidential electoral rules can result in a president's being elected with about 20 percent of total votes if the votes are gained efficiently.

References

Acemoglu, D., and J. Robinson. 2001. Inefficient redistribution. *American Political Science Review* 95: 645–661.

Babst, D. V. 1964. Elective government: A force for peace. *Wisconsin Sociologist* 3 (1): 9–14.

Bueno de Mesquita, B., and G. W. Downs. 2005. Strategic coordination, public goods, and political survival. Working Paper. Department of Politics, New York University.

———. 2006. Intervention and democracy. *International Organization* 60 (3): 627–649.

Bueno de Mesquita, B., and D. Lalman. 1992. *War and Reason: Domestic and International Imperatives.* New Haven, Conn.: Yale University Press.

Bueno de Mesquita, B., J. D. Morrow, R. M. Siverson, and A. Smith. 1999. An institutional explanation of the democratic peace. *American Political Science Review* 93 (4): 791–807.

———. 2004. Testing novel implications from the selectorate theory of war. *World Politics* 56 (3): 363–388.

Bueno de Mesquita, B., and A. Smith. 2006. Political survival and the logic of aid. Working Paper. Department of Politics, New York University.

Bueno de Mesquita, B., A. Smith, R. M. Siverson, and J. D. Morrow. 2003. *The Logic of Political Survival*. Cambridge, Mass.: MIT Press.

Chiozza, G. 2002. Is there a clash of civilizations? Evidence from patterns of international conflict involvement, 1946–1997. *Journal of Peace Research* 39 (6): 711–734.

Chiozza, G., and H. E. Goemans. 2003. Peace through insecurity: Tenure and international conflict. *Journal of Conflict Resolution* 47 (4): 443–467.

———. 2004. International conflict and the tenure of leaders: Is war still *ex post* inefficient? *American Journal of Political Science* 48 (3): 604–619.

Dixon, W. J. 1994. Democracy and the peaceful settlement of international conflict. *American Political Science Review* 88 (1): 1–17.

Downs, G. W., and D. M. Rocke. 1995. *Optimal Imperfection? Domestic Uncertainty and Institutions in International Relations*. Princeton, N.J.: Princeton University Press.

Elman, C., and M. F. Elman. 1997. Lakatos and neorealism: A reply to Vasquez. *American Political Science Review* 91 (4): 923–926.

Fearon, J. D. 1994. Domestic political audiences and the escalation of international disputes. *American Political Science Review* 88 (3): 577–592.

———. 1995. Rationalist explanations for war. *International Organization* 49: 379–414.

Fordham, B. 1998. The politics of threat perception and the use of force: A political economy model of U.S. uses of force, 1949–1994. *International Studies Quarterly* 42 (3): 567–590.

Gartner, S. 1997. *Strategic Assessment in War*. New Haven, Conn.: Yale University Press.

Gaubatz, K. T. 1999. *Elections and War*. Stanford, Calif.: Stanford University Press.

Gulick, E. V. 1955. *Europe's Classical Balance of Power*. Ithaca, N.Y.: Cornell University Press.

Henderson, E. A., and R. Tucker. 2001. Clear and present strangers: The clash of civilizations and international conflict. *International Studies Quarterly* 45 (2): 317–338.

Huntington, S. P. 1993. The clash of civilizations. *Foreign Affairs* 72 (3): 22–49.

Kim, W., and J. D. Morrow. 1992. When do power shifts lead to war? *American Journal of Political Science* 36 (4): 896–922.

Levy, J. S. 1988. Domestic politics and war. *Journal of Interdisciplinary History* 18: 653–673.

Maoz, Z., and N. Abdolali. 1989. Regime types and international conflict, 1816–1976. *Journal of Conflict Resolution* 33 (1): 3–35.

Maoz, Z., and B. Russett. 1993. Normative and structural causes of democratic peace, 1946–1986. *American Political Science Review* 87 (3): 624–638.

McGuire, M. C., and M. Olson. 1996. The economics of autocracy and majority rule: The invisible hand and the use of force. *Journal of Economic Literature* 34: 72–96.

Milner, H. V. 1998. Rationalizing politics: The emerging synthesis of international, American, and comparative politics. *International Organization* 52 (4): 759–786.

Morgenthau, H. J. 1978. *Politics among Nations.* 5th ed. rev. New York: Knopf.

Morrow, J. D. 1991. Electoral and congressional incentives and arms control. *Journal of Conflict Resolution* 35 (2): 243–263.

Nincic, M. 1997. Loss aversion and the domestic context of military intervention. *Political Research Quarterly* 50 (1): 97–120.

Niou, E., P. Ordeshook, and G. Rose. 1989. *The Balance of Power.* Cambridge: Cambridge University Press.

Niskanen, W. A. 1997. Autocratic, democratic, and optimal government. *Economic Inquiry* 35 (3): 464–479.

Organski, A. F. K. 1958. *World Politics.* New York: Knopf.

Powell, R. 1994. Anarchy in international relations theory: The neorealist-neoliberal debate. *International Organization* 48 (2): 313–344.

———. 1996. Uncertainty, shifting power, and appeasement. *American Political Science Review* 90 (4): 749–764.

———. 1999. *In the Shadow of Power: States and Strategy in International Politics.* Princeton, N.J.: Princeton University Press.

———. 2004. Bargaining and learning while fighting. *American Journal of Political Science* 48 (2): 344–361.

Prange, G. W. 1981. *At Dawn We Slept: The Untold Story of Pearl Harbor.* New York: Penguin Books.

Reiter, D., and A. C. Stam III. 1998. Democracy and battlefield military effectiveness. *Journal of Conflict Resolution* 42 (June): 259–277.

———. 2002. *Democracies at War.* Princeton, N.J.: Princeton University Press.

Rummel, R. J. 1983. Libertarianism and international violence. *Journal of Conflict Resolution* 27 (1): 27–71.

Russett, B. 1993. *Grasping the Democratic Peace: Principles for a Post–Cold War World.* Princeton, N.J.: Princeton University Press.

Russett, B., J. Oneal, and M. Cox. 2000. Clash of civilizations, or realism and liberalism déja vu? Some evidence. *Journal of Peace Research* 37 (5): 583–608.

Schultz, K. A. 1998. Domestic opposition and signaling in international crises. *American Political Science Review* 92 (4): 829–844.

———. 2001. *Democracy and Coercive Diplomacy.* Cambridge: Cambridge University Press.

Smith, A. 2004. *Election Timing.* Cambridge: Cambridge University Press.

Starr, H. 1972. *War Coalitions: The Distribution of Payoffs and Losses.* Lexington, Mass.: D.C. Heath.

Thucydides. 1959. *History of the Peloponnesian War.* 3 vols. Trans. T. Hobbes. Ann Arbor: University of Michigan Press.

Wagner, R. H. 2000. Bargaining and war. *American Journal of Political Science* 44 (3): 469–484.

Waltz, K. N. 1979. *Theory of International Politics*. Reading, Mass.: Addison-Wesley.

Werner, S. 1996. Absolute and limited war: The possibility of foreign-imposed regime change. *International Interactions* 22 (1): 67–88.

Wintrobe, R. 1990. The tinpot and the totalitarian: An economic theory of dictatorship. *American Political Science Review* 84 (3): 849–872.

Wittman, D. 1979. How a war ends: A rational model approach. *Journal of Conflict Resolution* 23: 743–763.

2 The Political Economy of Warfare

Edward L. Glaeser

Why do countries, both democracies and dictatorships, engage in massively self-destructive wars? As Mansfield and Snyder (2005) make clear, wars are often pursued by democracies and are often enthusiastically supported by the population as a whole. Given the enormous amount of destruction caused by armed conflict, it is remarkable that countries enthusiastically enter into wars when negotiated settlement is presumably always an option (Fearon 1994).

This chapter follows Marx (1859), Fearon (1994), and Hess and Orphanides (1995) and presents a model of warfare where leaders benefit from conflict even though the population as a whole loses.[1] Warfare creates domestic political advantages, both for insecure incumbents like Napoleon III and for long-shot challengers, like Islamic extremists in the Middle East, even though it is costly to the nation as a whole. Self-destructive wars can be seen as an agency problem where politicians hurt their nations but increase their probability of political success. This problem becomes more severe if the population can be falsely persuaded that another country is a threat.

The model here considers three different cases. First, I assume that ability at warfare is known only for current leaders.[2] As a result, current leaders with above-average skills in making war will have an incentive to start wars because once these wars begin, voters won't to want to switch horses in midstream for a leader of unproven ability. While the model relies on asymmetric knowledge of incumbents and challengers, any assumption that wars increase the costs of switching leaders can generate similar results. In this "wag-the-dog" version of the model, leaders will be more likely to support wars when their war-making ability is higher, when the war is less costly to the nation, and when the benefits of office are higher. Popular incumbents are less likely to start wars.

While this version of the model can explain why incumbents might favor warfare, it cannot explain why wars would ever be popular. In the second variant of the model, war can beneficial because another country poses a future threat.[3] In this case, both challengers and incumbents may be too pacific relative to the needs of the nation because they bear some costs of war and few future benefits. There is a strategic complementarity between incumbent and challenger decisions about war. If a challenger is bellicose, an incumbent may declare war first to reduce the challenger's electoral support.

This second version of the model can't explain why countries would ever start wars that have higher costs than benefits. To address the existence of extremely popular but costly wars, I allow the possibility that political leaders can send false messages incorrectly depicting another country as a threat. This model follows Glaeser (2005) and assumes that people can be misled by political entrepreneurs who vilify outsiders as a means of increasing support for their own policies. Wars become popular because the population has been convinced that the outside nation is a threat, but since the people have been misled, the wars are ultimately costly to the nation.

In this version of the model, incumbents can again be moved to war by the threat of a bellicose challenger. Outsiders who are unlikely to come into power otherwise support war as a strategy of political desperation. They may gain politically but are unlikely to pay the costs because they are unlikely to be elected. This result helps us to understand why out-groups in countries like Saudi Arabia and Egypt are today the strongest voices for an incredibly costly conflict with the United States and Israel. This version of the model also suggests that information costs are important. Trust in the government also makes war more likely. Dictatorial control over information may also help explain a dictatorial penchant for welfare.

While there is some debate about the facts (Mansfield and Snyder 2005), most political science work following Bueno de Mesquita (1981) finds a robust negative effect of democracy on war (Russett and Oneal 2001; Rousseau 2005). This model predicts this relationship, both because dictators have a greater ability to mislead the public because of their control over the media and because the gains from staying in power are much higher for a dictator than for a leader in a democracy. As I discuss in the case studies, there are many examples of nineteenth-century leaders like Napoleon III and Bismarck who were willing to go to war to stay in power, but that there is little evidence of any twentieth-century American or British incumbents going to war for political purposes.

The first case study looks at nineteenth-century Europe, where both Napoleon III and Bismarck used wars for domestic political purposes (Mansfield and Snyder 2005). Napoleon III's foreign adventures rallied support for his wobbly regime for understandable reasons. Given the unrest he faced in 1870, even the Franco-Prussian war doesn't seem like an irrational gamble. Bismarck also undertook three wars to create Prussian hegemony within Germany and to silence the critics of the Hohenzollern monarchy within Prussia. These wars helped ensure Hohenzollern authority in Germany until 1918.

I then turn to entry into World War I, a collectively disastrous act for the European powers. Austro-Hungarian action against Serbia was certainly motivated by internal politics; they were fighting to suppress an ethnic uprising and to reaffirm the primacy of the Hapsburg regime. German and Russian belligerency also had much to do with internal politics. The Kaiser and his ministers had regularly justified large army budgets (which funded a force used to eliminate internal opposition) by emphasizing foreign threats from England and Russia. The Czar similarly tried to build support by pushing Russian interests in the Balkans. In 1914 both Romanovs and Hapsburgs faced tremendous internal unrest, and it is unsurprising that both leaders sought popular support through a war that could be depicted as defense against outside aggression.

Finally, I turn to U.S. wars between 1896 and 1975. During this period, there is no solid evidence on incumbents' acting in a particularly bellicose way to further their own electoral chances. The decisions to enter World War I and World War II seem to have been made out of conviction with little or no political motivation. Cuba, Korea, and Vietnam fit a pattern of bellicose outsiders raising the costs for the incumbent. Nationalistic outsiders pushed war with Spain in 1898, and McKinley was forced to act before he lost control of his own foreign policy. In 1950, Truman faced a drumbeat of Republican hostility to his supposed weakness in Asia. Similarly, in Vietnam, the Johnson tapes show a leader who acted aggressively in part because he feared Republican opponents would use any weakness vis-à-vis Russia against him.

The phenomenon of incumbents' using war to shore up their power is real, but the case studies and the model suggest that this is primarily a feature of dictatorships rather than democracies. If anything, the tendency in democracies has often been for incumbents to be warier of conflict than are opposition groups or the public at large. Both in democracies and in dictatorships, the strongest voices for conflict are often outsiders who have little chance of having to lead a war-torn country but stand to gain politically by pushing warfare.

Aggressive Wars and Political Survival—Wagging the Dog

This model of warfare hinges on the fact that war can increase popular enthusiasm for a leader. There are abundant examples of leaders who saw their support increase dramatically after declaring war (Napoleon III, Czar Nicholas II, Kaiser Wilhelm II, Gamal Nasser, and U.S. presidents). The popular enthusiasm for war-making leaders is hard to understand, given the track record that wars have had in causing misery. The model explains this enthusiasm with two effects. First, war makes it costly to switch leaders. Second, people on both sides of a conflict can be enthusiastic about the war because of different beliefs about the threats posed by the other nation.

The first effect—war decreases opposition to the incumbent—stems from the fact that internal strife is costly in the face of a common enemy. Cooperation against a common enemy is rational. Opposing the current leader is an extreme form of noncooperative behavior, so we should expect this behavior to decrease during times of conflict. Failure to stand by one's monarch could easily lead to defeat; after all, it was the Duke of Burgundy's dispute with the King of France that led to Henry V's conquest of France.[4] The first variant of the model presents a simple model of warfare in which the crucial assumption is that changes in leadership are costly in a wartime setting. The complementarity between continuity of leadership and wartime success creates an incentive for incumbents to start wars even if those wars are detrimental to their countries.

I assume two countries: the home country and the rival country. I only concern myself with the events in the home country; the rival country will merely fight back in the case of a war. In this first model, I assume that the rival will not start a war itself (this possibility is addressed in the next section). Within the home country, there is an incumbent leader and an opposition. The incumbent leader and his citizens know his quality as a war leader; no one knows the opposition's quality as a war leader.

In this first version of the model, the incumbent leader only makes one decision: at time 1, he decides whether or not to start a war against the rival country. After the incumbent makes this decision, the opposition makes an announcement of its policy, which can be war or peace. This policy is assumed to be binding, so that if the opposition comes into power, it must carry out its proposed policy.

After the incumbent and the opposition have both declared their policies, during period 2 people vote (or in a nondemocratic society, decide whether to support the incumbent or the opposition). Voters have exogenous preferences for the two candidates, and they also make their decisions based on the costs to the country of the war or of changing leaders. We do not solve the voter's paradox but rather assume that each voter has an intrinsic preference, denoted η_i (which may well be negative), and will vote for the incumbent if and only if η_i is greater than the net war-related benefits that would be created by switching to the opposition. Formally, the utility if the incumbent stays in power is $\eta_i - D_A(Incumbent)$, and the utility if the challenger gets into power is $-D_A(Challenger)$. Voters therefore support the incumbent if and only if

$$\eta_i > D_A(Incumbent) - D_A(Challenger),$$

where $D_A(Incumbent)$ represents the war damages if the incumbent stays in office, and $D_A(Challenger)$ reflects the war damages if the challenger takes office.

In period 3, after the election, the payoffs from the war are realized. These payoffs affect both citizens and leaders, and people base their votes on the expected payoff from the war. The basic timing of the model is

1. incumbent decides whether to start a war;

2. challenger decides whether to have a prowar policy;

3. an election occurs and the winning politician becomes leader;

4. the war is completed, and utilities are received for both the politicians and the citizens.

I rule out the possibility that the leader may suffer in some future election for initiating a costly war; this is not one stage of a repeated game. If leaders did have longer time horizons, that would deter warfare in this case (but not in later versions of the model).

The war will create damages to each citizen of country A, denoted D_A, that are equal to $\theta R_B - \mu_A - I(peace) \times p$, where θ is a constant, R_B represents the resources of country B, μ_A represents the quality of country A's leadership, $I(peace)$ is an indicator function that takes on a value 1 if a challenger who seeks peace is elected, and p is a constant less than θR_B. The leadership parameter is meant to capture the full range of abilities that a leader can use to improve his country's well-being in time of war, including strategic sense, diplomatic skills, and charisma.

Implicitly, I assume that the quality of leadership in country B is equal to zero. The damages to country B, denoted D_B, are equal to $\theta R_A + \mu_A - I(peace) \times |p|$. The effect of moving toward peace is always to reduce the damage to country B, but country A may actually be hurt by moving toward peace if $p < 0$. The value of μ_A depends on whether the incumbent or the challenger is in power. I assume that a leader's value of μ is revealed in office but not before, and that the incumbent knew his value of μ before declaring war. As such, the decision of whether to go to war depends on the realized value of μ, which I denote μ_I. The value of μ is unknown for the incumbent, and the expected value of μ is zero.

Given these assumptions, if the incumbent doesn't declare war, then the expected net war-related advantages from supporting the challenger are zero if the challenger also doesn't declare war and $-\theta R_B$ if the challenger supports war. If the incumbent declares war and the incumbent says he will continue the war, then the net advantage from supporting the challenger is $-\mu_I$. If the incumbent declares war and the challenger opts for peace, then the net advantage from supporting the challenger is $p - \mu_I$.

To close the model, I assume that $\eta_i = \xi + \varepsilon_i$, where ε_i is an idiosyncratic preference distributed symmetrically around zero, and ξ is common across the population. The shock ξ is realized only on the eve of the election only after war-related decisions have been made, and ξ is distributed uniformly on the interval $[\hat{\eta} - .5q, \hat{\eta} + .5q]$. The incumbent is kept in power if he receives at least 50 percent of support, which requires that ξ plus the war-related support from endorsing the incumbent must be greater than zero. I further assume that q is sufficiently large so that both candidates always have a chance of being elected. While this framework is specifically democratic, I mean it also to capture the desire of dictators to retain some form of popular support.

The politicians choose their actions to maximize expected payoffs. Being out of leadership generates utility of zero. If a leader is in power during peace, his utility is $B_0 > 0$, and if he leads during war, then his utility is $B_0 - B_1$, where $B_1 > 0$. The term B_1 reflects the fact that it is less pleasant to be the leader of a war-ravaged nation, and I assume that this is paid whether the leader initiated war or inherited a country at war and is trying to lead toward peace. The political equilibria are characterized by propositions 2.1 and 2.2.

Proposition 2.1 If the incumbent declares war, then the challenger will support the war if and only if $p < 0$. If the incumbent doesn't declare war, then the challenger will never support war.

If the incumbent doesn't declare war, there is no reason for the challenger to declare war because it will be socially costly and unpopular. If the incumbent does declare war, then the challenger is forced to face the incumbency advantage that his opponent enjoys, but he can potentially reduce the costs of war by following a peace policy. The challenger has an incentive to follow the peace policy if and only if $p > 0$ and peace will reduce the costs to the country of the war.

Proposition 2.2 characterizes the incumbent's behavior under the assumption that the incumbent believes that the challenger will react rationally to his decision of war versus peace. As long as $\mu_I > 0$, the incumbent faces a trade-off when deciding whether to go to war. He compares the advantage that comes from increasing his probability of staying in power with the disadvantage that comes from leading a country at war.

Proposition 2.2 There exists a value of $\mu_I > 0$, denoted μ_I^*, at which the incumbent is indifferent between declaring war and not declaring war. At values of μ_I above μ_I^*, the incumbent always prefers to declare war, and at values of μ_I below μ_I^*, the incumbent prefers peace. The value of μ_I^* is falling with B_0; rising with B_1, q, $\hat{\eta}$; and rising with p, if $p > 0$.

Proposition 2.2 emphasizes that warfare, which hurts the country, is attractive to the incumbent if the incumbent has a comparative advantage in defending the country. Even though the country would have been better off if the incumbent had not declared war, voters will continue to support the current leader if the leader's ability as a war leader is sufficiently large.

The comparative statics can be interpreted by noting that μ_I^* determines the range of values c for which a war will be started, so that factors that increase μ_I^* narrow that range and make a war less likely. Increases in B_1 make war less likely because this variable makes the war more painful to the incumbent if he stays in power. Increases in p decrease the attractiveness of war (when $p > 0$) because higher values of p will make it more likely that the incumbent will lose to an opponent who offers to improve the country's welfare by decreasing the scope of the war. Increases in q make it less likely that declaring war will sway the election.

Increases in B_0 make war more likely because this variable determines how attractive it is to remain a leader of even a war-torn country. This result can explain why wars seem to be more popular in dictatorships than in democracies. A central feature of most democracies is that the ability of the chief executive to expropriate rents for himself is limited. As a result, staying in power in a democracy (especially given the pain of being a leader during a costly war) may not be worth all that much. Staying in power in a dictatorship may be worth much more and may be worth the costs of starting a war.

As $\hat{\eta}$ rises, the probability of war falls. If the leader is likely to stay in power anyway because he is extremely popular, then the costs of fighting the war become quite appealing. Since the benefit of wars is increasing the probability of staying in office, and the cost is an unpleasant time as leader, those leaders who expect to survive anyway will not engage in warfare. As in Downs and Rocke (1994), war is most politically appealing for the desperate. One interpretation of this comparative static is that leaders with a high value of μ_I but low values of $\hat{\eta}$ are good at war but not otherwise popular (presumably because they are ineffective). The model echoes Hess and Orphanides (1995) in predicting that those leaders who are good at war and bad at domestic policy will engage in external aggression.

Appeasement at Munich: Preventive Wars

In this section, warfare creates nothing but costs to the country and is only followed by incumbents who seek to use foreign conflict to create an incentive to avoid changes of leadership. Many wars, both in the past and today, have been favored as much by challengers as by incumbents. In many cases, like Sparta and Athens at the start of the Peloponnesian War, or all the great powers at the start of World War

I, war is popular among all combatants. One explanation of this phenomenon is overconfidence, which might be the result of steady political indoctrination where leaders have regularly trumpeted the vast power of even the tiniest nation. The Iraqi reporting on the U.S. invasion is a particularly clear example of overoptimistic propaganda.

A second explanation, which I rely upon here, is that wars are supported because of the perceived threat and misbehavior of the enemy. The population thinks that whereas war may be bad, the alternative is worse. As such, when Germany invaded Belgium or Iraq invaded Kuwait, war on the part of the British and Americans, respectively, was justified because the enemy had violated a social norm, and this violation distinguished the enemy as a potential threat. Indeed, no major war has been fought in the past 185 years without claims that the enemy is potentially dangerous.

In this second model, I introduce defensive wars by assuming that there is some probability that the other country will start a war at some future date. In this case, after the end of the third period in the previous model, I assume that there is a final period when the rival country may attack the home country. This period occurs after the leader has realized his utility from leading the country, but the citizens' expected welfare includes the expected losses from this war. When they consider the pros and cons of war policy in the election, they will take into account the impact of this future war. As such, the timing of the model is now

1. incumbent decides whether to start a war;

2. challenger decides whether to have a prowar policy;

3. an election occurs and the winning politician becomes leader;

4. the leaders receive their payoffs;

5. with some probability, the rival country starts a war against the home country, and the citizens receive their payoffs.

I assume that the citizens believe that this ultimate war in period 5 will occur with probability π, and that this probability is independent of whether there is a first war. This assumption is surely counterfactual because a war in period 5 may more likely follow a prowar policy in period 2. Still, the assumption captures the idea of a preventive war where the people in one country believe that regardless of their actions, some other country will attack them in the future. The formation of this belief is addressed in the next section, but at this point it is treated as an exogenous.

The damages done to the home country in this new war, denoted D'_A, are equal to $\theta R'_B$, where R'_B denotes the resources of the rival country in this final period. These resources are equal to $g_B(R_B - D_B)$, or a country-level growth rate g_B times the country's initial resources R_B minus the damage potentially done to the country in the first war D_B. I assume that in the home country citizens discount the damage done in the fourth period by a discount factor β. There is a cost from suffering the war today but also a benefit because weakening country B will reduce the damage from the next war.

The expected benefit to citizens of the home country from a preventive war is $\beta \pi g_B \theta D_B - D_A$. The country pays costs today in terms of war damage but receives benefits because by destroying country B, country A ensures that country B will be less effective in a future war. Thus, warfare is more attractive to the citizens of the home country if (1) their country is strong relative to country B, (2) the discount factor is high, (3) they believe that the other country will start a war, (4) the elasticity of damage with respect to country resources (θ) is high, and (5) the growth rate of country B is high. Preventive wars make most sense for powerful countries that are in the process of losing their dominance over a rival that seems quite likely to start a new war.

Given these adjusted war-related benefits, people will vote taking into account not only the impact of the current war on their well-being but also the impact that their current war has on the damage in the next war. The voting rule is now to support the incumbent if and only if

$$\eta_i + \beta \pi g_B \theta (D_B(Incumbent) - D_B(Challenger))$$

$$> D_A(Incumbent) - D_A(Challenger).$$

To embed this in the previous model, I assume that nothing else has changed and that the leaders receive their final payments in period 3, so that they are not affected by the potential fourth-period war except insofar as the possibility of that war changes voting behavior. I do, however, consider only the case where $p \geq 0$ to focus on the case where peace would be attractive to the challenger except for the possibility of preventive war. Proposition 2.3 characterizes the behavior of the opposition.

Proposition 2.3 If the incumbent does not initiate a war, then the challenger will propose a war if and only if

$$\beta \pi g_B \theta^2 R_A - \theta R_B > \frac{B_1(.5q - \hat{\eta})}{B_0 - B_1}.$$

If the incumbent does initiate a war, then the challenger will propose to continue the war if and only if $\beta \pi g_B \theta > 1$. There exists a value of μ_I, denoted μ_I^*, at which the incumbent is indifferent between declaring war and not declaring war. If μ_I is greater than μ_I^*, then incumbent always prefers to declare war, and if μ_I is less than μ_I^*, the incumbent prefers peace.

Proposition 2.3 describes the two conditions under which the challenger will support war. In both cases, the conditions are that the ratio of the increase in electoral support from supporting war divided by a baseline level of electoral support must be greater than the change in utility (conditional upon being elected) divided by a baseline level of utility. These formulas follow from the fact that the leader's utility is equal to the probability of being elected times the utility conditional upon being elected.

It is possible for a challenger to want to go to war even if the incumbent does not go to war, but this requires the war to be quite popular. According to this variant of the model, challengers are unlikely to be excessively prowar, but they can be too propeace. Challengers will only support wars if they are attractive to the citizenry and if the gain in votes offsets any natural advantage the incumbent has at war and the utility costs from leading a country at war.

Given the behavior of the challenger, the incumbent then decides whether to go to war. Proposition 2.4 parallels proposition 2.2; again, an incumbent will initiate war if he has a sufficient comparative advantage in war. The appendix details the four conditions that determine whether the incumbent will choose to initiate a war. Because these conditions are somewhat arduous algebraically, proposition 2.4, I assume here and throughout the rest of the chapter that $p = 0$.

Proposition 2.4 (a) μ_I^* discontinuously falls when the challenger decides to support the war at the point

$$\beta \pi g_B \theta^2 R_A - \theta R_B = \frac{B_1(.5q - \hat{\eta})}{B_0 - B_1},$$

and at this point the value of μ_I^* becomes negative if and only if

$$\frac{.5qB_1}{2B_0 - B_1} > \hat{\eta}.$$

(b) μ_I^* increases with q, B_1, and R_B, and decreases with β, π, g_B, B_0, and R_A; the impact of these variables is discontinuous where

$$\beta\pi g_B\theta^2 R_A - \theta R_B = \frac{B_1(.5q - \hat{\eta})}{B_0 - B_1}.$$

The value of μ_I^* decreases with θ. The value of μ_I^* increases with $\hat{\eta}$ everywhere except where

$$\hat{\eta} = .5q - \frac{(B_0 - B_1)(\beta\pi g_B\theta^2 R_A - \theta R_B)}{B_1},$$

where μ_I^* discontinuously falls with $\hat{\eta}$.

Part (a) of proposition 2.4 describes the effect of the challenger's behavior on the incumbent's behavior. If parameters are such that the challenger will declare war if the incumbent doesn't, this will push the incumbent toward being more bellicose. In this version of the model, the challenger only supports the war when the citizens also want the war, so the challenger's bellicosity is not suboptimal from the citizens' point of view, but it increases the costs to the incumbent of remaining at peace. There is a strategic complementarity across the candidates in their decisions about warfare.

For parameter values where war is on the margin of optimality for the challenger, the incumbent may declare war even if he has a comparative disadvantage at warfare. Even though the incumbent is bad at warfare, because the challenger will benefit from the war in the election if the incumbent doesn't move first, the incumbent has a strong incentive to start a war. This situation is most likely to come about when the incumbent is unpopular.

The comparative statics in part (b) combine two effects. First, there is the effect on the returns to the incumbent from declaring war. Second, there is the effect on the challenger's behavior. If the incumbent knows that the challenger will become warlike, even if he isn't, then this will increase the incentives for the incumbent to declare war himself. In most cases, parameters that increase the returns to the incumbent from declaring war will also increase the returns to the challenger from declaring war. In this case, these parameters have a monotonic effect on warfare but one that is discontinuous at the point where the challenger decides to go to war.

For example, as prevention becomes more valued by the electorate (which will be the result of increases in β, π, g_B, and R_A, and decreases in R_B), war becomes more likely because of both effects. As the country becomes more patient, preventive wars become more appealing. As the country believes that war in the future with country B is more likely, preventive wars become more likely. And as the growth rate of country B increases, war becomes more appealing. Finally, as country A's resources go up or country B's resources go down, warfare becomes more appealing because prevention comes on the cheap. These comparative statics relate to a political science literature that associates the start of war with changes in the relative power of nations (Organski and Kugler 1980; Gilpin 1981; Levy 1987).

The two preference parameters, B_0 and B_1, have the expected signs. As the innate returns to leadership rise, both incumbents and challengers want to stay in power more, which makes war more likely because the fundamental advantage of warfare to leaders is to increase electoral support. Increases in B_1 deter both challengers and incumbents from pursuing war because this increases the utility costs of leading a war-torn nation. Increases in θ both raise the damage that country A will suffer in the first war and raise the damage in the second war and the expected benefits from a preventive war. At the margin of going to war, the second effect dominates.

Finally, the comparative static on $\hat{\eta}$ is nonmonotonic. Almost everywhere, a more popular incumbent is less likely to engage in warfare because he expects to be in power with a higher probability and doesn't want to pay the personal costs of leading a war. The countervailing force is that increases in $\hat{\eta}$ also make it more likely that the challenger will declare war if the incumbent doesn't. If the incumbent is entrenched, then the challenger is unlikely to end up being a war leader (since he is unlikely to win), and it makes sense to trade off a greater probability of success in the election with a lower utility once elected. Greater entrenchment of incumbents makes the incumbent less willing to risk war because he is going to be elected anyway, but it makes war more likely because the challenger is more willing to risk war when he has a low probability of being elected.

The Formation of Hatred

In the previous model, challengers might be bellicose, but they only support wars when those wars are actually beneficial to the citizenry. This result seems hard to square with the bellicosity in many countries when external threats seem objectively small. Kaiser Wilhelm and Hitler and much of the German public saw their wars as justifiable acts of German self-defense. In 1898, Americans argued that Spain was not only evil but also a threat to American liberties in the Western Hemisphere. These beliefs are not random. Governments have often gone to great lengths to depict the atrocities and threats posed by their opponents, and these depictions seem generally to have been successful even when false. To capture this phenomenon, the model follows Glaeser (2005) and allows politicians to send misleading signals about the extent of an external threat from external enemies. I refer to this belief in an external threat as hatred for reasons outlined in my prior work.

To allow the spreading of hatred, I assume at the start of the model that citizens in the home country believe that people in the rival country will start a war with probability π_0, and with this probability they will start a war probability 1. With probability $1 - \pi_0$ the rival country will not start a war. If the rival is war-prone, with probability 1, the citizens of the home country will receive a signal indicating the warlike nature of the rival country. In the absence of any false signals the citizens will accurately assess the risk from the rival country.

To allow the spreading of hatred against the rival country, I allow either one of the politicians to disseminate a false signal that the rival country is in fact a threat. They choose to spread these stories at the same time as they make their policy decisions, and everything else in the structure of this model follows the previous subsection. The cost of spreading this story is k_I for the incumbent and k_C for the challenger. The incumbent makes this decision when he decides his policy and before the challenger decides his policy. The challenger decides whether to spread the story after he has decided his policy and after the incumbent has decided his policy. I assume that once the incumbent has spread the story, the challenger can neither attack the story nor spread additional confirming rumors. The citizens of the home country believe that with probability ϕ the story that has been spread about the rival country is false. In Glaeser (2005), I determined an equivalent ϕ parameter endogenously so that individuals' beliefs were always completely rational. Here I treat ϕ as an exogenous parameter reflecting general distrust in society.

The citizens of the home country therefore believe that the rival country will start a later war with probability $\pi_0/(\pi_0 + \phi(1 - \pi_0))$. If country B is in fact war-prone, then the model is exactly the same as that just discussed, with $\pi = \pi_0/(\pi_0 + \phi(1 - \pi_0))$. I assume that country B is inherently peaceful and focus on the waging war against an inherently peaceful country. In this case, warfare against country B is unproductive to the citizens of country A, although they will believe that it is productive.

I assume $p = 0$, so the only policy choice by the challenger is whether to declare war if the incumbent doesn't. The challenger also needs to decide whether to spread signals of the warlike nature of the rival country if the incumbent hasn't already sent such a signal, and this decision is made simultaneously with the decision about policy. First, I turn to the decision to spread false stories.

Proposition 2.5 The incumbent will spread false stories if and only if he is initiating a war and

$$\frac{\beta g_B \theta \pi_0 (B_0 - B_1)\mu_I}{q(\pi_0 + \phi(1 - \pi_0))} > k_I.$$

The challenger will always send false stories when he is initiating a war. When $\mu_I < 0$, k_C is small, R_B is large, $\theta \approx R_B/R_A$, and $\beta \pi g_B > 1$, the challenger will spread false stories after the incumbent has declared war without spreading false stories.

Proposition 2.5 emphasizes that hatred in this case, as in Glaeser (2005), appears when it is a complement to political policies. Neither politician spreads stories about the rival country unless they are going to war. The challenger won't go to war unless he spreads false stories about the rival. The condition on

$$\frac{\beta g_B \theta \pi_0 (B_0 - B_1)\mu_I}{q(\pi_0 + \phi(1 - \pi_0))} > k_I$$

just describes whether the benefits to an incumbent of spreading hatred outweighs those costs. This condition may imply that spreading hatred is more common in dictatorial regimes, where the government has control over the media.

It is harder, presumably, for leaders in a democracy to falsely portray an external threat. Still, there are forces that continue to make this feasible. First, the government, through its intelligence agencies, may be seen as having particular knowledge about the threat posed by outsiders. Second, once there is a widespread belief in the danger of an external threat, the media may fear looking either foolish or unpatriotic by challenging this threat.[5] Proposition 2.6 describes the challenger's willingness to spread hatred and endorse warfare.

Proposition 2.6 If the incumbent declares peace and does not send a signal, then there exists a value of k_C, denoted k_C^*, at which the challenger is indifferent between sending a signal and supporting war and not sending a signal and not supporting war. If k_C is less than k_C^*, then the challenger both sends a signal and supports war, and if k_C is greater than k_C^*, then the challenger neither sends a signal nor supports war. The value of k_C^* is falling with q, B_1, R_B, and ϕ, and rising with β, π_0, g_B, R_A, $\hat{\eta}$, and B_0.

The challenger will be more prone to be prowar when he has the ability to spread stories about the threat posed by the rival country. The value of k_C^* captures the range of propaganda costs that would lead to warfare; higher values suggest that the war-prone opposition is more likely to occur. The comparative statics tell us that a peaceful incumbent is more likely to face a bellicose opponent when trust is high (ϕ is low), because in that case the opponent will find it easier to convince the population that the other country is a threat. A bellicose opposition is more likely when the returns to office (B_0) are higher and when the costs of being a wartime leader (B_1) are lower. The challenger is also more likely to support war when his home country is strong relative to the opponent, when the population cares about the future more, when the other country is growing more quickly, or when wars are more destructive.

As in the previous version of the model, incumbent entrenchment makes it more appealing for a challenger to endorse warfare. This effect makes it particularly likely that challengers in nondemocratic regimes will be warlike. In those cases, the returns to leadership are huge, and outsiders have intrinsically a small chance of being elected.

Proposition 2.7 describes a sufficient condition for the incumbent to wage war. The full set of conditions under which an incumbent finds war optimal is described in the appendix.

Proposition 2.7 The incumbent will always prefer to declare war if μ_I is greater than μ_I^*, where μ_I^* decreases with β, π_0, g_B, and B_0, and increases with q, B_1, and ϕ.

The basic comparative statics are the same as in proposition 2.4 and for the same reasons. One new comparative static on ϕ concerns the level of trust. A sufficiently trusting population is more likely to be lied to and more likely to be taken to war.

In this case, the incumbent is more likely to go to war if parameters are such that the challenger will push war if the incumbent doesn't. Indeed, the incumbent won't declare war unless either he has a comparative advantage at warfare or he believes that the challenger will declare war if he doesn't. This feature of the model, a peaceful incumbent pushed to war by a bellicose challenger, will turn out to be a regular feature of the case studies that follow.

Napoleon III, Bismarck, and the Wag-the-Dog Strategy

In 1848 both France and Germany had revolutions that appeared to augur a new era of democracy and limits on executive power. But in the decades that followed, both nations got empires before they got republics. In both cases, warfare was an intrinsic element of domestic politics. Both Napoleon III and Bismarck used warfare to further a domestic agenda that consisted mainly of executive authority. I follow Mansfield and Snyder (2005) closely in my discussion of Napoleon III, who is particularly interesting because he admitted that he used warfare as a means of gaining domestic popularity.

There are at least four reasons why Napoleon III was particularly prone to warfare. Three of these reasons are captured by the model, and one is not. First, by virtue primarily of his famous name, Napoleon III was understood by the French public to have a comparative advantage at military activity (a high perceived value of μ_I). Louis Napoleon's hold on power was never all that secure (he had a low value of $\hat{\eta}$). He had neither the monarchical legitimacy of the Bourbons nor the authority of a real constitution. Napoleon III lived in extraordinary luxury as emperor and might well have lost his life if he lost his power (which means he had a high value of B_0). The factors behind Napoleon III's penchant for war, a high value of staying in power (B_0), combined with a reputation for military competence (μ_I) and a high degree of instability ($\hat{\eta}$) have been features of many of the war-prone dictatorships of the twentieth century.

Napoleon III fought five wars over 22 years. His first war was a hap-
hazard military operation against the Roman Republic. Louis Napoleon initially abstained from supporting this war, but when he was
elected president, he sent troops to fight the Republicans. In this war
Louis Napoleon, not yet emperor, tried to steer a middle course but
ended up supporting war to gain support from the politically dominant conservatives, who supported war to protect the Papacy.

In 1852, Louis Napoleon made himself emperor, and he spent the
next 18 years working hard to keep himself in power. Napoleon III first
went to war in Crimea. This war began in a dispute over Roman Catholic rights in Bethlehem and Jerusalem, where Napoleon III continued
his interest in appearing to be a protector of the faith. After this dispute
led to a full war between Turkey and Russia, Napoleon III joined with
England in a full-scale conflict with Russia that ran from 1854 to 1856.
Popular enthusiam for war was stoked by stories of Russian atrocities
(the "massacre of Sinope") and the belief that Russia presented a real
threat to English interests in the East.

Karl Marx and others have long argued that Napoleon III fought in
Crimea to further his domestic political agenda. Wawro (2000, 51)
writes that "to marginalize this ineradicable opposition [wealthy
English-style liberals...red republicans], Napoleon III embarked on a
series of foreign adventures." A. W. Kinglake, a member of Parliament
during Napoleon III's lifetime, argued that the emperor must "distract
France from thinking of her shame at home, by send her attention
abroad...if Prince Louis...were to continue quartered upon France
instead of being thrown into prison and brought to trial, it was indis-
pensable that Europe must be disturbed" (Kinglake 1874, 210, cited in
Gooch 1956).

In 1859, Napoleon III joined forces with Piedmont to fight Austria in
Northern Italy. In this case, the Emperor admitted the political advantages of the war. He told his cabinet "On the domestic front, the war
will at first awaken great fears; traders and speculators of every stripe
will shriek, but national sentiment will [banish] this domestic fright;
the nation will be put to the test once more in a struggle that will stir
many a heart, recall the memory of heroic times and bring together
under the mantle of glory the parties that are steadily drifting away
from one another day after day" (Plessis 1985, 146–147, cited in Mansfield and Snyder 2005, 184). Émile Ollivier, a republican opponent
declared, "Italian independence is only a pretext....Basically the Emperor is only concerned to strengthen his dynasty and silence the

slowly emerging internal opposition" (Mansfield and Snyder 2005, 188). The war started with vilification of the Austrians, and popular enthusiasm ensued: "Townsmen and villagers who had ignored the brewing crisis in the winter went berserk in the spring, rushing to join crowds and bellowing slogans like 'long live war' and 'death to the Austrians' when mobilization was announced" (Wawro 2000, 67). The Emperor's popularity soared. One contemporary observer describes how "it is impossible to give any idea of the enthusiasm with which [Napoleon III] was greeted when in field uniform, with tunic and kepi.... An overwhelming acclamation of 'Long Live the Emperor!'" (Case 1972, 75). France's mediocre performance in the war was transformed by the emperor's celebration into another great victory: "The celebrations and illuminations after Solferino were even more extensive than those in 1855" (Wawro 2000, 70).

Napoleon III's penultimate military adventure was his support for the Emperor Maximilian in Mexico. The official cause of Napoleon's intervention was the Juarez regime's failure to pay its debts to France, but there is little doubt that he was once again seeking military glory that would strengthen his regime.

Napoleon III's final war was his fight against Prussia in 1870. French entry into this war is typically described as a trap laid by Bismarck for Napoleon III and France. The precise cause was a Hohenzollern candidate for the Spanish throne. After initially supporting Prince Leopold of Hohenzollern-Sigmaringen, King Wilhelm of Prussia withdrew his support from contention but refused to promise the French that there would never be another Hohenzollern claim on the Spanish throne. The German threat was real (after all, Germany would invade France three times over the next 70 years), and newspapers allied with the government were quite able to depict Germany as a hostile power. Napoleon III declared war and personally led the French troops against Germany.

Napoleon III again saw that "the war would represent a displacement of internal into external politics." After public opinion was strongly built against Germany, the political gains from war were obvious; Foreign Minister Gramont declared that "the government will not survive in the Chamber tomorrow unless it is able to present definite Prussian concessions." But why did Napoleon III take this gamble?

First, Germany was a real and perceived threat, which made a "preventive" war popular. Second, Napoleon's popularity and hold on the government had continued to sag throughout the 1860s. In 1870 the Emperor's nephew had shot a journalist, and "the journalist's funeral on 7 March was the occasion for tumultuous anti-imperial demonstrations in Paris. Barricades went up, buses were overturned and great bonfires roared throughout the night" (Wawro 2000, 106). Without a war, Napoleon III would probably have been removed from power and either exiled or imprisoned. Third, it was far from clear *ex ante* that the Prussians would be capable of defeating the French. The French had better small arms (the Chassepot rifle), and historically the French army had been more than a match for their German rivals.

Of course, Napoleon III came up against Bismarck, who had been skillfully using foreign wars for domestic political purposes throughout the 1860s, and Bismarck had, it turned out, a far more formidable army at his disposal. Bismarck became Minister-President and Foreign Minister of Prussia in 1862 after the Prussian Diet had rejected Kaiser Wilhelm's budget. His first two years were marked by distinct unpopularity, and the House of Deputies called for his resignation: "During the Prussian Constitutional Conflict of 1862–6, a defeat of the crown did not seem impossible when the Progressive Party, representing the liberal bourgeoisie, gained a majority in the Diet and refused to approve the military budget" (Bergahn 1973, 11). Bismarck personally had a low probability of survival, and the Hohenzollern monarchy as a whole looked pretty shaky.

In Bismarck's first war, Prussia was allied with Austria, and the target was Denmark. Before the war, Bismarck "was beginning to see, in the foreign field, possibilities of confounding and, eventually, reconciling the parliamentary opposition" (Craig 1955, 167). While the conflict was initially unpopular with some, the victory strengthened the regime: "Bismarck had long held that, if they were given a foreign success sufficiently striking to inflate their self-esteem, the Prussian people would forget their internal grievances; and this now proved true" (Craig 1955, 170).

Bismarck pushed his second war against Austria as a fight for "the establishment in Frankfurt of a German Parliament elected by universal suffrage," because "he believed that universal suffrage would have a conservative effect." Moltke's victory over the Austrians at Sadowa did change Bismarck's domestic position enormously, and "within two months of the battle, the Prussian legislature voted budgetary credits to cover the government's expenses during its four-year breach of the constitution" (Mansfield and Snyder 2005, 199).

Bismarck's 1870 war with France also had political benefits: "Throughout North Germany swept a flame of impassioned patriotism fed by and reflected in the Press" (Howard 1961, 59). The enthusiasm for the Kaiser, Moltke, and Bismarck grew even greater after the stunning defeat of Napoleon III at Sedan. Unification of Germany under Prussian leadership was accomplished in a way that denigrated rather than supported the power of popular democracy. Bismarck's triumph ensured enough popularity that he was able to govern Germany in peace for almost another two decades. Finally, the enormous success of Moltke's general staff ensured that the Diet could no longer try to starve the army of resources without courting popular disfavor. Since the army was the bulwark of the *ancien regime* against popular discontent, funding for the army ensured political survival, at least until 1918.

The European Powers and World War I

In 1914 every major European power chose to engage in an enormously destructive conflict that would destroy three ancient regimes (Hohenzollerns, Hapsburgs, and Romanovs) and lead every incumbent government in those powers to lose control. Not only was World War I a spectacularly bad decision for Europe as a whole, none of the leaders in 1914 can possibly be said to have benefited *ex post* from the decision to go to war. Can the model shed some light on this seemingly irrational conflict?

Austro-Hungary was the first nation to start hostilities against a neighbor in 1914, and its actions are most clearly dictated by domestic political concerns. Serbian nationalists had shot the Hapsburg heir, and "street demonstrations insisted that Belgrade be punished and took up the cry *Serbien muss sterbien*, a play on words that meant 'Serbia must die'" (Wawro 2000, 213). The Serbian killers "had been supplied with weapons from a Serbian military arsenal and helped to cross the border by Serbian frontier guards," and this "information was sufficient to confirm Austria's rooted belief in Serbian malevolence and to arouse its equally ready desire to punish the small kingdom for its disturbance of order within the empire" (Keegan 1998, 50). The incident, stoked up by the press, ensured that both Foreign Minister Berchtold and Army Chief of Staff von Hotzendorf were eager for war.

The Emperor Franz Joseph knew that the war would be popular, and if successful, would both strengthen the regime and discredit ethnic separatists within the Empire. He also correctly feared defeat and change more generally, and he sought support from Germany before moving ahead. Indeed, the remarkable thing about Austrian intervention was the reticence of the Emperor given the strong domestic incentives for war.

The Romanov regime faced considerable internal opposition; there had been a revolution in 1905, and the first half of 1914 was marked by widespread strikes. Russian expansion into the Balkans was one means of gaining domestic support; acting as protector of the Orthodox Christians in the region was an attractive role for the Czar. According to Pipes (1990, 200), this foreign entanglement eventually produced the need for military action: "In several previous confrontations in the Balkans, Russia had yielded to the outrage of her conservative nationalists. To have done so again in the crisis that developed in July 1914 following the Austrian ultimatum to Serbia, worded with deliberate insolence and backed by Germany, could have spelled the end of Russia's influence in the Balkan Peninsula and possibly domestic difficulties. St. Petersburg, therefore, decided, with French concurrence, to support Serbia." Certainly, the Czar's domestic troubles quieted immediately after the outbreak of war as the nation rallied to his banner.

The Kaiser's decision to back Austro-Hungary and then to declare war on Russia (after Russian mobilization) was also related to internal politics. Starting in the 1890s, the Kaiser began a costly and belligerent naval arms race that was "nothing less than an ambitious plan to stabilize the Prusso-German political system and to paralyze the pressure for change" (Bergahn 1973, 29). The Germans and the English accompanied greater naval expenditures with an ongoing program of vilification that emphasized the threat posed by the other power.

Over time, the Kaiser's and his Chancellor Bethmann-Hollweg's domestic position weakened and "by the spring of 1911, the temptation to conduct 'domestic policy with the steam power of diplomacy' had become so great for Bethmann-Hollweg and Kiderlen that they decided to act" (93–94). The Kaiser then approved sending a gunboat, *Panther*, to challenge the French in Morocco, which resulted in an "upsurge of imperialist enthusiasm" (94). After the 1914 Zabern incident, the government faced a vote of no confidence from the Reichstag, and in early 1914 "the majorities in the Reichstag and the reactions of the press showed that a large section of the population had become alienated from the monarchy" (178). In this atmosphere, the government encouraged conflict with Russia, because "new enemies had to be found all the time... without them... the monarchy as a whole would suffer a severe setback" (181).

All three of the more dictatorial regimes, Austro-Hungary, Germany, and Russia, had clear internal political reasons for entering into World War I. The Emperor, the Kaiser, and the Czar all had strong incentives to stay in power, and all of them faced declining political support. The imperial houses all were perceived as having a special role leading the country in time of war. Finally, in all countries, vilification of their outsiders (Serbia, England, and Austro-Hungary, respectively) made the war popular as a seemingly necessary piece of preemptive defense.

Entry into the war by the more democratic nations, France and England, seems far less driven by internal politics. Support for war in France reflected both an immediate cause—the Franco-Russian alliance—and the long-standing post-1871 hostility toward Germany. When Russia got itself into war with Germany over Serbia, the French stood by this commitment, when it certainly would have been possible to abstain or at least council the Russians against war. Instead, "Messimy, the Minister of War, and Joffre, the Chief of Staff, were pressing the Russians to achieve the highest possible state of readiness" (Keegan 1998, 61). Decades of French discussion of the dangers of German aggression meant that pacifism was sure to be wildly unpopular, and after all, given German actions at the time, French fears were hardly inappropriate.

The British entered the war to stand by an 1839 treaty in which they pledged the neutrality of Belgium, but even this treaty only gave Britain were right, not the duty, to act militarily if Belgium were attacked. Entry into the continental war was chosen by the British liberal party, and this entry probably had more to do with the Liberal Foreign Minister Sir Edward Grey's belief in what was right than any political calculation. Still, political concerns certainly supported Grey's (and the Liberal cabinet's) decision. Decades of anti-German stories and sympathy for "neutral Belgium" encouraged vast prowar public demonstrations. The opposition Conservative party was sure to be more hawkish on the issue, and if the liberals failed to act, a prowar opposition party and strong public feelings seemed to ensure that the incumbents would have shortly lost power if they hadn't supported war.

U.S. Wars, 1898–1975

Between 1898 and 2000, the United States fought six wars with more than 100 battle deaths: the Spanish-American War, World War I, World War II, the Korean War, the Vietnam War, and the Gulf War.

The Spanish-American war and the Gulf War were wildly one-sided wars that involved less than 400 American battle deaths (and less than 2,500 deaths overall). The Korean War, the Vietnam War, and World War I were quite significant, involving 34,000, 47,000, and 53,000 battle deaths, respectively. Finally, World War II involved 292,000 battle deaths.[6]

The precipitating event leading to the Spanish-American War was the Cuban revolution against Spain, led by José Martí. Spain's harsh suppression of that revolution, led by Valeriano Weyler, provided grist for journalists and politicians seeking to vilify Spain. Support for U.S. intervention in Cuba was never led by the president. Cleveland was robustly noninterventionist, and McKinley only went to war under considerable outside pressure.

Support for the war came from a set of journalists and Cubans who vilified Spain and a set of domestic politicians outside the government who pushed for war. One set of vilifiers were Cuban exiles who started their own newspaper (*Patria*) and steadily spread anti-Spanish, prowar propaganda: "Aided by skillful propaganda churned out by the Cuban Junta in New York and Washington, the insurrection gained wide public sympathy, which the administration could not ignore" (Musicant 1998, 79–80).[7] Joseph Pulitzer, William Randolph Hearst, and Hearst star reporter Richard Harding Davis aided in the vilification by depicting the insurrection as a just uprising against a villainous Spanish regime. Weyler was described by Hearst's *New York Journal* as "a fiendish despot . . . a brute, the devastator . . . pitiless, cold, an exterminator of men" (75). As Mullainathan and Shleifer (2002) write, sharp categorization makes better stories than subtle discourse.

Political support for the war came from Republican outsiders like the Assistant Secretary of the Navy Theodore Roosevelt, Congressman Joe Cannon, and Senator Henry Cabot Lodge. In the wake of the destruction of the U.S.S. *Maine*, Cannon pushed through a $50 million defense appropriation in the "Cannon Emergency Bill," and Roosevelt leapt to the forefront of naval recruiting. Enthusiasm for war in Congress was so strong that McKinley faced the very real prospect that if he didn't take action, Congress would declare war without his support. Faced with great popular enthusiasm for war, and a profound threat to his authority as president, McKinley finally put an ultimatum to Spain to quit Cuba, and this ultimatum led to war. Outsiders saw great gains from belligerency, and just as the model suggests, the incumbent went ahead and declared war first.[8]

Outsiders were also more enthusiastic about U.S. intervention in World War I than was President Woodrow Wilson. Theodore Roosevelt became one of the strongest voices for U.S. preparedness and involvement on the allied side.[9] Still, between 1914 and 1916, neither Woodrow Wilson nor the Republican leadership firmly committed themselves to engagement. Like the Cuban Junta before them, both English and German agents worked to get favorable publicity for their side and build hatred against their opponents. The English proved far more capable than the Germans at building hatred, and in the face of changing public opinion and increasing German attacks on U.S. shipping, Wilson moved toward preparedness.

Still, in the election of 1916, Wilson ran as the more propeace candidate with the slogan, "He kept us out of war." The Republican party was slightly more bellicose, declaring that "we must have a coherent continuous policy of national defense, which even in these perilous days the Democratic party has utterly failed to develop, but which we promise to give to the country."[10] The public was not yet convinced that a preventive war was necessary, and neither political party was inclined to go against public opinion.

Wilson's decision to lead America into war came only in April 1917, after the German navy had pursued unrestricted submarine warfare against both allied and U.S. shipping for two months. During this period, the Zimmerman telegram was also published, exposing a German effort to bring Mexico into war against the United States. In the face of this German activity, Wilson finally moved. There is little evidence that he was acting to secure reelection in 1920, nor is it the case that congressional support for war was so strong that Wilson had little choice but to go to war. If anything, Wilson's calculation seems to have been an apolitical, idealistic decision.[11]

World War II seems almost unique among U.S. twentieth-century conflicts. Franklin Roosevelt was more interventionist than some of his Republican opponents (with the notable exception of Wendell Willkie), but his actions prior to Pearl Harbor were fairly modest considering the scale of worldwide carnage. War only came about after a direct attack on the United States, and as such, it is hard to see much of the model at work in the decision to go to war against Japan, especially since even after Pearl Harbor, the United States did not declare war against Germany. Formal intervention into the European war came only after Nazi Germany itself declared war on the United States.

The wars in Korea and Vietnam hark back to the pattern preceding 1941, where the strongest voices for war came from outsiders. Both wars were led by Democrats, whose opponents were more hostile toward the communist threat. After a North Korean attack on South Korea on June 25, 1950, the next day President Truman authorized General MacArthur to evacuate Americans and defend Seoul. Those orders were later extended to attacking any North Korean troops south of the 38th parallel. Truman eventually committed the United States to a full-scale war against both the North Koreans and eventually the Chinese to defend South Korea.

Truman was almost surely motivated by a strong sense of what was right, but he did face political incentives to intervene. Like McKinley in 1898, Truman faced a solid group of political opponents who had been attacking him for military weakness toward the Soviet Union and specifically for his failure to stop Mao Zedong's establishment of a communist China in 1949. After Mao's victory, Senator Styles Bridges called for a vote of censure against the Truman administration, and Senator Knowland called for Secretary of State Dean Acheson's resignation (Acheson 1969, 358). Joseph McCarthy made his first assault on the administration in Wheeling, West Virginia, on February 9, 1950. Truman (and Acheson's) Republican opponents consistently called for a more aggressive policy against communism, particularly in the Far East.

A failure to defend South Korea in 1950 would have cost Truman politically. His Republican opponents immediately claimed that Acheson had invited aggression in Korea by a failure to affirm the U.S. commitment to Asia. The American public was convinced of a communist threat, and many people thought Truman had already shown weakness on this issue. As in 1898, a strong prowar group outside of power increased the costs of peace for the incumbent.

The basic pattern of Democratic support for Vietnam mirrored Truman in Korea or McKinley in Cuba. There is clearer evidence than with Truman that Johnson's actions were motivated partially by a desire to reduce the ability of his Republican opponents to argue that he was soft. He was "especially worried about keeping Lodge mollified because Republicans are waging a Lodge-for-President write-in campaign in New Hampshire. He does not wish to give his Ambassador in Saigon a pretext for resigning in protest, coming home and running against him for President, complaining to Americans that LBJ is doing too little to save South Vietnam" (Beschloss 1997, 259). In the 1964 election against Goldwater, Johnson ran a campaign emphasizing that Goldwater was too prowar, but at the same time, he saw commitment to Vietnam as a means of combating the view that he was himself too propeace.

Even in his second term, Johnson was afraid of seeming too weak to stay committed to the war in Vietnam or to win that war. He correctly anticipated that the Republicans would run a hawkish candidate in 1968, and that a Democratic failure to win the war would be used against the Democratic candidate.[12] His support for the war came not from a wag-the-dog attempt to distract from domestic weakness but rather from an attempt to preempt his domestic opponents from arguing that he wasn't sufficiently strong on national defense.

This history of U.S. wars between 1896 and 1975 does not show an overwhelming pattern of political wars, perhaps because staying president for four more years isn't enough to make up for the terrible costs of war. If there is a political pattern, it is of less bellicose incumbents going to war to preempt prowar opposition groups, which is one scenario suggested by the model.

Conclusion

Does this model help us to understand conflict in the Middle East today? While the logic of the wag-the-dog section of the model has been used to explain U.S. intervention in Iraq, if the war was meant to increase popularity, then this seems to have been a profound miscalculation. It is hard to think that the change in the probability of staying in power (which in retrospect was probably negative) times the modest benefits of being president was even in expectation large enough to justify the difficulties inherent in leading the country through an unpopular war.

The one aspect of the model that is supported by recent events in the United States is that the supporters of the war, both in and out of the administration, worked hard to vilify Saddam Hussein. The fact that some allegations appear to be incorrect *ex post* is consistent both with the model and with almost every other example of wartime leadership. As Arthur Ponsonby said in 1928, "When war is declared, truth is the first casualty."

The model does better at explaining the political patterns in the Middle East. While previous Middle Eastern leaders, notably Nasser and Saddam Hussein, led their countries into wars, quite possibly to quiet domestic discontent, the current leadership of Islamic countries has not pushed toward war with Israel and has been generally allied with the United States. Egypt, Jordan, and Saudi Arabia have frequently cooperated with the United States. Although the leadership of these countries has generally sought to avoid conflict (after all, any conflict would be immensely costly to them), dissident groups within these countries have been far more bellicose. These groups have worked to demonize the United States and Israel. For these political actors, who have little chance of coming into power, supporting conflict increases political support, and there is little chance of having to actually lead the country in war.

Can the threat posed by these anti-U.S. and anti-Israel Arab leaders be reduced? The model suggests three parameters that might be changed and might matter. First, decreasing the returns to leading these countries, through checks on the power of the executive, should reduce the incentives to use military means to stay in power. Second, a greater rotation of leadership, where the current opposition has a higher probability of leading in the future, should reduce the attractiveness of promoting highly self-destructive policies. Third, policies that increase the costs of spreading hatred against Israel and the United States will also make war less popular and war-mongering less attractive.

Appendix: Proofs of Propositions

Proof of Proposition 2.1   In the event that both candidates declare for peace, the probability of the incumbent's remaining in power is $.5 + \hat{\eta}/q$, and the returns to being leader are B_0 for either leader, so the expected utility for the incumbent is B_0 times $.5 + \hat{\eta}/q$, and the expected utility for the challenger is B_0 times $.5 - \hat{\eta}/q$. If the incumbent is propeace but the challenger declares for war, then the probability of the incumbent's staying in power is $.5 + (\hat{\eta} + \theta R_B)/q$, and the expected utility of the incumbent is this probability times B_0. The expected probability of victory for the challenger is $.5 - (\hat{\eta} + \theta R_B)/q$, and the expected utility for the challenger equals $(.5 - (\hat{\eta} + \theta R_B)/q)(B_0 - B_1)$. This implies that the challenger will never declare war because $\theta R_B > 0$.

If the incumbent declares war and the challenger supports war, then the probability of electoral success for the incumbent is $.5 + (\hat{\eta} + \mu_I)/q$, and the expected benefits for the challenger are $(.5 - (\hat{\eta} + \mu_I)/q) \cdot (B_0 - B_1)$. If the incumbent declares war and the challenger promises peace, then the probability of electoral success for the incumbent is $.5 + (\hat{\eta} + \mu_I - p)/q$, and the expected benefits for the challenger are $(.5 - (\hat{\eta} + \mu_I - p)/q)(B_0 - B_1)$. The challenger will support peace if and only if $p > 0$. ∎

Proof of Proposition 2.2   The incumbent receives expected utility of $(.5 + \hat{\eta}/q)B_0$ if he doesn't declare war. If $p < 0$ so that the challenger will support war, then the incumbent's payoff from declaring war is $(.5 + (\hat{\eta} + \mu_I)/q)(B_0 - B_1)$. If $p > 0$ so that the challenger will support peace, then the incumbent's payoff from declaring war is $(.5 + (\hat{\eta} + \mu_I - p)/q)(B_0 - B_1)$. The incumbent's benefits from declaring war are therefore $(.5 + (\hat{\eta} + \mu_I - \max(0, p))/q)(B_0 - B_1)$, which is greater than $(.5 + \hat{\eta}/q)B_0$ if and only if

$$\mu_I > \frac{B_1}{B_0 - B_1}(.5q + \hat{\eta}) + \max(0, p) = \mu_I^*.$$

The value of μ_I^* is falling with B_0, and rising with B_1, q, $\hat{\eta}$, and p (when $p > 0$). ∎

Proof of Proposition 2.3   If the incumbent doesn't initiate a war and the challenger also declares for peace, then for voters there are no net war-related gains from supporting the challenger, and the probability of the incumbent's staying in power is $.5 + \hat{\eta}/q$. If the incumbent doesn't initiate a war but the challenger declares for war, then for voters the war-related gains in supporting the challenger are $\beta \pi g_B \theta^2 R_A - \theta R_B$, and the probability of victory for the incumbent is $.5 + (\hat{\eta} - \beta \pi g_B \theta^2 R_A + \theta R_B)/q$. As such, the challenger will benefit from initiating a war if and only if

$$\beta \pi g_B \theta^2 R_A - \theta R_B > \frac{B_1(.5q - \hat{\eta})}{B_0 - B_1}.$$

If the incumbent initiates a war and the challenger also supports the war, then the war-related gains from supporting the incumbent are $(\beta \pi g_B \theta + 1)\mu_I$; the incumbent's prowess as a war leader makes him both an advantage in the current war and an advantage in the next war. As such, the probability of incumbent success is $(.5 + (\hat{\eta} + (\beta \pi g_B \theta + 1)\mu_I)/q)$. If the incumbent declares war and the challenger supports peace, then the war-related benefits from supporting the incumbent equal $(1 + \beta \pi g_B \theta)\mu_I - p(1 - \beta \pi g_B \theta)$, and the probability of incumbent success is $(.5 + (\hat{\eta} + (\beta \pi g_B \theta + 1)\mu_I - p(1 - \beta \pi g_B \theta))/q)$. Putting these together, the challenger will support a war begun by an incumbent if and only if $\beta \pi g_B \theta > 1$.

Conditions for the incumbent to support war: For the incumbent there are four cases to consider: (1) the challenger favors war in either state, (2) the challenger favors war in neither state, (3) the challenger supports whatever policy is favored by the incumbent, and (4) the challenger is strictly contrarian and supports war if and only if the incumbent favors peace.

If the challenger favors war in either state, then the incumbent favors war if and only if

$$(.5 + (\hat{\eta} + (\beta \pi g_B \theta + 1)\mu_I)/q)(B_0 - B_1)$$

$$> (.5 + (\hat{\eta} - \beta \pi g_B \theta^2 R_A + \theta R_B)/q)B_0,$$

or

$$\mu_I > \frac{B_1(.5q + \hat{\eta}) - B_0(\beta \pi g_B \theta^2 R_A - \theta R_B)}{(B_0 - B_1)(\beta \pi g_B \theta + 1)}.$$

If the challenger does exactly what the incumbent does, then the challenger favors war if and only if

$$(.5 + (\hat{\eta} + (\beta \pi g_B \theta + 1)\mu_I)/q)(B_0 - B_1) > (.5 + \hat{\eta}/q)B_0,$$

or

$$\mu_I > \frac{B_1(.5q + \hat{\eta})}{(B_0 - B_1)(\beta \pi g_B \theta + 1)}.$$

If the challenger declares peace in either case, then the challenger favors war if and only if

$$(.5 + (\hat{\eta} + (\beta \pi g_B \theta + 1)\mu_I - p(1 - \beta \pi g_B \theta))/q)(B_0 - B_1) > (.5 + \hat{\eta}/q)B_0,$$

or

$$\mu_I > \frac{p(1 - \beta \pi g_B \theta) + \dfrac{B_1}{B_0 - B_1}(.5q + \hat{\eta})}{\beta \pi g_B \theta + 1}.$$

Finally, if the challenger always does the opposite of what the incumbent does, then the challenger supports war if and only if

$$(.5 + (\hat{\eta} + (\beta \pi g_B \theta + 1)\mu_I - p(1 - \beta \pi g_B \theta))/q)(B_0 - B_1)$$

$$> (.5 + (\hat{\eta} - \beta \pi g_B \theta^2 R_A + \theta R_B)/q)B_0,$$

or

$$\mu_I > \frac{p(1 - \beta\pi g_B\theta) - \dfrac{B_0}{B_0 - B_1}(\beta\pi g_B\theta^2 R_A - \theta R_B) + (.5q + \hat{\eta})\dfrac{B_1}{B_0 - B_1}}{(\beta\pi g_B\theta + 1)}.$$

In all four of these conditions, there is a cutoff point for μ_I that determines whether war is optimal for the incumbent.   ∎

Proof of Proposition 2.4   If $p = 0$ so that there effectively is no peace option once the war is started, then the conditions collapse to (1) the challenger declares war if the incumbent doesn't if and only if

$$\beta\pi g_B\theta^2 R_A - \theta R_B > \frac{B_1(.5q - \hat{\eta})}{B_0 - B_1},$$

(2) if this condition holds, then the incumbent declares war if and only if

$$\mu_I > \frac{B_1(.5q + \hat{\eta}) - B_0(\beta\pi g_B\theta^2 R_A - \theta R_B)}{(B_0 - B_1)(\beta\pi g_B\theta + 1)},$$

and (3) if the challenger's condition fails to hold, the incumbent declares war if the condition fails to hold if and only if

$$\mu_I > \frac{B_1(.5q + \hat{\eta})}{(B_0 - B_1)(\beta\pi g_B\theta + 1)}.$$

When

$$\beta\pi g_B\theta^2 R_A - \theta R_B > \frac{B_1(.5q - \hat{\eta})}{B_0 - B_1},$$

then

$$\mu_I^* = \frac{B_1(.5q + \hat{\eta}) - B_0(\beta\pi g_B\theta^2 R_A - \theta R_B)}{(B_0 - B_1)(\beta\pi g_B\theta + 1)},$$

and when

$$\beta\pi g_B\theta^2 R_A - \theta R_B < \frac{B_1(.5q - \hat{\eta})}{B_0 - B_1},$$

then

$$\mu_I^* = \frac{B_1(.5q + \hat{\eta})}{(B_0 - B_1)(\beta \pi g_B \theta + 1)}.$$

At the point where

$$\beta \pi g_B \theta^2 R_A - \theta R_B = \frac{B_1(.5q - \hat{\eta})}{B_0 - B_1},$$

μ_I^* drops discontinuously from

$$\frac{B_1(.5q + \hat{\eta})}{(B_0 - B_1)(\beta \pi g_B \theta + 1)}$$

to

$$\frac{B_1(.5q + \hat{\eta})}{(B_0 - B_1)(\beta \pi g_B \theta + 1)} \left(1 - \frac{B_0(.5q - \hat{\eta})}{(B_0 - B_1)(.5q + \hat{\eta})} \right),$$

which is positive if and only if

$$\hat{\eta} > \frac{.5qB_1}{2B_0 - B_1}.$$

To derive comparative statics in this case, it is necessary both to consider comparative statics holding challenger behavior constant and to include the effects that come when parameters change challenger behavior. Holding challenger behavior constant, the variables, $\hat{\eta}$, q, and B_1 cause μ_I^* to rise, and the variables B_0, β, π, and g_B cause μ_I^* to fall within region. Increases in R_A cause μ_I^* to fall, and increases in R_B cause μ_I^* to rise, when

$$\beta \pi g_B \theta^2 R_A - \theta R_B > \frac{B_1(.5q - \hat{\eta})}{B_0 - B_1}.$$

Increases in θ cause μ_I^* to fall unless

$$\beta \pi g_B \theta^2 R_A - \theta R_B < \frac{B_1(.5q - \hat{\eta})}{B_0 - B_1} \quad \text{and} \quad 2\beta \pi g_B \theta R_A < R_B.$$

Increases in $\hat{\eta}$, β, π, g_B, B_0, and R_A, and decreases in R_B, q, and B_1, make the condition

$$\beta \pi g_B \theta^2 R_A - \theta R_B > \frac{B_1(.5q - \hat{\eta})}{B_0 - B_1}$$

more likely to hold. If this condition holds, there is a discontinuous drop in μ_I^*. Increases in θ make the condition more likely to hold if $2\beta\pi g_B\theta R_A > R_B$, but this must always hold if the condition holds. As such, μ_I^* is smoothly increasing with q and B_1 and smoothly decreasing with β, π, and g_B almost everywhere, but at the point where

$$\beta\pi g_B\theta^2 R_A - \theta R_B = \frac{B_1(.5q - \hat{\eta})}{B_0 - B_1},$$

μ_I^* discontinuously jumps upward with q and B_1 and discontinuously jumps downward with β, π, and g_B. Increases in $\hat{\eta}$ cause μ_I^* to rise almost everywhere, except at the point where

$$\beta\pi g_B\theta^2 R_A - \theta R_B = \frac{B_1(.5q - \hat{\eta})}{B_0 - B_1},$$

at which point an increase in $\hat{\eta}$ causes a discontinuous jump downward in μ_I^*. ∎

Proof of Proposition 2.5 If the incumbent has not declared war and has not sent a signal, then there are four options for the challenger: (1) no war/no signal, (2) no war/signal, (3) war/no signal, and (4) war/signal. No war/no signal yields utility of $(.5 - \hat{\eta}/q)B_0$. No war/signal yields expected utility of $(.5 - \hat{\eta}/q)B_0 - k_C$, which is clearly dominated by no war/no signal. War/no signal yields utility of $(.5 - (\hat{\eta} + \theta R_B)/q)(B_0 - B_1)$, which is also clearly dominated by no war/no signal, and finally war/signal yields utility of

$$\left(.5 - \frac{1}{q}\left(\hat{\eta} - \beta\frac{\pi_0 g_B\theta^2 R_A}{\pi_0 + \phi(1 - \pi_0)} + \theta R_B\right)\right)(B_0 - B_1) - k_C.$$

This dominates no war/no signal if and only if

$$\beta\frac{\pi_0 g_B\theta^2 R_A}{\pi_0 + \phi(1 - \pi_0)} - \theta R_B > \frac{B_1(.5q - \hat{\eta}) + qk_C}{B_0 - B_1}.$$

If the incumbent has not declared war but has sent a signal, then the challenger only needs to decide whether to declare war, and as before, he will benefit from war if and only if

$$\frac{\beta\pi_0 g_B\theta^2 R_A}{\pi_0 + \phi(1 - \pi_0)} - \theta R_B > \frac{B_1(.5q - \hat{\eta})}{B_0 - B_1}.$$

For the incumbent, the no war/no signal strategy is always preferable to the no war/signal strategy. Indeed, if

$$\frac{\beta\pi_0 g_B \theta^2 R_A}{\pi_0 + \phi(1 - \pi_0)} - \theta R_B < \frac{B_1(.5q - \hat{\eta})}{B_0 - B_1} < \frac{B_1(.5q - \hat{\eta}) + qk_C}{B_0 - B_1},$$

then the challenger will pursue no war/no signal in either case, so the incumbent has utility $(.5 + \hat{\eta}/q)B_0$ if he chooses no war/no signal and utility $(.5 + \hat{\eta}/q)B_0 - k_I$ if he chooses no war/signal. If

$$\frac{B_1(.5q - \hat{\eta})}{B_0 - B_1} < \frac{\beta\pi_0 g_B \theta^2 R_A}{\pi_0 + \phi(1 - \pi_0)} - \theta R_B < \frac{B_1(.5q - \hat{\eta}) + qk_C}{B_0 - B_1},$$

then the challenger will pursue no war/no signal if the incumbent chooses no war/no signal, and the challenger will pursue war if the incumbent chooses no war/signal. For the incumbent, the expected utility from no war/no signal is $(.5 + \hat{\eta}/q)B_0$, and the utility from no war/signal is

$$\left(.5 + \frac{1}{q}\left(\hat{\eta} - \beta\frac{\pi_0 g_B \theta^2 R_A}{\pi_0 + \phi(1 - \pi_0)} + \theta R_B\right)\right)B_0 - k_I,$$

which is smaller than $(.5 + \hat{\eta}/q)B_0$ because

$$\frac{\beta\pi_0 g_B \theta^2 R_A}{\pi_0 + \phi(1 - \pi_0)} - \theta R_B > \frac{B_1(.5q - \hat{\eta})}{B_0 - B_1} > 0$$

by assumption. Finally, if

$$\frac{B_1(.5q - \hat{\eta})}{B_0 - B_1} < \frac{B_1(.5q - \hat{\eta}) + qk_C}{B_0 - B_1} < \frac{\beta\pi_0 g_B \theta^2 R_A}{\pi_0 + \phi(1 - \pi_0)} - \theta R_B,$$

then the challenger will choose war/signal if the incumbent pursues no war/no signal, and war/no signal if the incumbent pursues no war/signal. The incumbent's expected payoff from no war/no signal is

$$\left(.5 + \frac{1}{q}\left(\hat{\eta} - \beta\frac{\pi_0 g_B \theta^2 R_A}{\pi_0 + \phi(1 - \pi_0)} + \theta R_B\right)\right)B_0,$$

and his payoff from no war/signal is

$$\left(.5 + \frac{1}{q}\left(\hat{\eta} - \beta\frac{\pi_0 g_B \theta^2 R_A}{\pi_0 + \phi(1 - \pi_0)} + \theta R_B\right)\right)B_0 - k_I.$$

Thus no war/no signal is always preferable to no war/signal for the incumbent, and the incumbent will only send a signal if he is initiating a war.

For the incumbent, war/signal dominates war/no signal if and only if

$$\frac{\beta g_B \theta \pi_0 (B_0 - B_1) \mu_I}{q(\pi_0 + \phi(1 - \pi_0))} > k_I.$$

If the incumbent declares war without sending a signal, then the challenger will benefit from sending a signal if and only if

$$\left(.5 - \left(\hat{\eta} + \left(\frac{\beta g_B \theta \pi_0}{\pi_0 + \phi(1 - \pi_0)} + 1\right)\mu_I\right)\Big/q\right)(B_0 - B_1) - k_C$$

$$> (.5 - (\hat{\eta} + \mu_I)/q)(B_0 - B_1),$$

which is true if and only if

$$\frac{q k_C (\pi_0 + \phi(1 - \pi_0))}{(B_0 - B_1)\beta g_B \theta \pi_0} < -\mu_I.$$

If this inequality holds, then the incumbent's utility for war/signal is k_I less than his utility for war/no signal, so war/no signal dominates. If

$$\frac{q k_C (\pi_0 + \phi(1 - \pi_0))}{(B_0 - B_1)\beta g_B \theta \pi_0} > -\mu_I,$$

then the incumbent's utility for war/signal is

$$\left(.5 + \left(\hat{\eta} + \left(\frac{\beta g_B \theta \pi_0}{\pi_0 + \phi(1 - \pi_0)} + 1\right)\mu_I\right)\Big/q\right)(B_0 - B_1) - k_I,$$

and his utility for war/no signal is $(.5 + (\hat{\eta} + \mu_I)/q)(B_0 - B_1)$. War/signal dominates in this case if and only if

$$\frac{\beta g_B \theta \pi_0 (B_0 - B_1) \mu_I}{q(\pi_0 + \phi(1 - \pi_0))} > k_I,$$

and this inequality implies that $\mu_I > 0$, so in particular,

$$\frac{q k_C (\pi_0 + \phi(1 - \pi_0))}{(B_0 - B_1)\beta g_B \theta \pi_0} > -\mu_I.$$

Thus war/signal dominates war/no signal for the incumbent if and only if

$$\frac{\beta g_B \theta \pi_0 (B_0 - B_1) \mu_I}{q(\pi_0 + \phi(1 - \pi_0))} > k_I.$$

Now we turn to conditions under which the challenger will send a signal after the incumbent has declared war without sending a signal. As shown, the challenger will send a signal after the incumbent has done war/no signal if and only if

$$\frac{q k_C (\pi_0 + \phi(1 - \pi_0))}{(B_0 - B_1) \beta g_B \theta \pi_0} < -\mu_I, \tag{*}$$

so we assume this inequality. Then $\mu_I < 0$, so we have

$$\frac{\beta g_B \theta \pi_0 (B_0 - B_1) \mu_I}{q(\pi_0 + \phi(1 - \pi_0))} < k_I,$$

which ensures that war/no signal dominates war/signal for the incumbent. Assuming (*), the incumbent decides between war/no signal and peace/no signal. If

$$\frac{\beta \pi_0 g_B \theta^2 R_A}{\pi_0 + \phi(1 - \pi_0)} - \theta R_B < \frac{B_1(.5q - \hat{\eta}) + q k_C}{B_0 - B_1},$$

then peace/no signal by the incumbent induces the challenger to do peace/no signal. In this case, the utility for peace/no signal for the incumbent is $(.5 + \hat{\eta}/q)B_0$, and the utility for war/no signal is

$$\left(.5 + \left(\hat{\eta} + \left(\frac{\beta g_B \theta \pi_0}{\pi_0 + \phi(1 - \pi_0)} + 1\right)\mu_I\right) \middle/ q\right)(B_0 - B_1),$$

which is smaller than $(.5 + \hat{\eta}/q)B_0$ because $\mu_I < 0$. So, in this case, the incumbent chooses peace/no signal. If

$$\frac{\beta \pi_0 g_B \theta^2 R_A}{\pi_0 + \phi(1 - \pi_0)} - \theta R_B > \frac{B_1(.5q - \hat{\eta}) + q k_C}{B_0 - B_1}, \tag{**}$$

then peace/no signal by the incumbent induces the challenger to do war/signal. In this case, peace/no signal gives the incumbent utility

$$\left(.5 + \frac{1}{q}\left(\hat{\eta} - \beta \frac{\pi_0 g_B \theta^2 R_A}{\pi_0 + \phi(1 - \pi_0)} + \theta R_B\right)\right)B_0$$

and war/no signal gives the incumbent utility

$$\left(.5 + \left(\hat{\eta} + \left(\frac{\beta g_B \theta \pi_0}{\pi_0 + \phi(1 - \pi_0)} + 1\right)\mu_I\right) \Big/ q\right)(B_0 - B_1),$$

so war/no signal dominates if and only if

$$\frac{B_1(.5q + \hat{\eta}) - B_0(\beta\pi g_B\theta^2 R_A - \theta R_B)}{(B_0 - B_1)(\beta\pi g_B\theta + 1)} > \mu_I, \tag{***}$$

where $\pi \equiv \pi_0/(\pi_0 + \phi(1 - \pi_0))$. Thus the challenger will send a signal after the incumbent has done war/no signal if and only if (*), (**), and (***) hold, which is possible when $\mu_I < 0$, k_C is small, R_B is large, $\theta \approx R_B/R_A$, and $\beta\pi g_B > 1$.   ∎

Proof of Proposition 2.6   If the incumbent does not declare war, the challenger will do so if and only if

$$\beta\frac{\pi_0 g_B\theta^2 R_A}{\pi_0 + \phi(1 - \pi_0)} - \theta R_B > \frac{B_1(.5q - \hat{\eta}) + qk_C}{B_0 - B_1},$$

or equivalently,

$$k_C > \frac{1}{q}\left(\left(\beta\frac{\pi_0 g_B\theta^2 R_A}{\pi_0 + \phi(1 - \pi_0)} - \theta R_B\right)(B_0 - B_1) - B_1(.5q - \hat{\eta})\right) \equiv k_C^*.$$

Comparative statics follow directly.   ∎

Proof of Proposition 2.7   First, assume that

$$\beta\frac{\pi_0 g_B\theta^2 R_A}{\pi_0 + \phi(1 - \pi_0)} - \theta R_B < \frac{B_1(.5q - \hat{\eta}) + qk_C}{B_0 - B_1}.$$

Then, if

$$\frac{\beta g_B\theta\pi_0(B_0 - B_1)\mu_I}{q(\pi_0 + \phi(1 - \pi_0))} > k_I,$$

war/signal dominates peace/no signal if and only if

$$\mu_I > \frac{(B_1(.5q + \hat{\eta}) + qk_I)}{(B_0 - B_1)\left(1 + \dfrac{\beta g_B\theta\pi_0}{(\pi_0 + \phi(1 - \pi_0))}\right)}.$$

If

$$\frac{\beta g_B \theta \pi_0 (B_0 - B_1) \mu_I}{q(\pi_0 + \phi(1 - \pi_0))} < k_I,$$

then if

$$\frac{qk_C(\pi_0 + \phi(1 - \pi_0))}{(B_0 - B_1)\beta g_B \theta \pi_0} > -\mu_I,$$

war/no signal dominates peace/no signal if and only if

$$\mu_I > \frac{B_1(.5q + \hat{\eta})}{B_0 - B_1},$$

and if

$$\frac{qk_C(\pi_0 + \phi(1 - \pi_0))}{(B_0 - B_1)\beta g_B \theta \pi_0} < -\mu_I,$$

war/no signal dominates peace/no signal if and only if

$$\mu_I > \frac{(B_1(.5q + \hat{\eta}))}{(B_0 - B_1)\left(1 + \dfrac{\beta g_B \theta \pi_0}{(\pi_0 + \phi(1 - \pi_0))}\right)},$$

which is impossible because in this case $\mu_I < 0$. Thus the incumbent goes to war if and only if

$$\mu_I >$$

$$\max\left(\frac{(B_1(.5q + \hat{\eta}) + qk_I)}{(B_0 - B_1)\left(1 + \dfrac{\beta g_B \theta \pi_0}{(\pi_0 + \phi(1 - \pi_0))}\right)}, \frac{(qk_I)}{(B_0 - B_1)\left(\dfrac{\beta g_B \theta \pi_0}{(\pi_0 + \phi(1 - \pi_0))}\right)}\right),$$

or

$$\frac{B_1(.5q + \hat{\eta})}{B_0 - B_1} < \mu_I < \frac{(qk_I)}{(B_0 - B_1)\left(\dfrac{\beta g_B \theta \pi_0}{(\pi_0 + \phi(1 - \pi_0))}\right)}.$$

Now, assume that

$$\beta \frac{\pi_0 g_B \theta^2 R_A}{\pi_0 + \phi(1 - \pi_0)} - \theta R_B > \frac{B_1(.5q - \hat{\eta}) + qk_C}{B_0 - B_1}.$$

If

$$\frac{\beta g_B \theta \pi_0 (B_0 - B_1) \mu_I}{q(\pi_0 + \phi(1 - \pi_0))} > k_I,$$

then war/signal dominates peace/no signal if and only if

$$\mu_I > \frac{(B_1(.5q + \hat{\eta}) - B_0 P + q k_I)}{(B_0 - B_1)\left(1 + \dfrac{\beta g_B \theta \pi_0}{(\pi_0 + \phi(1 - \pi_0))}\right)}.$$

If

$$\frac{\beta g_B \theta \pi_0 (B_0 - B_1) \mu_I}{q(\pi_0 + \phi(1 - \pi_0))} < k_I,$$

then if

$$\frac{q k_C (\pi_0 + \phi(1 - \pi_0))}{(B_0 - B_1)\beta g_B \theta \pi_0} > -\mu_I,$$

war/no signal dominates peace/no signal if and only if

$$\mu_I > \frac{B_1(.5q + \hat{\eta}) - B_0 P}{B_0 - B_1},$$

and if

$$\frac{q k_C (\pi_0 + \phi(1 - \pi_0))}{(B_0 - B_1)\beta g_B \theta \pi_0} < -\mu_I,$$

war/no signal dominates peace/no signal if and only if

$$\mu_I > \frac{(B_1(.5q + \hat{\eta})) - B_0 P}{(B_0 - B_1)\left(1 + \dfrac{\beta g_B \theta \pi_0}{(\pi_0 + \phi(1 - \pi_0))}\right)}.$$

Thus the incumbent goes to war if and only if

$$\mu_I >$$

$$\max\left(\frac{(B_1(.5q + \hat{\eta}) - B_0 P + q k_I)}{(B_0 - B_1)\left(1 + \dfrac{\beta g_B \theta \pi_0}{(\pi_0 + \phi(1 - \pi_0))}\right)}, \frac{(q k_I)}{(B_0 - B_1)\left(\dfrac{\beta g_B \theta \pi_0}{(\pi_0 + \phi(1 - \pi_0))}\right)}\right),$$

$$\min\left(-\frac{qk_C(\pi_0 + \phi(1 - \pi_0))}{(B_0 - B_1)\beta g_B\theta\pi_0}, \frac{B_1(.5q + \hat{\eta}) - B_0 P}{B_0 - B_1}\right) < \mu_I$$

$$< \frac{(qk_I)}{(B_0 - B_1)\left(\dfrac{\beta g_B\theta\pi_0}{(\pi_0 + \phi(1 - \pi_0))}\right)},$$

or

$$\frac{(B_1(.5q + \hat{\eta})) - B_0 P}{(B_0 - B_1)\left(1 + \dfrac{\beta g_B\theta\pi_0}{(\pi_0 + \phi(1 - \pi_0))}\right)} < \mu_I < -\frac{qk_C(\pi_0 + \phi(1 - \pi_0))}{(B_0 - B_1)\beta g_B\theta\pi_0}.$$

I define μ_I^* as

$$\max\left(\frac{(B_1(.5q + \hat{\eta}) - B_0 P + qk_I)}{(B_0 - B_1)\left(1 + \dfrac{\beta g_B\theta\pi_0}{(\pi_0 + \phi(1 - \pi_0))}\right)}, \frac{(qk_I)}{(B_0 - B_1)\left(\dfrac{\beta g_B\theta\pi_0}{(\pi_0 + \phi(1 - \pi_0))}\right)}\right)$$

and comparative statics follow. ∎

Notes

1. While the core idea is in Fearon (1994) and in the work of earlier analysts such as Karl Marx, this chapter differs from most of its predecessors in providing a political micro-foundation for the electoral gains from combat. The work of Hess and Orphanides (1995) is a prominent exception because it shows war resulting from well-described electoral competition.

2. This is a primary difference between this model and Hess and Orphanides (1995), who write that, leaders go to war to show their war-making ability. In this model, leaders go to war so that their war-making ability becomes relevant to reelection.

3. Wars can serve a country's interest because countries lack the ability to commit to long-run contracts, where one country promises never to exploit another in the future. If one country thinks that the balance of power is increasingly favoring a neighbor, then preemptive war may be attractive, although in a world with complete contracts, both nations would happily commit never to start a conflict.

4. There are times when this logic is probably understood by all participants, but the tendency to cooperate and support current leaders in the face of a threat also seems emotionally hard-wired. The tendency to band together against outsiders has been shown in many experiments, like the famous Smuggler's Cove experiment, where boys were given artificial identities and then fought on the basis of these identities (Sherif 1961).

5. Both Mullainathan and Shleifer (2002) and Gentzkow and Shapiro (2006) provide models of media bias where the media may be unwilling to challenge widely held views.

6. Battle deaths are from ⟨http://www1.va.gov/opa/fact/amwars.asp⟩.

7. Their incentives were obvious. One member of the "Junta," Palma, became the first president of independent Cuba.

8. Roosevelt would, of course, become president largely because of his role in the war. Cannon would become Speaker of the House of Representatives, and Lodge secured a long career as the foreign policy leader of the Senate.

9. As the model predicts, Theodore Roosevelt was deeply hawkish when he wasn't in power and didn't need to bear the consequences of his bellicosity, but during his time in office, he was moderate enough to even win a Nobel Peace Prize.

10. Party platform text is from ⟨http://www.presidency.ucsb.edu/showplatforms .php?platindex=R1916⟩.

11. The only way in which the model is vindicated is the remarkable work of the U.S. government to vilify Germans after war was declared. This was the first war where an explicit agency, the Committee on Public Information, worked hard to convince the public of the evil of their wartime opponent.

12. He did, however, underestimate the extent to which propeace forces within his own party would eventually upset his goals for a second nomination.

References

Acheson, D. 1969. *Present at the Creation*. New York: W. W. Norton.

Bergahn, V. R. 1973. *Germany and the Approach of War in 1914*. New York: St. Martin's Press.

Beschloss, M. 1997. *Taking Charge: The Johnson White House Tapes, 1963–1964*. New York: Simon and Schuster.

Bueno de Mesquita, B. 1981. *The War Trap*. New Haven, Conn.: Yale University Press.

Case, L. 1972. *French Opinion on War and Diplomacy during the Second Empire*. New York: Octagon Books.

Craig, G. 1955. *The Politics of the Prussian Army*. Oxford: Oxford University Press.

Downs, G. W., and D. M. Rocke. 1994. Conflict, agency, and gambling for resurrection: The principal-agent problem goes to war. *American Journal of Political Science* 38 (2): 362–380.

Fearon, J. D. 1994. Domestic political audiences and the escalation of international disputes. *American Political Science Review* 88 (3): 577–592.

Gentzkow, M., and J. Shapiro. 2006. Media bias and reputation. *Journal of Political Economy* 114 (2): 280–317.

Gilpin, R. 1981. *War and Change in World Politics*. Cambridge: Cambridge University Press.

Glaeser, E. L. 2005. The political economy of hatred. *Quarterly Journal of Economics* 120 (1): 45–86.

Gooch, B. 1956. A century of historiography on the origins of the Crimean War. *American Historical Review* 62 (1): 33–56.

Hess, G. D., and A. Orphanides. 1995. War politics: An economic, rational voter framework. *American Economic Review* 85: 828–846.

Howard, M. 1961. *The Franco-Prussian War*. London: Routledge.

Keegan, J. 1998. *The First World War*. New York: Vintage Books.

Kinglake, A. W. 1874. *The Invasion of the Crimea*. London: Blackwood.

Levy, G., and R. Razin. 2004. It takes two: An explanation of the democratic peace. *Journal of European Economic Association* 21: 1–29.

Levy, J. S. 1987. Declining powers and the preventive motivation for war. *World Politics* 40 (1): 82–107.

Mansfield, E., and J. Snyder. 2005. *Electing to Fight*. Cambridge, Mass.: MIT Press.

Marx, K. 1859. Quid pro quo. *Das Volk*, July 30, August 6, 13, 20. ⟨http://www.marxists.org/archive/marx/works/1859/quid-pro-quo/⟩.

Mullainathan, S., and A. Shleifer. 2002. Media bias. NBER Working Paper 9295. Cambridge, Mass.: National Bureau of Economic Research.

Musicant, I. 1998. *Empire by Default: The Spanish-American War and the Dawn of the American Century*. New York: Henry Holt.

Organski, A. F. K., and J. Kugler. 1980. *The War Ledger*. Chicago: University of Chicago Press.

Pipes, R. 1990. *The Russian Revolution*. New York: Vintage Books.

Rousseau, D. L. 2005. *Democracy and War: Institutions, Norms, and the Evolution of International Conflict*. Stanford, Calif.: Stanford University Press.

Russett, B., and J. Oneal. 2001. *Triangulating Peace: Democracy, Interdependence and International Organizations*. New York: W. W. Norton.

Sherif, N. 1961. *Intergroup Conflict and Cooperation: The Robbers Cove Experiment*. Norman, Okla.: Institute of Group Relations.

Wawro, G. 2000. *Warfare and Society in Europe, 1792–1914*. London: Routledge.

3 Globalization and Insecurity: Reviewing Some Basic Issues

Michelle R. Garfinkel, Stergios Skaperdas, and Constantinos Syropoulos

The hidden hand of the global market would never work without the hidden fist. And the hidden fist that keeps the world safe for Silicon Valley's technologies to flourish is called the United States Army, Air Force, Navy and Marine Corps (with the help, incidentally, of global institutions like the U.N. and the International Monetary Fund). And those fighting forces and institutions are paid for by all the tax dollars that Washington is "wasting" every year.

Thomas Friedman, "Techno-Nothings," *New York Times*, April 18, 1998, p. A13

If we ask . . . what would be the most powerful mechanism for ensuring that the forces of economic convergence overwhelm those of divergence, the answer has to be jurisdictional integration.

Martin Wolf, *Why Globalization Works* (2004), p. 315

Concepts like Thomas Friedman's "hidden fist" and Martin Wolf's "jurisdictional integration" are rarely, if ever, invoked in economic analyses of trade and globalization. That is not surprising given that such analyses are based on—or at least are intellectually inspired by—models of trade in which concerns about security and governance are completely absent. However, while abstracting from security concerns might be analytically convenient, in practice many goods that are traded internationally or are important inputs in the production of tradeable goods—oil, diamonds, land, water resources—are subject to contestation, either domestically by rival groups or internationally by different countries.

We first argue that insecurity has costs that are economically important. These costs include direct costs such as those of arming and destruction as well as more indirect ones due to distortions in production, consumption, and investment that are brought about by insecurity and conflict. We then discuss the various costs of domestic insecurity and their economic importance, and examine the potential costs of transnational insecurity.

Different trading regimes can be expected to induce different costs of insecurity, but how these costs vary with trading regimes has barely been investigated in economics. The classical liberal viewpoint, which by default appears to be the position shared by many economists, is that more liberal trading regimes tend to reduce conflict because the gains from trade bring potential adversaries closer to one another.[1] To our knowledge, there is no precise mechanism to which classical liberalism appeals, but the positive effects of trade on security can work through a variety of channels. For example, business contacts become personal contacts, increased trade strengthens diplomatic ties, and increased human contacts improve intercultural understanding. According to the liberal view, breaking down barriers to trade brings not only the familiar gains from trade but also reduces costs of insecurity.

A sharply different perspective comes from the realist school of international relations. In particular, when one party trades with an adversary (actual or potential), that party provides its opponent with fuel for growth and enhanced military strength.[2] That increase in the adversary's military strength in turn induces the party to expend more resources on security itself, thereby detracting from the gains it realized from trade. Indeed, according to the realist perspective, the increased security costs could very well offset the gains.

Are the liberals or the realists right? Attempting to answer such a question requires a formal framework that can admit both trade and the costs of insecurity. We examine such a framework that borrows from our previous work (Skaperdas and Syropoulos 2001; Garfinkel, Skaperdas, and Syropoulos 2005). Two small adversaries compete for a contested resource that can be used in the production of tradeable goods.[3] The model we examine is simple enough in its symmetry such that it allows for the two adversaries to be interpreted as either small countries or groups within a single country. The costs of insecurity, measured by the value of resources diverted from productive uses, vary with the degree to which the countries in which the parties operate are open to trade. We study, in particular, the two polar opposite regimes of autarky and free trade. In determining welfare in such a setting, the gains from free trade need to be weighed against the possibly higher costs of conflict that emerge in the autarkic outcome. The findings we report include (1) importers of the contested resource gain unambiguously under free trade; (2) exporters of the contested resource lose under free trade when the international price of the resource is close enough to its autarkic price.

Thus, even this simple framework indicates that the question of whether the liberals or the realists are correct in their views about trade cannot be answered unconditionally. And yet, this framework identifies specific and different conditions under which the liberal and realist views hold. Moving beyond the liberal-realist debate, our framework also provides new insights into the "natural resource curse" and a distortion in trade patterns that is brought about by insecurity.

Ultimately, the costs of insecurity and, as our analysis indicates, the effects of globalization depend on how effectively individual countries and the relationships between countries are governed. We stress how economic globalization must be considered jointly with problems of governance and discuss dilemmas that are within today's time horizon and beyond.

The Economic Relevance of Domestic Insecurity

Since World War II civil wars have broken out in 73 countries, in many of them more than once, and the estimated death toll resulting directly from these conflicts is over 16 million (Fearon and Laitin 2003, 75).[4] The costs of arming and hiring combatants, the destruction of crops, structures, capital infrastructure, and many other collateral costs have been surveyed by researchers at the World Bank (Collier et al. 2003).

In addition, there are the usual—for economists—indirect costs of war that come from the static and dynamic misallocation of resources. Using the methodology developed by Lucas (1987) to estimate the welfare costs of the business cycle, Hess (2003) estimates the welfare costs of conflict from its effects on consumption alone for 147 countries spanning the period 1960–1992 to be on average 8 percent of steady-state consumption. The individual estimates for some countries are, not surprisingly, a bit smaller. For the United States, for example, the estimated cost is 3.2 percent. However, even this estimate is far greater than the Lucas-type estimate of the welfare cost of the business cycle in the United States (Hess 2003, 17). Moreover, the estimates for some lower-income countries are dramatically higher, e.g., the cost is 65 percent in Iraq and 40.5 percent in Angola.

Civil wars are not the sole source of conflict and security costs. Rodrik (1998; 1999), for example, has drawn attention to distributional and social conflict, and the costs associated with them: strikes and

lockouts, protests that sometimes become violent, military coups, ethnic, religious, or class rivalries, as well as common crime. The costs of
such conflicts would perhaps be more difficult to estimate, but surely
they are not negligible.

Another set of costs is associated with the public and private enforcement of property rights. Take as an example property rights in
land, a key factor of production, an issue we would expect to have
been settled by the twenty-first century. However, in many middle-
and low-income countries property rights in land are publicly unen-
forceable, if they exist at all. The Russian Parliament voted a land law
for urban areas a few years ago, but no such law exists for land in rural
areas yet. In India the problem is not the absence of law in land but the
hopeless conflict of too many contradictory laws, based on different
legal traditions that have not been resolved by the Indian state. Not
surprisingly, then, as Lewis (2004, 199) states: "It is not clear who
owns land in India. Over 90 percent of land titles are unclear." In
China numerous land disputes between local municipal enterprises
and peasant farmers with traditional rights have been reported, which
threaten the country's social stability and economic growth in the future (see, e.g., Jacques 2005). In the absence of effective public enforcement of law in land, which in itself is expensive but predictable, costly
contests often take place for its private capture. However, even those
who are able to privately appropriate land are unlikely to take the
more efficient long-term actions that someone with clear title would.

Thus, from civil wars, to distributional conflict, to the private appropriation of land, insecurity and conflict are associated with large costs.
It would be fair to say that these costs dwarf the (sometimes elusive)
deadweight losses from Harberger triangles that dominate much of
the study of inefficiency. Given the apparent economic significance of
conflict costs, especially for low-income countries, it is surprising how
little attention they have received among economists.

For our purposes here, it is important to note that many civil wars
and lower-level conflicts have taken place in countries with natural
resources like oil, diamonds, copper, and other minerals as well as
over the distribution of land. Many of these same countries also suffer
from the "natural-resource curse," the tendency to have low or negative income growth correlated with higher exports of natural resources.
We have a possible explanation for this puzzle that is based on the
costs of insecurity.

Insecurity in Interstate Relations

Trade and financial transactions between parties located in different nation-states naturally take place within an anarchic setting. That is, there is no interstate authority that can serve as arbiter of disputes between those parties. Not surprisingly, then, wars between states have continually taken place throughout recorded human history.

Since World War II, though, there have been fewer interstate wars than in the previous half century, with fewer fatalities than those in civil wars that took place over the same period. This relative calm, however, has not translated into lower levels of security costs. The superpower rivalry that existed between the United States and the Soviet Union throughout much of the latter half of the twentieth century left insecurity levels high. Whereas the economic costs of destructive warfare were relatively low, nations continued to pour resources into their respective militaries, and the costs of insecurity were far from negligible.

The cold war, while not a destructive war, was still a conflict. The standoff resulted partly from the threat of nuclear annihilation, aided by the presence of the United Nations and other international institutions that, though imperfect and weak, provided some semblance of predictability in international relations. For example, the concept of collective security and the reluctance of the two superpowers and their respective blocks to sanction changes in international borders provided a measure of cross-border stability that made states reluctant to engage in warfare against other states.[5]

The end of the cold war brought the breakup of the Soviet Union, Yugoslavia, and Czechoslovakia, a unipolar world, and arguably a weakening of the United Nations. Whether the relative interstate peace of the post–World War II period can continue into the future remains unclear. Two related though distinct problems have the potential to jeopardize that peace and thereby severely threaten economic globalization. As we argue, economic globalization in itself without appropriate governance could actually hasten the onset of more conflictual relations between states.

The first threat comes from regional wars with resource contestation as their primary though not sole source. According to Klare (2001), conflict between states over resources has become more serious lately. Oil is, of course, the most important resource, but other minerals and also fresh water resources are gaining importance as well. Here we provide only a few examples of such potential sources and areas of conflict. The discovered and yet-to-be-discovered oil wealth of Central Asia is fueling disputes and arming that could approach a new Great Game. The states surrounding the Caspian Sea—Russia, Kazakhstan, Turkmenistan, Iran, and Azerbaijan—have still not settled on a formula for dividing the rights of exploration and exploitation for oil. Where claims are settled, oil companies and their governments vie for contracts, rival pipeline routes, bids to buy local rights as well as local firms, and the whole endeavor is tinged with subterranean geopolitical calculations that involve the United States as well as all the powers of Russia, China, and Europe. Further South, with the Iraq war, the Middle East has already become a new battleground with much uncertainty about where it will lead. And areas with suspected oil reserves like the South China Sea (around the Spratly and Paracel islands) have been already contested in minor hot incidents as well as diplomatically by seven countries (China, Taiwan, Vietnam, the Philippines, Indonesia, Malaysia, and Brunei).

Beyond oil, fresh water has perhaps been underrated for its potential to create havoc in many areas with rapidly increasing populations, economic growth, and economic globalization. It is not well-known, for instance, that Egypt has threatened its upstream neighbors, especially Ethiopia, with bombing water facilities if they were to go ahead with irrigation projects on the Nile (Klare 2001, 153). In the coming years, the countries of the Upper Nile and the tributaries that drain into Lake Victoria (Sudan, Ethiopia, Kenya, Uganda, Tanzania, Rwanda, Burundi, Congo) will need to draw more water from the river, but any significant reductions in the downstream flow to Egypt could have catastrophic effects to the economy of that country.[6] We cannot predict how or whether such disputes will be resolved peacefully. In the meantime, it should surprise no one if impoverished Ethiopia buys state-of-the-art anti-aircraft batteries. Some other examples of rivers that have induced or are likely to induce contention include the Jordan river (Israel, Jordan, Syrian, and the Palestinians), the Tigris and Euphrates (Turkey, Syria, and Iraq), the Indus (Afghanistan, Pakistan, India), the Brahmaputra (China, India, and Bangladesh), and the Mekong (China, Thailand, Laos, Cambodia, and Vietnam).

The second type of insecurity that is looming on the horizon is the real or imagined rise of a peer competitor to the military and economic preeminence of the United States. The most widely mentioned candidate is China. Before September 2001 the role of China had been widely debated, especially in connection with its World Trade Organization accession. The proponents of China's admission to the WTO were offering the liberal gains-from-trade and peace-through-trade arguments, whereas its opponents were offering the realist it-will-come-back-to-bite-you argument as well as more ideological arguments regarding the nature of China's polity and its relation to Taiwan. Although it would take China decades to become a genuine peer competitor to the United States, in the absence of significant or prolonged measures not only to improve relations but also to eliminate all suggestions of hostile intent on either side, the present calm could well turn out to be the calm before the storm.[7] The experience of the first instance of modern globalization is not encouraging.

Before 1914 burgeoning trade flows and German bankers living in London made war unthinkable for many commentators because it was reasonably expected that war would economically destroy winners and losers alike. As Norman Angell wrote in his best-selling *The Great Illusion* (1909), "The capitalist has no country, and he knows, if he be of the modern type, that arms and conquests and jugglery with frontiers serve no ends of his, and may very well defeat them" (quoted in Joll 1992, 161). But the rivalries between the European great powers proved too great to overcome. The initial trade openness gave way gradually to tariffs, other protective measures, and eventually to the Great War.

Whether security costs are generated by neighboring states with resource disputes or by a potential geopolitical rivalry, the extent of trade openness can be expected to affect these costs. We turn next to an analysis of a setting with small countries that is more appropriate for regional resource disputes. While we have not yet examined the case of large countries in exactly the same setting, Skaperdas and Syropoulos (2002) analyze a setting in which the terms of trade are determined through bargaining, and Skaperdas and Syropoulos (1996) examine a case where prices are influenced by the contestants.

Contesting a Resource: A Simple Model of Globalization and Insecurity

We illustrate our main ideas within a framework that combines the key features of the model presented in Skaperdas and Syropoulos (2001) for the case of international conflicts and the model presented in

Garfinkel, Skaperdas, and Syropoulos (2005) for the case of domestic conflicts.[8] Consider two parties that can be, depending on the context, countries, groups, or individuals. Provided that the parties are identical, our analysis applies to both international conflict and domestic conflict. For most of the presentation, we need not specify the identity of the parties. They can be different groups within a single country, or each can represent a different country.

There are two factors of production. One factor is land. The other factor is labor. Neither party has secure claims to land. That is, all available land or "territory," denoted by T_o, is contested. Each party i, however, has a secure endowment of R units of labor resources, which can be transformed on a one-to-one basis into "guns," denoted by G_i, or used to produce also on a one-to-one basis "food," a final good valued for consumption. Given party i's guns choice, G_i, $R - G_i$ (≥ 0) units of labor will be available for the production of food; therefore, party i's maximal production of food will be $\max\{R - G_i, 0\}$.[9]

Goods for final consumption, food and oil, are produced under perfectly competitive conditions. Clearly, the names we are using here are not meant to imply that the model applies to environments that involve these commodities only but includes others that might be contestable (e.g., diamonds, precious metal, agricultural production). The goods can be traded domestically or, depending on the trade regime, internationally. Let O_i and N_i represent party i's consumption of oil and food ("nutrients"), respectively. The preferences of each party i take the Cobb-Douglas form,

$$U(O_i, N_i) = O_i^{\alpha} N_i^{1-\alpha}, \qquad i = 1, 2, \tag{3.1}$$

where $\alpha \in (0, 1)$.

We suppose that the two parties have secure possession of the goods they produce and those they exchange as well as over their labor endowments, R. Thus, the only matter of dispute between the two parties concerns the territory, T_o.[10] Both parties would like to take control of the contested territory, particularly for its oil. However, because of imperfect institutions of governance and enforcement, claims to this territory can be settled only via overt conflict or, equivalently in our model, under the threat of conflict.

It is precisely the contestability of this territory that motivates the two countries to allocate resources to guns. In particular, a party's production of guns enhances the share of T_o it can secure. More formally, the share of T_o that party i secures, q_i, depends positively on the relative number of guns it produces, as follows:

$$q_i \equiv q_i(G_1, G_2) = \begin{cases} \dfrac{G_i}{G_1 + G_2} & \text{if } G_1 + G_2 > 0, \\ \dfrac{1}{2} & \text{otherwise,} \end{cases} \qquad i = 1, 2. \qquad (3.2)$$

According to this specification,[11] the share of territory that party i secures in the contest is increasing in its own allocation of resources to arms,

$$\frac{\partial q_i(G_1, G_2)}{\partial G_i} > 0, \qquad i = 1, 2,$$

and decreasing in the allocation to arms by the other party,

$$\frac{\partial q_i(G_1, G_2)}{\partial G_j} < 0, \qquad j \neq i, i = 1, 2.$$

Once the contested land is divided between the two parties according to (3.2), each party engages in production. Party i produces $R - G_i$ units of food and $T_i = q_i(G_1, G_2)T_o$ units of oil, $i = 1, 2$. Each party i then chooses its consumption of oil and food, respectively O_i and N_i, to maximize (3.1) subject to the constraint that its aggregate expenditure is equal to the value of its output. Letting p_i denote the relative price of oil measured in units of labor, food, or guns, the value of party i's output or income, Y_i, is

$$Y_i(G_1, G_2) = p_i q_i(G_1, G_2)T_o + (R - G_i), \qquad i = 1, 2. \qquad (3.3)$$

As this expression reveals, the value of party i's output, Y_i, depends not only on i's own guns, G_i, but also on those of its opponent, G_j, $j \neq i$. This optimizing choice, using (3.1) and (3.3), generates the following indirect utility function:

$$V_i(G_1, G_2) = v(p_i)[p_i q_i(G_1, G_2)T_o + (R - G_i)], \qquad i = 1, 2, \qquad (3.4)$$

where $v(p) \equiv (1 - \alpha)^{1-\alpha}(\alpha/p)^{\alpha}$ represents the marginal utility of income.

We suppose each party i chooses G_i so as to maximize the group's welfare, V_i in (3.4). There are two potential channels through which guns have an effect. The first is the party's income, and here the effect is twofold. *Ceteris paribus*, a larger G_i raises the party's income Y_i

because it increases the party's share of the contested oil T_o. At the same time, an increase in G_i causes the party's income to fall because less labor is then available for the production of food. The second channel through which guns can affect welfare is through their possible impact on the relative price of oil. Exactly how this price may be affected depends on the trade regime in place. This dependence implies that the trade-off between guns and food itself is not invariant to trade openness.

In what follows, we explore the implications for security costs and welfare in the following two regimes: (1) autarky, where the two parties divide the contested land (oil) according to the relative amounts of guns and then consume only the oil and food produced domestically; and (2) trade, where the contested land is divided according to the relative amounts of guns but the oil is traded for food in international markets. In the former case, the domestic market-clearing relative price of oil is a function of that party's guns, resources, and preferences. In the case of trade, for simplicity and contrast, we assume both parties are small in world markets, and thus we treat the relative world price of oil, p, as a parameter.

Outcomes under Autarky

When barriers prevent trade across national borders, each party i chooses G_i to maximize its respective payoff, $V_i(G_1, G_2)$, shown in (3.4), where p_i is the autarkic price determined endogenously by domestic resource constraints, subject to the conflict technology shown in (3.2) and the labor resource constraint $G_i \leq R$.

To be more precise, if the parties are countries, for given guns, the domestic market-clearing price of oil in country i, p_i^A, is determined endogenously as

$$p_i^A = \frac{\alpha}{1 - \alpha} \frac{R - G_i}{q_i T_o}, \qquad i = 1, 2. \tag{3.5}$$

Given our symmetry assumptions, it should be clear that p_i^A will be identical across the two countries i: $p_i^A = p^A$, $i = 1, 2$.

If the parties are adversarial groups within a single country, then the possibility of integrated trade within the country between those groups implies that the autarkic price is determined endogenously by an aggregate domestic market-clearing condition that is common to the two groups. That is, given the groups' gun choices, the autarkic price for both parties, $p_i^A = p^A$, for $i = 1, 2$, depends on the country's aggregate endowments of labor and land as follows:

$$p^A = \frac{\alpha}{1 - \alpha} \frac{2R - G_1 - G_2}{T_o}. \tag{3.6}$$

However, because the conflict technology divides the contested resource among the participants, *ex ante* symmetry translates into *ex post* symmetry, and in the autarkic equilibrium our assumption that the two groups are identical implies that no trade between domestic groups takes place.[12] As (3.5) and (3.6) reveal, when parties devote more labor resources to guns production, the domestic supply of food falls relative to oil, and therefore the autarkic price of oil falls.

The conflict technology implies generally that if party i's opponent were to make no appropriative effort ($G_j = 0$, $j \neq i$), then party i could seize all of T_o by producing an infinitesimally small quantity of guns. But neither party would leave such an opportunity unexploited. As such, the "peaceful" outcome, where $G_i = 0$ for $i = 1, 2$, cannot be an equilibrium outcome. Accordingly, party i's optimizing choice of guns satisfies the following first-order condition:

$$\frac{\partial V_i}{\partial G_i} = v(p_i^A) \left[p_i^A T_o \frac{\partial q_i}{\partial G_i} - 1 \right] = 0, \qquad j \neq i, \, i = 1, 2. \tag{3.7}$$

The first term inside the brackets weighted by the marginal utility of income, $v(p_i^A)$, represents the marginal benefit of producing an additional gun. An increase in party i production of guns increases the share of land and thus oil that the party can secure. The marginal cost of producing an additional gun is represented by the second term inside the brackets, also weighted by the marginal utility of income. This marginal cost reflects the forgone opportunity for food production.

Under the assumption that the two parties are identical, the conditions in (3.7) for $i = 1, 2$, with (3.2) and either (3.5) for the case of interstate conflict or (3.6) for the case of intrastate conflict, imply a unique interior symmetric solution for guns under autarky:

$$G_i^A = G^A = \frac{\alpha}{2 - \alpha} R, \qquad i = 1, 2. \tag{3.8}$$

As revealed by this solution, the quantity of guns both parties produce is proportional to their labor endowment, R, and positively related to α, which measures the relative importance of oil to the two parties.

The solution for guns implies further that each party controls one half of the contested territory, $q_i = 1/2$ for $i = 1, 2$, and thus can extract and consume $O^A = T_i = (1/2)T_o$ units of oil. In addition, each party $i = 1, 2$ produces and consumes $N^A = R - G^A = [2(1 - \alpha)/(2 - \alpha)]R$ units of food in the autarkic outcome.

Outcomes under Free Trade

When the barriers to trade are removed, party i chooses G_i, subject to the resource constraint $G_i \leq R$, to maximize its respective payoff as shown in (3.4), with $p_i = p$, which indicates the international relative price of oil (or equivalently, land).[13] The first-order conditions to this problem for $i = 1, 2$, given by

$$\frac{\partial V_i}{\partial G_i} = v(p)\left[pT_o\frac{\partial q_i}{\partial G_i} - 1\right] = 0, \qquad j \neq i, i = 1, 2, \tag{3.9}$$

at an interior optimum, are essentially the same as the first-order conditions to the analogous problem under the assumption of no trade, (3.7) for $i = 1, 2$. But the conditions in (3.9) that treat p as fixed imply the following equilibrium choices for guns:

$$G_i^F = G^{F*} = \frac{1}{4}pT_o, \qquad i = 1, 2. \tag{3.10}$$

As the solution reveals, the optimizing choice of guns under free trade is increasing in the value of the contested resource, pT_o, whereas the equilibrium choice of guns under autarky, G^A, as shown in (3.8), is not related at all to the contested resource but instead to the secure resource, R, and the parameter that indicates the relative importance of oil in the determination of payoffs. Thus, despite the apparent similarities between the two sets of first-order conditions, (3.7) and (3.9), the incentives to arm under the two regimes are quite different, both qualitatively and quantitatively. The production of guns is higher under trade relative to that under autarky, the larger is the endowment of contested land relative to that of labor (T_o/R), the higher is the price of oil relative to food (p), and the less important is oil (α).

The Relative Appeal of Free Trade

Is it possible for the extra cost of guns to be high enough to outweigh the gains from trade relative to autarky? To make such a comparison, we need to calculate equilibrium welfare under the two regimes.

Combining the solution for guns (3.8) under autarky with either (3.5) or (3.6) shows the following solution for the autarkic price:

$$p_i^A = p^{A*} = \frac{4\alpha}{2-\alpha}\frac{R}{T_o}, \qquad i = 1, 2. \tag{3.11}$$

In turn, using this expression with (3.8) and the payoff function (3.4), we can find the equilibrium payoff obtained by each player i under autarky, V_i^A:

$$V_i^A = V^{A*} = \left[\frac{1}{2}\right]^\alpha \left[\frac{2(1-\alpha)}{2-\alpha}\right]^{1-\alpha} T_o^\alpha R^{1-\alpha}, \qquad i = 1, 2. \tag{3.12}$$

Similarly, combining (3.10) with (3.4) gives us the parties' equilibrium payoffs under trade, $V_i^F(p)$:

$$V_i^F(p) = V^{F*}(p) = v(p)\left[\frac{1}{4}pT_o + R\right], \qquad i = 1, 2, \tag{3.13}$$

which can be shown to be strictly quasi-convex in the price of oil, p, reaching its minimum at a price, $p_{min} = [4\alpha/(1-\alpha)]R/T_o$. This critical price is greater than the autarkic price, p^{A*}, shown in (3.11). Furthermore, given the strict quasi-convexity of $V^{F*}(p)$, there exists another price, $p' > p_{min}$, which is defined uniquely by the condition, $V^{F*}(p^A) = V^{A*} = V^{F*}(p')$, such that for a range of international prices, $p \in (p^{A*}, p')$, both parties prefer autarky to trade.

Figure 3.1, which depicts the parties' payoffs under free trade (V^{F*}) relative to their payoffs under autarky (V^{A*}) as a function of the world price of oil (p), illustrates the central results of this model of trade and conflict:

- For $p < p^{A*}$ and $p > p'$, welfare under autarky is higher than welfare under trade $(V^{A*} > V^{F*}(p))$.
- For $p^{A*} < p < p'$, welfare under trade is higher than welfare under autarky $(V^{F*}(p) > V^{A*})$.

Thus, even in the presence of contestable resources, importing countries unambiguously benefit from removing barriers to trade. Exporting countries are more likely to benefit the higher is the world price, but more generally increasing the degree of trade openness is not necessarily welfare-enhancing.

The underlying logic here is straightforward: When the international price of land or oil is sufficiently low $(p < p^{A*})$, the two parties

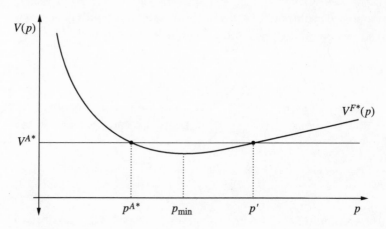

Figure 3.1
Free trade versus autarchy in the presence of conflict.

anticipate the opportunity to buy oil cheaply—in exchange for a relatively small fraction of their output of food—and accordingly devote fewer labor resources to guns relative to what they would choose under autarky $(G^{F*} < G^{A*})$. In this case, the shift away from the autarkic regime to free trade brings with it not only the familiar gains from trade but also a reduction in the cost of conflict. When the world price equals the autarkic price, $p = p^{A*}$, the particular trade regime in place has no relevance for the valuation of the contestable good $(G^{F*} = G^{A*})$, implying that the costs of conflict under trade are identical to those under autarky; at the same time, there are no gains from trade. But when the international price of the contested resource is higher than its autarkic price, $p > p^{A*}$, the stakes of the contest between the two parties exceed those under autarky. Thus, a shift from autarky to free trade would imply that the two parties allocate more labor resources to guns under the free trade regime relative to the autarkic regime, $G^{F*} > G^{A*}$. Of course, when $p > p^{A*}$, there are positive gains from trade, too. However, provided $p^{A*} < p < p'$, those gains are not sufficiently large to offset the added cost of conflict under free trade. That is, a shift from autarky to trade induces a welfare loss. Only when the price of land is sufficiently high $(p > p')$ will the gains from trade again be greater than the additional costs of guns under trade, as depicted in figure 3.1.[14]

It is important to emphasize that though our presentation has been based on some very simple specifications for utility and technology, the possible negative effects of increasing globalization we have identified here are very general. This robustness can be verified simply by differentiating party i's indirect utility function with respect to p while invoking the envelope theorem:

$$\frac{dV_i^F}{dp} = v(p)\left[-M_i^F + T_o\frac{\partial q_i}{\partial G_j}(dG_j^F/dp)\right], \qquad j \neq i, i = 1, 2,$$

where $M_i^F = \alpha Y^F/p - q_i T_o$ is the excess demand for oil, obtained from Roy's identity and the fact that $\partial Y_i/\partial p = q_i T_o$. The first term inside the brackets weighted by the marginal utility of income represents the welfare effect of an exogenous increase in the relative price of oil on the gains to trade. If party i is an importer of oil ($M_i^F > 0$), the effect is negative; otherwise ($M_i^F < 0$), the effect is positive. Hence, the gains from trade are convex in the world price, reaching a minimum at the point where the world price equals the autarkic price, $p = p^A$. The second term inside the brackets weighted by the marginal utility of income represents the welfare effect of the price increase on the costs of conflict. To be more precise, an increase in the international price of oil raises the stakes of the contest, thereby inducing the opponent to devote more labor resources to guns, as can be seen in (3.10): $dG_j^F/dp > 0$. From equation (3.2), the increase in the opponent's guns choice implies a reduction in party i's share of land and thus oil: $\partial q_i/\partial G_j < 0$ for $i \neq j = 1, 2$. As such, the costs of conflict under trade are monotonically increasing in the world price. At $p = p^A$, the costs are identical to those realized under autarky, but for $p < p^A$ ($p > p^A$) they are smaller (larger).

Furthermore, the particular assumption of price-taking behavior is convenient and can easily be relaxed without changing the main findings. Skaperdas and Syropoulos (2002), for example, allow for bargaining the price of land. By the same token, the findings do not hinge on the particular way in which conflict has been modeled here. Findlay and Amin (2000), for instance, consider a trade model in which security is modeled as a public good and is increasing in one party's defense expenditures and decreasing in the defense expenditures of the another party. They find that the gains from trade can be outweighed by the higher defense costs brought about by trade.

Other Implications and Issues
Interstate conflicts had been frequent and very costly up to World War II. World War I, in particular, took place just after the first big wave of

globalization, which was also a time of intense competition for colonies and resources between the great powers. Since World War II, however, while the frequency of interstate wars has fallen, civil wars have increased in frequency. Indeed, most of the carnage and arguably much economic stagnation and even retrogression since World War II can be attributed to civil wars (Collier et al. 2003). Yet, as we have already hinted, the approach we have presented applies to intrastate conflicts as well as to interstate conflicts.

Our approach further provides an explanation for the "natural resource curse," the tendency of many resource-rich parties to have low or negative rates of growth despite the high prices of their exports. Trade not only makes exporters of contested resources worse off relative to the autarkic regime; it also leaves them vulnerable to declining welfare as increases in the prices for their exports would tend to increase the cost of domestic conflict. As Mehlum, Moene, and Torvik (2006) argue, the key appears to be the security and governance of potentially contestable resources. Countries that have solved the problem of conflict over resources do well, whereas those that have not solved the problem can face declining welfare in the face of the seeming (and fleeting) prosperity that can come from higher oil or other export prices.

In addition, Garfinkel, Skaperdas, and Syropoulos (2005) find that the presence of insecure land endowments distorts the pattern of trade between that country and others relative to the hypothetical scenario where land endowments are perfectly secure. In particular, when the world price of oil falls within a certain price range, the contest between domestic groups over valuable resources reverses the direction of trade. Whereas the country as a whole would be a net importer of the good that uses the contestable resource (oil) intensively in production, if groups had secure claims on T_o in the presence of conflict, the country is a net exporter. More generally, for all world prices, the presence of domestic conflict imparts a positive bias on the country's exports.

The comparison between autarky and complete trade openness is too stark for many contexts. In practice, there are a number of other instruments that parties, groups, or individual actors could employ to minimize the potentially harmful conflict costs of greater openness to trade and exchange. Authors in different but similar contexts have argued that wage subsidies (Zak 1995; Grossman 1995), land reform (Horowitz 1993; Grossman 1994), and market interventions in general (Dal Bo and Dal Bo 2004) can be optimal in the face of various types of conflict, from common crime, to low-level political conflict, to insurrections, civil wars, and interstate wars. In a somewhat different vein, Martin, Mayer, and Thoenig (2005) have examined, both theoretically and empirically, the effects of multilateral trade relative to those of bilateral trade on the probability of conflict, and found how an increase in multilateral trade openness may increase such a probability.

Another way to think of the conflict costs that we have explored in this section in relation to trade and exchange is as a large component of the often-discussed, yet rarely modeled or operationalized, concept of transaction costs. Taking these costs into account indicates that exchange is neither likely to emerge nor necessarily optimal in a second-best world, and can explain many practices and institutions that would be difficult to comprehend in a world with zero enforcement and conflict costs.

Looking Ahead at Governance and Insecurity

Economic globalization without security is like putting the cart before the horse, especially when the terrain is not flat. The danger for both the cart and the horse of tumbling down a hill (or worse, into a crevasse, as occurred in the first part of the twentieth century) is high. Though economists have emphasized the importance of the security of property rights for economic performance, scant attention has been paid to the costliness of either security or insecurity, how these concretely affect resource allocation and efficiency, and how security might be achieved.

Thomas Friedman's "hidden fist" and Martin Wolf's "jurisdictional integration" point, respectively, to the role of coercive capacity as the ultimate source of enforcement and the importance of uniform or harmonized governance in providing security and predictability in economic transactions. Both are necessary for the effective security of property rights. They are also costly and difficult to achieve, and economists know very little about how to do it. There are, however, some trends and options regarding the future of governance that have been identified by some social scientists, which we briefly discuss next.

Governance in Low-Income Countries
Most countries in the world today do not have anything resembling modern governance, with effective laws, functioning courts, police, and bureaucracies. To have, for example, property rights in land, a

country needs a legislative body with the ability to commit to the staying power of the laws it creates, a title agency and trained civil servants, police and courts that will enforce the laws, the professional infrastructure of lawyers, judges, surveyors, or bureaucrats (and the universities to train them), and the belief that the process of securing title is routine and free of corruption. A break anywhere in this chain of property rights enforcement brings the whole edifice down. Clearly, it is expensive to have modern governance, and therefore it should not be surprising that most countries do not. Not only is that the case, but there are signs that governance and insecurity might be getting worse in many low-income countries. That is part of the general trend identified by Fukuyama (2004, 119): "For well over a generation, the trend in world politics has been to weaken stateness.... The growth of the global economy has tended to erode the autonomy of sovereign nation-states by increasing the mobility of information, capital, and, to a lesser extent, labor."

Furthermore, economic liberalization itself reduces tariff revenue, a major source of government revenue for low-income countries, and therefore reduces the state's capacity to accomplish the objectives it sets. With reference to sub-Saharan Africa, Herbst (2000) has argued that external recognition of states whose borders were determined by former colonial masters instead of by geography, similarity of culture, and internal political development has led to the severe underdevelopment of African states. In addition, Fukuyama argues, the governments of the West, the international financial institutions, and NGOs actually undermine state capacity in many low-income countries.[15]

"Failed" states and barely functioning states span the globe. In the Americas, from Bolivia and Peru in the south all the way north to Guatemala; all of Africa with the exception of South Africa; much of southeastern Europe; all of the Middle East and Central Asia; much of Southeast Asia, including Indonesia; as well as Papua New Guinea and Vanuatu in Oceania.[16] It is by now recognized across almost the whole spectrum of informed opinion that weak states do not serve anybody's interests (with the possible exception of those who run such states). Thus, Fukuyama (2004, 120) writes, "Strengthening these states through various forms of nation-building is a task that has become vital to international security but is one that few developed countries have mastered. Learning to do state-building better is thus central to the future of world order." If, however, international institutions with the targeted interventions they undertake tend to weaken already weak states, as Fukuyama (2004) argues, how could developed countries engage in successful nation building without negating the very idea of a strong state, unless of course it is a wholly owned subsidiary of the developed countries, the international community, or some other outside entity? Would that ever be achievable? Is this what the future holds?

It appears, however, that internal insecurity in low-income countries is very much connected to what occurs in the rest of the world. Thus, transnational governance appears to be important for the internal governance of low-income countries, not just for resolving disputes between individual countries and avoiding future superpower confrontations.

Transnational Governance
The power vacuum that exists and arguably is expanding in many countries will be filled one way or another. Local strongmen, one possible way of filling the vacuum, are not likely to serve today's economic prerequisites or share international and domestic legitimacy (which has economic functions as well). If, as another option of filling the power vacuum, nation building by outsiders were to take place, how much would the interests of the insiders—the inhabitants of the countries—be taken into account? Wouldn't there be a need to have checks on the outsiders by the insiders? Would it even be possible, even if the outsiders were to know perfectly well how to build nations (a highly doubtful proposition with the current state of knowledge), to do so without provoking internal reactions that would negate such attempts? Is, then, old-style imperialism an option?

The old-style, allegedly liberal, British imperialism has received a second positive look by Ferguson (2002) and others. But before imperialism had a serious chance at revival, it experienced a rude reversal in the dust and sands of Mesopotamia. Thus, with a Hobbesian solution to the world's governance problems appearing to be out of the question for now, Lockean or Rousseauian contractual solutions are more promising.

One possibility is strengthening international organizations like the UN by providing it with some enforcement powers, sources of independent or at least predictable revenues, and mechanisms of decision making that would allow greater representation of those who are affected by its decisions (like the citizens of countries that require building or rebuilding).

Another, complementary, possibility is the continued evolution and expansion of regional organizations like the European Union or Mercosur. Leonard (2005) argues that the European Union model holds great promise because its transnational organizational structure is well adapted to the problems of the twenty-first century in the sense that it strengthens governance in those countries that aspire to join, improves transnational decision making—especially when compared to other eras when the risk of war was continually looming over Europe—and has multiple layers of checks and balances so as to allow for as much representation and legitimacy as would be feasible in such transnational organizations.

Both international and regional institutions and organizations are likely to be strengthened in this century. The main question is how fast will they be strengthened. They need strengthening so as to forestall upheaval and wars that are unforeseeable in terms of their precise timing, nature, and length but that are generally predictable when the insecurity that exists today within and across many countries is allowed to evolve unchecked. Economic globalization without politically harmonized globalization is more dangerous the longer it lasts without adjustments.

Notes

We thank Peter Rosendorff and other participants at the 2005 CESifo conference as well as two anonymous referees for helpful comments. We also thank the Center for Global Peace and Conflict Studies and the Center for the Study of Democracy, both at University of California, Irvine, for financial support.

1. Polachek (1980) is a rare articulation by an economist of the classical liberal perspective of the effect of trade on conflict.

2. Waltz (1979) and Gowa (1995) give two notable elaborations of the realist perspective. Barbieri and Schneider (1999) report on the results of different recent political science studies from both schools.

3. The parties are small in the sense that they have no effect on international prices.

4. Fearon and Laitin (2003) base their findings on the *Correlates of War* project, among other sources. The definition of civil war uses the 1,000 deaths per year threshold.

5. That practice along with the principle of noninterference in the internal affairs of other states meant that whoever controlled the capital of a country had international recognition as the legitimate government. That recognition and the high economic value it conferred to its holder might have made internal instability and civil warfare more likely than otherwise. Herbst (2000) has argued with reference to sub-Saharan Africa partly on those grounds against the recognition of international borders.

6. Economic globalization intensifies demand for water resources primarily through the demand for water-intensive agricultural products, as in the case of Egyptian cotton.

7. Of course, there is the possibility of other states becoming peer competitors to the United States, even some seemingly unexpected ones at the moment. For example, Japan possesses the nuclear and missile technologies to become a major nuclear power within a short period of time. While Japan might not now aspire to become a nuclear power, a confirmation of North Korea's nuclear status or higher perceived threats from China could well make Japan a nuclear power, after sufficient preparation of its domestic opinion. A nuclear Japan would radically change world balance of power, even if it does not evolve to a U.S. peer competitor.

8. The model we present here is a generalization of the model in Skaperdas and Syropoulos (2001), allowing us to examine additional issues. It is also a special case of the model in Garfinkel, Skaperdas, and Syropoulos (2005), which allows for different degrees of insecurity and includes a number of other findings and in-depth analyses of issues like the relation to the "natural resource curse."

9. Note that "guns" can stand for any costly appropriative activity that subtracts from useful production and welfare, e.g., ordinary rent seeking, influence activities, or litigation.

10. Insofar as exchange reflects the factor content of goods traded, it should not matter for our central results whether the commodities or the factors used to produce them are subject to dispute. Furthermore, that all territory is insecure simplifies the algebra considerably but is not critical, as shown in Skaperdas and Syropoulos (2001; 2002) and Garfinkel, Skaperdas, and Syropoulos (2005).

11. This functional form, first introduced by Tullock (1980) and used extensively in the rent-seeking literature as well as in the literatures on tournaments and conflict, falls within the general class of contest success functions axiomatized by Skaperdas (1996):

$$q_i(G_1, G_2) = \frac{f(G_i)}{\sum_{j=1}^{2} f(G_j)},$$

where $f(\cdot)$ is a non-negative, increasing function. Also see Hirshleifer (1989), who investigates the properties of two important functional forms of this class, including the ratio success function, where $f(G) = G^m$ with $m > 0$, which simplifies to equation (3.2) when $m = 1$.

12. By contrast, in Garfinkel, Skaperdas, and Syropoulos (2005), conflict between groups is modeled as a winner-take-all contest such that the model predicts trade, despite the assumption of *ex ante* symmetry. Nevertheless, the equilibrium price under autarky is independent of the *ex post* and *ex ante* distribution of guns. Furthermore, even if each group factors in the effect that its own choice of guns has on the domestic relative price, p^A, the symmetry assumption implies that they behave as if they can have no influence on the party's autarkic price at all.

13. Assuming that parties are small relative to the global economy, their choices take that price as given.

14. Our discussion here has implicitly assumed, for convenience, that the labor resource constraint, $R - G_i \geq 0$, is not binding. However, as the solution for G^{F*} in (3.10) shows, there exists some world relative price of oil, denote it by $\tilde{p}$, such that at $p = \tilde{p}$, the parties fully exhaust their labor resource; any further increase in p beyond $\tilde{p}$ yields only the

gains from trade. Nevertheless, since $G^{A*} < R$, as shown in (3.8), $\tilde{p} > p^{A*}$. Therefore, the *effective* welfare-minimizing world price, given by $\min\{\tilde{p}, p_{\min}\}$, is strictly greater than the autarkic price, p^{A*}, implying that even when the labor resource constraint binds, there exists some range of world prices under which both parties prefer autarky to trade.

15. "Policymakers in the development field should at least swear the oath of doctors to "do no harm" and not initiate programs that undermine or suck out institutional capacity in the name of building it" (Fukuyama 2004, 42).

16. An illuminating map of such a division of the world can be found in Barnett (2004), where the world is divided into a "functioning core" of states and the "nonintegrating gap" of either failed or barely functioning states. Although one could argue with Barnett's particular designation of boundaries, we think the basic dichotomy is analytically useful. Barnett's own analysis, however, leaves much to be desired and could be characterized as utopian. For example, he characterizes the United States as having a "unique capacity to export security aound the planet" (7) and appears to call for massive interventions to do so.

References

Barbieri, K., and G. Schneider. 1999. Globalization and peace: Assessing new directions in the study of trade and conflict. *Journal of Peace Research* 36 (4): 387–404.

Barnett, T. P. M. 2004. *The Pentagon's New Map: War and Peace in the Twenty-First Century.* New York: G. P. Putnam's Sons.

Collier, P., V. L. Elliott, H. Hegre, A. Hoeffler, M. Reynal-Querol, and N. Sambanis. 2003. *Breaking the Conflict Trap: Civil War and Development Policy.* Policy Research Report. Washington, D.C.: World Bank.

Dal Bo, E., and P. Dal Bo. 2004. Workers, warriors, and criminals: Social conflict in general equilibrium. Working Paper. Berkeley: University of California.

Fearon, J. D., and D. D. Laitin. 2003. Ethnicity, insurgency, and civil war. *American Political Science Review* 97 (1): 75–90.

Ferguson, N. 2002. *Empire: The Rise and Demise of the British World Order and the Lessons from Global Power.* New York: Basic Books.

Findlay, R., and M. Amin. 2000. National security and international trade: A simple general equilibrium model. Working Paper. New York: Columbia University.

Fukuyama, F. 2004. *State-Building: Governance and World Order in the 21st Century.* Ithaca, N.Y.: Cornell University Press.

Garfinkel, M. R., S. Skaperdas, and C. Syropoulos. 2005. Globalization and domestic conflict. Working Paper 05-05-01. Irvine: University of California.

Gowa, J. 1995. *Allies, Adversaries, and International Trade.* Princeton, N.J.: Princeton University Press.

Grossman, H. I. 1994. Production, appropriation, and land reform. *American Economic Review* 84 (3): 705–712.

———. 1995. Robin Hood and the redistribution of property income. *European Journal of Political Economy* 11 (3): 399–410.

Herbst, J. 2000. *States and Power in Africa: Comparative Lessons in Authority and Control.* Princeton, N.J.: Princeton University Press.

Hess, G. D. 2003. The economic welfare cost of conflict: An empirical assessment. CESifo Working Paper 852. Munich: CESifo Group.

Hirshleifer, J. 1989. Conflict and rent-seeking success functions: Ratio vs. difference models of relative success. *Public Choice* 63 (2): 101–112.

Horowitz, A. W. 1993. Time paths of land reform: A theoretical model of reform dynamics. *American Economic Review* 83 (4): 1003–1010.

Jacques, M. 2005. Victims of the convulsions now transforming China. *The Guardian*, October 11.

Joll, J. 1992. *The Origins of the First World War.* 2d ed. New York: Longman.

Kaplan, R. D. 2002. *Warrior Politics: Why Leadership Demands a Pagan Ethos.* New York: Random House.

Klare, M. T. 2001. *Resource Wars: The New Landscape of Global Conflict.* New York: Henry Holt.

Leonard, M. 2005. *Why Europe Will Run the 21st Century.* New York: Public Affairs.

Lewis, W. W. 2004. *The Power of Productivity: Wealth, Poverty, and the Threat to Global Stability.* Chicago: University of Chicago Press.

Lucas, R. E. 1987. *Models of Business Cycles.* Oxford: Blackwell.

Martin, P., T. Mayer, and M. Thoenig. 2005. Make trade not war? CEPR Working Paper 5218. London: Centre for Economic Policy Research.

McGuire, M., and M. Olson. 1996. The economics of autocracy and majority rule: The invisible hand and the use of force. *Journal of Economics Literature* 34 (1): 72–96.

Mehlum, H., K. Moene, and R. Torvik. 2006. Institutions and the resource curse. *Economic Journal* 1161: 1–20.

Polachek, S. W. 1980. Conflict and trade. *Journal of Conflict Resolution* 24 (1): 55–78.

Rodrik, D. 1998. Where did all the growth go? External shocks, social conflict, and growth collapses. NBER Working Paper 6350. Cambridge, Mass.: National Bureau of Economic Research.

———. 1999. *The New Global Economy and Developing Countries: Making Openness Work.* Baltimore: Johns Hopkins University Press.

Skaperdas, S. 1996. Contest success functions. *Economic Theory* 7 (2): 283–290.

Skaperdas, S., and C. Syropoulos. 1996. Competitive trade with conflict. In *The Political Economy of Conflict and Appropriation*, ed. M. R. Garfinkel and S. Skaperdas. New York: Cambridge University Press.

———. 2001. Guns, butter, and openness: On the relationship between security and trade. *American Economic Review* 91 (2): 353–357.

———. 2002. Insecure property and the efficiency of exchange. *Economic Journal* 112: 133–146.

Tullock, G. 1980. Efficient rent-seeking. In *Toward a Theory of the Rent-Seeking Society*, ed. J. M. Buchanan, R. D. Tollison, and G. Tullock. College Station: Texas A&M University Press.

Waltz, K. N. 1979. *Theory of International Politics*. Boston: McGraw-Hill.

Wolf, M. 2004. *Why Globalization Works*. New Haven, Conn.: Yale University Press.

Zak, P. J. 1995. Institutions, property rights, and growth. Working Paper. Claremont, Calif.: Claremont Graduate University.

4 Investing in Regimes with Stationary or Roving Bandits

Kai A. Konrad

When the former socialist countries in Central and Eastern Europe started to transform their economic systems, many observers expected that there would be large inflows of foreign direct investment (FDI) and a quick catch-up. However, in most of these countries, this investment boom did not occur. Some countries did reasonably well, whereas others performed very poorly. To illustrate, consider FDI in the early transformation years 1988–1998. The cumulative FDI (gross) inflow for those years in Eastern European, Baltic, and European CIS countries was US$235 per capita. The figures for Hungary (US$1,720) and the Czech Republic (US$1,010) were about sixteen and nine times that of the Russian Federation (US$111), and the latter did more than twice as well as Ukraine (UNECE 1999, 170). In comparison, FDI inflow, 1990–1998, into the United States was US$2,241 per capita, almost ten times the aggregate per capita inflow over ten years in the transforming countries of Central and Eastern Europe (OECD 1999).

A central problem in these countries that may explain these figures is the lack of security for property rights, as a number of researchers have pointed out. Investors face the threat of possible nationalization, possible confiscatory taxation that amounts to de facto expropriation, and extortion by private "protection" agencies such as the Russian mafia and similar structures.[1] Typically, there is no single group that has the power to fully control and (re)allocate property rights. Instead, private "protection" agencies often enter the picture and assume the role of private government. Johnson et al. (2000), for instance, report that firms state that they suffer extortion not only from bureaucrats but also from criminal gangs. According to their survey, around 90 percent of the managers in Russia and Ukraine said firms in their industry pay for "protection" of their activities.

Extortion generates a serious holdup problem for investment. The Russia that Shleifer and Treisman (1999), Berkowitz and Li (2000), Cai and Treisman (2005), Treisman (1999; 2002), Frye and Zhuravskaya (2000), and Ponomareva and Zhuravskaya (2004), and others considered, both theoretically and empirically, lacked well-secured property rights and had multiple players who tried to appropriate or protect their properties. This uncertainty, plus the effort and cost that investors had to expend to protect their properties from expropriation, are likely to be key factors in explaining the lack of investment.

The investment of Knauf, a German building materials firm, in Russia illustrates the nature of the property rights conflict (*Moscow Times*, October 15, 1998). Knauf battled with the tax police about whether a given investment of US$1.68 million was tax-free or not, in circumstances where the tax police tried to collect a penalty, including a collection fee, in the amount of US$10.8 million. Knauf officials hinted that the tax police were collaborating with a third party that was trying to get control of the plant. Knauf also had trouble with another of its subsidiaries, Kubansky Gips–Knauf, at Psebai near the Georgian border. The *Moscow Times*, in a series of articles (November 29, 1997; December 9, 1997; February 10; March 10, 1998; December 5, 2001), reported the story in which local employees tried to gain control of Knauf's plant, kicking out the company's German owners. The local director, Alim Sergiyenko, physically prevented employees of Knauf from entering the plant for about two years. According to the *Moscow Times* (February 10, 1998), Sergiyenko had the support of the head of local administration and arbitration judges. High officials from Germany intervened via a telegram to Boris Yeltsin (*Petersburg Times*, February 5, 2002), and the governor finally helped install a legally elected director. Similar stories are reported for other firms.[2]

The problem of possible nationalization in foreign direct investment has been discussed with respect to the nationalization that took place in many developing countries between the mid-fifties and the late seventies (for empirical evidence and further references, see, e.g., Andersson 1991).[3] In the analysis here I focus on an aspect that has not been discussed in this literature.

Whether expropriation occurs is not just a decision made by the player who carries out the expropriation. Whether an investor is expropriated is often the outcome of fighting between the owner and the player, who attempts to appropriate the investment project for himself. As in the Knauf case, both the original owner and the parties trying to expropriate him expend wasteful effort in this fight, and this effort neg-atively affects the investor's willingness to make an investment and is also relevant for welfare. The type of effort in expropriation contests depends on the nature of the expropriation threat. Expropriation may lack a legal basis, in which case violence and making and carrying out threats may be used, whereas the foreign investor may invest in vari-ous types of self-protection.[4] Sometimes bureaucrats or government agencies may try to bend existing national or international laws in order to expropriate an investor. In this case, both sides may invest resources in achieving favorable changes in the legal, institutional, or contractual framework and in the legal dispute. I do not specify the precise nature of the different types of game here. Instead, I use a general model of conflict to describe the nature of the expropriation contest.[5]

Two regimes with insecure property rights that can be seen as benchmarks for a wide range of possible institutional regimes are ana-lyzed and compared. In both regimes, an investor decides whether to make an investment, for instance, to build a plant. If he invests, he must fight to defend his property against expropriation attempts, not only once but in a sequence of periods. In the first regime, one player may try to take over the property rights in the investment and may be in a position to make such an attempt in each of an infinite sequence of periods up to the point when he is finally successful. Once this has happened, this player enjoys the returns from this investment asset. This player is called a *stationary bandit*. The term *bandit* should not be taken too literally here because this player might be a member of the government, a bureaucrat, or a governmental agency. In the other re-gime, the identity of the player who attempts to expropriate the inves-tor changes from one period to the next, so that each contender has only one single opportunity to attempt to get hold of the investment project. Different contenders show up, one in each period, up to the point where a contender is successful in his appropriation effort. This successful contender then enjoys the returns from this investment asset safely for all future periods. These contenders are called *roving bandits*.

I solve for a Markov perfect equilibrium in these cases and compare the investment incentives in the respective equilibria. The analysis is related to studies of repeated property rights conflict more generally. Aidt and Hillman (2006) consider repeated property rights conflict among a given set of players who compete for an infinitely lived asset that yields a constant flow of period returns. In their analysis, all players are perfectly symmetric with respect to the appropriation contest, and the asset may be reallocated many times between these players as an outcome of repeated conflict. Similarly, Mehlum and Moene (2005) consider repeated fights between two rivals, also for an infinitely lived asset with a constant flow of period returns. Property rights can be reallocated between the two players as the outcome of conflict in each period. Mehlum and Moene focus on the role of incumbency advantages for the rival who was the winner of the fight in the previous period. General structures of multibattle contests in which a player needs more than one victory to win the prize are reviewed and studied in Konrad and Kovenock (2005; 2006a) and Polborn (2006). Bester and Konrad (2005) consider problems of the timing of an attack in a multiperiod framework if the players' fighting abilities or endowments can change over time.

Returning to the problem of FDI, note that in the present framework the security of property rights is very asymmetric between the initial foreign investor and the player who successfully appropriates the investment asset for himself. The foreign investor who has not been expropriated must continue to defend his investment asset in each period. The player who expropriated the investor successfully enjoys the asset throughout all future periods. The foreign direct investment problem motivates this asymmetry: the foreign investor and original owner of the investment project is exposed to repeated expropriation threats. The player who succeeds in expropriating the foreigner is typically a local. He is much less exposed to further expropriation threats. Stephan and Ursprung (1998) analyzed such a structure. Their framework is similar to the stationary bandit regime in what follows, except for the way they describe the period conflict. In comparison to the stationary bandit, a roving bandit who has only one chance to appropriate an asset for himself should be expected to fight more aggressively. Hence, one could expect that investment is less likely to occur in a country with roving bandits than in a country with a stationary bandit. One of the purposes of the formal analysis that follows is to show that this need not be the case.

The Structure of the Conflict

Suppose an investor considers building a plant in a host country in period $t = 0$. The cost of this investment is an amount $k > 0$. This investment is observable, irreversible, and immobile. Should the investor decide in the future to shut down the plant, this amount is irreversibly lost.

The plant generates a flow of revenue in all future periods, $t = 1, 2, \ldots$ The revenue in each period t is normalized to 1 if the investor controls the plant in the respective period, and is smaller if the investor loses the control rights in the plant.[6]

If the plant is still controlled by the original owner in period t, before the plant generates revenue in that period, a player (the bandit) may attempt to appropriate the plant. As mentioned before, using the term *bandit* should not suggest only the type of agent who tries to appropriate for himself. The agents could be members of organized crime, corrupt government officials or bureaucrats, goverment agencies that simply try to (re)nationalize firms or other assets, or businessmen, entrepreneurs, or managers who try to increase their wealth by acquiring the property of other players. The investor tries to ward off this attempt. The respective efforts determine whether the initial owner continues to control the plant or whether the control right is transferred to the bandit. In the latter case, the game ends, and the bandit controls the plant from then on.

Types of Expropriation Threat

For the investor who is in possession of the plant and has to defend this property against bandits, the type of bandit may matter. Two types are considered. I refer to these as the *stationary bandit* and the *roving bandit* regimes, in line, for instance, with Hillman and Krausz (2005). A stationary bandit is a player who can make an attempt to appropriate the plant in each of a potentially infinite series of periods. Whenever the appropriation attempt is successful, the plant is turned over to the bandit, and the loss for the investor is final. A regime with roving bandits is as follows. An investor has to ward off a bandit in each of a series of periods, much like in the regime with a stationary bandit, and if the bandit is successful, the loss of control and ownership is final in this regime also. However, the identity of the bandit changes from one period to the next. Formally, there is a large set of potential bandits in the host country, and in each period where appropriation has not yet taken place in a previous period, a new bandit (randomly chosen from a set with uncountably many identical bandits) gets his one and only chance to make an attempt to appropriate the plant.[7]

Intuitively, a stationary bandit does not lose as much as a roving bandit if the appropriation attempt fails in a given period. He can simply start another attempt in the next period, whereas the roving bandit, by definition, does not have this option.[8] Other contexts with similar structures suggest that stationary bandits may internalize their future opportunities and that this may make them less aggressive than roving bandits, causing a smaller efficiency loss and more efficient investment choices. It turns out that the latter need not be the case.

I assume that the present value of the bandit's benefit from appropriating the project for himself is $w \in (0, \infty)$. For the analysis, no specific assumptions about the determination of w need be made. To make the regimes more comparable, however, I assume that w is the same for roving bandits and for a stationary bandit.[9]

The two regimes should be seen as theoretical benchmarks that differ as regards their predicted outcomes. Countries with multiple rival private providers of "protection" or gangs might be examples for the regime with roving bandits. Countries with a dominant but extortionary government may be closer to the stationary bandit regime.

The Fighting Technology
Consider the foreign owner of a plant. As long as he is in possession of the plant, bandits can show up, trying to appropriate the plant. I assume they show up sequentially, one bandit per period, and number the periods $t = 1, 2, \ldots$. If the foreign owner has not been expropriated up to period t, he and the bandit of this period expend efforts, $a_t \geq 0$ and $b_t \geq 0$, respectively. The relative size of defensive effort a_t and aggressive effort b_t will determine who wins this competition. More formally, the control of the firm will be allocated according to a contest success function for which the probability $q_t = q(a_t, b_t)$ that the foreign owner wins is

$$q_t(a_t, b_t) = \begin{cases} 1 & \text{if } a_t \geq \gamma b_t, \\ 0 & \text{if } a_t < \gamma b_t. \end{cases} \tag{4.1}$$

The bandit wins the contest with the residual probability $1 - q_t$. Here, $\gamma > 0$ is a parameter that measures the quality of property rights. If $\gamma = 0$, then the property rights of the investor are perfectly secured without his expending any cost on property rights protection. A zero effort suffices to ward off any bandit. The larger γ, however, the more expensive it is to ward off bandits. For instance, if $\gamma = 1/2$, the investor needs half the amount of resources used by the bandit to defend his investment from being appropriated.

The contest success function of the all-pay auction without noise as in (4.1) has been used in many contexts.[10] It could be given a number of microeconomic underpinnings and has some crucial features of a contest: both contestants have a cost of effort that cannot be recovered even if they lose in the all-pay auction. Each side improves its chances for winning (weakly) if it uses more effort.

Property Rights Regime

When the investor makes his decision whether to invest, he does not perfectly know the quality of the property rights. In the most simple nontrivial case, property rights can be good (γ_0) or bad (γ_1), with $\gamma_0 < \gamma_1$ and probabilities p_0 and $p_1 = 1 - p_0$. For investment to yield positive gross returns for the investor, it turns out that this requires that the condition $\gamma w < 1$ hold. Hence, I assume this condition is fulfilled for the case of the good property rights regime. The investor will obtain zero gross returns if $1 < \gamma_1 w$. Hence, I assume that this condition is fulfilled for the bad property rights regime. Summarizing, I consider the case $0 < \gamma_0 w < 1 < \gamma_1 w$, such that the two property rights regimes differ in a qualitatively relevant way.

The investor (and everyone else who did not know it previously) learns the true quality γ of property rights as soon as the investment is made and prior to any fighting efforts. Moreover, the quality of property rights stays the same for all subsequent periods. When making the investment decision, the investor thinks that p_0 and $p_1 = 1 - p_0$ are the probabilities that property rights will be good or bad.

The uncertainty about γ at the investment stage is assumed for two reasons. First, it allows study of the investment that takes place but is *ex post* unprofitable. Second, it allows study of the role of an investor's uncertainty about the true property rights quality.

The Static Contest Equilibrium

Suppose the two players A and B value winning the prize in the all-pay auction by z_A and z_B. Let the contest success function that determines the winner by comparing their efforts be defined by equation (4.1). The players choose efforts a and b, and the costs of these efforts are equal to a and b by appropriate normalization. To determine the equilibrium efforts chosen by A and B is in this case not trivial. The equilibrium of a static all-pay auction with the contest success function (4.1) has been fully characterized by Baye, Kovenock, and deVries

(1996), and I use their results here.[11] For a wide range of possible costs of effort, each player would like to expend just a tiny amount of effort more than the rival because this is sufficient for him to win the prize. This is intuitively the reason that the problem does not have an equilibrium in pure strategies. The equilibrium does exist, however, in mixed strategies and is unique. What is used in what follows is that the equilibrium payoffs from participating in this all-pay auction are

$$\pi_A = \max\{z_A - \gamma z_B, 0\} \quad \text{and} \quad \pi_B = \max\{z_B - (z_A/\gamma), 0\}. \tag{4.2}$$

Moreover, because the equilibrium is in mixed strategies, each of the players wins with some positive probability, and the equilibrium win probabilities are $q_A = 1 - \gamma z_B/2z_A$ if $z_A \geq \gamma z_B$, and $q_A = z_A/2\gamma z_B$ if $z_A < \gamma z_B$, with $q_B = 1 - q_A$. The equilibrium is characterized in detail in the appendix.

To make some of this intuitively plausible, note that no contestant will expend effort that exceeds his valuation of winning. Player A will not expend more effort than z_A, and player B will not expend more than z_B. Knowing this, no one will expend more than is needed to top the maximum effort that the other contestant may reasonably choose. Accordingly, if, for instance, $z_A > \gamma z_B$, player A can guarantee that he will win the contest by making an effort that exceeds γz_B by an arbitrarily small positive amount. By (4.1), this amount is sufficient to win against any effort of player B that is lower or equal to z_B. If A makes this choice, A's payoff is equal to $z_A - \gamma z_B$. Hence, A has a strategy that guarantees A a payoff arbitrarily close to $z_A - \gamma z_B$. Although this strategy does not characterize the equilibrium, it does indicate a lower bound of A's equilibrium payoff. Indeed, this difference is the equilibrium payoff for A, as can be seen in this case by (4.2). Moreover, given the option of player A's certainly winning this amount, it is natural for player B not to be able to obtain a positive payoff in this case. In what follows, (4.2) is used as an important building block when analyzing the different regimes.

Stationary Bandits

Suppose that investment took place in period 0 and the quality of property rights was revealed to all players. Consider the conflict subgame where the same bandit can again try to appropriate the investment project in period $t + 1$ if his attempt in t was unsuccessful, for each $t = 1, 2, \ldots$. The gross payoff of the investor (prior to deducting the initial investment cost k that was expended in period $t = 0$) can then be written as

$$u_t = -a_t + q(a_t, b_t)[1 + \delta u^*_{t+1}]. \tag{4.3}$$

The investor expends effort a_t on defensive measures. He wins the conflict with probability q, implying that he earns the returns from the current period and stays in possession of the project for this period and up to the beginning of the next period. The present value of staying in possession up to the beginning of the next period is u^*_{t+1}, and $\delta \in (0, 1)$ is the investor's discount factor, which is exogenous here and constant across periods, for simplicity. Accordingly, the investor's valuation of winning the contest in period t ("A's prize in the competition taking place in period t") is $1 + \delta u^*_{t+1}$.

Similarly, the payoff of a stationary bandit in the host country in period t who has not been successful in appropriating the investment project in a previous period can be written

$$v_t = -b_t + (1 - q(a_t, b_t))w + q(a_t, b_t)\delta v^*_{t+1}. \tag{4.4}$$

The stationary bandit expends effort b_t in period t. This effort is sunk, whether the bandit's attempt is successful or not. He wins with probability $(1 - q)$. In this case he receives w, which is the present value of future returns. With the remaining probability q, the expropriation attempt in period t is not successful. The bandit attributes value v^*_{t+1} to entering into period $t + 1$ in a situation in which the appropriation attempt in period t (and in previous periods) was unsuccessful, but in which he can continue to attempt to appropriate the investment project. Equation (4.4) can be rewritten as

$$v_t = -b_t + w - q(a_t, b_t)(w - \delta v^*_{t+1}). \tag{4.5}$$

Accordingly, the bandit's valuation of winning the contest in period t is the payoff difference between winning and losing as in (4.5), that is, $[w - \delta v^*_{t+1}]$.

This game has a potentially infinite horizon and a stationarity property. Restricting consideration to Markov strategies, all relevant history at a period t is summarized in whether the investment took place initially (otherwise there is no interaction in future periods) and whether the investor is still in possession of the investment project at the beginning of t. If an investment took place in period 0, the following holds (see appendix).

Proposition 4.1 Suppose investment did take place. A stationary Markov perfect equilibrium of the repeated conflict subgame with the same bandit exists as follows. The continuation values in periods in which no previous appropriation attempt was successful are

$$u^* = \frac{1 - \gamma_0 w}{1 - \delta} \quad \text{and} \quad v^* = 0$$

if the property rights quality is good ($\gamma = \gamma_0$), and $u^* = 0$ and $v^* = w - 1/\gamma_1$ if the property rights quality is bad ($\gamma = \gamma_1$).

The equilibrium is such that the investor has a positive value from possessing the plant at the beginning of the next period if and only if his period return from operating the plant in this period (which was normalized to 1) exceeds γw, that is, the product of the parameter measuring property rights quality and the long-term benefit to the stationary bandit from owning the plant in that and all subsequent periods. Intuitively, the bandit has a long-run benefit from winning. The investor only has an immediate period gain but has to defend his property again next period. This explains intuitively why the period benefit 1 is compared with w. In addition, the property rights quality comes into play. The investor needs only a share γ of the cost of effort expended by the bandit to be successful when trying to defend his property.

If $1 > \gamma w$ does not hold, the investor's required equilibrium effort from defending his property in a given period dissipates his period benefit from this effort. This also holds for all future periods, so the investor cannot really gain in this competition. His overall benefit from initial ownership of the plant is zero because all possible future earnings just compensate for the his expected return from this defense effort.

Turning to the investment decision in period $t = 0$, investment takes place if and only if net present value of the expected returns that the investor receives from investing in the equilibrium, net of the effort expended, exceeds the investment cost. Assuming that the Markov perfect equilibrium that is characterized in proposition 4.1 is chosen if the investment took place in period $t = 0$, then the investor is willing to make this investment if the present value of the expected returns that he can keep net of fighting cost at least matches the investment cost. The present value of these net returns depends on the value of

γw. If the property rights quality is bad $(1 < \gamma_1 w)$, then these net returns are zero for the investor. If the property rights quality is good $(1 > \gamma_0 w)$, then the net present value from the returns net of contest efforts at period 0 is

$$\delta u^* = \frac{\delta}{1 - \delta}(1 - \gamma_0 w).$$

Given that the property rights regime is good with probability p_0, the expected net returns from investment exceed the investment cost, and investment takes place if

$$k \leq p_0 \frac{\delta}{1 - \delta}(1 - \gamma_0 w). \tag{4.6}$$

Note that what matters for the decision to invest is not the expected gross return the investor receives but the expected return net of his future cost of defending his own property. For instance, if $\gamma = \gamma_0$, the investor could defend his property in each period by a defense effort equal to $\gamma_0 w$ and have a present value of his gross return of

$$\frac{\delta}{1 - \delta} \cdot 1.$$

However, period return net of fighting cost is only $(1 - \gamma_0 w)$, and its present value is

$$\frac{\delta}{1 - \delta}(1 - \gamma_0 w).$$

This shows that investment considerations based on exogenous expropriation probabilities, or on expropriation probabilities that are empirically observed and taken as exogenous, will typically underestimate the actual underinvestment problem. They do not take into consideration that insecure property rights also cause considerable costs for defending one's own property, and these reduce the net returns investors can recover from their investment.

Equation (4.6) also shows another interesting result. It is not the expected value of property rights quality that matters for whether the investment pays or not. What matters is how large the expected return is in those states in which the return is positive, and how likely those states are. If the property rights quality is bad $(\gamma = \gamma_1$, with $\gamma_1 w > 1)$, how bad it is does not matter for the investor's payoff: in these cases the payoff is zero in any case. If the property rights quality is good ($\gamma = \gamma_0$, with $\gamma_0 w < 1$), however, the size of γ_0 is relevant for the investor's payoff. Konrad and Kovenock (2006b) show that contestants may benefit from an increase in the dispersion of their own stochastic ability. Their fundamental result can be applied to the problem here. The investor prefers *ex ante* uncertainty about the property rights quality. To illustrate this, let $p_0 = p_1 = 1/2$ and compare two cases. For one case, $\gamma_0 w = \gamma_1 w$. Uncertainty is absent. For the other case, $\gamma_0 w = 1/2$ and $\gamma_1 w = 3/2$. Hence, there is uncertainty about the quality of property rights. In both cases expected property rights quality is the same, but the payoff of the investor is different. In the first case, applying proposition 4.1, investment yields zero expected return for the investor because $\gamma w \equiv 1$. No investment will take place if $k > 0$. In the second case, applying proposition 4.1, the expected return for the investor is

$$\frac{\delta}{1 - \delta} \frac{1}{4},$$

and investment will take place if the cost of investment is smaller than this amount.

Roving Bandits

Consider now an investor who is threatend by roving bandits. Each roving bandit has at most one chance to try appropriating the investment project for himself. He will never have a second chance. This case may also describe the situation in a country with many competing players who all wait for an appropriation opportunity. When Knauf made the investments that led to its clash with the tax administration, the tax administration used a particular window of opportunity in which a confiscatory threat had a reasonable chance of being successful (even though it was not, in the end). The administration did not just dream up some demands for money; they used some transaction that provided a reasonable basis for their claims, given the set of rules that applied at the time. Similarly, when some oligarchs took over major public enterprises for low market values, this happened during a small window of opportunity that made such a transaction feasible. Indeed, it is likely that the situation in many transition countries is appropriately described by multiple public and private agents with sufficient power to become a player in this game, where each of them are waiting for the opportunity to make an appropriation attempt in the knowledge that the opportunity is probably unique rather than a situation in which there is a whole series of opportunities for each agent.

Consider the problem again more formally. The continuation value of the investor in period t if he is still holds the investment project at the end of period $t-1$ is

$$u_t = -a_t + q_t[1 + \delta u^*_{t+1}]. \tag{4.7}$$

The expression is similar to (4.3). Again u^*_{t+1} is the equilibrium continuation value in period $t+1$ if the investor is in possession and control of the investment project at the end of period t, but for the case of roving bandits. This continuation value need not be the same as in (4.3).

The identity of the roving bandit B_t changes from period to period and is labeled with subscript t. The value that player B_t attributes to being the roving bandit in period t who has only one opportunity to try appropriating the plant for himself in period t and uses effort $b_{t,t}$ is

$$v_{t,t} = -b_{t,t} + (1 - q_t)w + \delta q_t v^*_{t,t+1}. \tag{4.8}$$

The variable w denotes the present value of what B_t gets from winning the appropriation contest, and $v^*_{t,t+1}$ is what this player receives as a present value in period $t+1$ if his attempt fails. This $v^*_{t,t+1}$ is exogenously given here, and we assume that the unsuccessful attempt in period t does not lead to any benefits or options that are not available in the case of appropriation success, such that

$$v^*_{t,t+1} = 0. \tag{4.9}$$

The following result is shown in the appendix.

Proposition 4.2 Suppose investment did take place. A stationary Markov perfect equilibrium of the repeated conflict subgame with roving bandits has the following properties. The continuation values in periods in which no previous appropriation attempt was successful are

$$u^* = \frac{1 - \gamma_0 w}{1 - \delta} \quad \text{and} \quad v^* = 0$$

if the property rights quality is good ($\gamma = \gamma_0$), and $u^* = 0$ and $v^* = w - 1/\gamma_1$ if the property rights quality is bad ($\gamma = \gamma_1$).

The continuation value u^* again constitutes the value that the investor attributes to being in possession of the plant at the beginning of a given period, and v^* is the value that a roving bandit attributes to being in the unique position of being able to challenge the investor in one given period. Note that these values do not differ from those in the case with a stationary bandit. This may be surprising because the stakes for a bandit who does not have a second chance seem to be higher than for a bandit who can simply try again in the next period if he made an unsuccessful attempt in the previous period. The intuition is as follows. In the case in which the property rights quality is good, compare the roving bandit and the stationary bandit if they lose the competition at period t. The roving bandit does not get another chance. The stationary bandit gets another chance, but his expected equilibrium payoff from this second chance is zero. Hence, he is allowed to try again, but he does not attribute a positive value to this option in the equilibrium outcome. Accordingly, in the competition in period t, the roving bandit and the stationary bandit are more similar than they first appear to be. This explains why the investor is indifferent about fighting with a stationary or a roving bandit.

Equality of payoffs in the two regimes does not imply that the equilibrium outcomes are perfectly identical. There is one difference that does not show up in the propositions, and it relates to the equilibrium probabilities by which expropriation occurs in the two regimes. For the case with good property rights quality, the probability of successful appropriation in each given period is the same in both regimes. However, for bad property rights quality, successful appropriation in the Markov perfect equilibrium of the conflict subgame is more likely to occur for a roving bandit. The bandit who can repeatedly attempt to appropriate the investment project attributes a lower price to winning, and this makes it more likely that successful appropriation takes place in the future.

Turning to the investment stage, it follows from a comparison of the payoffs in the conflict subgames for the investor that the critical value of k for which investment may take place is the same in the two regimes.

Moreover, the result on the beneficial effects of downside risk in terms of a low γ_0 and the irrelevance of the actual size of $\gamma_1 w$ for $\gamma_1 w > 1$ carry over to this regime. It also holds in the case with roving bandits that the investor prefers a large downside risk with respect to γ for a given expected quality of property rights.[12]

Discussion and Conclusions

In the formal analysis the properties of the stationary Markov perfect equilibrium in the two regimes were characterized. Tacit collusion, negotiations, side payments, and binding contracts on current or future behavior were ruled out. In addition, the investor and the respective bandit had to choose their fighting efforts simultaneously in a given period.

Of course, some of these assumptions are crucial for the results. When discussing wasteful conflict, political scientists have pointed to the central question of whether wasteful resource effort could not be avoided by efficient negotiations. Fearon (1995) for instance, discusses several issues that may cause such negotiations to fail, among them problems of incomplete information, commitment, or time consistency. For this reason, it is important to ask whether, and under what conditions, players A and B can avoid expending wasteful efforts and reach a peaceful agreement. In the absence of information asymmetries, such an agreement is feasible if players A and B can commit to abstaining from expending appropriation effort or defense effort and on binding side payments for all future periods. It is reasonable to assume that such negotiations or tacit collusion might be easier if the bandit is stationary. However, even in this case, the mechanisms discussed by Fearon may operate and prevent any peaceful settlement. It is this framework with weak property rights that has motivated my work reported here.

Summarizing, appropriation fights between a foreign investor and local players in the host country characterize the investment climate in many countries, particularly in countries with weak and fragmented government. The various power groups in the host country may expend effort, attempting to appropriate property rights and control rights in an investment project or revenues from the project, whereas the investor tries to ward off these attempts. Whether an investor loses ownership and control of his property is the outcome of a fight in which the investor and his rival(s) expend resources to improve their odds. Typically, it is not simply the sovereign decision of some government agency in the host country. This is important for assessing the investment climate in such countries and the incentives for foreign direct investment. In particular, the cost of defending one's property rights lowers the net return on foreign direct investment. In turn, this cost is important for whether investment occurs or not.

The investment incentives of a foreign direct investor depend on various aspects, some of which showed up here: the discount rate of the host government, which can be seen as a proxy for the government's own security of property rights; whether the appropriation conflict is symmetric or it grants an effectiveness advantage to one of the players; and whether the player who might be successful in appropriating the investment project can run the project as efficiently as the investor. The uncertainty that the investor faces *ex ante* as regards the quality of property rights in the host country is also important. Investment conditions are more favorable if the investor is more cost-efficient in expending contest effort; if the loss in the value of future returns that emerges when appropriation takes place is large; if the quality of property rights is good; or if at least the *ex ante* uncertainty about the quality of the property rights regime in the host country is high.

Appendix

Proof of Proposition 4.1   Consider the candidate equilibrium of the conflict game in which investment has taken place that is described in proposition 4.1. For the proof we take the equilibrium values of continuation values for future periods $t + i$ as given and apply the one-stage deviation principle to solve for the mutually optimal behavior of A and B, confirming that this behavior yields the continuation values in the stationary candidate equilibrium.

In the candidate equilibrium, A's prize of winning a period contest is $z_A \equiv 1 + \delta u^*$, and B's prize of winning a period contest is $z_B \equiv w - \delta v^*$. The unique equilibrium of the all-pay auction with prizes z_A and z_B and a contest success function (4.1) is obtained from the general results in Baye, Kovenock, and de Vries (1996) as follows.   ∎

Lemma 4.1   In the static all-pay auction with two contestants A and B who value winning by z_A and z_B and a contest success function as in (4.1), the equilibrium is in mixed strategies with supports $[0, \min\{z_A, \gamma z_B\}]$ and $[0, \min\{z_A/\gamma, z_B\}]$. The equilibrium distribution of bids has no mass points other than at zero, and at most for one of the players. The payoffs are $\pi_A = \max\{z_A - \gamma z_B, 0\}$ for A and $\pi_B = \max\{z_B - z_A/\gamma, 0\}$ for B. The win probability for A is

$$q_A = \begin{cases} 1 - \dfrac{\gamma z_B}{2z_A} & \text{if } z_A \geq \gamma z_B, \\[3mm] \dfrac{z_A}{2\gamma z_B} & \text{if } z_A < \gamma z_B, \end{cases}$$

and $q_B = 1 - q_A$. The cumulative distribution functions characterizing the equilibrium strategies for $z_A \geq \gamma z_B$ are

$$F_A(a) = \begin{cases} \dfrac{a}{\gamma z_B} & \text{for } a \in [0, \gamma z_B], \\[3mm] 1 & \text{for } a > \gamma z_B, \end{cases} \tag{4.10}$$

and

$$F_B(b) = \begin{cases} 1 - \dfrac{\gamma z_B}{z_A} + \dfrac{b\gamma}{z_A} & \text{for } b \in [0, z_B], \\[3mm] 1 & \text{for } b > z_B, \end{cases} \tag{4.11}$$

and for $z_A < \gamma z_B$ they are

$$F_A(a) = \begin{cases} 1 - \dfrac{z_A}{\gamma_1 z_B} + \dfrac{a}{\gamma_1 z_B} & \text{for } a \in [0, z_A], \\[3mm] 1 & \text{for } a > z_A, \end{cases} \tag{4.12}$$

and

$$F_B(b) = \begin{cases} \dfrac{\gamma b}{z_A} & \text{for } b \in \left[0, \dfrac{z_A}{\gamma}\right], \\[3mm] 1 & \text{for } b > \dfrac{z_A}{\gamma}. \end{cases} \tag{4.13}$$

Consider the case $\gamma = \gamma_0$ with $1 > \gamma_0 w$. Let

$$u_{t+1}^* = \frac{1 - \gamma_0 w}{1 - \delta} \quad \text{and} \quad v_{t+1}^* = 0.$$

In the all-pay auction in period t player A competes for a prize of size

$$z_A = 1 + \delta \frac{1 - \gamma_0 w}{1 - \delta},$$

and B competes for a prize of size $z_B = w$, where

$$1 + \delta \frac{1 - \gamma_0 w}{1 - \delta} > \gamma_0 w.$$

Note that this inequality is equivalent to $1 > \gamma_0 w$, given that $\delta \in (0,1)$. Accordingly, the case $z_A > \gamma z_B$ in lemma 4.1 applies. Inserting these prize values yields a payoff from participating in the auction for player A equal to

$$z_A - \gamma_0 z_B = 1 + \delta \frac{1 - \gamma_0 w}{1 - \delta} - \gamma_0 w = \frac{1 - \gamma_0 w}{1 - \delta} = u^*. \tag{4.14}$$

By (4.3), the continuation value u_t is equal to A's equilibrium payoff in the period conflict, as in (4.14). The continuation value for B is given by $v_t = \pi_B + q\delta v_{t+1}^*$ and follows from (4.4). Using $v_{t+1}^* = 0$, the result $v_t = 0$ follows.

Consider the case $\gamma = \gamma_1$ with $1 < \gamma_1 w$. Let the anticipated continuation values be $u_{t+1}^* = 0$ and $v_{t+1}^* = w - 1/\gamma_1$. In the all-pay auction in period t player A competes for a prize of size $z_A = 1$, and B competes for a prize of size $z_B = w - \delta(w - 1/\gamma_1)$. Note that for these values of z_A and z_B, $1 < \gamma_1 w$ is equivalent to $z_A < \gamma_1 z_B$ for $\delta \in (0,1)$. The unique equilibrium for a contest with these prizes is therefore characterized by Lemma 4.1: A randomizes on the interval $(0, z_A]$, and B randomizes on the interval $[0, z_A/\gamma_1]$, with cumulative distribution functions that are given by (4.12) and (4.13). Note that $u_t = \pi_A$ by (4.3), and inserting yields $u_t = 0 = u^*$. The continuation value v_t can be obtained by choosing one of the effort levels that are within the equilibrium support of player B, for instance, $b = 1/\gamma_1$. This effort level makes B win with probability 1. Accordingly, inserting into (4.4), this yields

$$v_t = w - \frac{1}{\gamma_1}.$$

Note that for B the payoff from winning the period competition differs from this continuation value:

$$\pi_B = z_B - \frac{z_A}{\gamma_1} = w - \delta\left(w - \frac{1}{\gamma_1}\right) - \frac{1}{\gamma_1} = (1 - \delta)v^* = v^* - \delta v^*.$$

Proof of Proposition 4.2 In a stationary Markov perfect equilibrium, $u_t = u_{t+1}^* \equiv u^*$, and $z_A = 1 + \delta u^*$ is the prize value that the investor attributes to winning the contest in period t. Moreover, the payoff of winning for the roving bandit is $z_B = w$.

Suppose that for given γ_0 in the candidate equilibrium, $1 + \delta u_{t+1}^* > \gamma_0 w$ holds. Bandit B_t wins w if he wins the all-pay auction at t and receives zero otherwise. His maximum effort expended is w, implying that the investor will never expend more than $\gamma_0 w$ in the equilibrium. The investor therefore wins with probability 1 if he expends $a_t = \gamma_0 w$. Accordingly, the payoff of the investor is $u_t = 1 + \delta u_{t+1}^* - \gamma_0 w$. Using $u_t = u_{t+1}^* = u^*$ in the equilibrium, this has a unique solution,

$$u^* = \frac{1 - \gamma_0 w}{1 - \delta}, \tag{4.15}$$

and u^* is non-negative if and only if $\gamma_0 w \leq 1$. Hence, this will be the continuation value for the case with high property rights quality.

Suppose now that $1 + \delta u_{t+1}^* < \gamma_1 w$ in the candidate equilibrium. The valuation for winning the all-pay auction in period t for the investor is $1 + \delta u_{t+1}^*$, and this defines the maximum effort that the investor is willing to expend. In turn, the roving bandit B_t wins with probability 1 if he expends

$$\frac{1 + \delta u_{t+1}^*}{\gamma_1}$$

defining an upper bound for the effort expended by the bandit. By the properties of the static all-pay auction and invoking the one-stage deviation principle, $a_t = 1 + \delta u_{t+1}^*$ is an effort choice that is in support of the investor's equilibrium strategy and makes the investor win with probability 1. Accordingly, $u_t = 1 + \delta u_{t+1}^* - (1 + \delta u_{t+1}^*) = 0 = u^*$. Moreover, for the bandit

$$v_{t,t} = -\frac{1 + \delta u_{t+1}^*}{\gamma_1} + w + 0.$$

Using $v_{t,t} = v^*$ and $u_{t+1}^* = u^* = 0$ yields

$$v^* = w - \frac{1}{\gamma_1} \tag{4.16}$$

as the unique continuation value for bandit B_t at the beginning of period t. ∎

Notes

A previous version of this chapter was circulated as Konrad (2001). I thank Toke Aidt, Arye Hillman, Ram Mudambi, Joe Smolik, Donald Wintrobe, and Alfons Weichenrieder for helpful comments on the previous version; Florian Morath, Johannes Münster, Ethan Bueno de Mesquito, Edward L. Glaeser, and other participants at the 2005 CESifo conference for comments on this version; Jürgen Ehrke for valuable research assistance; and Greg Hess and an anonymous referee for helpful comments.

1. For a theoretical and empirical analysis of the Russian mafia and further references, see Skaperdas (2001).

2. The Knauf case is not unique. As Jeanne Whalen points out in an article in the *Moscow Times* (January 13, 1998), "U.S.-Russian Cable venture Kosmos TV and German building materials manufacturer Knauf spent a good part of the year battling for control of their companies against general directors they'd hired to run those enterprises. Both foreign investors reported their executives had turned into Frankensteins, kicking the owners out of their offices, dipping into the company till and wreaking havoc on business in general. Working through official channels hasn't helped either party. A series of court rulings have upheld the right of Kosmos TV's general director to continue running the company. Although two federal courts have empowered Knauf to take back its factory and fire its general director, the Germans have been unable to enforce the decisions."

3. Eaton and Gersovitz (1983; 1984) and many other researchers considered expropriation as a choice made at free will by the host government. The governments' ability to expropriate generates a holdup problem: the government may have an incentive to expropriate a foreign investor once the investment has been made. Because investors anticipate this, in the extreme case no investment takes place and high-yield investment opportunities are not used unless the government can commit itself not to fully confiscate the returns on this investment. Hence, the problem was typically seen as a commitment problem. The government is considered to make a free decision whether to expropriate the foreign direct investor, and it does not expropriate investors if the present value of the costs of an expropriation exceeds the benefits, or if the government is able to commit itself not to expropriate the investor. For some theoretical analyses of commitment considering repeated games, see, for instance, Cole and English (1991; 1992), Thomas and Worrall (1994), Cohen and Michel (1991). Further commitment devices are discussed in Schnitzer (1995; 1999; 2002), Konrad and Lommerud (2001), and Boadway and Keen (1998).

4. Self-protection can take interesting directions. Frantisek Mojzs was the former owner of a company with a US$150 million per year business. When faced with the option to adopt the mafia as a silent partner, he signed over ownership of his firm to the Roman Catholic Church (*International Herald Tribune*, March 6, 1998).

5. Conflict as an important mechanism has been emphasized in many contexts for determining resource allocation in the absence of well-defined property rights. See, for instance, Skaperdas (1992) and Garfinkel and Skaperdas (1996) on the allocation of property rights in social conflict more generally.

6. For instance, if the factory has been turned over to some other player, the investor may withdraw some intangible factors, causing a loss in managerial or production efficiency, and the new owner may have different skills to run production.

7. A different interpretation of this regime is as follows. Suppose that the investor faces a large set of possible contenders in each period who differ in their abilities to fight and their valuations of appropriating the project both within a period and across periods. In the framework with all-pay auctions, there are typically at most two contestants active, with the investor and one contender among them, where the contender is the strongest among the set of contenders in this period. In this second interpretation w, the present value of the bandit's benefit from appropriating for himself, may change over time, pos-

sibly as a random process. However, in the formal analysis I hold to the first interpretation or assume that w is constant over time in the second interpretation.

8. This first regime is very similar to the one considered by Stephan and Ursprung (1998). The main differences are that Stephan and Ursprung consider a Tullock (1980) contest success function instead of the all-pay auction without noise and that there is no investment stage.

9. Note that, in principle, the successful bandit may, after becoming the project owner, be exposed to some future threats as well, and such a threat and its implied fighting costs are generally determinants of w.

10. Variants of this contest success function are used to describe contests in fields ranging from military conflict (Bester and Konrad 2005), political conflict (Polborn 2006), promotional contests (Meland and Straume 2005), to litigation (Baye, Kovenock, and deVries 2005) and lobbying by interest groups (Ellingsen 1991).

11. The full characterization for the case considered here is also outlined in the appendix.

12. This could be shown drawing on the results in Konrad and Kovenock (2006b).

References

Andersson, T. 1991. *Multinational Investment in Developing Countries: A Study of Taxation and Nationalization.* London: Routledge.

Baye, M. R., D. Kovenock, and C. G. de Vries. 1996. The all-pay auction with complete information. *Economic Theory* 8: 291–305.

———. 2005. Comparative analysis of litigation systems: An auction-theoretic approach. *Economic Journal* 115 (505): 583–601.

Berkowitz, D., and W. Li. 2000. Tax rights in transition economies: A tragedy of the commons. *Journal of Public Economics* 76: 369–397.

Bester, H., and K. A. Konrad. 2005. Easy targets and the timing of conflict. *Journal of Theoretical Politics* 17 (2): 199–216.

Boadway, R., and M. Keen. 1998. Evasion and time consistency in the taxation of capital income. *International Economic Review* 39: 461–476.

Cai, H., and D. Treisman. 2005. Does competition for capital discipline governments? Decentralization, globalization, and corruption. *American Economic Review* 95 (3): 817–830.

Cohen, D., and P. Michel. 1991. Laissez-faire and expropriation of foreign capital in a growing economy. *European Economic Review* 35: 527–534.

Cole, H. L., and W. B. English. 1991. Expropriation and direct investment. *Journal of International Economics* 30: 201–227.

———. 1992. Two-sided expropriation and international equity contracts. *Journal of International Economics* 33: 77–104.

Eaton, J., and M. Gersovitz. 1983. Country risk: Economic aspects. In *Managing International Risk*, ed. R. J. Herring, 75–108. Cambridge: Cambridge University Press.

———. 1984. A theory of expropriation and deviations from perfect capital mobility. *Economic Journal* 94: 16–40.

Ellingsen, T. 1991. Strategic buyers and the social cost of monopoly. *American Economic Review* 81: 648–657.

Fearon, J. D. 1995. Rationalist explanations for war. *International Organization* 49: 379–414.

Frye, T., and E. Zhuravskaya. 2000. Rackets, regulation, and the rule of law. *Journal of Law, Economics and Organization* 16 (2): 478–502.

Garfinkel, M. R., and S. Skaperdas. 1996. Conflict and appropriation as economic activities. In *The Political Economy of Conflict and Appropriation*, ed. M. R. Garfinkel and S. Skaperdas, 1–14. Cambridge: Cambridge University Press.

Hillman, A., and M. Krausz. 2005. Credit markets and corruption. Unpublished paper.

Johnson, S., D. Kaufmann, J. McMillan, and C. Woodruff. 2000. Why do firms hide? Bribes and unofficial activity after communism. *Journal of Public Economics* 76: 495–520.

Konrad, K. A. 2001. Repeated expropriation contests and foreign direct investment. CEPR Discussion Paper 2695. London: Centre for Economic Policy Research.

Konrad, K. A., and D. Kovenock. 2005. Equilibrium and efficiency in the tug-of-war. CESifo Working Paper 1564. Munich: CESifo Group.

———. 2006a. Multi-battle contests. CEPR Discussion Paper 5645. London: Centre for Economic Policy Research.

———. 2006b. Multi-stage contests with stochastic ability. CEPR Discussion Paper 5844. London: Centre for Economic Policy Research.

Konrad, K. A., and K. E. Lommerud. 2001. Foreign direct investment, intra-firm trade and ownership structure. *European Economic Review* 45 (3): 475–494.

Mehlum, H., and K. O. Moene. 2005. Fighting against the odds. Memorandum. Department of Economics, University of Oslo.

Meland, F., and O. R. Straume. 2007. Outsourcing in contests. *Public Choice* 131 (3): 315–331.

OECD (Organisation for Economic Cooperation and Development). 1999. *Recent Trends in Foreign Direct Investment*. Paris.

Polborn, M. 2006. Investment under uncertainty in dynamic conflicts. *Review of Economic Studies* 73 (2): 505–529.

Ponomareva, M., and E. Zhuravskaya. 2004. Federal tax arrears in Russia: Liquidity problems, federal redistribution or regional resistance? *Economics of Transition* 12 (3): 373–398.

Rothschild, M., and J. E. Stiglitz. 1970. Increasing risk: A definition. *Journal of Economic Theory* 2: 225–243.

Schnitzer, M. 1995. Solutions to the sovereign debt problem: Countertrade and foreign direct investment. Habilitation thesis, University of Bonn.

———. 1999. Expropriation and control rights: A dynamic model of foreign direct investment. *International Journal of Industrial Organization* 17 (8): 1113–1137.

——. 2002. Debt vs. foreign direct investment: The impact of sovereign risk on the structure of international capital flows. *Economica* 69 (273): 41–67.

Shleifer, A., and D. Treisman. 1999. *Without a Map: Political Tactics and Economic Reform in Russia.* Cambridge, Mass.: MIT Press.

Skaperdas, S. 1992. Cooperation, conflict, and power in the absence of property rights. *American Economic Review* 82: 720–739.

——. 2001. The political economy of organized crime: Providing protection when the state does not. *Economics of Governance* 2 (3): 173–202.

Stephan, J., and H. Ursprung. 1998. The social cost of rent seeking when victories are potentially transient and losses final. In *Trade, Growth, and Economic Policy in Open Economies: Essays in Honour of Hans-Jürgen Vosgerau*, ed. K.-J. Koch and K. Jaeger, 369–380. Berlin: Springer.

Thomas, J., and T. Worrall. 1994. Foreign direct investment and the risk of expropriation. *Review of Economic Studies* 61: 81–108.

Treisman, D. 1999. Russia's tax crisis: Explaining falling revenues in a transitional economy. *Economics and Politics* 11 (2): 145–169.

——. 2002. Postcommunist corruption. In *Political Economy of Transition Institutions: Politics and Policies*, ed. J. Fidrmuc and N. Campos. Dordrecht: Kluwer.

Tullock, G. 1980. Efficient rent seeking. In *Towards a Theory of the Rent-Seeking Society*, ed. J. Buchanan, R. Tollison, and G. Tullock, 97–112. College Station: Texas A&M University Press.

UNECE (United Nations Economic Commission for Europe). 1999. *Economic Survey of Europe, 1999, No. 1.*

II Terrorism

5 A Gravity Model of Globalization, Democracy, and Transnational Terrorism

S. Brock Blomberg and B. Peter Rosendorff

The "liberal peace" hypothesis alleges that democracies are less likely to engage in militarized disputes with each other, that they are less likely to initiate conflicts with other democracies, and when they do, they allocate significantly more resources to the conflict than other polities (Bueno de Mesquita et al. 1999). Democracies trade more with each other and are more cooperative with respect to multilateral trading arrangements by forming trade blocs and joining preferential trade agreements (Mansfield, Milner, and Rosendorff 2002; Rosendorff 2006). Countries that trade more with each other are also less likely to engage in militarized disputes (Mansfield and Pevehouse 2000; Bearce, Mansfield, and Pevehouse 1999). Conversely, countries that are conflict-prone deter trade and investment and experience slower growth (Blomberg, Hess, and Orphanides 2004; Blomberg and Mody 2005; Blomberg and Hess 2006). This association between trade, conflict, and democracy has been a central concern of scholars in international relations, who have worked to establish the precise causal processes and mechanisms. How these dynamics fit together has been a subject of significant dispute among scholars in the field.

In the recent period, however, an alternative form of cross-border conflict has garnered closer attention: transnational terrorism.[1] Although terrorism is not war waged between states per se, it has many similar features: it is a cross-national violent process that threatens people and property, with attendant political and economic consequences. Moreover, observers have argued that terrorism is responsive to changes in the same underlying variables: democracies are less prone to terrorism, and terrorism is a response to increased globalization. This chapter investigates the links between democracy, commercial integration, and terrorism in a systematic manner.

These themes have dominated public debate with regard to current U.S. foreign policy. The Bush administration, for instance, insists that instilling democracy in the Arab world will stem the flow of anti-American terrorism and increase the security of U.S. assets and people, both at home and abroad. President Bush's speech at the Veterans of Foreign Wars annual meeting in August 2005 explicitly equates "peace" with "freedom." Chuck Hagel (2004), Republican senator from Nebraska, argues that the war on terrorism must be guided by principles that expand democracy abroad. It is not clear where this hypothesis emerges from, but one likely candidate is the administration's reading of the literature on the democratic peace. Similarly, the U.S. National Intelligence Council (2004) argues that globalization is a source of insecurity for the United States; and the *New York Times* columnist Thomas Friedman (2005) alleges that a "flatter" world (one without barriers to the flow of resources) makes transnational terrorism more likely. These support the popular view that globalization and terrorism are linked.

The questions, however, remain. Does democracy abroad reduce the flow of terrorism, and does increased globalization make terrorism more likely? Key to an answer is to realize that there are two sets of issues at work. What are the characteristics relevant to a country as a target, and do democracy and commercial integration matter as characteristics of the source country?

In this chapter we bring a methodology from the literature in international trade and apply it to another flow across international borders: transnational terrorism. Using a dyadic approach akin to the gravity model of empirical international trade, we simultaneously explore the determinants of terrorism in source and target countries. We show that the effects of democracy and globalization differ depending on whether the country is a source or a target state. Democracy in the source state reduces the incidence of terrorism, and in the target state, increases it. Commercial openness in the source country reduces terrorism, and in the target country, increases it.

Terrorism and Global Trends

World foreign direct investment (FDI) flows, which amounted to less than $13 billion in 1970, quadrupled every ten years, reaching $54 billion in 1980 and $209 billion in 1990. During the last half of the 1990s, however, FDI practically exploded, reaching a peak of $1.4 trillion in 2000. Worldwide trade also increased dramatically over the same period. Trade as a percent of gross domestic product (GDP) grew from 27 percent in 1970, to 38 percent by 1980, and to 45 percent by the year 2000.

During the latter half of the twentieth century there has been an increase in democratization across the globe. The percentage of countries that are nondemocracies (as calculated by Freedom House) starts at 46 percent in 1972, falls to 35 percent by 1980, and steadily declines to 25 percent by the year 2000.

While the run-up of FDI, trade, and democracy in the 1990s, and especially in the second half of that decade, has several explanations, it is strikingly correlated with a decline in transnational terrorism during that period. In the late 1980s and early 1990s, approximately 1.5 transnational terrorist events occurred every day. As globalization and democratization grew at an ever faster rate, the frequency of terrorist events declined sharply, reaching less than 0.5 events a day by 2000. Did this shift toward a more integrated and democratic world contribute to the large increase in peace during that same period?

In order to understand the effects that democracy and globalization might have on terrorist activity, we need an underlying view of the decision-theoretic mechanisms that determine terrorist choices. We define terrorism as the premeditated or threatened use of extranormal violence to obtain a political, religious, or ideological objective through the intimidation of a large audience. We assume that terrorists are rational actors, choosing strategies to maximize the chance of success with respect to particular objectives, taking full account of the constraints under which they operate (Sandler, Tschirhart, and Cauley 1983). The levels of activity undertaken and the location in which they occur depend on the costs, benefits, and resources available. Higher costs mean fewer activities; higher benefits and resources imply more activity.[2]

Enders and Sandler (1993) establish that terrorists respond to changes in incentives. An increase in the cost of one mode of operation across the international system (metal detectors in airports, for example) leads to changes in terrorist operations (fewer skyjackings) and an increase in other modes. Democracy and globalization work to influence terrorist activity through all three avenues: costs, benefits, and resources.

Terrorism and Democracy

Democracy, it is often alleged, provides a set of rules that facilitate the peaceful resolution of political conflicts. It offers access to the powerful decision makers and political institutions for citizens to seek redress for their grievances. It makes political organization cheaper and lowers the costs of (legitimate) political action, making illegal activities relatively more expensive, and therefore in expectation less terrorist violence.

On the other hand, key to the success of any terrorist act is recruitment and organization, both of which are made easier in environments with civil liberties and freedom of religion, association, and movement. All these are characteristic of democracies, of course. Moreover, the terrorist act must spread fear and anxiety through the population at large, facilitated by a free and well-functioning press and freedom of speech, which are also characteristic of democracy.

Eubank and Weinberg (1994) find that terrorist groups are more frequently hosted by democratic societies. Following Sandler (1995), Eubank and Weinberg (2001) find that terrorist events occur more frequently in stable democratic countries. Similarly, Li and Schaub (2004) find more incidents in democratic countries. It may not be democracy per se at work; the experience of less democratic or newly democratizing countries such as Afghanistan and Iraq suggests that the transitional period between authoritarianism and democracy is a particularly susceptible one for terrorist activity (Eubank and Weinberg 1998).

Other evidence on the link between democracy and transnational terrorism is mixed. Li (2005) attempts to disaggregate the many dimensions of democracy; he finds that voter turnout reduces terrorist incidents in a country but constraints on government authority increase incidents; press freedom raises incidents. Overall, the effect of democracy on terrorism is unclear.

Assessing the motives of terrorists leads to little insight. Although the targets of terrorism are more frequently democracies, rarely is the terrorists' manifesto one of installing democracy in their home countries; rather it is often about self-determination and removing foreign military occupation (Pape 2003).

The effects of democracy on a country's likelihood of being a source for transnational terrorism are not firmly established. Nondemocracies create fewer outlets for political grievances to be addressed, making violent means of political action more likely. This might lead to increased domestic terrorism, but it doesn't speak to the country as a source of transnational terrorism. When an autocratic government is perceived to have its authority bolstered by its foreign relations with democracies, however, we might expect that terrorist groups advocating the removal of the illegitimate autocrat would indeed target its foreign allies, some of whom may be democracies. We might expect therefore that nondemocracy abroad could increase transnational terrorism at home.

As to what makes a country a source of terrorists, there is little evidence of any kind. Discussion in this regard has rarely distinguished between domestic and transnational terrorism. Where political conflict is domestic, the lack of outlets for political discontent make violent means of protest more likely. Where a wider variety of groups get to participate in the political process, nonviolent means are at least attempted first. Others have argued that in a more democratic regime, more political action of all kinds, violent and nonviolent, is likely. For transnational terrorism, Eubank and Weinberg (2001) surprisingly find that "terrorist events are more likely to be carried out by the citizens of stable democracies than the citizens of any other type of country, from absolutism to insecure democracy." But their approach is merely to look for modal categories without looking to explain observed variations in the data.

Overall, the lack of clarity on the issue stems, in our view, from treating the source and target countries in the same manner. When the effects of democracy are permitted to differ conditional on whether the observation is a source or a target, one obtains a more precise view of the determinants of transnational terrorism.

Globalization and Terrorism

Globalization also affects the costs, benefits, and resources available for terrorist activities. If terrorism emerges from a sense of relative deprivation, then globalization, insofar as it encourages economic growth, may mitigate terrorist tendencies. On the other hand, if globalization is associated with increased inequality across countries and groups, then we might expect globalization to lead to more violence. On the cost side of the equation, the lowered barriers to flows of goods, money, people, and ideas make the networks of terrorist operations cheaper to operate. Terrorists themselves find it easier to move across increasingly permeable borders. Resource flows across borders necessary to finance terrorist operations become more difficult to monitor by authorities overwhelmed by the growth of the international financial system. Norms of privacy in international banking make information about these resource flows scarce. The fact that customs agents inspect only a small fraction of goods imported makes the smuggling of terrorist matériel cheaper, and the freer flow of information makes the knowledge and techniques of terrorist action more easily transferred. Globalization, like democracy, affects the costs, benefits, and resources of terrorists in many ways. The literature has focused on some of these mechanisms, and the evidence has been substantially inconclusive.

The popular discourse seems to put some of the blame for transnational terrorism on globalization, the increased flow of goods, services, ideas, people, and culture across international borders. The Economist (2002) suggests that the relative ease with which resources and people move around the world increases the risks associated with transnational terrorism. Paul Martin (2001), the Canadian Finance Minister, claims that terrorists themselves are hostile to the process of globalization—witness the choice of target by the 9/11 hijackers: a center of world trade and finance.

Krug and Reinmoeller (2004) argue that globalization is an important determinant of terrorism. They build a model to explain the internationalization of terrorism as a natural response to a globalizing economies. As countries become more economically integrated and market-oriented, there is no discrimination between what certain terrorist groups might see as bad products and good products or investments. Moreover, the same advances in technology that allow for easy access of goods and services also allow for easy access to military hardware and technology. In the short run, globalization may have the consequence of creating a series of winners and losers. These same losers will have easier access to retaliate in response to their losses, thereby multiplying the effect of globalization on terrorism.

An alternative view put forth by Crenshaw (2001) is that it is naive to believe that globalization is encouraging international terrorism. Although globalization and terrorism may be seemingly affecting one another, there is something more complicated at work. Put differently, the latest incidence of terrorism is not necessarily driven by globalization. Instead, the latest wave of terrorism should be seen as a series of civil wars that may be motivated by a strategically unified reaction to U.S. power rather than directly by globalization.

In a pooled cross-section analysis of globalization and transnational terrorism, Li and Schaub (2004) explore some of these links. On the one hand, reduced transaction costs of international trade and finance make tracing terrorist funds difficult and reduce the effective costs of financing terrorist activity. Similarly, as trade accelerates, illegal smuggling becomes cheaper, permitting weapons to travel with a higher chance of not being intercepted. On the other hand, if globalization and growth are associated, terrorism, a problem of underdevelopment and poverty, will take care of itself. Li and Schaub use the ITERATE data set (Mickolus et al. 2002) of 112 countries from 1975 to 1997. They find that international trade and investment have little effect on the number of terrorist events.

Others argue that globalization encourages terrorism for yet further reasons. If globalization increases world inequality, then it will increase feelings of relative deprivation. These feelings produce political action, some of it violent. Or merely, globalization results in a kind of cultural imperialization, significantly reducing the quality of life of people committed to a particular set of norms governing social behavior, norms that are broken by foreign influences.

Dyads and the Gravity Model

How can we possibly make sense of these conflicting theoretical claims and the even less satisfying empirical record? Here we make use of the concept of the directed dyad, which differentiates explicitly between the characteristics of the state that is the source of the terrorist activity and the state that is the target. By separating out the effects of democracy and globalization on the source and target states we generate much clearer and precise hypotheses and results than are available using standard panel regression techniques.

We start by focusing our attention on transnational terrorism and recognizing that this type of terrorism is fundamentally dyadic in nature. Hence it is amenable to investigation using an approach similar to the gravity of model of international trade.

Our focus is on the determinants of transnational terrorism. Following the definition adopted by Mickolus et al. (2002, 2), a transnational terrorist event is defined as "the use, or threat of use, of anxiety-inducing, extra-normal violence for political purposes, by any individual or group, whether acting for or in opposition to established government authority, when such action is intended to influence the attitudes and behavior of a target group wider than the immediate victims and when, through the nationality or foreign ties of its perpetrators, its location, the nature of its institutional or human victims, or the mechanics of its resolution, its ramifications *transcend national boundaries"* [italics added].

Transnational terrorism requires a flow of resources across international borders, whether it is foreign terrorists attacking domestic (and other foreign) targets, or domestic nationals attacking the property and lives of foreign nationals on domestic soil. As a result, it seems appropriate in any investigation of the determinants of transnational terrorism to consider the characteristics of both the source and target countries. Moreover, the characteristics of a country that might make it a likely target country may indeed be very different from the characteristics that make it a likely source of international terrorism. The features of the polity that make a country a terrorist producer may be different from the political structures, institutions, and environment that make a state a terrorist target.

We adopt here an explicitly dyadic approach, and we follow the insights drawn from international economics. A country's willingness to engage in international trade—to import and export—depend on key features of both the underlying economies. Following Heckscher-Ohlin, a country's trading patterns (whether it is an importer or exporter of a particular good) depend crucially on its factor endowments relative to its trading partner. A country relatively well endowed with a particular factor will export goods that use that factor intensively. We draw the obvious analogy when considering transnational terrorism: what matters are the underlying political conditions present in both the sending and receiving country, not just in the country in which the event took place or the nationalities of the victims.

For several decades, the most frequently used empirical specification for linking trade volumes with underlying economic conditions is known as the gravity model, which is an analogy borrowed from physics. When considering the flow of gravitational force between two bodies, it has long been understood that this depends on the mass of the two bodies and the distance between them. From international trade theory (Anderson and Van Wincoop 2003; Deardorff 1984), the volume of trade between two countries depends on the size of their economies and the physical distance between them. This specification has been further refined by adding variables such as income per capita, language differences, the regime types of the two countries. We claim here that the flow of transnational terrorism between states similarly depends on the incomes of the two countries, the distance between them, language differences, the regime types of the two states, and a number of other variables that describe the underlying economic and political conditions of both states.[3]

Our central hypotheses are these:

H1 The effects of democracy and globalization on terrorism differ for source and target countries.

H2 Terrorism falls with democracy and globalization in the source countries.

H3 Terrorism rises with democracy and globalization in the target countries.

We find that differences in income, democracy, and openness go a long way toward explaining transnational terrorism. Democratic institutions in a source country significantly reduce conflict, but these same institutions in host countries increase conflict. Source country openness has a negative, statistically significant effect on conflict, but host country openness has a positive, statistically significant effect on conflict. The effect for a source country of being a democracy or participating in the World Trade Organization is to decrease the number of terrorist strikes by about two to three per year, which is more than 2 standard deviations greater than the average number of strikes between any two countries in a given year.

The Data and Empirical Regularities

Terrorism is adopted from the ITERATE data set (Mickolus et al. 2002). The ITERATE project began as an attempt to quantify characteristics, activities, and impacts of transnational terrorist groups. The data set is grouped into four categories. First, there are incident characteristics, which code the timing of each event. Second, the terrorist characteristics yield information about the number, makeup, and groups involved in the incidents. Third, victim characteristics describe analogous information on the victims involved in the attacks. Finally, life and property losses attempt to quantify the damage from the attack.

A central contribution of our present work is to employ the data in a different manner than has been previously employed in the literature. We consider a *bilateral* definition of terrorism, which we measure in a number of ways. First, we measure terrorism T as the number of events in a host country h from attackers whose nationality comes from a source country s. Second, we define terrorism as the number of events perpetrated on individuals from the host country h by attackers whose nationality comes from the source country s. In addition, we measure T as the number of victims rather than as the number of incidents in a given year.

We present several caveats before we proceed. First, one may be concerned that the nationality of the source attacker may not represent the views of the country with which he is associated. While this is possibly true, this problem is no less severe than what we encounter when we try to measure any international variable. How do we properly account for a Mercedes manufactured in Alabama using parts imports from Asia, for example? Second, one may be concerned that there may be more than one nationality included in the attacking force. So, how does one decide which country is responsible for the attack? Although this is a serious consideration in theory, it turns out to be less of an issue in practice because 98 percent of attacks are reported with only one source country. Finally, one may be concerned that we may be undercounting the number of incidents because not all attacks are identified with a particular group. Even so, the vast majority of attacks do have an identified source country, amounting to over 8,000 incidents.

For several decades, the gravity model has been the workhorse of empirical trade research and, more recently, empirical FDI literature. One reason is that the model is relatively intuitive. The gravity equation simply states that there is a positive relation between trade/financial flows and the sizes of countries and a negative relation between trade/financial flows and distance.

A central contribution of this chapter is to introduce transnational terrorism T as the dependent variable into these various gravity models. To include T in the aforementioned approaches, consider the following gravity equation for log trade (x_{hst}) for country pair h, s at time t and its determinants:

$$x_{hst} = f(Y_{hst}, Z_{hst}, p_{hst}), \tag{5.1}$$

where Y is log of real GDP, Z is a vector of observables to include trade costs τ (e.g., distance and language barriers), p are multilateral resistance terms such as prices, which refer to the bilateral barrier between countries relative to the average trade barrier each country faces with all trading partners. These multilateral resistance terms may be thought of as product variables that create wedges to trade.

For traditional trade gravity models, one representation of equation (5.1) is (suppressing time subscripts for convenience)

$$x_{hs} = \alpha_0 + \alpha_1 y_h + \alpha_2 y_s + \alpha_3 Y_h + \alpha_4 Y_s + \delta Z_{hs} + \varepsilon_{hs}, \tag{5.2}$$

where y is the log of real GDP per capita, Z is a vector of variables including distance (both physical and technological measures), and language barriers and the error may be specified to control for random or time/country fixed effects. We modify equation (5.2) by specifying Z and redefining the left-hand side variable as T, so that we have

$$T_{hst} = \alpha_0 + \alpha_1 \cdot y_{ht} + \alpha_2 \cdot y_{st} + \alpha_3 \cdot Y_{ht} + \alpha_4 \cdot Y_{st} + \alpha_5 \cdot logdistance_{hs}$$

$$+ \alpha_6 \cdot comlang_{hs} + \alpha_7 \cdot area_{hs} + \alpha_8 \cdot DEM_{ht}$$

$$+ \alpha_9 \cdot DEM_{st} + \alpha_{10} \cdot WTO_{ht} + \alpha_{11} \cdot WTO_{st} + \varepsilon_{ijt}, \tag{5.3}$$

where h, s denote countries, t denotes time, and the variables are defined as follows: T is the number of terrorist attacks on country h from group representing country s; Y is the log of real GDP; y is the log of real GDP per capita; *logdistance* is the natural log of distance between two countries; *comlang* is a dummy variable that is 1 if countries have a common language and 0 otherwise; *area* is the natural log of the product of the size of the countries; DEM is defined both as an index of democratization from polity and as a dummy variable if the country is a democracy; WTO is defined both as trade/GDP and as an index of integration such as trade or participation in the WTO.[4] The purpose of estimating the gravity equation would be to consider the importance of DEM and WTO in affecting the likelihood of terrorism and to compare the relative magnitude to other factors highlighted in Blomberg and Hess (2006) as relevant in explaining terrorism, for instance, GDP per capita.[5]

It is also worthwhile to note that many of the bilateral conflict observations are zero. To correctly estimate the elasticities, then, it is necessary to consider the bias on account of censoring. We employ the Tobit model, which estimates the coefficients through a maximum likelihood procedure.

Empirical Results

Cross-Country Empirical Motivation

We begin motivating our discussion by considering the link between conflict that occurs within a county's borders from outsiders and conflict that occurs by the citizens of a country in other countries. In a crude way we are examining terrorist imports and terrorist exports. The purpose of this preliminary exercise is to see if the same countries that experience significant international conflict are those countries

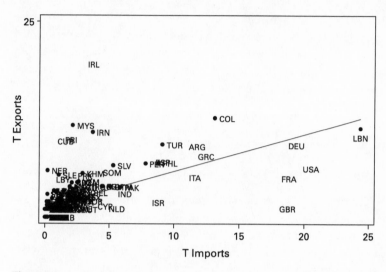

Figure 5.1
Imports and exports of terrorist events, 1968–2003.
Note: Dots denote poor, nonglobalized, nondemocracies.

whose citizens are terrorizing abroad. This is useful because it may
shed some light on some of the causes of terror: whether conflict is
driven by civil strife between countries who may have been given arbitrary borders by colonial powers; whether conflict is linked to particular countries such as the United States that may have very strong
international policies; whether conflict is due to globalization/
democratization/development such that those countries are more apt
to be net importers than net exporters.

Figure 5.1 plots countries by the number of terrorist exports versus
the number of terrorist imports and a line of best fit. If countries are
just as likely to import conflict as they are to export it, we would expect there to be a 45 degree line that relates each event. In fact, the line
of best fit is measured at 43 degrees—in line with such a hypothesis.

However, there are several important differences. First, there are notable net importers of conflict—they include Israel, the United States,
France, and Great Britain. There are also several notable net exporters
of conflict—Ireland, Iran, and Cuba. While there may be many factors
that shift countries away from the diagonal line, it is interesting to note
that the net importers mentioned are clearly more democratic and
developed than the net exporters. We denote the least democratic/
developed/open countries with dots. Most appear to be net exporters

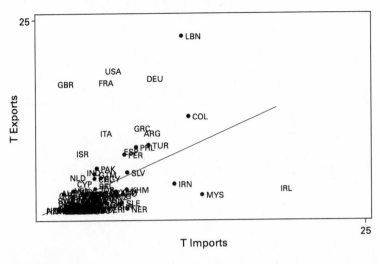

Figure 5.2
Imports and exports of terrorist events, conditional on democracy, openness, and income, 1968–2003.
Note: Dots denote poor, nonglobalized, nondemocracies.

of conflict. Hence, when developing our gravity model, it would appear that the traditional variables included in gravity models would also apply to conflict, namely, income, trade, and institutions.

This can be seen once we do the same experiment controlling for democracy, openness, and income. In this case, there does not appear to be such a difference in estimated imports or exports from conflict. Figure 5.2 plots this conditional regression. In this case there are just as many dots below and above the estimated line. Interestingly, it is still estimated to be a 45 degree line.

While these figures may be illuminating, they do not provide any direct evidence regarding the relation between globalization, democratization, and transnational terrorism. The problem is that these data conflate the characteristics of the host with the characteristics of the source country. As a gross first cut at the problem, we simply divide the data along source and host country lines. In table 5.1, a clearer picture emerges. The number of terrorist incidents by source country is larger when the source is nondemocratic and closed (especially after 1970); the number of incidents by host country conversely is larger in democracies and in open, globalized societies (although this association appears to be somewhat less strong in the recent period). These observations, of course, do not control for a number of factors that

Table 5.1
Global Trends for Terrorism, by Governance and Openness

Decade	1 Average	By Host Country				By Source Country			
		2 DEM	3 NODEM	4 OPEN	5 CLOSED	6 DEM	7 NODEM	8 OPEN	9 CLOSED
1960s	0.719	0.716	0.719	0.402	2.643	0.716	0.712	0.705	0.775
1970s	1.694	2.476	1.139	1.250	6.230	1.528	1.776	1.598	2.550
1980s	2.143	3.632	0.718	1.971	4.309	1.671	2.475	1.930	4.135
1990s	1.546	1.938	1.036	1.503	2.244	1.005	2.374	1.527	1.329
2000s	0.725	0.754	0.662	0.715	0.948	0.622	0.930	0.725	0.500
Average	1.616	2.358	0.917	1.414	3.803	1.277	1.983	1.524	2.325

Note: Each column provides the mean number of incidents for subsampled decades, 1968–2003. Column 1, averages across all countries during the subsampled time period; columns 2–5, averages from the location of the incident or host country; columns 6–9, averages from the nationality of the terrorist or source country; columns 2 and 6, averages for democracies (DEM is a dummy variable $= 1$ if *polity* > 7 or *executive* $+$ *legislative veto points* > 14, $= 0$ otherwise); columns 3 and 7, averages for the remaining nondemocracies (NODEM); columns 4 and 8, averages for more open countries (OPEN $=$ total trade/GDP > 30); and columns 5 and 9, averages for the remaining closed economies (CLOSED).

may be associated both with democracy and globalization. In the sections that follow, we add those controls and offer a more thorough analysis.

Baseline Results

We begin by explaining the results from estimating the gravity model, (5.3). In table 5.2, terrorism is measured by the number of incidents by location; our globalization variable is OPEN, which represents imports and exports as a percentage of GDP to and from all countries in columns 4 and 6; we also use an alternative measure of globalization by examining participation in the WTO and the IMF as indicators of commercial integration (columns 5, 7, and 8). DEM is a dummy variable that takes value 1 if the country's polity measure in that year is larger than 7 or if the sum of legislative and executive veto points is larger than 14.[6]

Columns 1–7 in table 5.2 include variables that do not change over time. These include distance, land mass, and dummy variables for language. Column 8 estimates the model to include controls for time. Each of these models is estimated using the Tobit estimator with standard errors clustered by the income level of each country pair.

Consider first the traditional gravity variables. Greater distance between the source and host countries reduces conflict (as has been well documented for trade and FDI). Traditional barriers to trade such as borders and language also appear to increase conflict. In this sense, conflict appears to be more of a regional threat than a global one.

Larger country size (higher GDP) increases conflict. One way to interpret this result is that "larger" means more of everything, including conflict. Even so, conflict is significantly more responsive to country size of the host rather than of the source.

But perhaps the most interesting and robust result comes from analyzing differences in income. Richer host countries (higher per capita GDP) generate more conflict, whereas richer source countries generate less conflict. This result is consistent across each specification, with the impact of source income being slightly greater in magnitude than the impact of host income. Taken literally, the estimation results from table 5.1 imply that a 1 percentage point increase in a source country's income should decrease the number of terrorist events by two per year. A 1 percentage point increase in a host country's income would invite about one more terrorist event per year.[7]

Table 5.2
Gravity Model for Terrorist Incidents, by Location, 1968–2003, Full Country Sample

	1 Base	2 DEM	3 DEM	4 GLO	5 GLO	6 DEM&GLO	7 DEM&GLO	8 F.E.
y_h	1.146***	0.949***	0.880***	1.428***	0.958***	1.219***	0.788***	0.528***
	[0.159]	[0.181]	[0.167]	[0.182]	[0.166]	[0.210]	[0.172]	[0.173]
y_s	−1.860***	−1.754***	−1.741***	−2.068***	−1.916***	−2.021***	−1.817***	−2.071***
	[0.165]	[0.187]	[0.176]	[0.207]	[0.176]	[0.236]	[0.184]	[0.191]
Y_h	2.583***	2.749***	2.658***	2.445***	2.655***	2.618***	2.654***	2.730***
	[0.137]	[0.157]	[0.145]	[0.152]	[0.144]	[0.180]	[0.149]	[0.152]
Y_s	0.824***	0.708***	0.941***	0.914***	0.990***	0.850***	0.983***	1.079***
	[0.120]	[0.137]	[0.130]	[0.148]	[0.132]	[0.174]	[0.137]	[0.141]
distance	−3.674***	−3.312***	−3.386***	−3.416***	−3.479***	−3.160***	−3.388***	−3.376***
	[0.220]	[0.239]	[0.226]	[0.227]	[0.224]	[0.247]	[0.230]	[0.231]
comlang	2.842***	2.890***	3.002***	2.798***	3.051***	2.897***	3.139***	2.925***
	[0.352]	[0.391]	[0.363]	[0.367]	[0.362]	[0.409]	[0.371]	[0.373]
border	1.202**	1.825***	1.728***	1.609***	1.549***	2.105***	1.777***	1.879***
	[0.513]	[0.570]	[0.532]	[0.533]	[0.529]	[0.591]	[0.543]	[0.546]
area	0.039	−0.215**	−0.148*	−0.413***	−0.103	−0.540***	−0.155*	−0.277***
	[0.078]	[0.096]	[0.087]	[0.097]	[0.088]	[0.114]	[0.092]	[0.095]
$polity_h$		0.126***				0.108***		
		[0.022]				[0.022]		
$polity_s$		−0.037***				−0.037***		
		[0.011]				[0.011]		
DEM_h			2.089***				1.919***	2.947***
			[0.377]				[0.400]	[0.422]

DEM$_s$			-1.926*** [0.410]				-1.153*** [0.442]	-0.682 [0.449]
OPEN$_h$				-0.038*** [0.006]		-0.028*** [0.008]		
OPEN$_s$				-0.024*** [0.007]		-0.012 [0.008]		
WTO$_h$					1.707*** [0.445]		1.409*** [0.471]	1.372*** [0.469]
WTO$_s$					-2.305*** [0.420]		-2.042*** [0.453]	-2.138*** [0.452]
IMF$_h$					0.438 [0.384]		0.375 [0.393]	0.628 [0.400]
IMF$_s$					-1.260*** [0.411]		-1.356*** [0.424]	-1.331*** [0.429]
Observations	209,208	136,963	183,276	191,368	200,236	129,543	179,332	179,332

Note: Brackets indicate clustered standard errors, and ***, **, *, statistical significance at .01, .05, .10 levels, respectively. Each column is the basic gravity model estimated over full country sample, 1968–2003. Columns 1–8 were estimated using the Tobit method to allow for substantial number of zero value observations; column 8 includes year fixed effects.

Regression includes Real GDP Y_i and Real GDP per capita y_i for host $i = h$ and source $i = s$ countries; log physical distance (*distance*); log physical area (*area*); dummy variable for language (*comlang*); dummy variable for border (*border*); measures of democracy (*polity* is index of democracy on 0–10 scale, with 10 most democratic; DEM is a dummy variable = 1 if *polity* > 7 or *executive + legislative veto points* > 14, = 0 otherwise); and measures of globalization (OPEN = total trade/GDP > 30; GLO is a dummy variable = 1 if member of WTO/GATT, = 0 otherwise).

This finding provides a segue into the chapter's main question. It might mean that conflict is the unfortunate consequence of the divide between rich and poor countries. During a process of sweeping change over the past 20 years, as countries have become more globalized and democratized, some countries have been left behind while others have flourished. Perhaps terrorists in the economies left behind have chosen to strike against those countries that have become more advantaged during the period in question.

We directly address this point as we consider the effect of these dynamic forces—globalization and democratization—on conflict. There are two main results from this estimation. First, democratic institutions in a source country significantly reduce conflict but in a host country increase conflict (this supports our conjectures). Second, source country openness has a negative and statistically significant effect on conflict, but host country openness often has a positive and statistically significant on conflict. *Ceteris paribus*, the impact in a source country of being a democracy or participating in the World Trade Organization is a decrease in the number of terrorist strikes by about one or two, which is more than 2 standard deviations greater than the average number of strikes between any two countries in a given year.

Moreover, as the results in table 5.3 show, our baseline estimates of the traditional gravity specification in equation (5.3), reported in table 5.2, are generally robust across modifications to take into account region, time, and income class. Columns 1–7 of table 5.2 report the results from a gravity specification where we include dummy variables for globalization and democratization in each specification.[8]

Greater distance, borders, and language appear to have similar statistically significant impacts (table 5.3). In this way, conflict appears to be more regional than global. Larger country size continues to increase conflict. Richer host countries continue to generate more conflict in each case except when only rich countries are considered.[9] Poorer source countries continue to generate more conflict.[10]

Finally, and most important, the effect on globalization and democratization continues to hold as well. As can be seen from the appropriate rows of table 5.3, the estimate associated with host democracy is statistically significant at below the 0.01 level in most cases, and the coefficient estimates are positive in each case (except in sub-Saharan Africa), varying between 0.8 in Asian countries and 1.3 in Latin America. The estimate associated with source democracy is statistically significant at below the 0.01 level in most cases, and the coefficient estimates vary between −0.6 in Latin American countries and −1.3 in Asia.

The estimates associated with globalization continue to be positive for host countries, ranging from 0.5 in sub-Saharan Africa to 1.4 in Asia. They are statistically significant at the 0.01 level in each case but one, in sub-Saharan Africa. The impact from source country globalization remains negative. All these effects are more pronounced in high-income countries than in low-income countries.

Columns 7 and 8 of table 5.3 explore what happens when we split the sample in 1985. Interestingly, the estimated impact of the gap from globalization and democratization is much lower, though still statistically significant, for the 1986–2003 subsample. The coefficient is two times larger for the second half of the sample.

Robustness across Measures of Terrorist Activity

In the previous section we defined host conflict from the perspective of the location of the event. We now define host conflict by the nationality of the victim (table 5.4). In national income accounting terms, we consider a nationality measure of host/source conflict rather than a location measure of host/source conflict. We employ the same specification as in table 5.2. We find that in general the coefficients have the same sign, similar magnitude, and similar statistical significance as those in table 5.2.

The remarkable similarity in results between tables 5.2 and 5.4 also gives us some information about possible measurement error. As discussed earlier, there may be some concerns that we are unable to capture the intent of the terrorist, given the inherent challenges to using media-based measures of conflict. Yet, when we select a different way of measuring the target for conflict, namely, by the nationality of the victim, we get precisely the same results. Clearly, this cannot account for all the possible problems associated with measuring conflict, but it is remarkable how similar are the results. Other possible measurement issues are analyzed in tables 5.5 and 5.6.

In table 5.5 we consider a different measure of conflict to account for the intensity of the violence. In this case, we define conflict as the number of victims rather than as the number of incidents.[11] The advantage to considering this measure is that it may better account for the actual damage of each attack. The disadvantage would be that often terrorists

Table 5.3
Robustness Checks: Gravity Model for Terrorist Incidents, 1968–2003, Subsamples by Region

	1 asia	2 ssafr	3 menaf	4 latca	5 highi	6 lowin	7 68-85	8 86-03
y_h	0.369* [0.191]	0.575*** [0.219]	0.435*** [0.119]	0.379** [0.180]	-0.494** [0.243]	0.667*** [0.161]	0.767*** [0.253]	0.664*** [0.237]
y_s	-0.554*** [0.159]	-0.104 [0.205]	-1.213*** [0.183]	-0.797*** [0.224]	-4.679*** [0.339]	-0.370*** [0.129]	-2.224*** [0.299]	-1.910*** [0.251]
Y_h	0.658*** [0.146]	0.925*** [0.219]	1.055*** [0.137]	0.762*** [0.128]	3.397*** [0.229]	0.748*** [0.109]	3.271*** [0.248]	2.340*** [0.192]
Y_s	0.675*** [0.158]	0.492** [0.195]	1.163*** [0.174]	0.576*** [0.144]	-0.032 [0.194]	0.644*** [0.112]	0.752*** [0.206]	1.216*** [0.191]
distance	-1.573*** [0.317]	-2.326*** [0.520]	-1.621*** [0.219]	-1.145*** [0.201]	-4.446*** [0.335]	-1.895*** [0.281]	-2.591*** [0.315]	-4.068*** [0.342]
comlang	1.526*** [0.377]	1.649*** [0.463]	0.371 [0.322]	0.973*** [0.299]	3.673*** [0.577]	1.899*** [0.330]	1.631*** [0.575]	4.411*** [0.507]
border	1.232* [0.669]	-0.131 [0.670]	1.234*** [0.415]	1.948*** [0.409]	-1.17 [0.941]	1.206** [0.469]	1.25 [0.869]	1.576** [0.704]
area	0.155 [0.109]	0.021 [0.114]	-0.048 [0.086]	-0.093 [0.075]	0.213 [0.130]	0.149* [0.088]	-0.557*** [0.136]	0.109 [0.132]
DEM_h	0.800** [0.355]	0.343 [0.418]	1.173*** [0.284]	1.283*** [0.305]	3.247*** [0.646]	1.028*** [0.293]	2.510*** [0.592]	2.632*** [0.582]
DEM_s	-0.307 [0.395]	-0.447 [0.500]	-0.553 [0.347]	-0.611** [0.278]	0.311 [0.800]	-0.461 [0.310]	-0.92 [0.684]	-0.91 [0.609]
WTO_h	1.481*** [0.533]	0.453 [0.603]	0.805*** [0.300]	-0.636** [0.258]	3.242*** [0.924]	0.532 [0.353]	2.998*** [0.730]	0.006 [0.617]

WTO$_s$	−0.394	−1.317***	−1.478***	−0.122	−2.807***	−0.259	−1.348**	−2.865***
	[0.505]	[0.502]	[0.332]	[0.302]	[0.924]	[0.342]	[0.680]	[0.621]
IMF$_h$	0.064	0.51	0.289	−0.157	1.439**	0.059	1.884***	−0.025
	[0.384]	[0.372]	[0.277]	[0.253]	[0.628]	[0.280]	[0.627]	[0.518]
IMF$_s$	−0.41	0.183	−0.507	−0.464*	−0.425	−0.273	−2.366***	−0.681
	[0.415]	[0.400]	[0.354]	[0.256]	[0.743]	[0.304]	[0.717]	[0.537]
Observations	44,416	68,713	27,746	59,508	90,579	81,922	67,397	111,935

Note: Brackets indicate clustered standard errors, and ***, **, *, statistical significance at .01, .05, .10 levels, respectively. Each column is the basic gravity model estimated over subsamples by region (*asia, ssafr, menaf, latca*), income (*highi, lowin*), and time (1968–1985, 1986–2003). Columns 1–8 were estimated using the Tobit method to allow for substantial number of zero value observations.

Regression includes Real GDP Y_i and Real GDP per capita y_i for host $i = h$ and source $i = s$ countries; log physical distance (*distance*); log physical area (*area*); dummy variable for language (*comlang*); dummy variable for border (*border*); and measures of democracy (DEM is a dummy variable = 1 if *polity > 7* or *executive + legislative veto points > 14*, = 0 otherwise).

Table 5.4
Gravity Model for Terrorist Incidents, by Nationality, 1968–2003, Full Country Sample

	1 Base	2 DEM	3 DEM	4 GLO	5 GLO	6 DEM&GLO	7 DEM&GLO	8 F.E.
y_h	1.722*** [0.088]	1.639*** [0.102]	1.514*** [0.092]	1.880*** [0.098]	1.689*** [0.092]	1.808*** [0.116]	1.525*** [0.095]	1.312*** [0.094]
y_s	-1.592*** [0.086]	-1.544*** [0.100]	-1.533*** [0.092]	-1.617*** [0.104]	-1.640*** [0.089]	-1.489*** [0.121]	-1.560*** [0.094]	-1.792*** [0.098]
Y_h	2.126*** [0.071]	2.151*** [0.082]	2.094*** [0.075]	1.952*** [0.080]	2.091*** [0.073]	2.027*** [0.098]	2.067*** [0.076]	2.132*** [0.077]
Y_s	0.349*** [0.061]	0.289*** [0.072]	0.365*** [0.065]	0.300*** [0.075]	0.350*** [0.065]	0.161* [0.088]	0.334*** [0.068]	0.399*** [0.069]
distance	-1.619*** [0.109]	-1.357*** [0.124]	-1.416*** [0.114]	-1.475*** [0.114]	-1.485*** [0.112]	-1.325*** [0.128]	-1.410*** [0.116]	-1.361*** [0.116]
comlang	2.303*** [0.186]	2.279*** [0.211]	2.320*** [0.191]	2.173*** [0.193]	2.289*** [0.187]	2.184*** [0.219]	2.292*** [0.192]	2.127*** [0.192]
border	1.226*** [0.295]	1.859*** [0.331]	1.572*** [0.305]	1.473*** [0.303]	1.390*** [0.301]	1.914*** [0.338]	1.587*** [0.308]	1.664*** [0.309]
area	0.362*** [0.040]	0.282*** [0.051]	0.287*** [0.045]	0.033 [0.049]	0.334*** [0.045]	0.05 [0.058]	0.317*** [0.047]	0.213*** [0.048]
polity_h		0.074*** [0.011]				0.064*** [0.011]		
polity_s		-0.019*** [0.006]				-0.016*** [0.006]		
DEM_h			1.827*** [0.212]				1.600*** [0.226]	2.192*** [0.237]

	(1)	(2)	(3)	(4)	(5)	(6)	(7)	(8)
DEM$_s$	-0.778*** [0.205]						-0.729*** [0.214]	-0.234 [0.218]
OPEN$_h$				-0.025*** [0.004]		-0.026*** [0.004]		
OPEN$_s$				-0.030*** [0.003]		-0.024*** [0.005]		
WTO$_h$					1.389*** [0.243]		0.963*** [0.262]	0.885*** [0.262]
WTO$_s$					-0.549** [0.219]		-0.342 [0.233]	-0.268 [0.233]
IMF$_h$					0.591*** [0.204]		0.554*** [0.207]	0.708*** [0.210]
IMF$_s$					-0.589*** [0.198]		-0.560*** [0.203]	-0.614*** [0.205]
Observations	209,208	136,963	183,276	191,368	200,236	129,543	179,332	179,332

Note: Brackets indicate clustered standard errors, and ***, **, *, statistical significance at .01, .05, .10 levels, respectively. Each column is the basic gravity model estimated over full country sample, 1968–2003. Columns 1–8 were estimated using the Tobit method to allow for substantial number of zero value observations; column 8 includes year fixed effects.

Regression includes Real GDP Y_i and Real GDP per capita y_i for host $i = h$ and source $i = s$ countries; log physical distance (*distance*); log physical area (*area*); dummy variable for language (*comlang*); dummy variable for border (*border*); measures of democracy (*polity* is index of democracy on 0–10 scale, with 10 most democratic; DEM is a dummy variable = 1 if *polity* > 7 or *executive* + *legislative veto points* > 14, = 0 otherwise); and measures of globalization (OPEN = total trade/GDP > 30; GLO is a dummy variable = 1 if member of WTO/GATT, = 0 otherwise).

Table 5.5
Gravity Model for Victims of Terrorism, 1968–2003, Full Country Sample

	1 Base	2 DEM	3 DEM	4 GLO	5 GLO	6 DEM&GLO	7 DEM&GLO	8 F.E.
y_h	1.279*** [0.173]	1.109*** [0.196]	1.001*** [0.180]	1.559*** [0.191]	1.080*** [0.179]	1.426*** [0.221]	0.907*** [0.185]	0.523*** [0.172]
y_s	-2.082*** [0.182]	-1.968*** [0.205]	-1.912*** [0.192]	-2.178*** [0.218]	-2.129*** [0.192]	-2.130*** [0.250]	-2.001*** [0.200]	-2.231*** [0.194]
Y_h	2.736*** [0.155]	2.925*** [0.177]	2.813*** [0.162]	2.466*** [0.163]	2.802*** [0.162]	2.644*** [0.194]	2.810*** [0.166]	2.758*** [0.158]
Y_s	0.918*** [0.130]	0.816*** [0.150]	1.058*** [0.142]	0.929*** [0.155]	1.103*** [0.143]	0.871*** [0.184]	1.111*** [0.149]	1.172*** [0.143]
distance	-3.890*** [0.246]	-3.509*** [0.265]	-3.554*** [0.250]	-3.453*** [0.241]	-3.653*** [0.249]	-3.242*** [0.264]	-3.544*** [0.254]	-3.292*** [0.237]
comlang	2.803*** [0.389]	2.791*** [0.433]	2.930*** [0.399]	2.577*** [0.388]	2.994*** [0.398]	2.628*** [0.438]	3.067*** [0.408]	2.592*** [0.380]
border	0.664 [0.570]	1.228* [0.634]	1.234** [0.587]	1.045* [0.566]	1.023* [0.584]	1.443* [0.635]	1.277** [0.599]	1.264** [0.560]
area	0.083 [0.085]	-0.176* [0.104]	-0.118 [0.094]	-0.442*** [0.101]	-0.071 [0.096]	-0.561*** [0.120]	-0.127 [0.100]	-0.271*** [0.095]
$polity_h$		0.122*** [0.023]				0.101*** [0.022]		
$polity_s$		-0.046*** [0.011]				-0.043*** [0.011]		
DEM_h			2.138*** [0.405]				1.955*** [0.429]	3.189*** [0.423]

	(1)	(2)	(3)	(4)	(5)	(6)	(7)	(8)
DEM$_s$			−2.372*** [0.443]				−1.539*** [0.476]	−0.827* [0.447]
OPEN$_h$				−0.046*** [0.007]		−0.038*** [0.008]		
OPEN$_s$				−0.033*** [0.007]		−0.022*** [0.008]		
WTO$_h$					1.735*** [0.474]		1.450*** [0.501]	1.380*** [0.464]
WTO$_s$					−2.674*** [0.454]		−2.282*** [0.487]	−2.327*** [0.451]
IMF$_h$					0.457 [0.414]		0.4 [0.423]	0.645 [0.400]
IMF$_s$					−1.316*** [0.442]		−1.389*** [0.456]	−1.298*** [0.428]
Observations	209,208	136,963	183,276	191,368	200,236	129,543	179,332	179,332

Note: Brackets indicate clustered standard errors, and ***, **, *, statistical significance at .01, .05, .10 levels, respectively. Each column is the basic gravity model estimated over full country sample, 1968–2003. Columns 1–8 were estimated using the Tobit method to allow for substantial number of zero value observations; column 8 includes year fixed effects.

Regression includes Real GDP Y_i and Real GDP per capita y_i for host $i = h$ and source $i = s$ countries; log physical distance (*distance*); log physical area (*area*); dummy variable for language (*comlang*); dummy variable for border (*border*); measures of democracy (*polity* is index of democracy on 0–10 scale, with 10 most democratic; DEM is a dummy variable = 1 if *polity* > 7 or *executive + legislative veto points* > 14, = 0 otherwise); and measures of globalization (OPEN = total trade/GDP > 30; GLO is a dummy variable = 1 if member of WTO/GATT, = 0 otherwise).

Table 5.6
Gravity Model for U.S. Victims of Terrorism, 1968–2003, Full Country Sample

	1 Base	2 DEM	3 DEM	4 GLO	5 GLO	6 DEM&GLO	7 DEM&GLO	8 F.E.
y_h	1.024**	0.866*	0.721*	1.133***	0.707*	0.723	0.522	0.156
	[0.399]	[0.480]	[0.417]	[0.431]	[0.409]	[0.524]	[0.425]	[0.403]
y_s	-1.827***	-1.384***	-1.454***	-1.582***	-1.946***	-0.962	-1.656***	-1.930***
	[0.428]	[0.520]	[0.461]	[0.499]	[0.453]	[0.622]	[0.480]	[0.474]
Y_h	2.968***	3.477***	3.059***	2.767***	3.080***	3.508***	3.067***	3.068***
	[0.367]	[0.460]	[0.387]	[0.386]	[0.385]	[0.517]	[0.397]	[0.386]
Y_s	1.000***	0.932**	1.284***	0.787**	1.374***	0.617	1.441***	1.535***
	[0.311]	[0.384]	[0.345]	[0.364]	[0.347]	[0.463]	[0.367]	[0.358]
distance	-3.841***	-3.413***	-3.403***	-3.329***	-3.533***	-3.016***	-3.341***	-3.166***
	[0.573]	[0.656]	[0.584]	[0.557]	[0.576]	[0.650]	[0.593]	[0.565]
comlang	3.266***	3.902***	3.376***	3.106***	3.543***	3.993***	3.590***	3.319***
	[0.939]	[1.129]	[0.969]	[0.925]	[0.962]	[1.130]	[0.992]	[0.944]
border	-0.143	0.259	0.734	0.394	0.467	0.667	0.987	0.904
	[1.441]	[1.754]	[1.490]	[1.411]	[1.464]	[1.741]	[1.515]	[1.443]
area	0.122	-0.265	-0.126	-0.442*	-0.129	-0.709**	-0.204	-0.337
	[0.203]	[0.262]	[0.224]	[0.235]	[0.227]	[0.300]	[0.238]	[0.232]
$polity_h$		0.056				0.042		
		[0.045]				[0.042]		
$polity_s$		-0.065**				-0.062**		
		[0.029]				[0.028]		
DEM_h			2.901***				2.996***	4.117***
			[0.987]				[1.049]	[1.052]

	(1)	(2)	(3)	(4)	(5)	(6)	(7)	(8)
DEM$_s$	−4.615*** [1.127]						−3.521*** [1.195]	−2.584** [1.126]
OPEN$_h$		−0.041*** [0.015]	−0.015 [0.020]					
OPEN$_s$		−0.051*** [0.018]	−0.053** [0.023]					
WTO$_h$				1.571 [1.098]			0.869 [1.167]	0.997 [1.110]
WTO$_s$				−4.453*** [1.122]			−3.299*** [1.199]	−3.563*** [1.143]
IMF$_h$				−0.796 [1.043]			−0.761 [1.069]	−0.634 [1.025]
IMF$_s$				−2.078* [1.130]			−2.222* [1.179]	−1.955* [1.125]
Observations	209,208	136,963	183,276	191,368	200,236	129,543	179,332	179,332

Note: Brackets indicate clustered standard errors, and ***, **, *, statistical significance at .01, .05, .10 levels, respectively. Each column is the basic gravity model estimated over full country sample, 1968–2003. Columns 1–8 were estimated using the Tobit method to allow for substantial number of zero value observations; column 8 includes year fixed effects.

Regression includes Real GDP Y_i and Real GDP per capita y_i for host $i = h$ and source $i = s$ countries; log physical distance (*distance*); log physical area (*area*); dummy variable for language (*comlang*); dummy variable for border (*border*); measures of democracy (*polity* is index of democracy on 0–10 scale, with 10 most democratic; DEM is a dummy variable = 1 if *polity* > 7 or *executive + legislative veto points* > 14, = 0 otherwise); and measures of globalization (OPEN = total trade/GDP > 30; GLO is a dummy variable = 1 if member of WTO/GATT, = 0 otherwise).

may be less interested in targeting victims than in getting a response from the target. At the very least, this measure provides a robustness check to our early results.

The results in table 5.5 continue to support the earlier findings. The sign and statistical significance of each relevant coefficient is similar to those discussed earlier. However, the magnitude of the coefficients associated with income per capita, globalization, and democratization are slightly larger—on the order of 10 percent greater. Since the left-hand side variables in both tables 5.3 and 5.4 have been scaled to be of similar magnitude, one can only conclude that the effect of these variables is greater on the number of victims than it is on the number of incidents.

We find that a 1 percentage point increase in income in a host country causes the number of victims to rise by about one. A 1 percentage point increase in the income of the source country causes the number of victims to fall by approximately two. Democracy or participation in the WTO in a host country causes the number of victims to double to two. Participation in the WTO in a source country causes the number of victims to fall twofold, or by about two.

Finally, table 5.6 considers the same measure as in table 5.5 but only for victims in the United States. This provides a final robustness check because the United States may be the most likely target country, and the U.S. media may be more likely than media in other countries to report terrorist attacks.

The results in table 5.6 mirror those in table 5.5. However, the magnitudes are different. It appears that a source country's being a democracy has a greater effect than in the full sample; the United States creates a larger target because of its democratic policies; and openness provides a greater hedge to terrorist attacks from source countries than in the previous regressions.

Conclusion

We construct a new database on bilateral conflict and estimate a gravity model for conflict. We find that development, democracy, and openness are each positive influences in creating a more peaceful environment for an attacking country in terrorism source countries. However, these same factors in target countries can increase conflict.

What do these results mean for policymakers? The work reported here is one of the first to document the need for development, democracy, and openness in encouraging peace for terrorist source nations. This means that policies that can encourage more liberal institutions to facilitate political and economic freedom in countries that are traditionally sources for transnational terrorism will have a pacifying influence. This lends support to policy efforts designed to export democracy to terrorist states.

Our work also substantiates the notion that globalization creates relative deprivation or increased inequality that may spur terrorist recruitment and export. We suggest a virtue of globalization: integration into the world economic community of terrorism source states would have a beneficial impact on reducing exports of transnational terrorism.

Unfortunately, the results presented in this chapter also point to the fact that the countries that tend to be more politically and economically free are more likely to be the targets of terrorism. Clearly, reducing the degree of democracy in these countries is not a policy option. Slowing the process of globalization, a topic that frequently emerges from those disadvantaged by openness, may not reduce terrorism in the importing countries; reductions in openness in those countries may reduce the degree of integration of the source countries, too; the net effect is not clear.

More realistically, target countries must be prepared to invest more heavily in counterterrorist measures, and to engage in comprehensive cooperation to avoid simply shifting the incidence of the attacks from more secure to less secure globalized democracies.

Notes

1. See, for instance, the special issue of the *Journal of Conflict Resolution* on the Political Economy of Transnational Terrorism (Rosendorff and Sandler 2004).

2. An additional concern for any terrorist organization is the effect of their actions on recruitment of future cadres (Rosendorff and Sandler 2004).

3. For examples in the trade literature, see, among others, Anderson (1979), who championed use of the gravity equation in structural trade models, and Markusen and Maskus (1999) and Carr, Markusen, and Maskus (2001a; 2001b), who investigated gravity models for FDI. Blomberg and Hess (2006) focus on trade, especially on comparing the costs of conflict to measures for trade promotion. Alternatively, Blomberg, Hess, and Orphanides (2004) investigate the impact of various forms of conflict such as terrorism, internal wars, and external wars on a country's economic growth. Other papers that apply gravity-type models to conflict are Glick and Taylor (2005) and Polachek and Seiglie (2007).

4. We also considered measures of imports/GDP with little qualitative change in the results.

5. All the data reported are taken from sources in Blomberg and Hess (2006), where a detailed discussion is provided.

6. Both measures are conventional measures of democracy—*polity* is a 1–10 scale of democracy from the Polity IV database, and *executive + legislative index* is a 2–14 scale of electoral rules from the Keefer (2005) database.

7. The results on the effect of relative size point to the importance of the divide between rich and poor as an explanatory variable of terrorism. This may mean that transnational terrorism depends on increased inequality rather than on income. However, in different regressions we include measures of income inequality (e.g., Gini coefficients) and find no statistical significance.

8. The regions we consider are, respectively, South East Asia, East Asia, the Middle East and North Africa, Latin America and the Caribbean, and high- and low-income countries. The latter classification is from Rose (2003) and is obtained from the World Bank development indicators.

9. This may be due to the fact that rich countries are less like to commit terrorist acts.

10. Again, except for the low-income sample, which may be less likely to strike against its poor counterparts.

11. For comparative purposes, we divide the left-hand side variable by 10 so that the mean is similar to the mean of conflict in tables 5.2–5.4.

References

Anderson, J. 1979. A theoretical foundation for the gravity equation. *American Economic Review* 69 (1): 106–116.

Anderson, J., and E. Van Wincoop. 2003. Gravity with gravitas: A solution to the border puzzle. *American Economic Review* 93 (1): 170–192.

Bearce, D., E. D. Mansfield, and J. C. Pevehouse. 1999. Preferential trading arrangements and military disputes. *Security Studies* 9 (1/2): 92–118.

Blomberg, S. B., and G. D. Hess. 2006. How much does violence tax trade? *Review of Economics and Statistics* 88 (4): 599–612.

Blomberg, S. B., G. D. Hess, and A. Orphanides. 2004. The macroeconomic consequences of terrorism. *Journal of Monetary Economics* 51 (5): 1007–1052.

Blomberg, S. B., and A. Mody. 2005. How severely does violence deter international investment? Working Paper 2005-01. Claremont, Calif.: Claremont McKenna College.

Bueno de Mesquita, B., J. D. Morrow, R. M. Siverson, and A. Smith. 1999. An institutional explanation for the democratic peace. *American Political Science Review* 93 (4): 791–808.

Carr, D., J. Markusen, and K. Maskus. 2001a. Estimating the knowledge-capital model of the multinational enterprise. *American Economic Review* 91 (3): 693–708.

Carr, D., J. Markusen, and K. Maskus. 2001b. Estimating the knowledge-capital model of the multinational enterprise: Reply. *American Economic Review* 93 (3): 995–1001.

Crenshaw, M. 1981. The causes of terrorism. *Comparative Politics* 13 (4): 379–399.

Crenshaw, M. 2001. Why America? The globalization of civil war. *Current History* 100: 425–433.

Deardorff, A. V. 1984. Testing trade theories and predicting trade flows. In *Handbook of International Economics*, ed. R. W. Jones and P. B. Kenen. Amsterdam: North-Holland.

Economist, The. 2002. *The Economist* (March 9).

Enders, W., and T. Sandler. 1993. The effectiveness of antiterrorism policies: A vector-autoregression-intervention analysis. *American Political Science Review* 87: 829–844.

Eubank, W. L., and L. Weinberg. 1994. Does democracy encourage terrorism? *Terrorism and Political Violence* 6 (4): 417–435.

———. 1998. Terrorism and democracy: What recent events disclose. *Terrorism and Political Violence* 10 (1): 108–118.

———. 2001. Terrorism and democracy: Perpetrators and victims. *Terrorism and Political Violence* 13 (1): 155–164.

Friedman, T. L. 2005. *The World Is Flat*. New York: Farrar, Straus and Giroux.

Glick, R., and A. M. Taylor. 2005. Collateral damage: Trade disruption and the economic impact of war. CEPR Discussion Paper 5209. London: Centre for Economic Policy Research.

Hagel, C. 2004. A Republican foreign policy. *Foreign Affairs* 83 (4): 64–76.

Keefer, P. 2005. Database of political institutions. ⟨http://go.worldbank.org/2EAGGLRZ40⟩.

Krug, B., and P. Reinmoeller. 2004. The hidden cost of ubiquity: Globalization and terrorism. Mimeo, October.

Li, Q. 2005. Does democracy promote or reduce transnational terrorist incidents? *Journal of Conflict Resolution* 49 (2): 278–297.

Li, Q., and D. Schaub. 2004. Economic globalization and transnational terrorism: A pooled time-series analysis. *Journal of Conflict Resolution* 48 (2): 230–258.

Mansfield, E. D., H. V. Milner, and B. P. Rosendorff. 2002. Why democracies cooperate more: Electoral control and international trade agreements. *International Organization* 56 (3): 477–514.

Mansfield, E. D., and J. C. Pevehouse. 2000. Trade blocs, trade flows, and international conflict. *International Organization* 54 (4): 775–808.

Markusen, J., and K. Maskus. 1999. Multinational firms: Reconciling theory and evidence. NBER Working Paper 7163. Cambridge, Mass.: National Bureau of Economic Research.

Martin, P. 2001. Globalization, terrorism, and the world economy. Speech by the Honourable Paul Martin, Minister of Finance for Canada, at a luncheon organized by the Reinventing Bretton Woods Committee and the Conference Board of Canada. November 16. ⟨http://www.fin.gc.ca/news01/01-105e.html⟩.

Mickolus, E., T. Sandler, J. Murdock, and P. Flemming. 2002. International Terrorism: Attributes of Terrorist Events (ITERATE). Dunn Loring, Va.: Vinyard Software. ⟨http://ssdc.ucsd.edu/ssdc/ite00001.html⟩.

Pape, R. 2003. The strategic logic of suicide terrorism. *American Political Science Review* 97 (3): 1–19.

Polachek, S. W., and C. Seiglie. 2007. Trade, peace, and democracy: An analysis of dyadic dispute. In *Handbook of Defense Economics, Vol. 2*, ed. T. Sandler and K. Hartley. New York: Elsevier.

Polity IV Project. 2008. Political Regime Characteristics and Transitions, 1800–2006. ⟨http://www.systemicpeace.org/polity/polity4.htm⟩.

Rose, A. 2003. Do we really know the WTO increases trade? *American Economic Review* 94 (1): 98–114.

Rosendorff, B. P. 2006. Do democracies trade more freely? In *Democratic Foreign Policy Making: Problems of Divided Government and International Cooperation*, ed. R. Pahre. London: Palgrave.

Rosendorff, B. P., and T. Sandler. 2004. Too much of a good thing? The proactive response dilemma. *Journal of Conflict Resolution* 48 (5): 657–671.

———. 2005. The political economy of transnational terrorism. *Journal of Conflict Resolution* 49 (2): 171–182.

Sandler, T. 1995. On the relationship between democracy and terrorism. *Terrorism and Political Violence* 12 (2): 97–122.

Sandler, T., J. T. Tschirhart, and J. Cauley. 1983. A theoretical analysis of transnational terrorism. *American Political Science Review* 77: 36–54.

U.S. National Intelligence Council. 2004. *Mapping the Global Future: Report of the National Intelligence Council's 2020 Project, Based on Consultations with Nongovernmental Experts around the World*. Washington, DC. ⟨http://www.foia.cia.gov/2020/2020.pdf⟩.

White House. 2005. President honors veterans of foreign wars at national convention. Press release. ⟨http://www.whitehouse.gov/news/releases/2005/08/20050822-1.html⟩.

6 The Factionalization of Terror Groups

Ethan Bueno de Mesquita

Terror organizations are not monolithic nor is their structure stable. Rather, they are made up of heterogeneous factions that frequently splinter from one another as the political and economic landscape shifts. Consider a few examples.

Republican militants in Northern Ireland have experienced a variety of splinterings. In the late 1960s, the Provisional Irish Republican Army (IRA) split from the Original IRA because of disagreements over military policy. In the mid-1980s, the extremist Continuity IRA splintered from the Provisionals when the Provisionals abandoned their policy of refusing to participate in parliament. Another radical splinter group, the Real IRA, broke from the Provisionals in the 1990s because of the Provisionals' decision to embrace the peace process that led to the Good Friday Agreement.

Militant Palestinian nationalism has been represented by a variety of terrorist groups. These include factions of the Palestine Liberation Organization, such as the al Aqsa Martyrs, the Democratic Front for the Liberation of Palestine, Fatah Tanzim, and the Popular Front for the Liberation of Palestine, as well as Islamic groups such as Islamic Jihad and Hamas, a militant splinter from the Muslim Brotherhood.

Basque separatist terrorists have largely kept the same name (ETA) but have at times been divided into a variety of factions. For instance, in the late 1970s, ETA split into the extremist ETA-militar and the more moderate ETA-politico-militar. The split was over whether Basque separatists should participate in regular politics, given Spanish democratization and the grant of partial autonomy to the Basque country.

Several factions have represented Tamil separatists, although the LTTE (Tamil Tigers) have dominated the violent campaign. In 2004, however, the LTTE experienced a split, dividing along geographical lines between the eastern followers of Colonel Karuna and the southern followers of long-time Tamil Tiger leader Velupillai Prabhakaran.

Several scholars argue that the existence of such internal divisions has important implications both for patterns of terrorist violence and counterterrorism policy. Bloom (2004; 2005) contends that competition among factions for public support is a primary cause of escalation in terrorist conflicts as terrorist factions try to outbid one another with violence. Bueno de Mesquita (2005a) argues that government concessions can lead to an increase in violence because only moderate factions accept concessions, leaving a more radical residual terror group. But he notes that such divisions can also help solve commitment problems because moderate factions can offer the government counterterror aid against more extreme factions in exchange for concessions. This work also suggests that the extent of the ideological division between moderates and extremists affects the level of concessions that governments make and the likelihood of negotiated settlement. de Figueiredo and Weingast (2001) argue that counterterrorism policy radicalizes moderate terrorist factions, which can lead to cycles of violence.

Although scholars have made progress in understanding the effects of factionalization on the politics of terrorism, little work has examined why or how terrorist organizations splinter. In this chapter I ask when a faction will form and where that faction will it locate itself in the ideological space. The goal of the splinter group is to maximize support among the population relative to the support enjoyed by the original terror group. Members of the population choose between joining one of the two terrorist factions or not participating in the terrorist movement at all. Thus, part of the contribution is to provide some microfoundations for the ideological splintering that is taken as a primitive in a variety of existing models.

The model, while quite stylized, yields several results. The spatial logic suggests that there are two possible sources of interfactional conflict, ideological divergence and competition over contested adherents. Moreover, factors that tend to mitigate one of these sources of internecine fighting will exacerbate the other. The model provides predictions regarding conditions that tend to make splinter groups more or less extreme. A strong economy increases the ideological extremism of splinter groups. The more resources the original faction has access to, the more extreme is the splinter group, while the more resources the splinter has access to, the less extreme it will be. The model also shows that a splinter is more likely to form when the economy is weak and when the splinter is well funded. Finally, the model shows that in a splintered terrorist organization, the distribution of ideological preferences of the members of the factions will be skewed away from the ideological positions of the factions themselves.

The Model

Consider a simple model with two types of strategic players: the leader of a potential splinter terrorist faction (s) and a population of potential terrorists. Since I am interested here in how splinter groups break from existing terrorist organizations, I also assume that there is an existing terrorist organization (t) with a fixed ideological position ($x_t \in \mathbb{R}$). At the beginning of the game the splinter faction's leader decides whether to splinter and, if he does splinter, chooses an ideological position $x_s \in \mathbb{R}$. Then each member of the population chooses whether to affiliate with the original terror group, affiliate with the splinter faction, or refrain from joining the terror movement.

The payoffs are as follows. The splinter group is in competition with the existing terrorist organization. Hence, should a splinter form, the splinter faction's leader has utility that is increasing in the supporters his faction attracts and is decreasing in the supporters the other faction attracts. The splinter leader also bears a cost c for splintering. Let N_j be the number of supporters for faction $j \in \{t, s\}$. Then the splinter leader's payoffs from splintering are

$$U_s(x_s | x_t, \beta_t, \beta_s) = N_s(x_t, x_s, \beta_t, \beta_s) - \theta N_t(x_t, x_s, \beta_t, \beta_s) - c,$$

where $\theta \in [0, 1]$ is a weight reflecting how much the splinter leader cares about the size of the original terrorist faction. Intuitively, if $\theta = 0$, the splinter leader suffers no disutility from the size of the original terror faction. This case corresponds to an instance where the splinter and original faction interests are not in conflict. Conversely, if $\theta = 1$, the splinter leader dislikes membership in the original faction as much as he desires membership in the splinter faction. Here, the two faction interests are diametrically opposed.

The splinter leader does not have ideological preferences. Any divergence in ideology between the two factions is entirely driven by recruitment concerns. Of course, were I to assume that the leader also had ideological preferences that differed from the existing terrorist organization's position, this would strengthen the ideological separation between the factions that occurs in equilibrium. But such substantive disagreement is not necessary to get separation.

The splinter leader can also choose not to form a new faction. Since he is assumed not to have ideological preferences, in this case he receives a payoff from participating in the economy, just like a member of the population who does not mobilize receives (γ; described later) and continues to bear a cost for those mobilized for the other faction ($-\theta N_t$).

Each member of the population can take one of three actions. She can join one of the two terror factions or refrain from joining a terror group. If she refrains, she continues to participate in the economy and receives a payoff of γ. If she joins terrorist faction j, her payoff is

$$U_i(j|x_j, \beta_j) = \beta_j - u(|x_j - x_i|),$$

where β_j is a group-specific payoff, and I assume that $-u(\cdot)$ is strictly concave and achieves its maximum at zero. The idea behind the first term is that different terrorist factions provide their members with different private goods. The difference between β_t and β_s, then, can loosely be thought of as the difference in the size of the two factions' budgets. Both because it is intuitive, and to avoid triviality, I assume that $\beta_t > \beta_s$, that is, the original terror organization has more resources than the splinter faction. The second term represents the ideological payoffs associated with joining a terror group. The assumptions on functional form are consistent with, for example, a quadratic-loss payoff function. The closer the member's preferences are to the group's ideology, the better off the member is.

The ideologies of the members of the public are distributed according to a continuously differentiable distribution F, with density f, whose support is the real line. I assume that f is symmetric and single-peaked with arg max$_x f(x) = x_t$. That is, the existing terrorist organization is located at the point in the ideological space where the most potential supporters are. This implies that F is concave for all $x \geq x_t$. These assumptions are consistent with, for example, F being the normal distribution with mean x_t.

Equilibrium

The solution concept is subgame perfect Nash equilibrium. I solve by backward induction.

The Population

Given an ideological position for each of the two terrorist factions (x_t, x_s), a member of the population will join faction j if two constraints are satisfied. First, the population member must prefer joining faction j to refraining from joining the terrorist movement entirely. This individual rationality constraint is given by

$$IR = \beta_j - u(|x_j - x_i|) \geq \gamma.$$

Second, the member of the population must prefer faction j to the other faction. This incentive compatibility constraint is given by

$$IC = \beta_s - u(|x_j - x_i|) \geq \beta_t - u(|x_{-j} - x_i|).$$

To build intuition, consider an individual trying to decide whether to join a splinter faction. If there was no original terrorist faction, then the individual would have to choose either the splinter faction or the outside option (the IR constraint would always bind). In this case, the membership of the splinter faction with an ideological position $x_s \geq 0$ would be a closed set with ideal points symmetrically distributed about x_s. In particular, a potential member to the right of x_s would only join if

$$u(x_i - x_s) \leq \beta_s - \gamma \Leftrightarrow x_i \leq x_s + u_+^{-1}(\beta_s - \gamma),$$

where, if $u^{-1}(x) = \{-a, a\}$, then u_+^{-1} is the positive element a. Define $\Delta_s \equiv u_+^{-1}(\beta_s - \gamma)$. In the absence of an original terror group, the splinter group would have a membership consisting of all population members with ideologies contained in $[x_s - \Delta_s, x_s + \Delta_s]$ and would have a total membership $N_s = F(x_s + \Delta_s) - F(x_s - \Delta_s)$.

Of course, there is another faction, and this implies that sometimes an individual will prefer the splinter to the outside option but not to the other faction (the IC constraint will bind for some individuals). Without loss of generality, restrict attention to cases where the splinter group forms to the right of the original faction $(x_s \geq x_t)$. The case of splintering to the left is symmetric.

If there are individuals for whom the IC constraint binds (that is, who prefer both factions to the outside option), they will be located to the left of the splinter group's ideological position and to the right of the original group's ideological position. Such population members, whom I refer to as *contested*, join whichever faction they prefer.

Let $\underline{x}_j$ be the leftmost population member who joins faction j, and similarly $\bar{x}_j$ be the rightmost population member who joins faction j. If the IC constraint binds, then $\underline{x}_s = \bar{x}_t$. Further, population members who have ideologies located at that point are indifferent between the two factions. Thus, when the IC constraint binds, $\underline{x}_s$ is characterized by

$$\beta_s - u(x_s - \underline{x}_s) = \beta_t - u(\underline{x}_s - x_t). \tag{6.1}$$

We can use equation (6.1) to derive some properties of the lower bound of splinter group support when the IC constraint binds.

Lemma 6.1 When the IC constraint binds, $\underline{x}_s$ is increasing in x_t, x_s, and β_t and decreasing in β_s.

The proofs of this and all subsequent results are in the appendix.

Lemma 6.1 says that as the splinter faction becomes more extreme (higher x_s) and as the original faction becomes wealthy relative to the splinter faction (high β_t or low β_s), the most moderate member of the splinter faction becomes more extreme. This is because, in either of these cases, the splinter faction becomes less attractive to more moderate people. Intuitively, very extreme splinters only attract very extreme members. Moreover, poorly funded splinters competing with well-funded original factions are unable to compete very successfully for members, so they tend to attract only adherents who share their ideology very closely.

Of course, given parameter values, whether or not the IC constraint binds is a function of how ideologically disparate the two factions are. Figure 6.1 shows the two possible situations. In the left-hand panel, the IR constraint binds on both sides, whereas in the right-hand panel, the IC constraint binds to the left of the splinter group's ideological position, and the IR constraint binds to the right. The shaded region in the right-hand panel represents the contested adherents.

The Splinter Group's Location
Given the implied affiliation decisions, how will the splinter group position itself? The splinter group faces a trade-off. On the one hand, as it moves to the right, it increases the size of the interval defining its membership. On the other hand, as it moves to the left, it takes away members from the other faction *and* it moves the interval defining its membership into a part of the ideological space where the density of potential members is greater.

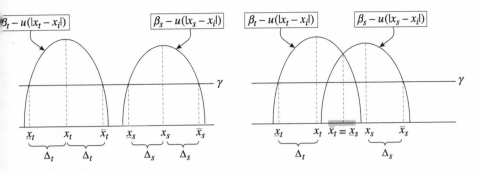

Figure 6.1
Left-hand panel: IR constraint binds on both sides; no adherents are contested. *Right-hand panel:* IC constraint binds on splinter group's left; all population members in shaded region are contested.

Substantively, one can think of this trade-off as follows. In deciding how extreme its demands and use of violence should be, a radical faction like Hamas or the Real IRA faces a trade-off. On the one hand, as it becomes more extreme, it becomes more appealing to disaffected members of society who might find groups like Fatah or the Provisionals unappealingly moderate. On the other hand, by becoming more moderate, such a faction can attempt to compete for more mainstream followers. Doing so confers two benefits. First, there are likely to be more people closer to the mainstream, so by choosing an ideology that appeals to these people the splinter faction puts itself in a position to grow. Second, in so doing, the splinter faction also steals adherents from its rival.

The splinter group never has an incentive to become more extreme than the point where the IR constraint just binds on its left. Define this point as $\hat{x}_s \equiv x_t + \Delta_t + \Delta_s$, as illustrated in figure 6.2. At this point the size of the interval defining the splinter group's membership reaches its maximum (the interval stays the same size as the group continues to move to the right), and the density of potential members is decreasing monotonically to the right of x_t. Moreover, since $\beta_s < \beta_t$, the splinter group will never locate itself at the same location as the original terrorist group because it would gain no recruits in this case.

Lemma 6.2 The optimal x_s satisfies $x_t < x_s \leq \hat{x}_s$.

The objective of the splinter group's leader is to maximize the difference between his group's membership and the original terror group's membership. He solves

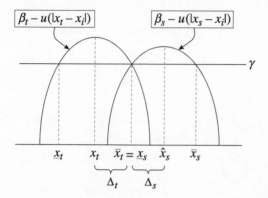

Figure 6.2
At $\hat{x}_s$, the IR constraint binds on splinter group's left.

$$\max_{x_s}[F(x_s + \Delta_s) - F(\underline{x}_s)] - \theta[F(\bar{x}_t) - F(x_{t,} - \Delta_t)] - c,$$

where $\underline{x}_s = \bar{x}_t$ is implicitly defined by equation (6.1).

Given this, we can characterize the optimal ideological position for the splinter group.

Proposition 6.1 The optimal ideological position x_s^* is characterized by

$$f(\bar{x}_s(x_s^*))\frac{\partial \bar{x}_s}{\partial x_s} = f(\underline{x}_s(x_s^*))\frac{\partial \underline{x}_s}{\partial x_s}.$$

This first-order condition says that at the optimum the marginal benefits of increasing the splinter group's extremism have to equal the marginal costs. As already discussed, the marginal benefit of choosing a more extreme ideology (increasing x_s) is attracting more adherents on the right. The marginal cost is that by moving to the extreme, the splinter group cedes contested adherents to the original faction. This has two effects. First, it diminishes the number of adherents to the splinter faction. Second, it increases the number of adherents to the original terrorist group by this same amount. Figure 6.3 illustrates the trade-off.

Whether to Splinter

A potential splinter leader, of course, need not form a splinter faction. Splintering from a terrorist organization is a risky endeavor. Terrorist

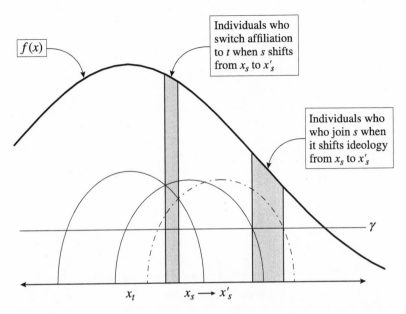

$f(x)$

Individuals who switch affiliation to t when s shifts from x_s to x'_s

Individuals who who join s when it shifts ideology from x_s to x'_s

γ

x_t $x_s \longrightarrow x'_s$

Figure 6.3
Marginal benefits and marginal costs of changing ideological positions from x_s to x'_s.

organizations regularly impose severe penalties on former members suspected of disloyalty. Chai (1993), for instance, describes the Japanese Red Army Faction's brutal murder, through burial in snow, of 14 of its members who were deemed disloyal. Similarly, following the bombing of Omagh, the Provisional IRA threatened to execute members of splinter groups who did not comport with Provisional negotiated cease fires (Dingley 1999).

Perhaps the most important determinant of the original organization's ability to impose costs on splinter groups is the level of centralization within the terrorist movement. In order to diminish the risk of infiltration, most terror groups are organized into somewhat decentralized cells (Chai 1993; Crenshaw 1981). However, there is variance in the degree of decentralization among terrorist movements. For instance, groups such as the IRA, ETA, and Hamas are divided into fairly autonomous cells, but they also have centralized commands that set strategy, allocate budgets, and so on. al Qaeda has taken decentralization much further, creating a network of only loosely affiliated factions and cells with a highly decentralized command apparatus (Arquilla and Ronfeldt 2001; Zanini and Edwards 2001).

The more decentralized a terrorist organization, the less able the leadership is to monitor the behavior of its cells, making it more difficult to identify and punish defectors. Thus, organizational structure can play an important role in determining the likelihood of splintering and, consequently, the level of extremism in the terrorist organization. The question remains, however, exactly when a splinter will form. Here, the potential leader will only splinter if the expected payoff of doing so is worth the risk, in particular, if

$$[F(x_s^* + \Delta_s) - F(\underline{x}_s)] - \theta[F(\bar{x}_t) - F(x_t - \Delta_t)] - c$$

$$\geq \gamma - [F(x_t + \Delta_t) - F(x_t - \Delta_t)].$$

Results

In this section I explore some comparative statics of the model and offer substantive interpretations of the results.

Two Forms of Interfactional Conflict

Competing terrorist factions often come into conflict with one another. The existence of such conflict is important to understanding the dynamics of terrorism for a number of reasons. First, interfactional competition can lead to internecine fighting. There is substantial variation in when terrorist factions fight one another. For instance, the Tamil Tigers have frequently used violence against other Tamil separatist groups. On the other hand, for most of its history Hamas steadfastly refused to engage in violence against competing Palestinian factions.

The spatial logic presented here highlights a heretofore overlooked subtlety in the conceptualization of the causes of interfactional conflict. There are, in the model, two possible sources of tension between factions: ideological divergence and competition for contested adherents. Avoiding one of these two types of conflict comes at the price of exacerbating the other type.

Consider again figure 6.3. As the splinter group becomes more ideologically extreme, moving from x_s to x_s', ideological conflict between the two factions increases for two reasons. First, the stated ideological positions of the two organizations are further apart. Second, the *memberships* of the two factions are more polarized on the ideological dimension. If ideological disagreement is the source of interfactional violence, then any factor that increases incentives for the splinter group to move to the right will exacerbate such conflict.

However, there is a second effect of a move to the ideological extreme by the splinter group. The set of contested adherents shrinks. Bloom (2004) argues that competition among factions for adherents is one of the major determinants not only of internecine violence but of terrorist escalation in general. Thus, the model suggests that terrorism and interfactional violence may actually diminish with an increase in ideological distance between the two factions.

Of course, the present model is silent on the issue of which type of interfactional conflict actually causes internecine violence or terrorism more generally. The model simply highlights the fact that interfactional conflict can take multiple forms—ideological divergence or competition for contested adherents—and shows that factors that increase one of these decrease the other.

Alignment of the Factions

Although terrorist factions may sometimes be in conflict, they can also serve as complements to one another in achieving common goals. For instance, at the time of this writing, it seems that because of intense competition for the loyalty of the Palestinian people, Fatah and Hamas view themselves as in deep conflict. However, at other times in the history of the Israeli/Palestinian conflict, Hamas was able to engage in violence that may have helped the Palestinian position in negotiations while allowing Fatah and its leadership to publicly distance themselves from the violent acts. In this mode, the two factions look more like complementary elements of an overall Palestinian movement.

In the model, the extent to which the mission of the two factions are complementary is formalized by the parameter θ, which measures the disutility the splinter faction suffers from an increase in membership of the original faction. A high θ represents a situation in which the two factions view each other as in tension, whereas a low θ represents a situation where the two factions are complementary.

When the splinter leader views the two factions as in competition (high θ), he suffers a greater loss from an increase in the original faction's membership. As a result, the marginal cost associated with becoming more extreme increases. This is because, as the splinter faction moves away from the original terror faction, the number of contested adherents diminishes, leaving the original faction with a larger following. This leads to the counterintuitive implication that when the splinter faction views itself as aligned with the original faction (in the sense that the size of the original faction does not have a large negative effect on the splinter faction), it will locate far from the original faction

in the ideological space. Conversely, when the splinter faction views itself as in competition with the original faction, it will locate close to the
original faction.

Proposition 6.2 The more disutility the splinter faction's leader suffers when the original terror faction's membership grows (higher θ),
the closer the splinter faction locates to the original faction in the ideological space (lower x^*).

Applying this result to the example of the Palestinian factions yields
the following prediction. At those times when Fatah and Hamas
viewed their missions as essentially complementary (before the decision by Hamas to compete for the leadership), they were expected to
distance themselves from one another ideologically so that they would
attract different adherents. However, now that they view each other as
rival factions, the expectation is that Hamas will move its ideology
closer to Fatah's in order to try to recruit adherents away from Fatah.
Interestingly, one interpretation of Hamas's decision to change its
long-standing policy of not running in Palestinian national elections
is precisely as an ideological move toward Fatah intended to coopt
support.

The Economy

How do changes in the state of the economy affect splinter groups'
incentives? The economy only has an effect on recruitment for a terrorist group when the IR constraint binds. Thus, the state of the economy
affects the marginal benefit of extremism but has no effect on the marginal cost.

A strong economy increases the marginal benefit of becoming more
extreme. When the economy is strong, for any given ideological position, the membership of the splinter group does not extend as far to
the right. Consequently, moving to the right incorporates new members in a part of the distribution with greater density. The strength
of the economy has no effect on the marginal costs of moving to the
right because the costs of becoming more extreme are due to losing
members to the more moderate terrorist faction, not to the regular
economy.

This logic can be seen in the figure 6.4. The marginal cost of becoming more extreme, regardless of the state of the economy, is shown in
area A. The marginal benefit depends on the economy. When the economy is strong (γ'), the marginal benefit is represented by areas B and

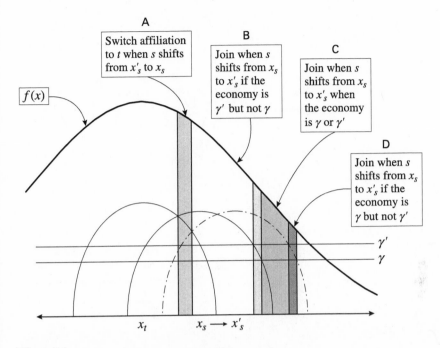

Figure 6.4
Strong economies lead to more extreme splinter groups.

C. When the economy is weak (γ), the marginal benefit is represented by areas C and D. Area B is larger than area D, reflecting the fact that there is a greater density of new adherents when the economy is strong. Thus, the marginal benefit of becoming extreme is larger with a strong economy.

Proposition 6.3 The stronger the economy (higher γ), the more extreme the position adopted by the splinter group.

A change in the economy does not only affect the extremism of the terrorist organization; it can also alter the total number of people who join the terrorist movement and the incentives to form a splinter in the first place.

There are three effects of an improvement in the economy on the decision of whether to splinter. First, for a fixed location, as the economy improves, the number of people the splinter faction is able to recruit decreases. This makes the splinter leader less likely to form a splinter faction. Second, as the economy improves, the number of people the original faction can recruit, even in the absence of a splinter, is smaller. This makes the appeal of forming a splinter and stealing some of the original faction's adherents less attractive, which also diminishes the likelihood of a splinter. Finally, as the economy improves, the opportunity costs of forming a splinter go up. Thus, as summarized in the following result, an improvement in the economy tends to decrease the likelihood of a splinter faction's forming.

Proposition 6.4 The stronger the economy (higher γ), the less likely a splinter faction is to form.

The effect of the economy on total mobilization is somewhat less clear. Clearly, if a splinter faction does not form, as a result of an economic improvement, total mobilization diminishes. However, if a splinter faction forms, the number of population members who mobilize is $F(x_s^* + \Delta_s) - F(x_t - \Delta_t)$. To assess the effect of an improvement in the economy on total mobilization in this case, we must examine

$$\frac{\partial F(x_s^* + \Delta_s) - F(x_t - \Delta_t)}{\partial \gamma} = f(x_s^* + \Delta_s)\left(\frac{\partial x_s^*}{\partial \gamma} + \frac{\partial \Delta_s}{\partial \gamma}\right) + f(x_t - \Delta_t)\frac{\partial \Delta_t}{\partial \gamma}.$$

There are three effects. First, as shown in proposition 6.3, when the economy improves, the splinter group becomes more extreme. This increases the number of people mobilized by adding members to the right of the splinter group's ideological position ($f(x_s^* + \Delta_s)\partial x_s^*/\partial \gamma > 0$). Second, for a fixed ideological position, as the economy improves, the interval of people around the splinter group's ideal point who are willing to join the terrorist organization shrinks because their outside option improves. This decreases mobilization to the right of the splinter group's position ($f(x_s^* + \Delta_s)\partial \Delta_s/\partial \gamma < 0$). Third, the same effect occurs to the left of the original terrorist organization's ideological position ($f(x_t - \Delta_t)\partial \Delta_t/\partial \gamma < 0$). Given these competing effects, it is not possible to conclusively determine the impact of an improvement in the economy on total mobilization without making further assumptions about the functional forms of $u(\cdot)$ and $f(\cdot)$.

Although the model does not yield a clear prediction regarding the effects of the economy on mobilization, the logic outlined has implications for the relation between terrorism and the economy.[1] Theorists have argued that economic contractions are likely to lead to increased mobilization due to decreased opportunity costs (see, for example, Blomberg, Hess, and Weerapana 2004 and Bueno de Mesquita 2005b).

The model suggests that the effect of the economy on mobilization may be somewhat more complicated. The mobilizing effect of the economy identified in earlier work is present in this model. When the economy is strong, the opportunity costs of mobilization are higher, decreasing mobilization on the margin. However, by considering the effect of the economy on the ideological positions of terrorist factions we find that there are other effects. In particular, a strong economy leads to a more radical splinter faction, should a splinter form. This tends to increase mobilization. A strong economy, however, also makes it less likely that a splinter will form at all, decreasing expected mobilization. Thus, on the one hand, economic growth tends to decrease mobilization by increasing the opportunity costs and decreasing the probability of a splinter. On the other hand, it may increase mobilization by allowing the splinter faction to reach further in the ideological space.

This raises two issues relevant to the debate over whether facilitating economic growth is an important tool for limiting terrorism. First, an improvement in the economy may create a more radical splinter faction, which presumably is bad from the government's perspective. Second, economic growth may increase or decrease total mobilization, depending on the shape of the utility functions, the distribution of preferences, and the effect on the decision to splinter. If total mobilization increases with economic growth, then growth has two negative consequences for terrorism: increased mobilization and increased extremism. If, however, mobilization decreases with economic growth, then facilitating growth presents a trade-off: less mobilization versus increased extremism.

It is also worth noting that the splinter group in the model need not be a group splintering toward the more radical end of the ideological spectrum. Instead, we could think of the splinter group as a *moderate* faction breaking with the original terrorist faction to pursue a negotiated settlement. In this scenario, the logic is reversed. Economic growth increases the moderation of the splinter group (causing it to position itself further to the left), which would presumably be to the government's advantage.

Original Faction's Resources

In addition to ideological payoffs, members of the population also gain a direct benefit β from joining a terrorist faction. One can think of this as actual compensation in private goods, expected future payoffs given the probability of victory, or other benefits associated with joining a terrorist group (Stern 2003). Under any of these interpretations, loosely speaking, we can interpret β_j as a measure of faction j's resources. The more resources a faction has, the better off are its members. What happens to the extremism of the splinter group as the original terror group's resource endowment increases?

When the original terrorist group has more resources, it captures a greater percentage of the contested adherents. Since the splinter group attracts relatively fewer members in the center, the marginal cost of becoming more extreme is lower. The marginal benefit of increased extremism is unaffected by the original terror group's resources because the rightmost members of the splinter group do not consider joining the original faction. Thus, the more resources the original terror group has access to, the more extreme is the splinter group.

This intuition is illustrated in figure 6.5. Area A represents the adherents lost by the splinter to the original terror group when it increases its extremism, if the original group has a relatively small resource endowment (β_t). Area B represents the adherents lost by the splinter to the original terror group when it increases its extremism, if the original group has a larger resource endowment (β_t'). The fact that the former is larger than the latter illustrates that the marginal cost of becoming more extreme is lower when the original group has more resources. This logic is formalized in the following proposition.

Proposition 6.5   The more resources the original terror group has access to (larger β_t), the more extreme is the splinter group.

Splinter Group's Resources
A related result obtains when the splinter group's resources change. However, the intuition is somewhat more complicated because an increase in the splinter group's resources affects both the IC and the IR constraints. As such, the splinter group's resources affect affiliation decisions on both its moderate and extreme wings. On the moderate (left) side, where the IC constraint binds, the effect of an increase in the splinter group's resources has exactly the opposite effect of an increase in the original group's resources. The more resources the splinter group has, the more effectively it can compete for contested adherents, and so the greater the marginal cost of becoming more extreme.

On the extreme (right) side, where the IR constraint binds, an increase in the splinter group's resources has the opposite effect of an

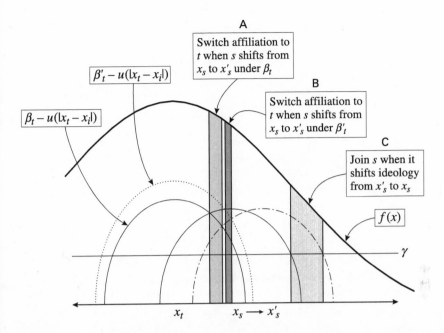

A

Switch affiliation to t when s shifts from x_s to x'_s under β_t

$\beta'_t - u(|x_t - x_i|)$

B

Switch affiliation to t when s shifts from x_s to x'_s under β'_t

$\beta_t - u(|x_t - x_i|)$

C

Join s when it shifts ideology from x'_s to x_s

$f(x)$

γ

x_t $x_s \longrightarrow x'_s$

Figure 6.5
Increasing the original terrorist faction's resources increases the extremism of the splinter group.

increase in the state of the economy. The more resources the terror organization has, the further into the extreme it can recruit. When resources are abundant, becoming more extreme garners relatively fewer new adherents because adherents are being added in a part of the ideological space where the density of people is small. Thus, the marginal benefit of becoming more extreme is lower.

These two intuitions suggest that when the splinter group has more resources, it will remain relatively moderate because the marginal cost of becoming more extreme is higher and the marginal benefit is lower. Substantively, well-financed splinter factions are able to compete fairly directly with the original faction in the center of the ideological space, whereas poorly funded splinters must move to the extreme to attract adherents. This is formalized in the following result.

Proposition 6.6 The greater the splinter group's resources (higher β_s), the more moderate the splinter group.

Because the splinter group competes more effectively for adherents when it has more resources, the splinter group's resources also affect the decision to splinter. Not surprisingly, the better able the splinter group is to provide these nonideological benefits to its adherents, the more likely a splinter is to form.

Proposition 6.7   The greater the splinter group's resources (higher β_s), the more likely a splinter is to form.

Ideological Skew of Terrorist Factions

Although this chapter does not address what leads to splintering within a terrorist organization, it seems reasonable to think that one important source of stability might be ideological balance. There are two senses in which the model allows us to evaluate whether a terrorist faction is ideologically balanced or ideologically skewed. The first criterion is to compare the total number of members to the left and to the right of the faction's ideological position. This, in some sense, measures the size of the moderate and extremist wings of the faction. The second criterion is how extreme the extremists in each wing of the faction are. That is, we can compare the distance from the faction's ideological position to the ideal point of the most extreme members on the right and left. This measurement does not speak to the relative size of the two wings but to the relative ideological extremism (or moderation) of the two wings of a terrorist faction.

As mentioned earlier, when there is only one terrorist faction, its membership consists of all population members within Δ_j of the faction's ideological position. If that ideological position is at the mean of the distribution, then there is no skew in the ideological preferences of the faction's members under either of the criteria discussed previously. There are as many members to the left of the faction's ideological position as to the right, and the leftmost and rightmost members are equidistant from that position. If the faction's ideological position is to the right (respectively, left) of the mean of the distribution, then there is skew under the first criterion. There are more total members to the left (respectively, right) of the ideological position than to the right (respectively, left). But the faction is still not skewed under the second criterion—the rightmost and leftmost members are equidistant from the faction's ideology.

The existence of splinter groups can disrupt even the weaker form of balance described by the second criterion. When a faction splinters, it generally creates contested adherents. Such adherents are then divided by the two competing factions. As shown in figure 6.2, this censors the membership of the splinter group on the left and the membership of the original group on the right. Thus, the most right-wing member of the splinter group is further to the right of the faction's ideological position than the most left-wing member of the splinter group is to the left of the faction's ideological position.

Both the splinter faction and the original faction will also typically fail to satisfy the first criterion—the two wings of each faction will not be of the same size. In the case of the splinter faction, however, it is not possible to say, generally, whether the right or left wing of the faction will be larger. Doing so would require further assumptions about the shapes of the utility functions and the distribution. This is because there are two competing effects. On the one hand, the right wing extends further from the ideological position of the group than the left wing, increasing the relative size of its membership. On the other hand, the left wing of the splinter faction is located in a part of the distribution that has greater density.

It is possible, however, to determine precisely the skew of the original terrorist organization. First, the most moderate (left-wing) member of the original terrorist faction is further from the faction's ideological position than the most extreme (right-wing) member. This is because the faction's membership is censored to the right by the presence of the splinter group. Second, because the distribution is unimodal and symmetric, and the faction is located at the mean, the fact that the left wing of the faction extends further than the right wing also implies that the number of people in the left wing of the original terrorist faction is larger than the number of people in the right wing of the original terrorist faction.

Proposition 6.8   Assume $x_s^* < \hat{x}_s$. Then the rightmost member of the splinter faction has an ideology further from the splinter faction's ideological position than does the leftmost member of the splinter faction. Further, the left wing of the original terrorist faction is larger than the right wing of the original terrorist faction, and the leftmost member of the original terrorist faction has an ideology further from the faction's ideological position than does the rightmost member.

Proof   The proof follows from the argument in the text.   ∎

Conclusion

I have presented a model of the splintering of a terrorist group in which affiliation decisions are endogenous and terrorist leaders are motivated by the desire to attract adherents. The model yields a number of results concerning the nature of interfactional conflict, factors that affect the ideological extremism of splinter factions, and the ideological balance of factionalized terrorist organizations.

The model presented here is intended as a small step in the ongoing project of unpacking the internal politics of terrorist organizations. In some sense, it can be viewed as providing some preliminary microfoundations for the ideologically heterogeneous factions that are taken as primitives in a variety of existing models (de Figueiredo and Weingast 2001; Kydd and Walter 2002; Bueno de Mesquita 2005a).

However, the model is incomplete in a variety of important ways. Most obviously, I have not considered several of the strategic decisions that are at the heart of terrorist politics. The model is silent on how ideological positions translate into levels of violence and counterterrorism (Berrebi and Klor 2006; Bueno de Mesquita 2005a), willingness to negotiate and compromise (Kydd and Walter 2002; Bueno de Mesquita 2005a), the types of tactics terrorists choose (Rosendorff and Sandler 2004), the willingness of group members to sacrifice for the organization (Berman 2003; Azam 2005), or the ability to secure the resources necessary to engage in a campaign of terror. Moreover, there is no government, and thus the model does not address how counterterrorism policy might affect affiliation decisions by the population (Rosendorff and Sandler 2004; Bueno de Mesquita 2005b) or position taking by the terrorist factions (de Figueiredo and Weingast 2001). Finally, the model assumes that terrorist leaders are motivated by a desire to attract adherents. However, there may be a variety of other factors that influence terrorist leaders' behavior, such as true ideological motivations, rent seeking, and signaling to donors or the government (Lapan and Sandler 1993; Overgaard 1994). More complete models will have to integrate strategic concerns regarding how terrorist campaigns are carried out with factors affecting the internal structure and politics of terrorist organizations themselves, such as those explored here.

Appendix

Proof of Lemma 6.1   Applying the implicit function theorem to equation (6.1) we find

$$\frac{\partial \underline{x}_s}{\partial x_t} = \frac{u'(\underline{x}_s - x_t)}{u'(\underline{x}_s - x_t) + u'(x_s - \underline{x}_s)} > 0,$$

$$\frac{\partial \underline{x}_s}{\partial x_s} = \frac{u'(x_s - \underline{x}_s)}{u'(\underline{x}_s - x_t) + u'(x_s - \underline{x}_s)} > 0,$$

$$\frac{\partial \underline{x}_s}{\partial \beta_t} = \frac{1}{u'(\underline{x}_s - x_t) + u'(x_s - \underline{x}_s)} > 0,$$

$$\frac{\partial \underline{x}_s}{\partial \beta_s} = \frac{-1}{u'(\underline{x}_s - x_t) + u'(x_s - \underline{x}_s)} < 0. \qquad \blacksquare$$

Proof of Lemma 6.2   The first inequality follows from the argument in the text. To see the second, note that

$$U_s(x_s|x_s \geq \hat{x}_s) = [F(x_s + \Delta_s) - F(x_s - \Delta_s)] - \theta[F(x_t + \Delta_t) - F(x_t - \Delta_t)].$$

Differentiating, we have

$$\frac{\partial U_s(x_s|x_s \geq \hat{x}_s)}{\partial x_s} = f(x_s + \Delta_s) - f(x_s - \Delta_s) < 0,$$

where the inequality follows from the fact that f is decreasing to the right of x_t. $\blacksquare$

Proof of Proposition 6.1   Lemma 6.2 implies that the optimal choice is interior. Since the objective is concave, the interior optimum is characterized by the first-order condition. $\blacksquare$

Proof of Proposition 6.2   The position adopted by the splinter is given by proposition 6.1. Taking the cross-partial of the objective with respect to x_s and θ yields

$$\frac{\partial^2 U_s}{\partial x_s \partial \theta} = -f(\underline{x}_s)\frac{\partial \underline{x}_s}{\partial x_s}.$$

Since, by lemma 6.1, $\partial \underline{x}_s/\partial x_s > 0$, the cross-partial is negative. Thus, theorem 3 of Edlin and Shannon (1998) implies that the optimal x_s is strictly decreasing in θ. $\blacksquare$

Proof of Proposition 6.3   The position adopted by the splinter is given by proposition 6.1. Taking the cross-partial of the objective with respect to x_s and γ yields

$$\frac{\partial^2 U_s}{\partial x_s \partial \gamma} = f'(x_s + \Delta_s)\frac{\partial \Delta_s}{\partial \gamma}.$$

Recall that $\Delta_s = u_+^{-1}(B_s - \gamma)$. The inverse function theorem then implies that

$$\frac{\partial \Delta_s}{\partial \gamma} = \frac{-1}{u'(u_+^{-1}(B_s - \gamma))}.$$

Moreover, notice that since $x_s + \Delta_s > x_t$, $f'(x_s + \Delta_s) < 0$. Combining these implies that the cross-partial is positive. Thus, theorem 3 of Edlin and Shannon (1998) implies that the optimal x_s is strictly increasing in γ. ∎

Proof of Proposition 6.4   The splinter faction forms if

$$[F(x_s^* + \Delta_s) - F(\underline{x}_s)] - \theta[F(\underline{x}_s) - F(x_t - \Delta_t)] - c$$

$$\geq \gamma - \theta[F(x_t + \Delta_t) - F(x_t - \Delta_t)].$$

Rearranging shows that a splinter forms if

$$[F(x_s^* + \Delta_s) - F(\underline{x}_s)] - \theta[F(\underline{x}_s) - F(x_t + \Delta_t)] - c - \gamma \geq 0.$$

The envelope theorem implies that the derivative of the left-hand side with respect to γ is

$$f(x_s^* + \Delta_s)\frac{\partial \Delta_s}{\partial \gamma} + \theta f(x_t + \Delta_t)\frac{\partial \Delta_t}{\partial \gamma} - 1 < 0,$$

where the inequality follows from $\partial \Delta_s / \partial \gamma < 0$ and $\partial \Delta_t / \partial \gamma < 0$. ∎

Proof of Proposition 6.5   Again taking cross-partials of the objective function, we have

$$\frac{\partial^2 U_s}{\partial x_s \partial \beta_t} = -(1 + \theta)f'(\underline{x}_s)\frac{\partial \underline{x}_s}{\partial \beta_t}\frac{\partial \underline{x}_s}{\partial x_s}.$$

Recall that $\underline{x}_s = \bar{x}_t > x_t$. This implies that $f'(\underline{x}_s) < 0$. Lemma 6.1 implies that $\partial \underline{x}_s / \partial \beta_t > 0$ and $\partial \underline{x}_s / \partial x_s > 0$. Thus, the whole cross-partial is positive. Theorem 3 of Edlin and Shannon (1998) then implies that the optimal x_s is strictly increasing in β_t. ∎

Proof of Proposition 6.6   Again taking cross-partials,

$$\frac{\partial^2 U_s}{\partial x_s \partial \beta_t} = f'(x_s + \Delta_s)\frac{\partial \Delta_s}{\partial \beta_s} - (1 + \theta)f'(\underline{x}_s)\frac{\partial \underline{x}_s}{\partial \beta_s}\frac{\partial \underline{x}_s}{\partial x_s}.$$

Applying the inverse function theorem, we find that

$$\frac{\partial \Delta_s}{\partial \beta_s} = \frac{1}{u'(u_+^{-1}(\Delta_s))} > 0.$$

Lemma 6.1 implies that $\partial \underline{x}_s / \partial \beta_s < 0$ and $\partial \underline{x}_s / \partial x_s > 0$. Thus, the entire cross-partial is negative, and theorem 3 of Edlin and Shannon (1998) implies that the optimal x_s is strictly decreasing in β_s. ∎

Proof of Proposition 6.7 From the proof of proposition 6.4, the splinter forms if

$$[F(x_s^* + \Delta_s) - F(\underline{x}_s)] - \theta[F(\underline{x}_s) - F(x_t + \Delta_t)] - c - \gamma \geq 0.$$

The envelope theorem implies that the derivative of the left-hand side with respect to β_s is

$$f(x_s^* + \Delta_s)\frac{\partial \Delta_s}{\partial \beta_s} - (1 + \theta)f(\underline{x}_s)\frac{\partial \underline{x}_s}{\partial \beta_s} > 0,$$

where the inequality follows from $\partial \Delta_s / \partial \beta_s > 0$ (see proof of proposition 6.6) and $\partial \underline{x}_s / \partial \beta_s < 0$ (lemma 6.1). ∎

Notes

Scott Ashworth, Bruce Bueno de Mesquita, Greg Hess, Edward Glaeser, Stergios Skaperdas, Peter Rosendorff, and other participants in the 2005 CESifo conference provided valuable comments and feedback. This chapter was written while I was a Lady Davis Fellow in the Department of Political Science and a Visiting Fellow in the Center for the Study of Rationality at Hebrew University in Jerusalem. I thank both organizations for their support and for providing congenial places to work.

1. For empirical studies on the economy's effect on terrorism, see, for example, Abadie (2006), Blomberg, Hess, and Weerapana (2004), and Krueger and Maleckova (2003).

References

Abadie, A. 2006. Poverty, political freedom, and the roots of terrorism. *American Economic Review* 96 (2): 50–56.

Arquilla, J., and D. Ronfeldt. 2001. Afterword (September 2001): The sharpening fight for the future. In *Networks and Netwars: The Future of Terror, Crime, and Militancy*, ed. J. Arquilla and D. Ronfeldt. Santa Monica: Rand.

Azam, J. P. 2005. Suicide bombing as intergenerational investment. *Public Choice* 122: 177–198.

Berman, E. 2003. Hamas, Taliban, and the Jewish underground: An economist's view of radical religious militias. NBER Working Paper W10004. Cambridge, Mass.: National Bureau of Economic Research.

Berrebi, C., and E. Klor. 2006. On terrorism and electoral outcomes: Theory and evidence from the Israeli-Palestinian conflict. *Journal of Conflict Resolution* 50 (6): 899–925.

Blomberg, S. B., G. D. Hess, and A. Weerapana. 2004. Economic conditions and terrorism. *European Journal of Political Economy* 20 (2): 463–478.

Bloom, M. M. 2004. Palestinian suicide bombing: Public support, market share and outbidding. *Political Science Quarterly* 199 (1): 61–88.

———. 2005. *Dying to Kill: The Global Phenomenon of Suicide Terror*. New York: Columbia University Press.

Bueno de Mesquita, E. 2005a. Conciliation, counterterrorism, and patterns of terrorist violence. *International Organization* 59 (1): 145–176.

———. 2005b. The quality of terror. *American Journal of Political Science* 49 (3): 515–530.

Chai, S.-K. 1993. An organizational economics theory of anti-government violence. *Comparative Politics* 26: 99–110.

Crenshaw, M. 1981. The causes of terrorism. *Comparative Politics* 13: 379–399.

de Figueiredo, R. J. P. Jr., and B. R. Weingast. 2001. Vicious cycles: Endogenous political extremism and political violence. Working Paper 2001-9. Berkeley: Institute of Governmental Studies, University of California.

Dingley, J. 1999. Peace processes and northern Ireland: Squaring circles? *Terrorism and Political Violence* 11: 32–52.

Edlin, A. S., and C. Shannon. 1998. Strict monotonicity in comparative statics. *Journal of Economic Theory* 81 (1): 201–219.

Krueger, A. B., and J. Maleckova. 2003. Education, poverty, and terrorism: Is there a causal connection? *Journal of Economic Perspectives* 17 (4): 119–144.

Kydd, A., and B. F. Walter. 2002. Sabotaging the peace: The politics of extremist violence. *International Organization* 56 (2): 263–296.

Lapan, H. E., and T. Sandler. 1993. Terrorism and signaling. *European Journal of Political Economy* 9 (3): 383–397.

Overgaard, P. B. 1994. The scale of terrorist attacks as a signal of resources. *Journal of Conflict Resolution* 38 (3): 452–478.

Rosendorff, P., and T. Sandler. 2004. Too much of a good thing? The proactive response dilemma. *Journal of Conflict Resolution* 48 (4): 657–671.

Stern, J. 2003. *Terror in the Name of God: Why Religious Militants Kill*. New York: Ecco-HarperCollins.

Zanini, M., and S. J. A. Edwards. 2001. The networking of terror in the information age. In *Networks and Netwars: The Future of Terror, Crime, and Militancy*, ed. J. Arquilla and D. Ronfeldt. Santa Monica: Rand.

7   Urban Structure in a Climate of Terror

Stephen Sheppard

Urban theorists and urban historians have identified a variety of reasons for the existence of cities. One of the foremost is that cities permit humans to share in the consumption of public goods that are either nonexcludable or most efficiently produced at some minimal scale that is sufficient to accommodate a large number of individuals. Perhaps original among these reasons was joint consumption of fortifications and other structures and mechanisms for defense.

Over time, other functions rose to importance, so that the role of the city as a center for trade and commercial interaction between producers and consumers and between different producers seemed paramount. Cities whose fortified walls were once a primary reason for existence found that economic incentives encouraged the walls' destruction so that interaction could more freely flow between residents and those drawn to the expanding urban centers. Market forces and the growth in factor productivity made possible through interaction in urban spaces dictated an evolving urban structure in which the importance of lower transportation costs led to cities that were more open but more vulnerable as well. In usual circumstances, this vulnerability was accepted because the benefits of open cities to the wider economy were clear.

While terrorism has been a component of political struggle and social conflict for millennia (the Zealot group known as the Sicarii attacked and killed individual Roman officials and Jews they regarded as collaborators in an unsuccessful effort to resist Roman occupation), it might be argued that terrorism and its impact on cities has changed in fundamental ways during the past century. Prior to this, terrorism mostly consisted of assassinations and attacks on specific target individuals and groups. The increase in destructive power of weapons that can be deployed by relatively small organizations or individuals has enabled them to affect the general climate of a community and the perceived risk of living or working in a city. It has therefore raised concerns about the fundamental viability of open cities and the central role they play in the economy.

Dedicated groups seem capable of creating a climate of terror that might have a significant impact on the economic viability of cities or at least the internal structure of urban areas. Thus, after the September 11 attacks in New York City, several writers predicted or urged a decline in the importance of large urban centers as a result of the terrorist attacks. Stephen Ambrose, writing in the *Wall Street Journal* (2001), urged adoption of a "defensive posture" made necessary by terrorism and made possible by improved electronic communication that would allow us to dispense with dense concentrations such as lower Manhattan. Similarly, Admiral William Crowe advised companies to decentralize away from dense urban centers toward low-profile locations. None of these recommendations were based on careful economic analysis, but economic concerns about the effects of terrorism and the appropriate response persist, most recently following the July 2005 bombings in London. Thus Seager, Moore, and Long, writing in the *Guardian* (2005), quote a CEBR economist as estimating that the bombings would reduce output in London by 0.6% and national output by 0.1%. This effect would be even greater if the July attacks were followed by a sustained terrorist campaign. Other experts expected little or no impact.

This chapter seeks to address the question in a more systematic fashion. I use a new source of data on urban structure based on a global sample of cities located around the world. These data provide measures of urban land use in each city and different points in time. After reviewing the recent theoretical and empirical literature addressing the effects of terrorism on urban structure, and providing a description of the data used, I provide some preliminary estimates of the effects of terrorism (or the climate of terror) on urban structure. Following these estimates, I discuss tentative conclusions and directions for future research.

Theory

Despite the potential importance of the topic, there have been surprisingly few recent theoretical expositions put forward to guide our thinking, assist in the design of policies, or provide a framework for empirical analysis of the effects of terrorism on urban form. One relatively complete analysis is provided by Rossi-Hansberg (2004), based on the dynamic models of Lucas (2001) and Lucas and Rossi-Hansberg (2002). These models concentrate on the positive externality that arises through increasing factor productivity when firms locate together in cities.

A second approach is provided by Harrigan and Martin (2002), whose analysis is based on a new economic geography model of the type used by Krugman (1991). This model concentrates on the risk of wage variability arising from shocks to individual firms, and the benefits to workers that result from locating where a large number of firms exist to smooth these fluctuations.

In addition to these theoretical approaches, there is a well-defined and widely used framework for understanding the broad determinants of urban structure and urban expansion that is relevant for empirical analysis. I first review these general (non-terror-related) determinants of urban structure, along with the hypotheses that would be suggested by this theory. Following this, I briefly review the Rossi-Hansberg and Harrigan and Martin analyses, identifying the suggested hypotheses concerning the effects of terrorism on urban structure.

Determinants of Urban Structure and Expansion

The expansion of urban areas is determined by the interaction of three broad types of phenomena: the physical constraints of geography and environment, the demand for land by the households and firms who inhabit the city, and the policy constraints that govern land use and spatial interactions in the city. The most useful models for informing public action on the management of urban expansion are those models that incorporate each of these factors in some way and that evaluate the relative contribution of each factor to urban expansion.

Unfortunately, we do not have the same level of theoretical understanding of the effects of the physical, economic, and policy environments on urban expansion. Very little work has been done on the effect of climate, ecological biomes, or topography on the form of cities. And while some models of expected policy effects do exist, for the most part such analyses have been limited to an *ex post* evaluation of the extent to which a particular type of policy appears to have been effective, *ceteris paribus*, in influencing urban structure. This type of analysis remains a potentially useful exercise because it provides important information to policymakers about where successes and failures have occurred.

The economic model of urban spatial structure is relatively well developed, although not necessarily more accurate in predicting actual outcomes. Several authors[1] provide clear expositions.

An urban area has an exogenously given population of L households having income y and preferences represented by a common quasi-concave utility function $v(c,q)$ that depends on consumption of a composite good c and housing q. Each household has a worker who is employed in the city center and must commute to the center to earn income. The household's annual transportation costs for this commute are $t \cdot x$ if it resides in a house x units of distance from the center.

Equilibrium requires that a common utility level u be achieved by a household at any location within the built-up area of the city, so the price per square meter of housing will vary with distance x. Households allocate their income to select the most preferred combination of the composite good and housing, so that in equilibrium one must have

$$\max_{q} \ v(y - t \cdot x - q \cdot p(x), q) = u \tag{7.1}$$

for all households.

Housing producers combine inputs of capital N and land l using a concave constant-returns production function $H(N, l)$ to produce square meters of housing. Housing production therefore exhibits diminishing marginal productivity of both capital and land. Constant returns to scale and free entry of housing producers is sufficient to determine an equilibrium land rent function $r(x)$ and a capital-land ratio (building density) $S(x)$ that depend upon distance x from the city center. These satisfy

$$\frac{\partial r(x)}{\partial x} < 0 \quad \text{and} \quad \frac{\partial S(x)}{\partial x}, \tag{7.2}$$

so both land value and building density decline with distance from the city center. Combining the solution for building density $S(x)$ with the housing $q(x)$ demanded by a household at distance x provides a solution for the population density $D(x, t, y, u)$ at distance x, given the exogenous levels of transport costs and income and the achieved utility level u.

The maximum extent of the urban area $\bar{x}$ depends on the ability of housing producers to bid land away from its alternative uses. Let r_A represent the alternative use value of land (often explained heuristically as the market rent of land in agricultural use). The maximum extent of the urban area is then given implicitly by

$$r(\bar{x}) = r_A. \tag{7.3}$$

Finally, equilibrium requires that all households be accommodated in the urban area. If θ represents the share of land available for development at each distance, this is ensured by the following equilibrium condition:

$$\int_0^{\bar{x}} 2\pi \cdot \theta \cdot x \cdot D(x, t, y, u) \, dx = L. \tag{7.4}$$

This basic theory provides an endogenous solution for the maximum extent of urban land use and relates this solution to several observable characteristics of the urban area. In particular, a number of comparative static results can be derived from this model that provide clear, testable hypotheses for analysis.

This model has housing producers (and agricultural producers outside the urban area whose demand for land generates the rents r_A) as the only direct consumers of land. It is easy to generalize this model so that firms who trade in the city center are included as well, combining inputs of capital and land according to $f(N, l)$ to produce an export good for external markets sold at price w. These firms provide a separate commercial demand for land. Assuming that the cost (in terms of reduced profitability) of moving production away from the urban center is greater than the aggregate commuting cost of the households who would occupy an equal amount of land, the firms will be more centrally located than the households. In this case two additional hypotheses can be derived concerning the effect of changes in the productivity of land in export-good production, and the effect of an increase in the world demand for the export good. All the hypotheses derived from this model of urban spatial structure are summarized in table 7.1.

Effects of Terrorism on Urban Structure

The models that serve as the foundation for the analysis in Harrigan and Martin (2002) provide less detail concerning urban structure than

Table 7.1
Hypotheses about Urban Spatial Structure Derived from the Standard Economic Model

	Comparative Static Result	Prediction and Hypothesis
1.	$\dfrac{\partial \bar{x}}{\partial L} > 0$	An increase in population will increase urban extent and urban expansion.
2.	$\dfrac{\partial \bar{x}}{\partial y} > 0$	An increase in household income will increase urban extent and urban expansion.
3.	$\dfrac{\partial \bar{x}}{\partial t} < 0$	An increase in transportation costs will reduce urban extent and limit urban expansion.
4.	$\dfrac{\partial \bar{x}}{\partial r_A} < 0$	An increase in opportunity cost of nonurban land will reduce urban extent and limit urban expansion.
5.	$\dfrac{\partial \bar{x}}{\partial H_l} > 0$	An increase in marginal productivity of land in housing production will increase urban extent and urban expansion.
6.	$\dfrac{\partial \bar{x}}{\partial \theta} > 0$	An increase in share of land available for housing development will increase urban extent and urban expansion.
7.	$\dfrac{\partial \bar{x}}{\partial f_l} > 0$	An increase in marginal productivity of land in production of export good will increase urban extent and urban expansion.
8.	$\dfrac{\partial \bar{x}}{\partial w} > 0$	An increase in demand for (world price of) export good will increase urban extent and urban expansion.

the traditional urban model. They use both a labor-pooling and a core-periphery model to examine the effects of terrorist attacks on urban centers. In the labor-pooling model, an increase in the probability of an attack in a particular location can introduce risk of wage variability that, because it affects all firms in the attacked region, can eliminate the advantages to workers from the labor pooling.

In both approaches it is important that the threat of attack be ongoing, and in this sense terrorism is fundamentally different from those types of conflict or warfare in which armistice, victory, or surrender provide an agreed and understood end to hostilities. For this reason, the observations of Davis and Weinstein (2002) concerning the recovery of the Japanese urban system to relative sizes similar to prewar levels despite significant differences in the damage inflicted on individual cities may not be relevant for understanding the effects of terrorism. Important factors with terrorism are that the threat is persistent and that the probability of attack may be positively related to density or to the magnitude of investment.

In both the labor-pooling model and the core-periphery model Harrigan and Martin (2002) find that a one-time attack will have no long-run effects on the equilibrium allocation of production and capital between locations. An ongoing threat, however, acts like a tax on particular locations. The effects are particularly striking in the core-periphery model, where there may be multiple equilibria. In this case an ongoing risk of terrorism causes workers to leave the larger city and reduces the incentive for agglomeration of firms. Eventually a locally stable equilibrium is reached, with equal distribution of production at all locations. Because this equilibrium is stable it persists even if the threat of terrorism is removed. Thus creation of a climate of terror leads to reduced size for the larger urban area.

The model presented in Rossi-Hansberg (2004) is more complex, providing both additional detail about the internal structure of urban areas and how they respond to an ongoing threat of terrorism, and also some policy recommendations capable of improving the economic outcome for urban residents. The cost of this complexity is some reduced specificity in the types of outcomes likely to emerge. A series of simulations are presented that indicate great sensitivity to transport costs and to the nature of interactions between nearby producers.

The interactions between firms are a central feature of the analysis and provide the basis for policy to improve the efficiency of the equilibrium outcome. A firm's productivity is positively affected when it locates near other productive firms. This means that firms have some incentive to cluster, although because the land is owned by absentee landlords, they cannot capitalize the benefits they create, and so in equilibrium there is too little clustering of firms. Policies that provide a subsidy for urban location can improve the outcome.

Rossi-Hansberg introduces the threat of terrorism by assuming that there is a risk of capital destruction at each location where the density of investment exceeds a certain level. This further reduces the incentive to cluster, robbing the urban area of some of its ability to enhance factor productivity through agglomeration. Applying the same subsidy scheme used in the absence of terrorism can still improve the outcome, and if the policymaker has better knowledge about the probability of a terrorist attack than individual agents in the economy, there is scope for further adjustment in the subsidy policy to improve economic outcomes.

Unlike Harrigan and Martin, Rossi-Hansberg's model has a fixed population in a single urban center. He proves several propositions that are relevant for the context here:

Table 7.2
Additional Hypotheses about Urban Spatial Structure

	Comparative Static Result	Prediction and Hypothesis
9.	$\dfrac{\partial \tilde{x}}{\partial T} < 0$	An increase in climate of terror will decrease urban expansion.
10.	$\dfrac{\partial^2 q}{\partial x \partial T} < 0$	An increase in climate of terror will decrease rate at which housing (residential capital) varies with respect to location.

$T =$ measure of level of terrorist activity.

• With no adjustment costs, the steady-state capital level in residential areas is higher before than after a shock that destroys part of the capital in the city (a terrorist attack reduces investment in residential areas in a steady state).

• With no adjustment costs, the range of steady-state capital levels across locations within the city decreases after a shock that destroys part of the capital in the city (a terrorist attack makes the capital density gradient flatter).

• In a model with adjustment costs, destruction of an area reduces productivity in nearby areas of the city and leads to a slower recovery of the destroyed area.

These provide the basis for two additional hypotheses to be examined and tested empirically (see table 7.2). In the present analysis hypothesis 9 is tested directly; the results for hypothesis 10 are not presented here.

The Data

The data used for the empirical analysis combine information on urban land cover in a global sample of cities, population for jurisdictional areas within each city, measures of income and relevant economic variables for the country in which each city is located, and measures of the number of terrorist incidents in each country. Use of national (rather than local) data for economic variables and the level of terrorism serves two important functions. First, it permits coverage of a much larger number of cities, including those in countries where local income, transport cost, or land value data are not available. Second, using these data allows us to estimate the effects of a climate of terror that is more extensive than the direct experience of terrorism within the city where investment and urban expansion decisions are being made. For example, recent experience in the United States has shown that cities very far removed from New York and Washington, including cities so much smaller and remote that they would presumably be exposed to very little risk of terrorist attack, have nevertheless devoted considerable effort toward preparing for a terrorist attack. Presumably these preparations signal a level of concern that could also distort investment activity and as a result affect the level of urban development and urban land cover.

The data are collected for a sample of 120 cities randomly selected from a larger random sample constructed by UN Habitat for data collection in connection with their Urban Observatory program. The larger sample has been constructed to be representative of the global urban population in cities having population over 100,000 persons. The sample of 120 cities used here was stratified so that it is representative of the global urban population by region, income class of country, and size of metro areas. Figure 7.1 shows the global distribution of the sample and lists the entire sample of cities.

For each of the cities in the sample, Landsat thematic mapper satellite images were obtained for dates that are near the national census dates and for which cloud-free images were available. Images were obtained for two time periods: approximately 1990 and approximately 2000. The images provide data on reflected light intensity in seven spectral bands (three visual and four infrared). These data are used to classify each point as urban (covered with impervious built structures or surfaces), water, or nonurban (everything else) in each time period.

Commercial products are available that provide this information, but the usual practice is to fill in small interior open spaces and classify them as urban. The approach here has been to regard such spaces as nonurban so that eventually it is possible to distinguish between new capital investment and building at the urban periphery and infill development building inside the built-up area. The contrast can be seen immediately in a side-by-side comparison of images showing estimated urban land cover from one of these commercial products and from the estimate obtained for this analysis. An example for Addis Ababa, Ethiopia, is shown in figure 7.2 (the contrast can be seen particularly well online). Such a comparison shows solid urban land cover within the boundaries of the city (commercial product) versus a more mottled pattern of urban land cover (data used here), reflecting the

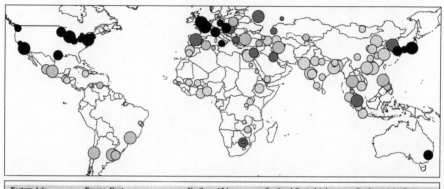

Eastern Asia	Europe, Cont.	Northern Africa	Southand Central Asia	Southeast Asia, Cont.
Shanghai, China	Thessaloniki, Greece	Cairo, Egypt	Mumbai, India	Cebu, Philippines
Beijing, China	Palermo, Italy	Alexandria, Egypt	Kolkota, India	Ipoh, Malaysia
Seoul, Korea	Sheffield, UK	Casablanca, Morocco	Dhaka, Bangladesh	Bacolod, Philippines
Hong Kong, China	Astrakhan, Russia	Algiers, Algeria	Teheran, Iran	Songkhla, Thailand
Guangzhou, China	Leipzig, Germany	Marrakech, Morocco	Hyderabad, India	**Sub-Saharan Africa**
Pusan, Korea	Le Mans, France	Port Sudan, Sudan	Pune, India	Addis Ababa, Ethiopia
Zhengzhou, China	Castellon, Spain	Aswan, Egypt	Kanpur, India	Johannesburg, South Africa
Yulin, China	Oktyabrsky, Russia	Tébessa, Algeria	Jaipur, India	Accra, Ghana
Yiyang, China	**Latin America and Caribbean**	**Other Developed**	Coimbatore, India	Harare, Zimbabwe
Leshan, China	Mexico City, Mexico	Tokyo, Japan	Vijayawada, India	Ibadan, Nigeria
Ulan Bator, Mongolia	Sao Paolo, Brazil	Los Angeles, USA	Rajshahi, Bangladesh	Pretoria, South Africa
Changzhi, China	Buenos Aires, Argentina	Chicago, USA	Ahvaz, Iran	Kampala, Uganda
Anqing, China	Santiago, Chile	Philadelphia, USA	Shimkent, Kazakhstan	Bamako, Mali
Ansan, Korea	Guadalajara, Mexico	Houston, USA	Jalna, India	Ouagadougou, Burkina Faso
Chinju, China	Guatemala City, Guatemala	Sydney, Australia	Gorgan, Iran	Ndola, Zambia
Chonan, Korea	Caracas, Venezuela	Minneapolis, USA	Saidpur, Bangladesh	Banjul, Gambia
Europe	San Salvador, El Salvador	Pittsburgh, USA	**Southeast Asia**	Kigali, Rwanda
Paris, France	Montevideo, Uruguay	Cincinnati, USA	Manila, Philippines	**Western Asia**
Moscow, Russia	Tijuana, Mexico	Fukuoka, Japan	Bangkok, Thailand	Istanbul, Turkey
London, UK	Kingston, Jamaica	Tacoma, USA	Ho Chi Minh City, Vietnam	Tel Aviv, Israel
Milan, Italy	Ribeirão Preto, Brazil	Springfield, USA	Singapore, Singapore	Baku, Azerbaijan
Madrid, Spain	Valledupar, Colombia	Modesto, USA	Bandung, Indonesia	Sana'a, Yemen
Warsaw, Poland	Guarujá, Brazil	St. Catharines, Canada	Medan, Indonesia	Yerevan, Armenia
Vienna, Austria	Ilhéus, Brazil	Victoria, Canada	Palembang, Indonesia	Kuwait City, Kuwait
Budapest, Hungary	Jequié, Brazil	Akashi, Japan	Kuala Lumpur, Malaysia	Malatya, Turkey
				Zugdidi, Georgia

City Sample by Size and Income

93,000 – 500,000	500,000 – 1.5 million	1.5 million – 4 million	4 million – 32 million
$610 – $3600	$610 – $3600	$610 – $3600	$610 – $3600
$3601 – $8500	$3601 – $8500	$3601 – $8500	$3601 – $8500
$8501 – $18000	$8501 – $18000	$8501 – $18000	$8501 – $18000
$18001 – $30000	$18001 – $30000	$18001 – $30000	$18001 – $30000

Figure 7.1
Sample of 120 cities, by size and income. Data compiled from world development indicators, national censuses, and author calculations.

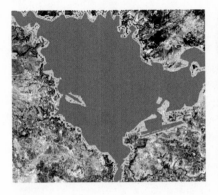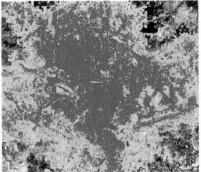

Figure 7.2
Addis Ababa, Ethiopia, January 5, 2000. *Left:* Urban land cover as portrayed in EarthSat's GeoCover Land Cover product. *Right:* Urban land cover as derived through computer-assisted processing of Landsat data. From Angel, Sheppard, and Civco (2005). Available at ⟨http://web.worldbank.org/⟩.

presence of open spaces within the urban areas that provide the potential for infill development. Further details concerning the remote sensing data and classification procedure are provided in Angel, Sheppard, and Civco (2005).

The remote sensing data provide measures of total urban land use at two points in time. These measures are then matched with population data for jurisdictional boundaries in each area, obtained from the Center for International Earth Science Information Network's Global Rural-Urban Mapping Project. Using growth rates observed for each jurisdiction from 1980 through 2000, I interpolate to obtain population estimates for the dates of each image. Similarly, national per capita gross domestic product (GDP) is interpolated to provide an estimate of income levels in each city at the date of the image. Data on biome type, availability of shallow groundwater aquifer, air transport links, national share of global IP address space, and the value of agricultural land (approximated by agricultural output per hectare) were obtained from world development indicators or from sources described more fully in Angel, Sheppard, and Civco (2005).

The data on terrorism and terrorist incidents come from the Memorial Institute for the Prevention of Terrorism Knowledgebase, which combines data from the RAND Terrorism Chronology and RAND-MIPT Terrorism Incident databases. These provide data from 1968 to the present on a variety of terrorist incidents, numbers of persons injured, and numbers of fatalities associated with each incident, categorized by country. The data are collected from open, publicly available sources, with information collected in an effort to capture all terrorist acts. Terrorism is defined as "violence, or the threat of violence, calculated to create an atmosphere of fear and alarm. These acts are designed to coerce others into actions they would not otherwise undertake, or refrain from actions they desired to take."

An argument could be made for seeking out (or collecting) data that would give information on the number of terrorist incidents in the individual cities themselves, and using this as an independent variable in the model. In addition to posing greater problems of endogeneity, using city-specific measures might significantly understate the climate of terror or atmosphere of fear and alarm that seems intrinsic to the problem of terrorism. Recent experience in both the United States and Britain, for example, suggests that individuals and organizations in cities far removed (and less significant) than the cities actually attacked still behave *as if* they were confronted by a serious risk of attack. Including the combined experience of the entire country may thus provide a better representation. Here, all terrorist incidents (or injuries or fatalities) that have occurred in the decade preceding the date of the image are summed and associated with measures of urban structure, population, income, and so on (see table 7.3).

Estimates of Terrorism Effects

The assembled data allow testing of several of the hypotheses related to urban structure and urban extent. Specifically, the cross-section data are used to estimate models to provide tests of hypotheses 1, 2, 4, 5, 7, 8, and 9. Table 7.4 presents the main model estimates (models 1, 2, and 3) as well as a series of intermediate specifications that provide insight into the robustness of parameter estimates to various specifications of the model.

All the models relate the logarithm of total urban cover (T_1 or T_2) with the logarithm of the variables (or value of dichotomous variables). There are three possible measures of terrorism that are available for use: the number of terrorist incidents, the number of injured persons in all terrorist incidents, and the number of fatalities. Each of these measures was tested using the data. Qualitatively, all performed similarly. The greater number of incidents and the much greater cross-sectional variation provided more precise estimates of the effect of incidents than of the effect of injuries or fatalities. The results reported

Table 7.3
Variables Used in Models

Variable	Mean	σ	Min	Max
Total urban land cover	402.805	635.114	8.92	4268.00
Population	3363025.000	4459765.000	93041.00	27200000.00
Income	9914.078	9916.698	609.88	35354.00
Terrorist incidents	52.608	88.276	1.00	622.00
Air linkages	108.208	133.390	0.00	659.00
IP share	0.058	0.163	0.00	0.59
Agricultural land value	3347.646	12569.780	68.84	150542.90
Fuel cost	0.620	0.357	0.02	1.56
Wage cost per km	0.245	0.301	0.01	1.73
East Asia	0.133	0.341	0	1
Europe	0.133	0.341	0	1
Latin America	0.133	0.341	0	1
North Africa	0.067	0.250	0	1
Other developed	0.133	0.341	0	1
South Central Asia	0.133	0.341	0	1
Southeast Asia	0.100	0.301	0	1
Sub-Saharan Africa	0.100	0.301	0	1
West Asia	0.067	0.250	0	1

here all use the number of incidents during the decade prior to the measurement of urban land cover as the measure of terrorism.

We also investigated using each of these measures on a per capita basis (number of incidents per person). Although this might serve as a better measure of risk to an individual, it is interesting to note that the per capita versions of these variables do not perform as well (either in terms of the precision of the parameter estimates or the fit of the overall model). In part, this is likely due to the logarithmic functional form and the fact that population is separately entered into the model. It may also be attributed to the particular way in which terrorism affects urban structure. Terrorist acts create a climate of terror that is translated into estimates of personal and commercial risk through interaction and social-psychological processes. This type of climate—just like other environmental factors—has the nature of a public good and is subject to little or no congestion. It therefore makes sense that the appropriate way to measure terrorism effects is to measure the total contribution toward creating this climate of terror rather than the per capita contribution.

Table 7.4
Model Estimates: Urban Structure and the Impact of Terrorism

	Total Urban Land Cover								
	Model 1	Model 2	Model 3	Model 4	Model 5	Model 6	Model 7	Model 8	Model 9
Population	0.5923***	0.4731***	0.7734***	0.7762***	0.774***	0.7656***	0.8135***	0.7926***	0.7677***
σ	0.093	0.114	0.063	0.065	0.064	0.065	0.032	0.036	0.04
Income	0.6737**	0.5114***	0.5134***	0.4959***	0.4957***	0.5124***	0.5161***	0.3447***	0.4964***
σ	0.277	0.071	0.065	0.068	0.068	0.069	0.069	0.078	0.057
Terrorist incidents	-0.2251***	-0.1861***	-0.0317	-0.0383	-0.0453	-0.0249	-0.0291	-0.0445	-0.0679**
σ	0.058	0.053	0.028	0.027	0.027	0.026	0.025	0.029	0.03
Air linkages	0.0947	0.1147*	-0.2094***	-0.2202***	-0.217***	-0.2446***	-0.2417***		
σ	0.064	0.063	0.038	0.038	0.037	0.038	0.04		
IP share	1.6991***	1.7226***	0.0335	0.0296	0.0273	0.038			
σ	0.508	0.459	0.045	0.045	0.045	0.046			
Agricultural land value	-0.235***	-0.1515***	1.1378***	1.3384***	1.3505***				
σ	0.061	0.035	0.349	0.336	0.356				
Fuel cost		-0.0199	-0.1204*						
σ		0.063	0.067						
Wage cost per km	-0.164								
σ	0.246								
Shallow ground water			0.119	0.1195					
σ			0.128	0.129					
East Asia			0.1443	0.1594	0.164	-0.0995	-0.1904	-0.7207***	
σ			0.222	0.229	0.235	0.247	0.224	0.263	
Regional Fixed Effects									

	(1)	(2)	(3)	(4)	(5)	(6)	(7)	(8)	(9)
Europe			0.028	0.0123	−0.0053	−0.3974***	−0.4031***	−0.4757**	
σ			0.15	0.148	0.156	0.136	0.135	0.183	
Latin America			−0.0706	−0.0397	−0.0233	−0.3804**	−0.3941**	−0.6743***	
σ			0.186	0.186	0.196	0.175	0.19	0.22	
North Africa			−0.0848	−0.0104	−0.0435	−0.4021	−0.4056	−0.8175**	
σ			0.301	0.286	0.286	0.282	0.293	0.315	
South Central Asia			−0.2306	−0.19	−0.2225	−0.5781**	−0.6457***	−0.9489***	
σ			0.229	0.247	0.253	0.246	0.235	0.299	
Southeast Asia			−0.1234	−0.0579	−0.0654	−0.3961	−0.4382*	−0.9505***	
σ			0.23	0.235	0.247	0.244	0.247	0.274	
Sub-Saharan Africa			0.3375	0.3161	0.3446	−0.0073	0.0006	−0.2439	
σ			0.206	0.217	0.223	0.208	0.212	0.284	
West Asia			0.42*	0.4532**	0.4194*	0.0678	0.0539	−0.402*	
σ			0.216	0.227	0.225	0.222	0.228	0.239	
Constant	−7.588**	−4.9061***	−9.0663***	−8.7964***	−8.7244***	−8.2869***	−8.8601***	−8.4225***	−9.8926***
σ	3.001	1.571	1.033	1.03	1.011	1	0.736	0.908	0.792
Observations	198	240	240	240	240	240	240	240	240
F	44.84	36.82	72.81	75.42	84.02	77.52	83.27	58.24	155.02
R^2	0.7652	0.7586	0.8461	0.8429	0.8417	0.8362	0.8346	0.8005	0.7536
Anderson LR	23.331	21.999							
Anderson LR P-value	0.1052	0.232							
Hansen J	11.712	12.791							
Hansen J P-value	0.7007	0.7501							
Cragg-Donald	24.76	23.04							
Cragg-Donald P-value	0.0741	0.1891							

Note: All models estimated with robust standard errors, clustered by city. Levels of significance: ***, 1% level or better; **, 5% level; *, 10% level.

Models 3–9 are standard OLS estimates. Model 9 provides the simplest possible model, expressing total urban land cover as a function of population, income, and level of terrorism. Model 8 adds controls for regions of the world, having as a component the "other developed countries" region that includes the United States, Canada, Japan, Australia, and New Zealand. Models 7 and 6 add controls for the extent to which the city is linked to the global economy and hence may experience an effective increase in the world price for its export good or an increase in the productivity of land for production of the export good. This linkage is measured by using the number of air linkages (the number of direct flights to airports out of the country from the municipal airport) and the share of global IP addresses assigned to Internet users in the country. Model 5 adds a control for the value of agricultural land surrounding the city (measured by the value added in agriculture per hectare of arable land). Model 4 adds a control for the productivity of land in providing housing services by having an indicator for the presence of shallow aquifers that permit the easy construction of wells for water and permit house building that is unbound from the constraints of water supply infrastructure. Model 3 adds a control for the effect of travel costs as measured by the price (in PPP constant dollars) of refined motor fuel.

A central concern that confronts any attempt to estimate the determinants of urban land use using cross-section data is the problem of endogeneity. Variables such as population, income, the number of air linkages, and terrorist incidents may all affect total urban land use, but they will also be affected by the level of urban land cover. If a city has, for some random reason, a large positive shock to its total stock of built-up urban space, the space may serve to attract new residents, create new income-earning opportunities, justify improved air service, and provide attractive targets to terrorists. To the extent that this is true, there is correlation between the independent variables and the regression error, resulting in biased and inconsistent estimates.

Models 1 and 2 address this concern by providing instrumental variables in estimates of the model, taking all the model variables except the region indicators used to correct for fixed effects as endogenous. In addition to the included region instruments, other instruments used are latitude and longitude, the slope of the land, and the biome (an indicator of the type of flora and fauna that inhabit the natural surroundings where the city is located).

The data and the models are sufficient to provide direct tests of hypotheses 1, 2, 3, 4, and 9, and (subject to interpretation) tests of hypotheses 5, 7, and 8. Analysis of hypothesis 6, concerning the effects of transport costs and the share of land available for residential development, respectively, is not discussed here but is dealt with in Angel, Sheppard, and Civco (2005). Testing of hypothesis 10 (that terrorism flattens the density gradient) is not discussed here.

Regarding the confirmation of the implications of the models, the first thing to note is that the models perform very well. A relatively large share of the cross-sectional variance in urban expansion and the amount of land in urban use is explained by these models. Furthermore, the parameters are estimated with high precision. Most of the estimates are significant at the 10 percent level or better, and in the more complete specifications all the key variables are correctly signed and comfortably significant.

Every model estimated has correctly signed and precisely estimated effects for population and income. There is unambiguous support for hypotheses 1 and 2. Every model that includes the value of agricultural land provides a parameter estimate that is also significant and signed as would be predicted by hypothesis 4.

Hypothesis 5 asserts that an increase in the productivity of land in production of housing should increase the amount of land in urban use. The effect of available groundwater provides an indirect or partial test of this assertion because in settings with shallow aquifers housing can be constructed without the added cost of providing piped water. A result of this kind has been found in the case of North America by Burchfeld et al. (2003). The present analysis provides only partial support for this, with parameter values in models 3 and 4 being qualitatively as expected but not statistically significant.

Hypotheses 7 and 8 relate to the productivity of land in producing the export good in the city, and the effect of world demand for the output of producers in the city. The connectedness of producers in the city (via air transport and the Internet) can be interpreted as indicative of both of these. The effect of both is correctly signed in all models where they are included. Interestingly, in the OLS models the effect of air linkages is statistically significant, whereas the effect of IP share often is not. In models 1 and 2, where endogeneity is accounted for using IV estimates, the IP share greatly increases in importance and is significant, whereas the air linkages, although still of the expected sign, are estimated with less precision.

What about the central question: the effects of terrorism on urban structure? The empirical analysis provides clear evidence, particularly in models 1 and 2, that terrorism reduces urban land use. This almost certainly implies reduced investment in residential capital and very likely implies reduced investment in productive capital. This is consistent with hypothesis 9 and provides support for the models I discussed.

It is interesting to note that models 1 and 2, estimated using instrumental variables, show a much larger effect of terrorism than the other models. This suggests some endogeneity in the level of terrorism to which a city is subject, which is not at all surprising. Correcting for this to the extent allowed by our instruments reveals a startling fact: doubling the amount of terrorist incidents is associated, *ceteris paribus*, with an 18–22 percent decline in urban land cover. Apparently a decade of terrorist attacks is a powerful deterrent to urban investment. It should be noted that this effect becomes clear after adjusting for population and income. In that sense, the analysis here is most directly linked to the model of Rossi-Hansberg (2004) and provides some empirical basis for further consideration of the policy prescription he derives.

Conclusion

The analysis has provided strong empirical support both for general predictions of urban models and for specific predictions concerning the effects of ongoing terrorism. Contrary to what is sometimes asserted, or what is inferred from urban reconstruction after traditional warfare, terrorism effects appear to be large. A doubling in the number of terrorist incidents (which is not uncommon) is associated with at least a 3–6 reduction in development of land for urban purposes and perhaps as much as a 22% reduction in such development after accounting for the feedback between city size and terrorism.

These effects are noted after accounting for population, income, and a variety of other relevant variables. Terrorism may indeed reduce the population in vulnerable cities (as suggested, for example, by the Harrigan and Martin models), but aside from this, terrorism has affects urban structure and the investment that creates the built environment. This shows up clearly in the cross-sectional data used for this study.

The analysis provides at least tentative support for the models of Rossi-Hansberg (2004) and Harrigan and Martin (2002) and for the idea that terrorism should be regarded as a type of tax on urban producers and residents. Such taxes can cause distortion, and there may be a useful role for public policy to be designed to correct these distortions and improve economic efficiency.

It was noted that the measurement of urban land use was undertaken so as to clearly identify unbuilt land in the interior of the urban area. This measurement is not yet complete, but this capability of the data will eventually provide for the possibility of testing hypothesis 10, concerning the effects of terrorism on the range of densities of investment in the urban area. Higher levels of terrorism should be associated with relatively more new development at the urban periphery and relatively less new development in the open areas within the interior of the city.

We are left with a tentative conclusion: terrorism appears to have significant effects on urban structure. The theoretical models with which the data are consistent also suggest that public policy can play a useful role in correcting the distortions caused by this tactic of political struggle.

Notes

Thanks to Brock Blomberg for stimulating conversation on this topic and for bringing data sources to my attention, and to Greg Hess, without whose encouragement this chapter would not have been written. The support of World Bank Research Committee and U.S. National Science Foundation grant SES-0433278 and the assistance of my co-principal investigators, Shlomo Angel and Dan Civco, in acquiring the data on urban expansion are gratefully acknowledged.

1. See, *inter alia*, Mills (1972); Henderson (1977); or Brueckner (1987). I use their notation and basic approach in this chapter.

References

Ambrose, S. 2001. Beware the fury of an aroused democracy. *Wall Street Journal*, October 1, A24.

Angel, S., S. Sheppard, and D. Civco. 2005. *The Dynamics of Global Urban Expansion.* Washington, D.C.: World Bank.

Brueckner, J. 1987. The structure of urban equilibria. In *Handbook of Regional and Urban Economics*, ed. E. Mills. New York: Elsevier.

Burchfeld, M., H. G. Overman, D. Puga, and M. A. Turner. 2006. Causes of sprawl: A portrait from space. *Quarterly Journal of Economics* 121 (2): 587–633.

Davis, D. R., and D. E. Weinstein. 2002. Bones, bombs and break points: The geography of economic activity. *American Economic Review* 92: 1269–1289.

Glaeser, E., and J. Shapiro. 2002. Cities and warfare: The impact of terrorism on urban form. *Journal of Urban Economics* 51: 205–224.

Harrigan, J., and P. Martin. 2002. Terrorism and the resilience of cities. *Federal Reserve Board of New York Economic Policy Review* 8 (2): 97–116.

Henderson, J. V. 1977. *Economic Theory and the Cities.* New York: Academic Press.

Krugman, P. 1991. *Geography and Trade.* Cambridge, Mass.: MIT Press.

Lucas, R. E. 2001. Externalities and cities. *Review of Economic Dynamics* 4: 245–274.

Lucas, R. E., and E. Rossi-Hansberg. 2002. On the internal structure of cities. *Econometrica* 70: 1445–1476.

Mills, E. 1972. *Studies in the Structure of the Urban Economy.* Baltimore: Johns Hopkins University Press.

Rossi-Hansberg, E. 2004. Cities under stress. *Journal of Monetary Economics* 51: 903–927.

Seager, A., C. Moore, and H. Long. 2005. Economy expected to hold fast: Amid fears for consumer confidence, it seems Britain can absorb such shocks. *The Guardian*, July 19.

III   The Costs of Warfare

8 War in Iraq versus Containment

Steven J. Davis, Kevin M. Murphy, and Robert H. Topel

Prior to the invasion of Iraq in March 2003, the United States, Britain, and their allies pursued a policy of containment authorized by the United Nations Security Council. Major elements of the policy included economic sanctions on Iraq, disarmament requirements, weapons inspections, Northern and Southern no-fly zones within Iraq, and maritime interdiction to enforce trade restrictions. Continued containment was the leading option to war and forcible regime change. We analyze these two policy options, war and containment, with attention to three questions. In terms of military resources, casualties, and expenditures for humanitarian assistance and reconstruction, is war more or less costly for the United States than a policy of continued containment? Compared to war and forcible regime change, would a continuation of the containment policy have saved Iraqi lives? And, is war likely to bring about an improvement or deterioration in the economic well-being of Iraqis? Our attention to these questions reflects strong and vocal concerns—before and after March 2003—about the costs of war, the loss of life in the event of war, and the longer-term effects of war on Iraqi society.

Our study is a revised and expanded version of an analytical essay that we circulated shortly before the March 2003 invasion.[1] Although the decision point for the Iraq invasion is past, we largely retain the *ex ante* perspective of our earlier essay. That is, we premise the analysis on data and facts that were known, or reasonably knowable, as of early 2003. This perspective is the one that confronts decision makers faced with the question of how to deal with "tyrants, rogue states and terrorists who threaten not only their own people but also others." In this regard, one of our goals is to show how basic economic principles and a quantitative approach can inform analyses of national security and humanitarian concerns presented by rogue states.

Several important issues pertaining to the Iraq intervention are beyond the scope of our study. For example, we do not consider whether the prewar containment policy could have been reformulated to achieve its main objectives with less harm to the Iraqi population. Nor do we evaluate the conduct of the war and ensuing occupation. Other important issues outside the scope of our analysis include the impact of war on oil prices, the broader costs and benefits of nation building in Iraq, the effects of military intervention in Iraq on other rogue states and on weapons proliferation, the war's effects on attitudes toward the United States in the rest of the world, and the implications of the war for U.S. relations with other nations. These issues merit careful attention, but we do not address them here.

In making the case for war, the U.S. and U.K. governments stressed threats posed by Iraqi weapons of mass destruction (WMD), i.e., long-range ballistic missiles and chemical, biological, and nuclear weapons. As it turns out, no large WMD arsenals were discovered in Iraq after the March 2003 invasion. This development undercut the case for war in the views of many and diminished the credibility of the U.S. and U.K. governments and their intelligence agencies. Our analysis, however, does not turn on the issue of whether Iraq possessed large WMD stockpiles prior to the 2003 invasion. Instead, we initially proceed under the assumption that containment was, and would remain, fully effective in preventing Iraq from using WMDs against the United States, its allies, and their interests. This assumption serves to focus attention on the relative costs of the two policy options. We also extend our analysis to consider several costly contingencies that might arise under a continuation of the containment policy.

Several other studies assess the economic consequences of the Iraq conflict. Nordhaus (2002) projects the costs of military spending, occupation, humanitarian assistance and reconstruction. He also considers the potential effects of war on oil markets and the U.S. economy. McKibbin and Stoeckel (2003) consider war-induced effects of potentially higher oil prices and greater uncertainty on macroeconomic outcomes in the world economy. Wallsten and Kosec (2005) take up some of the same questions as our study, but from an *ex post* rather than *ex ante* perspective. We rely on their study in assessing the cost of U.S. military casualties resulting from war in Iraq. Another recent study by Bilmes and Stiglitz (2006) estimates a variety of direct and indirect costs of the Iraq war. Several reports by the U.S. Congressional Budget Office and other government agencies address the budgetary consequences of the Iraq war. We draw heavily on these reports in constructing our projections for the economic costs of war and containment.[2] Our study differs from previous work in many respects, large and small, but perhaps the most significant difference is our systematic evaluation of the two leading policy options on the table prior to the Iraq war.

We proceed as follows. Section 8.1 considers the U.S. military resources required to carry out a policy of containment, the economic cost of those resources, and the likely duration of a hostile Iraqi regime under containment. Section 8.2 considers projected U.S. costs of war in Iraq including the costs related to postwar occupation, fatalities and injuries sustained by U.S. military personnel, humanitarian assistance and reconstruction aid. Section 8.3 draws on the inputs developed in sections 8.1 and 8.2 to calculate and compare U.S. costs of war and containment in present value terms. Section 8.4 extends the cost analysis to consider concerns related to the sustainability and effectiveness of containment and the effect of the war on the likelihood of major terrorist attacks on the United States. Section 8.5 builds a simple model to gauge the economic welfare of Iraqis under the containment and war options. We calibrate the model based on the economic record of the Saddam Hussein regime and assumptions about the duration of the regime under containment, the impact of war on Iraq's economy, and the path of economic development after regime change. Section 8.6 considers the issue of lost Iraqi lives, and section 8.7 concludes. Section 8.8 contains an afterword dated March 2008.

8.1 U.S. Military Resources and Costs under Containment

The military aspects of the containment policy were undertaken principally by U.S. and British forces.[3] Our analysis restricts attention to the size and cost of the U.S. military forces engaged in the containment of Iraq, but we would welcome a comparable analysis for Britain and other countries.

Baseline Case

Military Resources In September 2000, General Tommy R. Franks testified before the U.S. Senate Committee on Armed Services as follows: "By maintaining a significant forward presence in the region, the U.S. seeks to deter and, if need be, to defeat Iraqi aggression. To this end, at any given time, some 30 naval vessels, 175 military aircraft, and 17,000–25,000 soldiers, sailors, airmen and Marines are in the CENT-COM AOR [Area of Responsibility]."[4] In his testimony, Franks makes clear that EUCOM, which encompasses Turkey in its AOR, also played a key role in containing Iraq, particularly in the enforcement of the Northern no-fly zone. On this basis, we use a figure of 200 military aircraft devoted to Iraqi containment at the time of General Franks's testimony in 2000. His testimony also refers to a Maritime Interdiction Force, composed of naval vessels from the United States and seven other countries, charged with enforcing UN sanctions and restricting Iraqi exports and imports. Franks does not provide figures for the military resources devoted to Iraqi containment under EUCOM or the Maritime Interdiction Force, but it is clear that his figures for troops, aircraft, and naval vessels in the CENTCOM AOR constitute only a partial inventory of the full military resources deployed to contain Iraq.

A Department of Defense document on fiscal year (FY) 2001 budget requests for U.S. military operations in Bosnia, Kosovo, Southwest Asia, and East Timor provides more precise information about the troops devoted to containment.[5] For operations in Southwest Asia directed toward the containment and deterrence of Iraq, the document lists "troop strength" levels (including Guard and Reserve troops) of 3,550 for Army Requirements, 15,691 for Navy Requirements, 426 for Marine Corps Requirements, 8,457 for Air Force Requirements, and 40 for Defense Health Program Requirements, for a total of 28,164 troops. The document also shows expenditures for Southwest Asia under Defense-Wide Requirements but does not list troops in this category. Presumably, the U.S. also undertook other surveillance and intelligence-gathering activities to contain Iraq (including CIA and State Department activities) that are not reflected in the document.

These sources make clear that containment required a potent U.S. military presence in the Southwest Asia region, including many personnel and large amounts of military hardware. In short, the United States devoted roughly 28,000 troops, 30 ships (including a carrier battle group), and about 200 aircraft and other equipment to containment efforts prior to the prewar build-up. The next step in the analysis is to estimate the economic costs of these military resources. We are not aware of reports by the Department of Defense or other sources that provide economic cost figures for the full complement of military resources devoted to the containment of Iraq, so we construct our own cost estimates. We develop two methods that differ somewhat with respect to data requirements and underlying assumptions.

Cost Calculations: Method 1   Our first method calculates the economic cost of military resources devoted to containment as the sum of labor costs, capital costs, and the cost of expended munitions. Consider labor costs. In September 2002, the U.S. Congressional Budget Office (CBO) issued a document on the "Estimated Costs of a Potential Conflict with Iraq."[6] Based on the experience of U.S. Army peacekeepers in Bosnia and Kosovo, the document assigns costs of $226,000 per person/year for troops deployed in a prospective postwar occupation of Iraq.[7] We adopt this figure in calculating the labor costs of the military resources deployed in the containment of Iraq. We interpret the figure as capturing costs for compensation, personnel transport, and personnel support. We calculate capital costs and expenditures for munitions separately.

For our purposes, the CBO figure for labor costs has some problematic aspects. First, it appears to include certain capital costs such as spare parts for the operation and maintenance of equipment in theater. Second, and cutting the other way, it omits a large chunk of personnel costs, because CBO accounting practices do not include the basic pay of active-duty military personnel engaged in an overseas operation as part of the operation's cost.[8] This large omission is on the order of $40,000–$50,000 per person/year by our estimates.[9] The CBO figure also omits the cost of military personnel who support the operation but are stationed outside the theater of operations. Finally, the CBO figure does not include the costs of compensating, supporting, and training the additional troops who rotate through the theater of operations over time. These costs are large, because the number of troops required to sustain a long-term overseas operation is at least three times larger than the force in theater at a point in time.[10]

On net, the full economic cost of the personnel resources (including personnel support and transport) required to carry out the containment policy is probably larger than $226,000 per person/year. Nevertheless, we adopt this figure in constructing our first estimate for the cost of containment. To facilitate a consistent cost comparison between policy options, we use the same figure for personnel-related costs when estimating the economic cost of a postwar occupation of Iraq.

Multiplying $226,000 per person/year by 28,164 military personnel in theater yields annual labor costs of $6.4 billion for the containment policy.

To estimate the capital value of the ships, planes, and other military equipment engaged in the containment of Iraq, we rely on another document produced by the U.S. Congressional Budget Office, titled "Budgeting for Naval Forces."[11] According to this document, the CBO estimates that the average shipbuilding rate needed to maintain a 300-ship Navy is 8.5 ships per year at a cost of $10.8 billion, which implies that the capital value of 30 "average" ships is $38.1 billion. The same document estimates annual construction costs for 148 aircraft at $10.2 billion, so the capital value of 200 "average" aircraft is about $15.3 billion.[12] In our calculations we scale up these figures for ships and aircraft by 6 percent to express them in 2003 dollars.[13] In addition, we estimate that Army, Marines, and Air Force ground units required an additional $1.5 billion in military equipment in theater to carry out the containment policy.[14]

The next step is to estimate the annual costs of these capital inputs—depreciation, maintenance, fuel and other operating expenses, and the government's opportunity cost of funds tied up in capital goods. Table 8.1 provides estimates for the depreciation, maintenance, and operating costs of military equipment. Line 1 reports straight-line depreciation rates calculated from projected equipment lifetimes. Line 2 reports estimated operations and maintenance (O&M) spending on military equipment in peacetime use, expressed as a percentage of capital value. This category captures the costs of fuel, parts, and depot maintenance for military equipment at a peacetime operations tempo. To derive the estimates in line 2, we rely on the steady-state assumption that the ratio of O&M spending on military equipment to procurement spending for new capital goods is constant over time. We also assume that this ratio is the same for all types of military equipment.[15] Applying these assumptions to data on military spending in CBO (2001) yields the O&M spending rates in line 2. Actual O&M spending rates are higher for military equipment stationed in theater because of a higher operations tempo. Line 3 draws on CBO (2005b) estimates of the extra depreciation and maintenance costs incurred by in-theater military equipment in Iraq, Kuwait, and Afghanistan to illustrate the impact of a higher operations tempo. Summing the entries in lines 1–3 yields annual depreciation, maintenance, and operating costs of

Table 8.1
Annual User Costs of Capital for U.S. Military Equipment (as percent of capital value)

	Army Equipment	Marines Equipment	Air Force Aircraft	Navy Aircraft	Navy Ships
A. Estimated Rates of Depreciation, Operations, and Maintenance Costs					
1. Straight-line depreciation[a]	4.5	4.4	2.5–3.3	3.7	2.8
2. Normal rate of operations and maintenance spending in peacetime use (incl. Fuel)[b,c]	1.7	1.7	1.0–1.3	1.4	1.1
3. Extra depreciation and maintenance costs for in-theater equipment (excl. fuel)[d]	16.9	14.3	0.6–0.8	0.5	0.5
4. Sum of lines 1, 2, and 3	23.1	20.5	4.0–5.4	5.6	4.4
B. Cost of Capital: Containment					
5. Sum of depreciation, maintenance, and operations costs applied to the containment policy[e]	12.0	12.0	7.0	7.0	5.5
6. Opportunity cost of capital[f]	2.0	2.0	2.0	2.0	2.0
7. Real user cost of capital applied to the containment policy: sum of lines 5 and 6	14.0	14.0	9.0	9.0	7.5
C. Additional Capital Cost: War					
8. Prewar build-up and postwar redeployment[g,h]	6.5+	6.5+	6.8+	6.8+	5.6+
9. Major combat phase[g,i]	22.2+	22.2+	7.3+	7.3+	6.1+
D. Cost of Capital: Occupation					
10. Postwar occupation, no major insurgency[j]	16.0	16.0	8.0	8.0	7.5
11. Postwar occupation, major insurgency[j]	24.0	24.0	9.0	9.0	7.5

Source: Authors' calculations based on data in CBO (2000; 2001; 2005b, tables 2–5).
Notes:
a. Except for Navy ships, straight-line depreciation rates in line 1 are based on equipment lifetimes reported in CBO (2005b). The figures are value-weighted means over different types of equipment. The straight-line depreciation rate for Navy ships is calculated as (8.5/300) based on the annual shipbuilding rate needed to sustain a 300-ship Navy, as reported in CBO (2000).
b. According to CBO (2001, 5): "[Operations and maintenance] spending for equipment includes the costs of the parts and fuel used by military units, as well as the costs incurred in maintaining equipment at large centralized maintenance facilities called depots. Parts include what are termed 'consumables,' such as washers, filters, and gaskets, and 'depot-level reparables' (DLRs), such as spare parts, avionics, and engine components.

Table 8.1
(continued)

Major overhauls at depots, which are public (DoD) or private (contractor) repair facilities, involve major inspection and repair of weapon systems; the costs for them include both material and civilian labor costs. The cost of military personnel engaged in operating and maintaining the equipment are not included in O&M spending."

c. Data from CBO (2001, 1, fig. 1) indicate that operations and maintenance (O&M) spending on capital goods accounts for 7.4% of defense expenditures, which amounts to 39% of procurement spending. Applying the steady-state assumption yields an O&M spending rate equal to 39% of straight-line depreciation costs. Assuming that the ratio of O&M spending on capital goods to straight-line depreciation costs is the same for all types of military equipment yields the entries in line 2.

d. The extra rate of depreciation and maintenance in line 3 is calculated as the increase in annual depreciation for in-theater equipment divided by the value of the equipment as reported in CBO (2005b). These estimates are based on U.S. experience in Iraq, Kuwait, and Afghanistan in recent years. For Army and Marines equipment, the extra rate of depreciation includes an annual 2 percent loss rate for in-theater equipment. For Navy ships, we assume that the extra rate of annual depreciation and maintenance amounts to 0.5% of the capital value. Depreciation rates for Army and Marines equipment are much higher in theater because the equipment is used much more intensively. For example, miles per truck in theater are ten times as high as in peacetime use. Note that line 3 does not capture extra fuel costs due to a higher operations tempo for in-theater military equipment.

e. Line 5 reports our figure for the sum of depreciation, maintenance and operations costs for the military equipment devoted to containment. For Army and Marines equipment (mostly ground equipment), we use a much lower figure than in line 3 because the operating tempo of ground equipment under containment is lower than the one reflected in lines 3 and 4.

f. The opportunity cost of capital in line 6 reflects a real interest rate on government debt of 2 percent (see "Valuing the Policy Options" in section 3).

g. Lines 8 and 9 report additional user costs of capital that we apply to military equipment deployed in an Iraq war over and above the costs for operations support projected by the CBO (2002). That is, the entries in lines 8 and 9 are not intended to capture the full user cost of capital in an Iraq war. Rather, they capture the portion that, in our judgment (based principally on other CBO sources), is missing from the prewar projections in CBO (2002).

h. For Army and Marines (ground) equipment, line 8 is the sum of straight-line depreciation in line 1 and the opportunity cost of capital in line 6. For aircraft and ships, we also add the normal rate of operations and maintenance spending in line 2 less 0.3 percentage points for fuel usage during peacetime operations.

i. For Army and Marines (ground) equipment, line 9 is a weighted average of the Army and Marines entries in line 4 less 0.3 percentage points for fuel usage during peacetime operations. We weight the Army entry three times as heavily as the Marines entry. For aircraft and ships, line 9 is the sum of lines 4 and 6 less 0.3 percentage points for fuel usage during peacetime operations.

j. The real user cost of capital in lines 10 and 11 are educated guesses based on adjustments to line 4 for fuel consumption and operations tempo. These numbers include 2 percentage points for the opportunity cost of capital.

roughly 4.5–5.5 percent of capital value for aircraft and naval vessels and more than 20 percent for ground equipment. These figures, reported in line 4, do not capture the extra fuel costs associated with a higher operations tempo for equipment in theater.

Table 8.1, line 5, reports the rate of depreciation, maintenance, and operating costs that we apply to military equipment used in the containment policy. For Army and Marines equipment (mostly ground equipment), we use a much lower figure than in line 3 based on the view that containment involved a much lower operations tempo for such equipment than engagements in Iraq, Kuwait, and Afghanistan. For naval vessels and aircraft, we adjust the line 3 entries upward to account for the missing extra fuel consumption. To account for the opportunity cost of government funds, line 6 adds 2 percentage points, which is consistent with the evidence that the U.S. government faces a 2 percent real interest rate.

We now have in place the required elements for our first method of calculating the economic cost of the military resources devoted to the containment policy. Table 8.2, panel A summarizes the calculations. Applying the real user cost of capital inputs from table 8.1, line 8, to the capital asset values just derived yields capital costs of $4.7 billion per year. Adding $6.4 billion for labor costs and $0.2 billion per year for expended munitions yields total containment costs of about $11.3 billion per year.[16]

Cost Calculations: Method 2   As a check on this cost figure, consider a simpler set of calculations that relies on different inputs and assumptions. First, CBO (2000, table 5) provides a figure of $94.7 billion as the annual cost of maintaining a 300-ship navy (excluding $10.3 billion for research and development). This figure encompasses procurement costs, operating costs, personnel costs, military construction, and other items. The implied all-in cost for an average 30-ship naval force is about $9.5 billion per year, or $10.0 billion in 2003 dollars. Second, recall that naval forces (including Marines) account for 16,117 out of 28,164 military personnel devoted to the containment of Iraq. Multiplying $10 billion by (28,164/16,117) yields $17.5 billion per year as the implied cost of containing Iraq.

This calculation does not adjust for differences in labor intensity among the armed services. Defense budget figures for FY 2001 imply that military personnel account for 24.4 percent of total costs in the Air

Table 8.2
Annual Costs of U.S. Military Resources Devoted to Containment, Summary of Calculations

A. Summary of Cost Calculations: Method 1

	Ground Equipment	Aircraft	Naval Vessels
Capital value (billions of 2003 $)	1.5	16.2	40.4
Real user cost of capital (% per year; table 8.1, line 8)	14.0	9.0	7.5
Annual capital costs ($ billions)	0.21	1.46	3.03
No. of military personnel in theater			28,164
Annual cost per person (thousands of 2003 $)			226
Annual labor costs (billions of 2003 $)			6.37
Annual cost of expended munitions (billions of 2003 $)			0.2
Capital, labor, and munitions costs (billions of 2003 $)			11.26

B. Summary of Cost Calculations: Method 2

	Navy (30 ships)	Air Force	Army	All Forces
No. of military personnel in theater	16,117	8,457	3,590	
All-in costs per person/year (2003 $)	620,463	734,893	443,846	
Total costs (billions of 2003 $)	10.0	6.21	1.59	17.81

C. Annual Containment Cost Figures Used in Policy Comparison

Baseline case: average of method 1 and method 2 costs	14.54
Higher costs, to account for extra forces; one-third higher than baseline case	19.38
Lower costs, to account for dual-use nature of deployment; one-third lower than baseline case	9.69

Sources: CBO (2000; 2002) and authors' calculations using data, estimates, and assumptions described in text and table 8.1.

Force, 40.4 percent in the Army, and 28.9 percent in the Navy.[17] To adjust for these differences, think of the Air Force, Army, and Navy as three different technologies for producing "military output," and assume that the value of military output per dollar of expenditure is the same across the three services. This condition must hold on the margin if Department of Defense funds are allocated efficiently among the services. Next, divide the all-in cost estimate for the U.S. naval force devoted to the containment of Iraq ($10 billion) by the number of naval personnel (16,117). This calculation yields an all-in annual cost per person for U.S. naval forces devoted to containment of $620,463. Given this figure, and using the data on labor cost shares and number of military personnel devoted to Iraq by service, we have

$620,463[(28.9/24.4)8,457 + (28.9/40.4)3,590 + 16,117] = \$17.8$ billion

as the estimated annual cost of containing Iraq.[18]

This figure is substantially larger than the \$11.3 billion figure calculated using method 1. In the absence of a compelling reason to prefer one estimate over the other, we adopt the simple average of \$14.5 billion in 2003 dollars as our baseline figure for the estimated annual costs of containment. By way of comparison, outlays by the U.S. Department of Defense were \$344 billion in fiscal year 2002.[19] So \$14.5 billion for the containment of Iraq amounts to about 4.2 percent of the prewar U.S. defense budget.

Higher Containment Costs

One might reasonably argue that the \$14.5 billion figure is too small for at least two reasons. First, containment efforts also drew on U.S. military resources that were stationed outside the Southwest Asia region or that were stationed in the region only on an occasional basis for particular operations. These additional military resources helped to deter Iraq and to support and execute particular operations, but their costs are not included in the \$14.5 billion figure. A noteworthy example is Operation Desert Fox, a four-day bombing campaign carried out by U.S. and British forces against Iraqi targets in December 1998. The execution of Desert Fox relied heavily on out-of-area military resources and military resources temporarily deployed to the Middle East.[20] As we discuss in section 8.4, the United States also undertook large additional force deployments to the Persian Gulf region in 1994 and 1996 to deter Iraqi aggression against other states.

Second, containment efforts in 2000 and 2001 involved a level of military pressure that was insufficient to compel Iraq's full compliance with UN Security Council resolutions. Prior to the prewar build-up of U.S. and British forces, Iraq had for several years refused to admit UN weapons inspectors.[21] Iraq had a long history of stalling, evading, undermining, and circumventing the UN weapons inspection process (Pollack 2002, ch. 3), an essential element of the containment policy.[22] Even on the brink of war, Iraq continued to resist and impede UN weapons inspections, often with considerable success.[23] Given this history of continual resistance to inspection and limited disarmament by the Saddam Hussein regime, an effective containment policy apparently required a larger commitment of U.S. military resources and a more aggressive posture by U.S. forces. That is, a fully effective containment policy would have cost substantially more than $14.5 billion per year.

It is not obvious how best to adjust for the incomplete effectiveness of the containment policy. It is also difficult to quantify the cost of the out-of-area military resources that contributed to containment efforts and that provided a deterrent to Iraqi aggression. As a crude adjustment for these factors, we consider a higher containment cost figure of $19.4 billion, which is one-third greater than our baseline figure. Section 8.4 develops an alternative approach to concerns about the containment policy.

Dual-Use Military Deployment

Another criticism of our containment cost calculations cuts the other way. The military resources that the United States devoted to Iraqi containment prior to March 2003 projected U.S. power in the region and functioned as forward bases in a critical and volatile part of the world. Hence, a friendlier Iraqi regime would only mitigate, not obviate, the need for the deployment of U.S. military resources to the region. According to this argument, some portion of the calculated costs is not fully attributable to the policy of containing Iraqi.[24] This argument is logically sound, but its quantitative force is unclear. On the one hand, the United States had no major military bases and few ground forces in the Middle East prior to the Iraqi invasion of Kuwait in August 1990.[25] This fact suggests that few U.S. ground forces would be stationed in the Middle East if Iraq were governed by a stable, unthreatening regime. On the other hand, U.S. military bases in southern Turkey and a strong naval presence near the Middle East were significant features of U.S. policy long before the invasion of Kuwait. As a crude adjustment for the dual-use character of U.S. military resources deployed in the containment of Iraq, we consider a lower containment cost figure of $9.7 billion, which is one-third smaller than our baseline figure.

Spontaneous Regime Change

Containment is necessary only so long as a dangerous regime, or a like-minded successor, remains in power. So our calculation of containment costs should account for the possibility that the prewar Iraqi regime would peacefully evolve into a far less dangerous one. It is hard to precisely assess the probable duration of a dangerous Iraqi regime, absent war, but history offers some guidance.[26] The regime of Saddam

Hussein survived a devastating war with Iran in the 1980s, a crushing military defeat in the Gulf War of 1991, twelve years of draconian sanctions, and a tremendous decline in living standards during the war with Iran and again in the 1990s under containment. These facts suggest that the regime was hard to dislodge under a policy of containment. Other highly repressive regimes, such as Cuba and North Korea, also show much staying power.

The key issue is not how long Saddam Hussein himself would continue to rule Iraq, absent external intervention. Rather, the real issue is the expected duration of a regime that presents a similar threat to the United States and others. The experience of North Korea provides a case in point. When the North Korean leader Kim Il-sung died in 1994, many doubted the ability of his son and designated successor, Kim Jong-il, to secure the reins of power. Those doubts turned out to be misplaced, and the regime continued in essentially the same repressive and hostile form. Moreover, North Korea under Kim Jong-il continued to advance its nuclear weapons program and its long-range missile delivery systems.[27] In the case of Iraq, expert accounts suggest that Saddam's sons had a firm grip on the apparatus of terror, repression, and security prior to the March 2003 invasion. Pollack (2002, ch. 4) indicates that Saddam's sons, especially Qusay, were well positioned to continue in their father's place after his death. Pollack's account also stresses that much of the regime's leadership was closely linked to Saddam by ties of family and clan. In sum, it does not appear that the continuity of the regime rested on the personal survival of Saddam Hussein.

In this light, consider an optimistic scenario in which the prewar Iraqi regime peacefully morphs from malign to benign at an annual hazard rate of 3 percent. This assumption implies an expected duration for a hostile regime, absent external intervention, of 33 years beyond March 2003. If one dates the onset of a dangerous Iraqi regime to Saddam's assumption of the presidency in 1979, then the 3 percent hazard rate implies an expected total duration for the regime of about 57 years.[28] In comparison, the Soviet Union survived 69 years after its founding in 1922 until its dissolution in 1991, including more than four decades under a policy of containment by the West. The containment of North Korea has involved a large U.S. military presence on the Korean Peninsula for more than 50 years.[29] These historical facts are consistent with our assumption of a 3 percent hazard rate for peaceful regime change in Iraq.[30]

8.2   U.S. Military, Reconstruction, and Humanitarian Costs under War

Incremental Appropriations versus Economic Costs

News reports and commentary on the economic costs of the Iraq war typically focus on incremental appropriations in government budgets. In September 2002, for example, the Democratic staff of the House Budget Committee (HBC) issued a report that projected a new war in Iraq would increase U.S. budget costs by $47 billion to $93 billion for military operations alone, not counting the costs of an extended occupation. A report issued by the U.S. Congressional Budget Office in the same month reached similar conclusions.[31] In March 2003 the Bush Administration requested supplemental spending authority of $62.6 billion, mostly to fund U.S. war efforts in Iraq.[32] These and other budget projections and budget requests are heavily reported by the news media and widely interpreted as measuring the actual or projected economic costs of the U.S. resources devoted to the Iraq war. This interpretation is incorrect.

The economic costs of military resources are appropriately measured in terms of what they cost to produce (production cost) or the value they provide in their next-best use (opportunity cost). In contrast, CBO (2002) captures only "the incremental costs of deploying a force to the Persian Gulf (the costs that would be incurred above those budgeted for routine operations)."[33] Similarly, "All of the costs described in the [HBC 2002] report represent incremental costs—those that would not have occurred but for the military operation."[34] These incremental budget effects fail to capture the full cost of producing the military resources deployed in the Iraq war. For example, CBO "estimates reflect only the costs of aircraft flying hours and ship steaming days above those normally provided in DoD's regular appropriations."[35] Depreciation costs and normal maintenance costs for military hardware devoted to the Iraq war are also omitted from the CBO and HBC projections, as are the costs of training U.S. military forces. The "incremental costs" in budget documents also fail to reflect opportunity costs, except under the extreme view that U.S. military resources have zero value in their next-best use. These same points apply to the incremental appropriations that the Bush administration sought and obtained from Congress in connection with the Iraq war. In short, cost measures based on budget requests and budget projections fail to capture the full economic costs of the military resources devoted to the war.

Table 8.3
Incremental Budgetary Costs under Alternative Deployment Options for Extra Troops in Iraq

Deployment Option	Extra Forces for Use in Iraq	Incremental Budgetary Costs (billions of 2004 $)	
		Upfront	Annual
A. Create two new Army divisions	18,000–23,000 (after 3–5 years)	18.0–19.4	9.5–10.1
B. Eliminate rapid reaction requirement	18,000–23,000	–	3.6–4.2
C. Use Army National Guard units			
D. Withdraw forces from the Sinai Peninsula, Bosnia, Kosovo, and Okinawa	9,000–11,000	"... could have significant diplomatic and political consequences ... [but] this action would probably not result in substantial incremental costs because the savings that would accrue from withdrawing forces from those other commitments would largely offset the costs of sustaining additional forces in Iraq."	

Source: CBO (2003a).

A focus on "incremental costs" also results in misleading cost comparisons across deployment scenarios. For example, the CBO and HBC reports exclude the basic pay of active-duty military personnel in their cost projections but include pay for reservists called to full-time duty. As a result, deployment scenarios that involve greater reliance on reserve troops appear costlier than otherwise identical scenarios that rely more heavily on active-duty personnel. Table 8.3 illustrates the point in starker fashion, drawing on CBO (2003a) cost projections for alternative options to deploy additional forces in Iraq. The CBO assigns zero "incremental costs" to option D, which involves a withdrawal of forces from the Sinai Peninsula, Bosnia, Kosovo, and Okinawa, "because the savings that would accrue from withdrawing forces from those other commitments would largely offset the costs of sustaining additional forces in Iraq." Such savings are true savings only if those forces generate zero benefits in their current deployment or any other alternative deployment. Put differently, it would be unwise to conclude from table 8.3 that option D is the least costly, or most desirable, option simply because it triggers the lowest incremental budgetary costs. A focus on "incremental costs" may be useful for government budgeting and planning purposes, but it does not deliver sensible measures for the economic costs of the military resources devoted to the Iraq war. By the same logic, these "incremental costs" do not provide a sensible basis for comparing the economic costs of the military resources required under war and containment.

Measuring the Direct Economic Costs of War

We seek to measure the full production costs of the projected military resources devoted to the Iraq war and postwar occupation; any additional transport, munitions, and supply costs required to prosecute the war and carry out the occupation; the projected cost of casualties incurred by U.S. military forces; and projected costs for humanitarian assistance and reconstruction aid. Our cost calculations consider the military scenarios sketched out in CBO (2002). Because this document focuses on war and its near-term aftermath, we provide additional economic cost figures for longer-term occupation and peacekeeping roles by U.S. forces. We consider costs for the United States only.

With respect to military resources, we focus on production costs rather than opportunity costs for two reasons. First, a production cost approach parallels our treatment of containment costs and thereby facilitates an apples-to-apples cost comparison between the two policy options. Second, direct measurement of (historical) production costs is more straightforward and less reliant on subjective judgments than efforts to measure the opportunity costs of military resources. Nevertheless, there are potential problems with a production cost approach. For example, if a country accumulates an oversized military relative to its national security goals, then historical production costs are likely to exceed the opportunity cost of ready military resources. In this case, a production cost approach to a particular military operation would overstate its true economic cost (i.e., opportunity cost). We do not think this case applies to the United States in the wake of 9/11 and an expanding set of U.S. security concerns. More plausibly, the U.S. military is at least temporarily undersized relative to its national security goals, in part because of the Iraq war.[36] In this situation, historical production costs may understate opportunity costs.

Initial Deployment, Major Combat, and Redeployment

Table 8.4 summarizes military force requirements in the major combat phase of a war in Iraq, as projected in the two war scenarios considered by CBO (2002). Both scenarios envision a much larger, more

Table 8.4
Summary of Projected Military Force Requirements for War in Iraq, Major Combat Phase, Two Scenarios from U.S. Congressional Budget Office

	Heavy Ground Option	Heavy Air Option
	Personnel in Theater (thousands)	
Army	213	93
Marines	45	25
Navy	63	63
Air Force	34	60
Special Ops	12	12
Total personnel	367	253
	Heavy Ground Equipment	
Tanks	800	300
	Naval Forces	
Carrier battle groups	5	5
Amphibious ready groups	1	1
Surface action groups	1	1
Total Navy battle force ships	60	60
	Aircraft	
Attack and transport helicopters[a]	800	500
Marine air wings[b]	1	1
Navy carrier air wings[b]	5	5
Air Force fighter wings[b]		
Wings	5 1/3	0
Combat planes	384	720
Air Force bombers	72	72
Total aircraft	1,500	2,500

Source: CBO (2002).
Notes:
a. It is unclear whether helicopters are included in the CBO figures for "total aircraft." Moseley (2003) reports that 1,666 U.S. aircraft (excluding helicopters) actually participated in Operation Iraqi Freedom, including some aircraft that supported operations but did not deploy into theater. The 1,666 figure includes 655 fighters and 51 Air Force bombers.
b. According to CBO (2002), each Air Force tactical fighter wing "represents a force with sufficient aircraft to ensure that 72 combat planes can be sustained and supported." CBO (2002) does not report exact figures for the number of combat aircraft in Marine air wings and Navy carrier air wings.

Table 8.5
Estimated Capital Values of Deployed Military Equipment during War in Iraq, Two Scenarios from U.S. Congressional Budget Office (billions of 2003 dollars)

	Ground Equipment, incl. Helicopters	Aircraft[a]	Naval Vessels[a]	All Equipment[b]
Heavy ground option	72.3	109.6	80.8	262.7
Heavy air option	27.9	182.6	80.8	291.4

Source: Authors' calculations based on data in CBO (2000; 2002; 2005b).
Notes:
a. Capital values for "aircraft" and "naval vessels" are estimated by applying the method described in "Cost Calculations: Method 1" in section 1 to the force requirements listed in table 8.4. For this purpose, we assume that the figure for total aircraft reported in table 8.4 excludes helicopters.
b. Capital values for "all equipment" are based on the recent experience of U.S. ground troops. According to CBO (2005b, table 2), Army equipment use in theater in Afghanistan, Kuwait, and Iraq during 2005 had a capital value of 31.34 billion 2005 dollars for 100,000 to 150,000 troops. Using the midpoint value for number of troops and deflating by 5 percent to express in 2003 dollars yields $238,781 for the value of "ground equipment, including helicopters" per Army personnel in theater. Similar calculations using data in CBO (2005b, table 3) yield $154,286 per Marines personnel. (In computing this figure, we exclude the value of fighters and tanker aircraft operated by the Marines because they are included under "aircraft.") We multiply the per person equipment values by the corresponding number of Army and Marines personnel listed in table 8.4 to obtain the capital value of "ground equipment, incl. helicopters." For Special Operations personnel, we use the per person equipment value for Marines.

ground-intensive force than the one deployed under containment. The heavy air option involves 253,000 troops deployed in theater and 2,500 aircraft; the heavy ground option involves 367,000 troops and 1,500 aircraft. Both options involve 60 Navy battle force ships, including five carrier battle groups.

Based partly on these CBO projections, table 8.5 provides estimates for the capital value of deployed military equipment during the combat phase of an Iraq war. Capital values for naval vessels and (fixed-wing) aircraft are estimated by the same method as in table 8.2. Capital values for ground equipment (including helicopters) reflect the recent experience of Army troops and Marines engaged in Afghanistan, Kuwait, and Iraq, as detailed in the table notes. Our estimated capital value for the military equipment required during the combat phase of a war in Iraq is $263 billion under the heavy ground option and $291 billion under the heavy air option.

Table 8.6 reports data on the projected cost of an Iraq war by phase of engagement and type of costs. The cost figures in the table reflect upward adjustments to the figures in CBO (2002) to account for basic pay of active-duty military personnel and the additional user costs of capital not captured in the CBO figures. Based on our calculations, the projected costs of the U.S. military resources devoted to an Iraq war—initial deployment, major combat, and redeployment—range from $46 to $80 billion depending on force option and duration of major combat. As also indicated in the table, our projected costs are 56–67 percent greater than the CBO projections for the same scenarios. Thus, our adjustments to capital and labor costs have a major impact on projected costs relative to the CBO figures.[37]

Postwar Occupation, Reconstruction Aid, and Humanitarian Assistance

Table 8.7 summarizes several other projected costs associated with war and forcible regime change in Iraq. Panel A shows projected costs for the deployment and use of ground troops, naval forces, and air forces during a postwar occupation. We construct these projections using method 1 for containment costs. Relative to containment, however, we apply a much higher value for the user cost of capital on ground equipment, and we allow user costs to vary with operations tempo. These assumptions capture the fact that depreciation, maintenance, and operating costs are sensitive to operations tempo, as detailed in CBO (2005b). A high operations tempo (table 8.7) is intended to reflect a postwar situation that involves a significant insurgency, whereas a low operations tempo is intended to reflect one that primarily involves peacekeeping operations and the maintenance of stability. Occupation scenarios with a high operations tempo also entail extra munitions costs.[38]

Table 8.7 does not impose any particular assumption about the level of U.S. military forces engaged during a postwar occupation of Iraq. Rather, the entries in panels A and B provide information about projected annual costs for a given level of military resources, such as 100,000 armed forces in theater and their equipment, supplies, munitions, and so on. For example, the last row of panel A implies that the U.S. cost is $62.8 billion per year for an occupation force of 200,000 military personnel operating at a high tempo.[39] In the analysis below, we scale the figures for occupation costs up or down in proportion to the

Table 8.6
Estimated Costs of a Projected War in Iraq: Initial Deployment, Major Combat Phase, and Redeployment (billions of 2003 dollars)

A. Costs of Heavy Ground Option

	Initial Deployment (3 months)	First Month of Combat	Each Additional Month of Combat	Redeployment (3 months)
Personnel and personnel support[a]	7.7	0.5	2.5	7.7
Operations support, incl. munitions[b]	5.4	7.1	5.4	1.5
Transport to and from theater	2.8	0.7	0.7	1.5
Additional capital costs[c]	4.2	2.4	2.4	2.9
Total	20.1	12.8	11.1	13.6

B. Costs of Heavy Air Option

	Deployment (3 months)	First Month of Combat	Each Additional Month of Combat	Redeployment (3 months)
Personnel and personnel support[a]	5.3	1.8	1.8	5.3
Operations support, incl. munitions[b]	4.2	6.2	4.7	1.1
Transport to and from theater	1.9	0.5	0.5	1.0
Additional capital costs[c]	4.7	2.0	2.0	2.6
Total	16.1	10.5	9.0	10.0

C. Undiscounted Total Costs of Initial Deployment, War, and Redeployment

	From Panels A and B	CBO (2002) Projections	Ratio of A and B to CBO (2002)
Heavy ground option			
2 months	57.5	36.3	1.58
3 months	68.6	43.6	1.57
4 months	79.6	50.9	1.56

Heavy air option			
2 months	45.6	27.3	1.67
3 months	54.6	33.4	1.63
4 months	63.6	39.5	1.61

Sources: CBO (2002) and authors' calculations.

Notes:

a. For "personnel and personnel support" we adjust the corresponding entries in CBO (2002, tables 3, 4) by adding an estimate for the basic pay of active-duty military personnel. The adjustment is equal to the number of projected active-duty military personnel in CBO (2002, table 2) multiplied by $51,223/12 per month. See text notes 8 and 9 for our derivation of the average basic pay figure per full-time equivalent military personnel.

b. According to CBO (2002, tables 3, 4), "operations support" includes "all incremental costs related to the operation and maintenance of air, land, and sea forces involved in the Persian Gulf. It includes costs associated with the incremental increase in flying hours and steaming days, such as costs for increased fuel consumption and repair parts. It also includes the costs of equipping and maintaining ground troops and purchasing equipment as well as costs associated with command, control, communications, and intelligence. In addition, the category covers force reconstitution, which includes the replacement of munitions stocks and repair or replacement of damaged equipment, and the incremental cost of increased depot maintenance for items such as aircraft, tanks, and ships."

c. "Additional capital costs" are computed by applying the entries in table 8.1, lines 8 and 9, to the capital value estimates in table 8.5. We assume that all equipment is engaged for three months during the deployment phase, that naval vessels and ground equipment are engaged for three months during the redeployment phase, and that aircraft are engaged for one month during the redeployment phase.

Table 8.7
Estimated Costs of a Projected War in Iraq: Postwar Occupation, Casualties, Reconstruction, and Humanitarian Assistance (billions of 2003 dollars)

	Operations Tempo	Billions of 2003 $	Time Frame
A. Postwar Occupation Costs: Method 1			
Per 100,000 ground troops in theater, incl. capital costs on ground equipment[a]	Low High	26.4 29.3	Annual
Naval forces, one-fifth of force level during major combat phase (12 ships, 6,276 personnel)[b]	Low High	2.6 2.6	Annual
Air forces, one-fifth of force level under heavy ground option (300 aircraft, 12,686 personnel)[c]	Low High	4.8 5.4	Annual
Total occupation costs for ground troops, naval forces, and air forces (118,962 armed forces)	Low High	33.9 37.3	Annual
Occupation costs per 100,000 armed forces in theater[d]	Low High	28.5 31.4	Annual
B. Postwar Occupation Costs: Method 2			
Occupation costs per 100,000 armed forces in theater[e]		48.4	Annual
C. Reconstruction Aid and Humanitarian Assistance[f]			
Humanitarian assistance		1–10	2–4 years
Reconstruction aid (HBC 2002)		9.2–18.4	10+ years
Reconstruction aid (HBC 2003)		28.3–73.3	10+ years
D. Cost of U.S. Casualties			
Per 1,000 U.S. fatalities[g]		6.9	
Per 7,153 U.S. injuries		9.0	

Sources: HBC (2002; 2003), Nordhaus (2002), Viscusi and Aldy (2003), Wallsten and Kosec (2005), and authors' calculations.
Notes:
a. Postwar occupation costs for "ground troops in theater" are the sum of labor costs per person (table 8.2, panel A; $226,000 per person/year) plus capital costs. Drawing on table 8.5, we use a capital value of $238,781 per person for ground equipment. We apply a user cost of capital of 16 percent per year (table 1, line 11) at a low operations tempo and 24 percent at a high operations tempo. In the case of high operations tempo, we add another $10,000 per person/year for munitions.
b. Postwar occupation costs for "naval forces" are the sum of capital costs for naval vessels and labor costs for naval personnel. Applying the same figure for capital value per ship as in table 8.2 and a user cost of capital of 7.5 percent per year yields annual capital costs of $1.2 billion. Applying the same ratio of naval personnel to naval vessels as in section 1, "Baseline Case," for the containment policy, and using a figure $226,000 per year for personnel yields annual labor costs of $1.4 billion. Summing the capital and labor costs yields $2.6 billion.

Table 8.7
(continued)

c. Postwar occupation costs for "air forces" are the sum of capital costs for fixed-wing aircraft and labor costs for Air Force personnel. Applying the same figure for capital value per aircraft as in table 8.2 and the user cost figures for aircraft from table 8.1, lines 10 and 11, yields annual capital costs of $1.9–$2.2 billion, depending on operations tempo. Applying the same ratio of Air Force personnel to fixed-wing aircraft as in section 1, "Baseline Case," for the containment policy, and using a figure $226,000 per year for personnel yields annual labor costs of $2.9 billion. We sum the capital and labor costs to derive the figures reported in this table, adding another $300 million for munitions under a high operations tempo.
d. "Occupation costs per 100,000 armed forces in theater" are calculated as "total occupation costs" divided by 118,962 armed forces.
e. "Occupation costs per 100,000 armed forces in theater" are calculated using "all-in costs per person/year" for Army, Navy, and Air Force personnel (table 8.2, panel B). The force composition (ground troops, Navy personnel, Air Force personnel) is the same as in panel A of this table.
f. The projected cost range for "humanitarian assistance" is from Nordhaus (2002, 67), and the projected cost ranges for "reconstruction aid" are from HBC (2002, 22) and HBC (2003, 2).
g. The figure of $6.9 million per fatality is the midpoint value of a statistical life in the studies reviewed by Viscusi and Aldy (2003), as reported in Wallsten and Kosec (2005) and adjusted to 2003 dollars. Based on experience through August 25, 2005, for U.S. military personnel and contractors, the Iraq engagement has involved 7.153 injuries per fatality. Wallsten and Kosec classify these injuries by severity into several categories and assign welfare costs based on estimates of the willingness to pay to avoid injury. They add lifetime medical costs for injury treatment to obtain the economic cost of injuries, discounting future medical costs at 5 percent annual rate.

size of the armed forces engaged, while maintaining fixed ratios of ground troops to other personnel. The figures for "Occupation costs per 100,000 armed forces in theater" in table 8.7 involve a ratio of ground troops to Navy and Air Force personnel that is twice as high as in the Heavy Air Option.[40]

The projected costs for humanitarian assistance and postwar reconstruction aid are drawn from three sources. Nordhaus (2002) projects U.S. costs for humanitarian assistance to the Iraqi people in the range of $1 billion to $10 billion over a period of two to four years. HBC (2002) projects U.S. costs for reconstruction aid in the range of $9.2 billion to $18.4 billion over a period of ten years. An update in HBC (2003), issued six months after the Iraq invasion, projects much higher U.S. reconstruction costs in the range of $28.3 billion to $73.3 billion. As of July 5, 2005, actual U.S. budget allocations for the Iraq Relief and Reconstruction Fund total about $18.4 billion, which includes more than $5 billion in allocations for security and law enforcement activities such as training and equipping Iraqi security forces. Cumulative fund outlays amount to $6.3 billion as of June 28, 2005, largely for security services and law enforcement.[41]

U.S. Casualties

To project the cost of casualties sustained by U.S. military personnel in an Iraq war, we rely on the estimates in Wallsten and Kosec (2005). Their estimates are designed to capture the economic value of lost lives, the welfare losses suffered by injured soldiers, and the lifetime medical costs of treating injuries sustained in Iraq. In table 8.7, panel D, we report a projected cost of $6.9 billion per 1,000 U.S. fatalities. This figure, drawn from Wallsten and Kosec, reflects the midpoint estimate for the value of a statistical life in the literature reviewed by Viscusi and Aldy (2003). Based on the experience of U.S. forces through August 25, 2005, the Iraq engagement has involved 7.153 injuries per fatality. Wallsten and Kosec classify these injuries by severity and assign welfare costs based on estimates of the willingness to pay to avoid injury. They add lifetime medical costs for injury treatment to obtain the economic cost of injuries. Their estimates imply a cost of $9.0 billion per 7,153 injuries.

War Scenarios

Table 8.8 describes several scenarios for an Iraq war that we consider in the present value cost analysis. The scenarios differ in key respects: length of major combat phase; duration, size, and operations tempo of a postwar U.S. occupation force; fatalities and injuries sustained by U.S. forces; and U.S. outlays for humanitarian assistance and postwar reconstruction aid. For all scenarios, initial deployment commences in December 2002, major combat commences in March 2003, and redeployment of the invasion force takes three months from the end of major combat and is followed immediately by occupation. Fatalities occur at a rate proportional to troop levels during occupation, and injuries occur at the rate of 7.153 per fatality.

These scenarios capture a broad range of preinvasion views about the likely outcome of a military intervention in Iraq.[42] Scenario 1, the most hopeful, entails a two-month major combat phase, a small-scale occupation that ends by December 2005, one thousand U.S. fatalities, and relatively modest outlays for humanitarian assistance and reconstruction aid. This scenario is consistent with the view that the Iraqi people would welcome a U.S.-led invasion force as liberators—initially and after euphoria over Saddam's overthrow wanes—and that regime change and reconstruction would proceed smoothly with little interference from terrorists, insurgents, or outside powers. Scenarios 2–6 entail a progressively longer occupation, larger occupation force, higher operations tempo during occupation, greater casualties, and larger outlays for humanitarian assistance and reconstruction. The length of the major combat phase also increases. Two variants each of scenarios 4 and 5 differ in postwar reconstruction costs.

Scenarios 1–3 describe considerably more favorable outcomes than scenarios 4 and 5, which are in turn much more favorable than scenario 6. In particular, scenario 6 envisions an occupation force of 200,000 U.S. military personnel in theater through September 2007 and a smaller force level through 2013, with forces engaged at a high operations tempo throughout. Scenario 6 also entails 7,000 U.S. fatalities, about 50,000 U.S. injuries, and $60 billion in undiscounted costs for humanitarian assistance and reconstruction aid. Scenario 7 describes an even worse outcome: a dangerous new regime emerges in Iraq after a long and costly occupation, and the U.S. reverts to its prewar containment policy.

8.3   War versus Containment: Direct U.S. Costs

Valuing the Policy Options

War and containment are two strategies for responding to the threats posed by a dangerous regime in Iraq. Under each strategy, the United States (and other intervening powers) incurs a stream of costs over time to produce benefits in the form of lowered threats to national security. In this respect, war and containment can be seen as alternative costly investments intended to produce a flow of future benefits. We initially assume that the two policies are equally effective in dealing with the threats posed by a dangerous regime. We also assume that at least one policy has a positive net present value. Given these assumptions, the choice between policy options reduces to present value cost comparisons. We seek to estimate the cost of establishing a stable regime in Iraq that does not threaten the national security interests of the United States and that does not engage in large-scale oppression of its own people or others.

We calculate the present value cost of containment as

$$\sum_{i=0}^{\infty} (\text{Annual Containment Cost})(1 - \lambda)^i R(i), \qquad (8.1)$$

Table 8.8
Alternative Scenarios for a Projected War in Iraq

Scenarios, Ordered by Costliness	Length of Major Combat Phase	Size of Occupation Force, Duration, and Operations Tempo	U.S. Fatalities Major Combat	U.S. Fatalities Occupation	Undiscounted Cost of Humanitarian Assistance	Undiscounted Cost of Reconstruction Aid
1. Short war; 2 1/3-year occupation, little postwar conflict	2 months	100,000 troops initially, declining linearly to zero in January 2006; low operations tempo	500	500	$1 billion over 2 years	$9.2 billion over 5 years
2. Short war; 3-year occupation, greater postwar conflict	2 months	150,000 troops initially, declining linearly to zero in September 2006; high operations tempo through December 2004	500	1,000	$2 billion over 3 years	$12 billion over 5 years
3. Medium war; 3-year occupation, small insurgency	3 months	150,000 troops initially, declining linearly to zero in October 2006; high operations tempo through September 2005	800	2000	$4 billion over 3 years	$15 billion over 5 years
4. Medium war; 5-year occupation, larger insurgency; two reconstruction cost levels	3 months	200,000 troops initially, declining linearly to zero in October 2008; high operations tempo through September 2006	1,000	3,000	$6 billion over 4 years	(a) $30 billion over 7 years (b) $50 billion over 10 years
5. Same as (4) except larger occupation force, more casualties; two reconstruction cost levels	3 months	200,000 troops through October 2006, declining linearly to zero in October 2008; high operations tempo through September 2006	1,000	4,000	$6 billion over 4 years	(a) $40 billion over 7 years (b) $75 billion over 10 years

| 6. Longer war; 10-year occupation, major insurgency | 4 months | 200,000 troops for four years, declining linearly to zero in November 2013; high operations tempo | 2,000 | 5,000 | $10 billion over 4 years | $50 billion over 10 years |
| 7. Same as (6) but regime change fails and containment resumes in 2014 at baseline cost level (table 8.2, panel C) | | | | | | |

Note: Following are common assumptions for the scenarios in this table:

- Initial deployment commences in December 2002, major combat commences in March 2002, and redeployment concludes three months after the end of major combat.
- Costs of initial deployment, major combat, and redeployment of forces engaged in major combat as specified in table 8.6.
- Occupation force levels and costs commence immediately following redeployment phase. For example, if major combat phase lasts two months, then postwar occupation costs commence in August 2003.
- Fixed ratio of ground troops to Navy and Air Force personnel during occupation phase as specified in table 8.7, panel A.
- Occupation costs as specified in table 8.7, panel A.
- Fatalities occur at a constant rate during major combat phase, and at a rate proportional to the number of troops in theater during occupation phase.
- Cost of fatalities and injuries as specified in table 8.7, panel D, with a fixed ratio of 7.153 injuries per fatality.
- Humanitarian assistance and reconstruction aid dispensed at a constant level over the indicated time frame.

where λ is the annual hazard rate for spontaneous regime change, and $R(i)$ is the discount factor applied to containment costs incurred i periods hence. We use the annual flow costs of containment reported in table 8.2, and we assume that containment remains in effect until Iraq undergoes a spontaneous regime change. Similarly, we calculate the present value cost of the war scenarios in table 8.8 as

$$\sum_{i=0}^{\infty}(\text{War Costs})_i R(i). \tag{8.2}$$

To obtain the cost of occupation and casualties for the war scenarios, we rescale the flow costs reported in tables 8.6 and 8.7 based on force size, operations tempo, and casualties.

In selecting a discount rate for the present value calculations, a sensible approach is to use the real-time cost of funds facing the U.S. government. As of early 2003, the real annual yield on ten-year inflation-indexed U.S. Treasury bonds was about 2 percent.[43] We use this figure as our baseline discount rate. An alternative approach relies on expert opinions regarding the appropriate social discount rate for public policy decisions with long-lived consequences. Weitzman (2001) surveys about 2,000 professional economists on this issue and finds a mean discount rate of 4 percent. To accommodate the heterogeneity in expert opinion, he also fits a model to the survey responses and obtains a schedule for certainty-equivalent discount rates that declines with the time horizon—from about 4 percent for 1–5 years hence to 3 percent for 6–25 years hence and 2 percent for 26–75 years hence.[44]

The appropriate discount rate also depends on whether the costs incurred under a given policy are correlated with the opportunity cost of government funds in future states of the world. This opportunity cost is likely to be higher when economic growth is lower. We see no obvious reason for future costs under containment or war to be correlated with future growth in an important way, but some readers may hold a different view. Hence, we also consider higher discount rates in our calculations, in line with the view that the costs associated with a given policy are concentrated in states of the world with a relatively high opportunity cost of government funds.

Present Value Cost Results

Table 8.9 reports results for the containment policy. At a 2 percent discount rate on future costs and a 3 percent annual hazard rate for re-

Table 8.9
Present Value Cost of Military Resources Required for Continued Containment, as of 2003

| | | Present Value Cost, Billions of 2003 $[b] | | | |
| | | Exponential Discounting,[c,d] Annual Discount Rate | | | Gamma Discounting,[c] $\mu = .04$ and |
Containment Scenario	Annual Costs[a]	2%	4%	6%	$\sigma = .03$
Baseline case	14.54	297	216	171	247
Extra forces and higher costs	19.38	395	288	228	329
Dual-use deployment and lower costs	9.69	198	144	114	164

Sources: CBO (2000; 2002) and authors' calculations using data, estimates, and assumptions described in text and table 8.1.
Notes:
a. Annual costs are computed as the average of the method 1 and method 2 cost calculations summarized in table 8.2. Relying only on method 1 yields annual and present value cost figures that are 22.5 percent smaller.
b. The present value cost of containment is calculated according to equation (8.1) with $\lambda = .03$ and exponential or gamma discounting, as indicated. λ is the annual hazard rate of spontaneous transition from a dangerous to a benign regime in Iraq.
c. Under exponential discounting, $R(i) = (1 + r)^{-i}$ for $i = 0, 1, 2, \ldots$. Under gamma discounting, $R(i) = [1 + i\sigma^2/\mu]^{-z}$, where $z = (\mu/\sigma)^2$. The gamma discounting parameters are drawn from Weitzman (2001). The implied effective discount rate is 4 percent per year initially and declines for more distant years.
d. The impact of expected regime duration can be read from table 8.8 by recognizing that, to a close approximation, the present value cost of containment under exponential discounting depends on the sum of the hazard rate and the discount rate. For example, the present value cost of containment at a hazard rate of .03 and a discount rate of .04 is nearly the same as the present value cost at a hazard rate of .05 and a discount rate of .02.

gime change, the present value cost of containment is $297 billion in our baseline scenario. If effective containment requires extra military forces per the discussion in section 1, "Higher Containment Costs," the cost rises to nearly $400 billion. The precise cost also depends on the discount rate, the likelihood of spontaneous regime change, and other details. Thus our analysis does not establish a precise value for the economic cost of sticking with the containment policy. It does show that the containment policy was an expensive option for the United States under a broad range of reasonable assumptions. This conclusion holds even under the assumption, which we have maintained thus far, that containment would remain completely effective in protecting U.S. national security interests.

Table 8.10 reports results for the war scenarios. At a 2 percent discount rate, the cost of war ranges from $106 billion in scenario 1 to $872 billion in scenario 7.[45] The present value cost is $320 billion for scenario 4(b), which involves an occupation force that declines from 200,000 troops in September 2003 to zero in October 2008, $56 billion in undiscounted costs for postwar aid, 4,000 fatalities, and nearly 30,000 injuries. More generally, table 8.10 shows that the duration and size of the postwar occupation have a profound effect on the overall cost of the war option. For example, the cost of military resources engaged in occupation ranges from $35 billion in scenario 1 to $153 billion in scenario 4 and $410 billion in scenario 6. The intensity of postwar conflict also has a large impact on U.S. costs related to casualties and reconstruction aid.

In sum, our analysis shows that both containment and war were costly policy options for the United States. The analysis also identifies key factors that influence the cost of each policy option. For example, the expected duration of a hostile regime in Iraq, absent war, has a dramatic effect on the cost of containment. To see this point, consider our baseline containment scenario with a 2 percent discount rate and a 3 percent hazard rate for peaceful regime change. Raising the hazard rate to 5 percent lowers the cost of containment from $297 billion to $212 billion. Lowering the hazard rate to 2 percent raises the cost of containment to $371 billion. Hence, under the containment option, policies or developments that promote peaceful regime change generate large economic benefits for the United States.

How costly will the Iraq intervention ultimately become for the United States, both in absolute terms and relative to containment? As of January 2006, it appears quite possible that the Iraq intervention will ultimately unfold along lines similar to scenario 5(a), though perhaps with fewer U.S. casualties. At a 2 percent annual discount rate, the projected cost of this scenario is $414 billion (in 2003 dollars), according to our analysis. In comparison, the projected cost of containment in our baseline case is $297 billion. A somewhat more pessimistic view about the cost of effective containment and the likelihood of peaceful regime change yields containment costs similar to the $414 billion figure. Thus, despite the undeniably high cost of the Iraq intervention, our analysis indicates that containment may well have been equally costly for the United States.

It also appears possible (as of January 2006) that the Iraq intervention will unfold along lines not too different from scenario 6, though

Table 8.10
Present Value Cost of War in Iraq, as of 2003, Alternative Scenarios

Scenario[a]	Total	Initial Deployment, Major Combat, Redeployment	Military Resources Engaged in Occupation	U.S. Fatalities and Injuries	Reconstruction Aid and Humanitarian Assistance
Present Value Cost[b,c] at 2% Annual Discount Rate, Billions of 2003 $					
1	106	45.4	34.6	15.8	9.8
2	152	45.4	70.2	23.3	13.5
3	187	54.3	71.4	43.3	18.3
4(a)	302	54.3	152.6	61.2	34.1
4(b)	320	54.3	152.6	61.2	51.6
5(a)	414	54.3	239.7	75.9	43.5
5(b)	445	54.3	239.7	75.9	74.5
6	633	63.3	409.5	105.0	55.5
7	872	63.3	409.5	105.0	55.5
Present Value Cost[b,c] at 6% Annual Discount Rate, Billions of 2003 $					
1	103	45.1	32.9	15.8	9.2
2	146	45.1	66.2	22.3	12.6
3	179	53.9	67.0	41.3	17.2
4(a)	284	53.9	140.0	57.2	30.9
4(b)	296	53.9	140.0	57.2	44.5
5(a)	380	53.9	216.7	69.9	39.3
5(b)	404	53.9	216.7	69.9	64.0
6	552	62.6	347.4	93.5	48.2
7	642	62.6	347.4	93.5	48.2

Source: Authors' calculations.
Notes:
a. See table 8.8 for scenario descriptions and assumptions.
b. Present value costs for the heavy air option. The present value costs of "initial deployment, major combat and redeployment" for the heavy ground option are about $11 billion to $16 billion higher.
c. Present value calculations use a monthly time unit and exponential discounting.

with fewer U.S. casualties. The projected cost of scenario 6 is $633 billion. It is hard to argue that continued containment would have involved comparable or greater expected economic costs for the United States than an intervention experience similar to scenario 6, unless one dispenses with the assumption that containment would be fully effective in protecting U.S. national security interests. We take up that issue in section 8.4.

Departures from Constant Supply Costs

In our cost calculations we assume constant supply costs within the relevant range for all military inputs. This assumption is less appealing when war involves an extended, intense engagement that leads to shortages of critical equipment, higher costs of recruiting and retention, reductions in the combat effectiveness of U.S. troops, or an impaired ability to meet other national security threats. News reports of body armor shortages, under-armored transport vehicles, missed recruiting targets, and large reenlistment bonuses suggest that the Iraq engagement has been big enough and long enough to move the United States up the supply schedule for its ground forces. Cutting in the other direction are static scale economies achieved by large-scale operations and dynamic scale economies that arise from learning by doing on the battlefield. News accounts suggest that U.S. military experience in the Gulf War of 1991 and later in Bosnia, Kosovo, and Afghanistan led to improvements in the combat effectiveness of U.S. forces. The Iraq intervention is also likely to be a source of lessons, albeit hard won, that will improve the effectiveness of the U.S. military in potential future conflicts. Of course, opponents can also draw lessons from battlefield experience. On balance, it is unclear whether these departures from constant supply costs are quantitatively significant, and which way they cut. This is a ripe area for careful research.

Nation Building and Postoccupation Deployments

Our analysis of the war scenarios in table 8.8 is designed to assess the cost of establishing a stable regime in Iraq that does not threaten the national security interests of the United States and that does not engage in large-scale oppression of its own people or others. Some advocates of the Iraq war have appealed to and argued for more ambitious goals, such as transforming Iraq into a beacon of liberty in the Middle East and an exemplar of market-based capitalism. These are worthy goals, but a serious effort to attain them would probably involve significant additional costs for reconstruction aid and other nation-building efforts. Achieving these goals would also yield benefits not factored into our analysis. For these reasons, our analysis does not deliver an assessment of the more ambitious nation-building goals in connection with the Iraq intervention.

A similar point applies to the longer-term costs and benefits of a U.S. strategic alliance with a new Iraqi regime. An analogy may be helpful in this regard. The United States has maintained a significant military presence in Japan for more than 60 years after the allied victory in World War II. It would be inappropriate to treat U.S. military forces stationed in Japan decades after victory as part of the cost of victory. Instead, the cost of these military forces should be weighed against their strategic benefits. Similarly, if the United States maintains a military presence in Iraq after the defeat of insurgents and the establishment of a stable, peaceful regime, it would be inappropriate to count those forces as part of the cost of war in Iraq without also factoring in their benefits.

8.4   Concerns about Containment and Implications for the Cost Calculus

Concerns about Containment

Many war advocates argue that the Iraqi regime posed an unacceptable security risk in a post-9/11 world. Shawcross (2004, 69–70) stresses Saddam's obsession with WMDs, his demonstrated willingness to use them, and the dangers of his potential collaboration with terrorists:

Now, in the early twenty-first century, threats have changed, and so must the responses to them. The proliferation of weapons of mass destruction, and of terrorists who stalk from the shadows and are susceptible to no kind of deterrence, alter the concept of imminent danger. . . .

There was no doubt that Saddam, alone among the dictators, had long shown an absolute obsession with obtaining such weapons [WMDs] and had actually used them. He had also refused to accede to more than a decade of international demands that he desist. There was ample reason to believe that he already possessed biological and chemical weapons capacity and that he would seek to restart his nuclear weapons program if he were able. He had the knowledge and the intent—he lacked only the fissile material. . . .

Whether or not [Al Qaeda and Saddam] collaborated directly, the very existence of a new global terrorist network made Iraq's presumptive possession of WMD much more threatening. Theoretically it offered Saddam (and others) a way to attack the United States by proxy and perhaps without identification.

Prudent policymakers could not ignore the fact that Saddam and Osama bin Laden shared a hatred of the United States.

In fact, Saddam Hussein had a long history of harboring and supporting international terrorists when it suited his purposes.[46]

Pollack (2002, xxiv) stresses doubts about whether it was feasible to sustain an effective containment policy: "Perhaps the single most important reason why the United States must act soon to adopt a new policy toward Iraq is that our old policy, the policy of containment, is eroding." In support of this conclusion, Pollack points to Iraq's eviction of UN weapons inspectors in the fall of 1998, rising discontent in Arab countries and Muslim communities over the basing of U.S. military forces in the Persian Gulf region, the erosion of sanctions' effectiveness over time, and declining international support for containment.[47]

A related argument for preemptive action in 2003 stresses the potential for a future military conflict with Iraq that would involve much higher costs. According to Pollack (2002, xv–xvi),

In the case of Iraq, if we do not act soon to topple Saddam Hussein's regime, we are likely to face a much worse conflict with Saddam down the road after he has acquired nuclear weapons and advanced conventional weapons. An invasion of Iraq in the near term, when Saddam has only a limited stockpile of weapons of mass destruction and his conventional forces remain weak, is likely to seem effortless and cost-free compared to a war with Saddam after he has crossed the nuclear threshold. Given Saddam's propensity to miscalculate, his penchant for aggression, and his willingness to absorb horrific punishment, it would be a terrible mistake for the United States to allow him to acquire such capabilities and risk war with a nuclear-armed Iraq.... This book argues that war with Saddam's Iraq is well nigh inevitable and that it would be far, far better for the United States to face this challenge sooner rather than later.[48]

Shawcross (2004, 71–73, 93, 115–116) develops a similar argument. He applauds Israel's bombing of Iraq's Osirak nuclear reactor in 1981 because it set back Saddam's efforts to acquire nuclear weapons. He also asks whether preemptive action against Al Queda and the Taliban regime in Afghanistan would have prevented the 9/11 attacks.

O'Hanlon (2002c) summarizes the state of affairs this way in September 2002:

Saddam continues to have chemical weapons in abundance and probably biological agents as well, but we have already proved we can deter him from using these weapons over the past dozen years, and there is no reason to think he has transferred either type to al-Qaida. By contrast, a nuclear weapon is

something Saddam almost surely does not now have, but that he might someday acquire—and that, if ever used, could clearly dwarf 9/11 in its effects....
Letting Saddam get a nuclear weapon and then seeing what if anything he
might do with it is a social science experiment we can live without. Simply
having such a weapon could give Saddam "defensive cover" for aggression,
fundamentally changing the balance of power in the region.

   That, in a nutshell, is the case for a preemptive war. Whatever one thinks
of this case, it should not depend on advocates producing a "smoking
gun."...Saddam is trying to get the bomb...[and] it would make more sense
to fight before he had the bomb than after.

   O'Hanlon also notes that "Iraq was disturbingly close—perhaps
only months away—from building a nuclear weapon at the time of
Desert Storm" in 1991.

   But unlike Pollack and Shawcross, O'Hanlon favors containment
over war. He wraps up his essay by stating, "Even a war skeptic such
as me must acknowledge that President Bush has a reasonable case
when he describes the risk involved in Iraq's nuclear program. Rigorous inspections and disarmament would, to my mind, be an acceptable
solution. But to get that outcome, we may have to threaten war, threat-
en it quite credibly." O'Hanlon does not spell out the dimensions or
costs of a credible threat.

   These arguments by Shawcross, Pollack, and O'Hanlon—and related arguments by many others—partly turn on underlying views
and implicit assumptions about the prospective costs of war and containment. To help evaluate these arguments, we extend our analytical
framework to consider concerns related to the cost of credible threats,
the effectiveness of containment, and the likelihood and cost of future
conflict with Iraq under a policy of containment. In the same spirit, we
also consider how the cost calculus depends on the potential impact of
the war-versus-containment choice on the likelihood of major terrorist
attacks on the United States.

Costly Credible Threats

There was widespread agreement prior to the Iraq invasion that an effective containment policy required a rigorous program of inspections
and disarmament. So, what did it take in the way of military resources
to compel Iraqi compliance with an effective inspections program?
What constituted a credible threat forceful enough to inspire Iraqi cooperation? Precise answers to these questions are not at hand, but the
historical record offers some guidance.

Iraq repeatedly resisted the UN weapons inspections process, a fact evident from the many UN Security Council resolutions on the matter. On November 1, 1998, Iraq halted all cooperation with UN weapons inspectors. Four days later, UN Security Resolution 1205 demanded that Iraq "provide immediate, complete and unconditional cooperation" with inspectors and warned of the threat to "international peace and security" posed by noncooperation.[49] Later the same month, the United States aborted a missile strike on Iraq when its government agreed to cooperate with the inspections process. After the Iraqi government failed to follow through, the United States and Britain launched Operation Desert Fox, an extensive four-day aerial bombardment of Iraqi targets. The U.S. portion of the operation involved over 40,000 troops, 300 aircraft, and 40 ships.[50] Despite its destructive intensity, Operation Desert Fox failed to compel the readmission of UN weapons inspectors to Iraq.

In fact, weapons inspectors did not return to Iraq for four long years. It is instructive to briefly recount the sequence of events leading up to their return. On September 12, 2002, President Bush addressed the United Nations, "challenging the organization to swiftly enforce its own resolutions against Iraq. If not, Bush contends, the U.S. will have no choice but to act on its own against Iraq." On October 11, 2002, the U.S. Congress authorized an attack against Iraq. On November 8, 2002, the UN Security Council unanimously approved resolution 1441 calling for "tough new arms inspections on Iraq and [providing] precise unambiguous definitions of what constitutes a 'material breach' of the resolution." Resolution 1441 also warned that Iraq would face "serious consequences" if it violated the resolution. By this point in time, the likelihood and prospects of an Iraq war were major sources of concern and discussion throughout the world. There was no doubt about the seriousness of the threat confronting the Iraqi regime. In the face of this rather considerable pressure, Iraq finally relented and allowed UN weapons inspectors to return on November 18, 2002.[51]

This historical summary highlights two points. First, aerial bombardments on the scale of Operation Desert Fox were insufficient to compel Iraqi compliance with a rigorous inspections and disarmament regime. Second, not until the approach of a full-scale, regime-ending war did Iraq finally relent and permit the resumption of a viable inspections program. Credible threats of this sort are costly to mount.

The same point applies to the occasional extra deployments required to deter Iraqi aggression under the containment policy. For example, in

October 1994, Iraqi forces began massing near the border with Kuwait. The United States responded by rapidly increasing troop levels in the Persian Gulf region to about 60,000 and by deploying another 350 military aircraft and a carrier battle group to the region. Britain also reinforced its military presence in the region. Faced with an impending attack by the United States and Britain, Iraq withdrew its forces well away from the Kuwaiti border, ending the confrontation. But two years later, in response to the mobilization of Iraqi military forces and fears of an Iraqi attack on Jordan, Kuwait, or Saudi Arabia, the United States engaged in a similarly large deployment of military forces to the Persian Gulf region.[52]

In light of this historical record, consider a containment policy that relies on costly credible threats, as needed, to compel compliance with inspections and disarmament and to deter Iraqi aggression. The present value cost of containment now becomes

$$\sum_{i=0}^{\infty} [(\text{Annual Containment Cost})$$

$$+ p(\text{Credible Threat Cost})](1 - \lambda)^i R(i), \tag{8.3}$$

where p is the probability that, in any given year, effective containment requires the mounting of a credible threat. In calculating equation (8.3), we consider two values for the cost of a credible threat, \$13.05 billion and \$26.1 billion. The latter figure is the sum of deployment and redeployment costs under the heavy air option (table 8.6). We also use the baseline annual containment costs of \$14.54 billion (table 8.2), a 2 percent annual discount rate, and a 3 percent annual probability of peaceful regime change.

Figure 8.1 illustrates how the need for costly credible threats affects the present value cost of containment. For comparison, the figure also shows the present value cost of war under scenarios 5(a) and 6. As shown in the figure, the probability and cost of credible threats have important effects on the cost calculus. For example, the cost of war in scenario 5(a) exceeds the baseline containment cost by about \$115 billion, but this gap vanishes if effective containment involves a 22 percent chance of mounting a high-cost threat in any given year. Similarly, war scenario 5(a) and an effective containment policy are equally costly, if there is a 44 percent chance of mounting a low-cost threat.

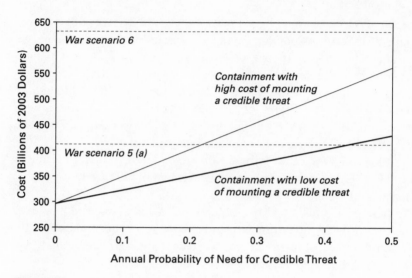

Figure 8.1
Present value cost of war compared to containment, with costly credible threats.

Limited Wars

With some probability, an effective containment policy might require a limited war against Iraq, that is, a war that reverses or prevents some hostile action by Iraq but does not proceed to forcible regime change, occupation, and reconstruction. Contingencies that might lead to limited war include Iraqi aggression against neighboring states, large-scale slaughter of civilians by Iraqi security forces, and information that Iraq was on the verge of acquiring or building a nuclear weapon. Limited war followed by the resumption of containment implies a present value cost expression with the same form as equation (8.3). The cost of a limited war replaces the credible threat cost in (8.3), and p now refers to the probability of a limited war in any given year.

As illustrated in figure 8.2, the prospects for limited war also have important effects on the cost calculus. In constructing this figure, we assume that a limited war involves the same level of military resources and U.S. casualties as scenario 1 in table 8.10 (excluding the postwar costs and casualties). Recall that scenario 1 involves the heavy air option with two months of major combat and 500 U.S. fatalities. Based on our earlier analysis, the projected cost of such an engagement is $53.3 billion.[53] Other assumptions underlying figure 8.2 are the same as in figure 8.1.

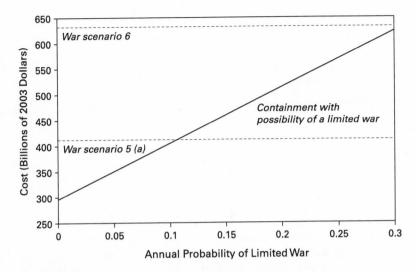

Figure 8.2
Present value cost of war compared to containment, with possibility of a limited war.

As shown in figure 8.2, containment is as costly as war scenario 5(a) when there is a 10 percent chance of a limited war in any given year. Containment is as costly as war scenario 6 when there is a 31 percent chance of a limited war in any given year.

War and Forcible Regime Change, Now or Later?

Some argued for preemptive war and forcible regime change in Iraq on the grounds that war was highly probable in any event and likely to be much costlier at a later date. To assess the force of this argument, let P denote the probability of war and forcible regime change in the next N years under a policy of containment, and suppose that the undiscounted cost of a future war is m times the cost of an immediate war. Let p_i denote the probability of war in year i conditional on the survival of a dangerous Iraqi regime through year $i - 1$. p_i can be thought of as the conditional probability that the United States faces a war of "necessity" with Iraq in year i.

If $p_0 = 0$ in the initial year (2003), $p_i = p > 0$ for the next N years, and $p_i = 0$ thereafter, the probability of a future war of "necessity" under a policy of containment is

$$P = p \sum_{i=1}^{N} (1 - \lambda - p)^{i-1} = \frac{p[1 - (1 - \lambda - p)^N]}{\lambda + p}, \tag{8.4}$$

where λ is the annual hazard rate for peaceful regime change, as before. The present value cost of the containment policy now becomes

$$(\text{Annual Containment Cost})\left[1 + \sum_{i=1}^{N}(1 - \lambda - p)^{i}R(i)\right]$$

$$+ p[m(\text{Cost of Immediate War})]\sum_{i=1}^{N}(1 - \lambda - p)^{i-1}R(i)$$

$$+ (1 - \lambda - p)^{N}\sum_{i=N+1}^{\infty}(\text{Annual Containment Cost})(1 - \lambda)^{i-N}R(i).$$

$$(8.5)$$

Figure 8.3 applies equation (8.5) to illustrate how the present value cost of the containment policy varies with the probability and cost of a future war. We allow for a possible war in the next ten years, through 2013. War costs are based on scenario 5(a), and annual containment costs are set to the benchmark value in table 8.9. As in figures 8.1 and 8.2, we assume a 2 percent discount rate and a 3 percent hazard rate for peaceful regime change.

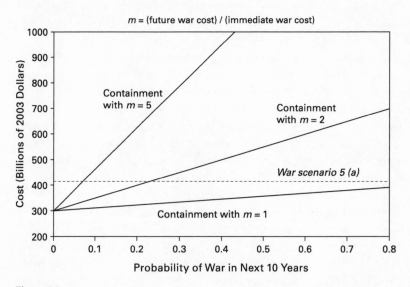

Figure 8.3
Present value cost of immediate war compared to containment, with possibility of a future war.

Figure 8.3 shows that the possibility of a future war can profoundly alter the cost calculus. For example, if a future war is twice as costly as an immediate one, and the probability of such a war in the next ten years exceeds 25 percent, then containment is more costly than an immediate, preemptive war. If a future war is five times as costly and occurs with probability greater than 8 percent in the next ten years, then containment is more costly than immediate war. If a future war is five times as costly and occurs with a 50 percent chance in the next ten years, then the present value expected cost of the containment policy exceeds $1.1 trillion.

We think this analysis helps to clarify the wide divergence of opinion about the wisdom of the Iraq war. The precise probability and cost of a future war with Iraq matter greatly for the cost of containment, but there is no sure method for assessing the probability and cost of a future war. Even modest differences of opinion about, say, the probability of a future war translate into sizable differences in the costliness of containment. From this perspective, it is unsurprising that the decision to invade Iraq in 2003 and overthrow the regime remains a matter of intense controversy.

Our analysis also highlights a problematic aspect of the oft-drawn distinction between a war of "choice" and one of "necessity." In particular, the analysis shows that a war of "choice" can be highly desirable when it forecloses the possibility of a more costly war of "necessity." This statement continues to hold when the possibility of a war of "necessity" is remote, provided that a future war is costly enough relative to an immediate one. In this respect, there is no clean separation between a war of "choice" and one of "necessity." Of course, the mere possibility of a costly war of "necessity" at some future date does not ensure that immediate war is the best policy choice.

Future Terrorist Attacks
Views also differ widely about the likelihood that the prewar Iraqi regime would support or facilitate a major terrorist attack against the United States. For some, this danger became a major plank in the case for war. Others dismissed the possibility of Iraqi participation in a terrorist attack against the United States. Indeed, many argued that war in Iraq raised the likelihood of a major terrorist attack against the United States. We do not try to settle these differences of opinion. Instead, we offer brief remarks about the magnitude of the stakes.

To gauge the potential cost of a future terrorist attack, it is helpful to review the economic scale of the 9/11 attack. Bram, Orr, and Rapaport (2002) estimate direct costs of the attack on the World Trade Center—"comprising earnings losses, property damage, and the cleanup and restoration of the site"—of $33 billion to $36 billion. Their calculations understate the direct costs, however, because they equate the value of lost lives to the value of forgone earnings. In fact, as common sense suggests and economic analysis shows, a lost life is worth more than forgone earnings. Murphy and Topel (2005), for example, estimate the value of a human life to be about three times earnings capacity. Tripling the Bram, Orr, and Rapaport (2002) estimate of lost earnings yields a figure of about $50 billion for the direct costs of the 9/11 attack on the World Trade Center. This figure is highly conservative as an estimate for the overall costs of 9/11 because it omits indirect costs associated with disruption to the U.S. financial system and the regional economy in the New York area. The economic costs of a future terrorist attack could be considerably larger, especially if it involves chemical weapons, biological agents, or nuclear weapons.

Suppose, for example, that a dangerous Iraqi regime raises the probability of a major terrorist attack by 4 percentage points in any given year, and that the economic cost of such an attack is $100 billion. These figures imply an expected cost from (additional) terrorist attacks of $4 billion per year. Capitalizing this flow at the factor $1/(r + \lambda)$, with $r = .02$ and $\lambda = .03$, yields a present value cost of $80 billion. This is a sizable effect and potentially large enough to tilt the scale in favor of war. Of course, if war raises the probability of a major terrorist attack on the United States, then the effect cuts in favor of the containment policy.[54]

Integrated Treatment of Costly Threats, Wars, and Terrorist Attacks
Costly threats, terrorist attacks, limited wars, and a full-scale regime-changing war are possible contingencies under a policy of containment. Our earlier analysis considers these contingencies one at a time; table 8.11 considers all four at the same time. The table shows present value containment costs for three new scenarios plus a scenario with no contingencies, as in table 8.9. The table considers the baseline annual containment costs of $14.5 billion and lower annual costs of $9.7 billion, annual discount rates of 2 and 6 percent, and an annual hazard for peaceful regime change of 3 percent. Our discussion focuses on the baseline case with a 2 percent annual discount rate.

Table 8.11
Present Value Cost of Containment Allowing for Costly Credible Threats, Terrorist Attacks, and Future Wars (billions of 2003 dollars)

Contingencies	No Contingencies	Optimistic Scenario	Middle Scenario	Pessimistic Scenario
Costly credible threats				
Annual probability of mounting threat	0	.05	.10	.15
Cost of mounting threat	–	13.05	26.1	26.1
Limited wars				
Annual probability of fighting limited war	0	.03	.03	.05
Cost of fighting	–	53.3	53.3	53.3
Terrorist attacks				
Annual probability, relative to case with a peaceful Iraqi regime	0	0	.03	.05
Economic cost of attack	–	–	100	250
Regime-changing war				
Probability of war in next ten years	0	.05	.10	.15
Cost, multiple of costs for war scenario 5(a)	–	1	1.5	2
Present Value Cost of Containment				
Baseline, $14.54 billion per year plus contingencies at 2% discount rate	297	346	441	705
Lower costs, $9.69 billion per year plus contingencies at 2% discount rate	198	251	351	620
$14.54 billion per year plus contingencies at 6% discount rate	171	205	269	437
$9.69 billion per year plus contingencies at 6% discount rate	114	150	216	386

Source: Authors' calculations.
Note: The present value calculations are carried out using an expanded version of equation (8.5) with $\lambda = .03$. Regime change, whether peaceful or forcible, eliminates the possibility of additional threats or wars and reduces the (relative) probability of terrorist attacks to zero.

In the "optimistic scenario," a hostile Iraqi regime has no effect on the likelihood of a terrorist attack, but there is a 5 percent annual chance that the United States mounts a costly threat and a 3 percent annual chance that it fights a limited war against Iraq. These contingencies apply so long as a hostile Iraqi regime persists. There is also a 5 percent chance that the United States fights a full-scale regime-changing war against Iraq at some point in the next ten years in the optimistic scenario, where the undiscounted cost of such a war is the same as for war scenario 5(a) in table 8.10. Factoring in these contingencies yields a present value containment cost of $346 billion for the optimistic scenario, as compared to $297 billion when all contingencies have zero probability.

The "middle scenario" posits a greater probability of mounting a costly threat and a greater probability of engaging in a regime-changing war. Credible threats and a regime-changing war are also more costly in the middle scenario. Finally, the middle scenario posits that the annual probability of a major terrorist attack on the United States is 2 percentage points higher with a hostile Iraqi regime. The economic cost of such an attack, if it occurs, is set to $100 billion. Factoring in these contingencies yields a present value containment cost of $441 billion for the middle scenario.

The "pessimistic scenario" posits yet higher probabilities for all contingencies and higher costs for threats, terrorist attacks, and regime-changing wars. Factoring in these contingencies yields a present value containment cost of $705 billion. We have designated the assumptions that underlie this large cost figure as "pessimistic," but they seem well within the range of prewar assessments offered by some knowledgeable observers. This is not to say that these prewar assessments were correct, but neither were they easily dismissed. For those who held such views, or even more pessimistic ones, continued containment was a highly unattractive option.

8.5   War versus Containment: Effects on Iraqi Economic Well-Being

Economic Collapse under Saddam Hussein
After Saddam Hussein became president and secured his position as dictator in 1979, the Iraqi population suffered a catastrophic collapse in living standards, largely as a consequence of Saddam's rule. Nordhaus (2002, 53) estimates that Iraq's real GDP per capita (at 2002 prices) fell from around $9,000 in 1979 to $1,000–$1,200 in 2001. The upper fig-

ure for 2001 implies a staggering 87 percent decline in per capita output. The most significant factors in the collapse were the devastating war with Iran in the 1980s, draconian economic sanctions imposed on Iraq in response to its 1990 invasion of Kuwait and its later refusals to comply with UN Security Council resolutions, and the destruction of Iraq's infrastructure during allied efforts to expel Iraqi forces from Kuwait in 1991. The militarization of Iraqi society, the diversion of resources to Saddam's palaces and monuments, and declines in the relative price of oil amplified the collapse in Iraqi living standards.

After 1990 lost oil revenues alone were enormous. According to Nordhaus (2002, 53), "Under sanctions, oil production during the 1991–2002 period averaged 1.4 million bpd. Assuming Iraq could have produced 3 million bpd during this period, the revenue shortfall since the first Persian Gulf War was about $150 billion." The implied average annual revenue shortfall of $12.5 billion is 40–50 percent as large as Iraq's estimated GDP in 2001. This figure for lost oil revenues is almost certainly too low, if the comparison benchmark is a stable Iraqi economy with ready access to export markets and international oil exploration and extraction technologies. Iraq's oil production peaked at more than 3.4 million bpd in 1979 and had been trending sharply upward since 1973.[55] Further, as Nordhaus (2002, 72) remarks, "Experts believe that, if restructuring operations can operate effectively, Iraq's production capacity can be raised to between 3 and 4 million bpd within two years.... Iraq has enormous reserves relative to its current production...[and] has negotiated $40 billion of contracts with Russia, China, and France to develop approximately 5 million bpd of new capacity."

Much of Iraq's greatly diminished output was diverted to an oversized military, an apparatus of terror and repression, and the relentless glorification of Saddam Hussein. Prewar Iraq employed nearly 500,000 persons in various intelligence, security, and police organizations, and a total of nearly 1.3 million when the armed forces and paramilitary units are included. All together, the various security organizations and military units accounted for about one-quarter of employment in prewar Iraq.[56] This militarization of Iraqi society occurred principally under Saddam Hussein—the army rose from 180,000 men in 1980 to 1 million men (6 percent of the population) in 1988.[57] Despite the sanctions imposed on Iraq after the Gulf War, the regime "embarked upon a series of costly projects to build victory monuments and palaces for Saddam (fifty of them at last count), which cost Iraq as much as another $2.5 billion per year.... Many of the fifty new palaces Saddam has built for himself since the Gulf War have gold-plated faucets and artificial rivers, lakes, and waterfalls that employ pumping equipment that could have been used to address the country's desperate water and sanitation problems."[58]

The foregoing assessment based on prewar data sources is broadly consistent with the analysis in Foote et al. (2004), four economists who worked for the Coalition Provisional Authority in Baghdad and who had access to additional data on Iraq's economy. They estimate that real GDP per capita at constant 2002 prices fell by 60 percent from 1979 to 2001. Living standards fell much more because of two other factors under the regime's control—the militarization of Iraqi society and the diversion of output to Saddam's palaces and monuments— and because of declines in oil prices after 1979. Based on this review of the evidence, we conclude that real income per capita fell by roughly 75 percent as a consequence of Saddam's rule and the regime he established.

Assessing the Impact of War and Regime Change

To assess the impact of regime change on Iraqi economic welfare, we consider an extended transition period to a higher level of GDP per capita. During the transition, output grows by enough to recover much or all of the declines in Iraqi GDP per capita caused by Saddam's misrule. Our analysis treats GDP per capita as a measure of living standards. However, since war and containment imply different time paths for GDP per capita, we carry out the analysis in terms of economic welfare, which captures current and future levels of GDP per capita.

Baseline Model   Let V^T denote per capita welfare at the outset of transition, immediately after regime change. The regime change may occur spontaneously or as the result of external intervention (war). In the latter case, welfare is $V^T - W$, where W denotes the direct one-time impact of war on GDP per capita. Let V^S denote per capita welfare under the current regime assuming no external intervention.

We make the following assumptions:

- Prior to regime change, GDP per capita grows at annual rate g.

- After regime change, GDP per capita grows at rate g plus, during an N-year transition period, an additional rate h.

• The extra component of the growth rate h during the transition period equals $M^{1/N} - 1$, where M is a multiple of initial output (just prior to regime change) that captures the favorable long-run effect of regime change on the level of GDP per capita.

• Absent external intervention, there is a probability λ in any give year of spontaneous, peaceful regime change.

• The discount rate applied to future income is a constant denoted by r.

Under these assumptions, per capita welfare at the outset of transition is

$$V^T = \sum_{i=0}^{N} \left[\frac{(1+g)(1+h)}{1+r} \right] + \frac{M(1+g)^{N+1}}{(1+r)^N(r-g)}. \tag{8.6}$$

Given no external intervention, per capita welfare satisfies the following relation:

$$V^S = 1 + \lambda \left(\frac{V^T(1+g)}{1+r} \right) + (1-\lambda)\left(\frac{V^s(1+g)}{1+r} \right). \tag{8.7}$$

The first term on the right side is GDP per capita at the initial output level, which we have normalized to unity. The second term is the probability of a spontaneous regime change multiplied by the present value of welfare under transition. The third term is the continuation probability for the current regime multiplied by the present value of welfare. Solving this equation for V^S yields

$$V^S = \frac{1 + r + \lambda V^T(1+g)}{[(1+r) - (1-\lambda)(1+g)]}. \tag{8.8}$$

Using equations (8.6) and (8.8), we can compare the effects of war and containment on Iraqi economic welfare. The ratio $(V^T - W)/V^S$ provides a convenient measure for the impact of war relative to containment. When this ratio exceeds unity, war improves Iraqi welfare relative to containment. Subtracting 1 from this ratio gives the impact of war on Iraqi welfare, expressed as a percentage of initial welfare.

Model with Forgone Growth Prior to Regime Change   The baseline model of how regime change affects Iraqi welfare is conservative in the sense that it assumes identical long-term growth rates before and after regime change. An alternative model allows for slower long-term growth in the absence of regime change. So consider an alternative model with growth rate g^S under the initial regime. For this model, assume that regime change brings about an N-year transition period to a higher level of income per capita *and* a higher long-term growth rate $g \geq g^S$. In addition, assume that output growth forgone prior to regime change is never made up. In other words, the catchup process after regime change recovers the drop in output per capita under Saddam, but it does not return the economy to its initial baseline growth path. This alternative model involves only slight modifications to the preceding equations. In particular, the g terms in equations (8.7) and (8.8) are replaced by g^S.

Effect of War on Iraqi Welfare

We now use the model to project the effect of war on the average economic well-being of Iraqis. For our baseline case, we assume a 20-year transition period following regime change. We set $M = 4$ based on the evidence that Iraqi living standards declined by 75 percent or more under Saddam Hussein. Given $N = 20$ years, this choice for M implies $h = 7.18$ percent per year. As before, we assume that the probability of spontaneous regime change is 3 percent per year. We set the long-term growth rate at $g = 2$ percent per year, and we set the annual discount rate on future income flows at $r = 5$ percent. We assume that the destruction associated with war amounts to 50 percent of a year's GDP.

Plugging these values into the baseline model, we calculate that $(V^T - W)/V^S$ equals about 1.5. That is, war raises Iraqi welfare by 50 percent relative to containment in the baseline case. This is an enormous improvement in economic welfare. Table 8.12 quantifies the impact of war on Iraqi welfare for several alternative parameter choices. The table shows that war leads to large gains in Iraqi welfare under a wide variety of alternative parameter choices. Even in the least favorable case for war—involving higher war costs, little catchup during the transition, and a high rate of peaceful regime change—war leads to a substantial improvement in Iraqi welfare compared to a policy of containment.

Table 8.13 quantifies the impact of war on Iraqi welfare in the model with forgone growth prior to regime change. In contrast to the table 8.12 results, we now assume that regime change, whether peaceful or forcible, raises the long-term growth of GDP per capita by 2 percentage points. This modified model implies that war brings very large welfare

Table 8.12
Impact of War on Iraqi Economic Welfare, Baseline Model

Scenario Description	War Cost, Years of GDP	g, Long-Term Output Growth Rate	M, Catchup as Multiple of Initial GDP	λ, Annual Probability of Peaceful Regime Change	Impact of War on Iraqi Welfare as Percent of Initial Welfare
Baseline case	0.5	.02	4	.03	49.8
Slow long-run growth	0.5	0	4	.03	62.8
Higher war cost	1	.02	4	.03	49.0
Less catchup after regime change	0.5	.02	2	.03	25.1
More catchup after regime change	0.5	.02	7	.03	65.6
Higher rate of peaceful regime change	0.5	.02	4	.07	24.5
Lower rate of peaceful regime change	0.5	.02	4	.02	66.8
Highly unfavorable case for war	1	.02	2	.07	12.2
Highly favorable case for war	0.25	.02	7	.02	91.5

Source: Authors' calculations.

Note: All calculations use exponential discounting with an annual discount rate of $r = .05$ on future income. The effective discount rate under containment, inclusive of the regime change probability, is $r + \lambda$.

Table 8.13
Impact of War on Iraqi Economic Welfare, Model with Forgone Growth

Scenario Description	War Cost, Years of GDP	M, Catchup as Multiple of Initial GDP	λ, Annual Probability of Peaceful Regime Change	Impact of War on Iraqi Welfare as Percent of Initial Welfare
Baseline case	0.5	4	.03	100.7
Higher war cost	1	4	.03	99.8
Less catchup after regime change	0.5	2	.03	67.3
More catchup after regime change	0.5	7	.03	122.3
Higher rate of peaceful regime change	0.5	4	.07	49.9
Lower rate of peaceful regime change	0.5	4	.02	134.8
Highly unfavorable case for war	1	2	.07	35.0
Highly favorable case for war	0.25	7	.02	170.0

Source: Authors' calculations.
Note: All calculations use a long-term growth rate after regime change of $g = .02$, a long-term growth rate prior to regime change of $g^S = 0$, and an annual discount rate on future income flows of $r = .05$. The effective discount rate under containment, inclusive of the regime change probability, is $r + \lambda$.

gains for Iraqis, ranging from 35 to 170 percent (table 8.13). War has a more favorable effect because regime change now has a positive effect on long-term growth.

The results in tables 8.12 and 8.13 strongly suggest that war is an economic blessing for Iraqis compared to the alternative policy of containment. How is this possible, given the obvious destructive consequences of war? The answer has two parts. First, the Iraqi economy was in terrible condition before the war, and it would have remained in a sorry state under the policy of containment. Second, as we discussed, economic well-being underwent an extraordinary collapse under Saddam Hussein. If, over the course of a generation, Iraqis recover even half of the economic losses they suffered under Saddam Hussein, then economic welfare will rise significantly as a consequence of forcible regime change.

8.6 War versus Containment: Lost Iraqi Lives

This section briefly reviews evidence on Iraqi casualties in the 1991 Gulf War, the number of premature Iraqi deaths from 1991 to 2003 under the containment policy, and the broader record of war, death and repression under Saddam Hussein. Our account draws heavily on Pollack (2002) and Welch (2002). After reviewing the evidence, we reach a rough judgment as to whether continued containment would have saved Iraqi lives compared to a policy of war and forcible regime change.

Lost Lives under Saddam Hussein

The regime of Saddam Hussein was a ghastly enterprise that brought death and torture to hundreds of thousands of Iraqis and others. Pollack (2002) recounts the following:

• 200,000 Iraqi troops killed in battle during the 1980–1988 war with Iran, and another 400,000 to 500,000 wounded (24). Iranian casualties were much greater.

• In reprisal for Kurdish assistance to the Iranians, the Iraqi regime slaughtered Kurds and destroyed their homes in 1988 and 1989. "When the campaign finally ended in 1989, some two hundred thousand Kurds were dead, roughly 1.5 million had been forcibly resettled, a huge swatch of Kurdistan had been scorched by chemical warfare, and four thousand towns had been razed" (20).

• The Gulf War initiated by Saddam "probably caused no more than 10,000 to 30,000 Iraqi military casualties and another 1,000 to 5,000 civilian casualties" (139).

• In 1991, after the Gulf War, "anywhere from 30,000 to 60,000 Shi'ah were killed in the suppression of the *intifadah* in the south" (51).

• In 1992 and 1993, the regime drained about 4,500 square kilometers of wetlands in the south. "In so doing, [the regime] created an ecological catastrophe and destroyed the way of life of several hundred thousand Marsh Arabs who had made their homes among the rushes and reeds for more than a millennium" (125).

• In addition, perhaps 200,000 or more Iraqis died after the 1991 Gulf War and the postwar *intifadah* through some combination of sanctions and internal repressions (138–139). More than half of the premature deaths were children under five.

The issue of child deaths under sanctions attracted much attention. Welch (2002) provides an informative discussion and a helpful assessment of conflicting claims. He cites Richard Garfield, clinical professor of international nursing at Columbia University, as the most credible source for estimates of how sanctions affected mortality among Iraqi children.[59] According to Welch,

Garfield concluded that between August 1991 and March 1998 there were at least 106,000 excess deaths of children under 5, with a "more likely" worst-case sum of 227,000. (He recently updated the latter figure to 350,000 through this year.) Of those deaths, he estimated one quarter were "mainly associated with the Gulf war." The chief causes, in his view, were "contaminated water, lack of high quality foods, inadequate breast feeding, poor weaning practices, and inadequate supplies in the curative health care system. This was the product of both a lack of some essential goods, and inadequate or inefficient use of existing essential goods." ... It seems awfully hard not to conclude that the embargo on Iraq has been ineffective (especially since 1998) and that it has, at the least, contributed to more than 100,000 deaths since 1990.

All told, the regime of Saddam Hussein killed or caused the deaths of well over half a million Iraqis. Under the policy of containment after the Gulf War, a reasonable estimate is that 200,000 or more Iraqis died prematurely at the hands of the regime or as a direct consequence of its policies, including its refusal to comply with UN Security Council resolutions and the diversion of oil revenues and other resources to construct palaces and monuments.

Despite their sobering quality, the raw numbers fail to convey the sheer horror of the regime. Pollack (2000, 123) succinctly captures some of the horror in a gut-wrenching passage that tells of gouging out the eyes of children to force confessions from parents and grand-parents, lowering victims into huge vats of acid, cutting out the tongues of regime critics, the systematic rape of women and girls in front of male relatives, and other extreme forms of torture and abuse.

War and Containment Compared

How does the tally of human misery and repression under contain-ment compare to the likely consequences of war? Under the policy of containment in effect after the end of the 1991 Gulf War, premature Iraqi deaths numbered at least 10,000 per year and probably two or three times as many. If we discount future lost lives at a rate of 2 per-cent per year and assume a 3 percent annual hazard for spontaneous and peaceful regime change, then a continuation of the containment policy could be expected to result in another 200,000 to 600,000 dead Iraqis. In comparison, the Gulf War of 1990–1991 killed as many as 35,000 Iraqis, mostly troops who died during a long and intensive ae-rial bombardment by the United States and its allies.[60] Iraqi troops might be expected to adopt more effective tactics in reaction to their crushing defeat in the 1991 war. Or they might be expected to fight harder in response to an invasion. Either way, a more effective re-sponse by Iraqi military forces would prolong combat and probably lead to greater Iraqi casualties.

O'Hanlon (2002a; 2002b) looks to the 1989 U.S. invasion of Panama and the 1993 U.S. engagement in Somalia to assess the probable loss of lives in a 2003 Iraq war. Scaling up from these conflicts, he estimates that "Iraqi troop losses might be expected to be anywhere from 2,000 to 50,000, with civilian casualties in the same relative range." He stresses that a key unknown is the willingness of Iraqi troops to fight. He also cautions that Iraqi use of chemical or biological weapons against U.S. troops or its own population could substantially raise Iraqi casualties. However, even his most pessimistic projections involve fewer fatalities than the 200,000–600,000 expected premature deaths that we project under a continuation of the containment policy.

There is a great deal of uncertainty about the number of premature Iraqi deaths under both war and containment. We think the weight of evidence points to a greater Iraqi death toll from a continuation of the prewar containment policy than from a policy of war and forcible regime change. Perhaps the strongest reason to question this assessment is the possibility that a postwar Iraq could devolve into an extended and large-scale civil war. This possibility cannot be ruled out. What can be ruled out in light of the evidence is that the leading alternative to war involved little loss of Iraqi lives.

8.7   Concluding Remarks

Forcible regime change in Iraq has proved to be a costly undertaking. As of January 2006, it appears likely that the Iraq intervention will ultimately unfold along a path that implies present value costs for the United States in the range of $410 billion to $630 billion in 2003 dollars. These figures reflect a 2 percent annual discount rate. They capture the estimated economic costs of U.S. military resources deployed in the war and postwar occupation, the value of lost lives and injuries sustained by U.S. soldiers, the lifetime medical costs of treating injured soldiers, and U.S. outlays for humanitarian assistance and postwar reconstruction. Preinvasion views about the likely course of the Iraq intervention imply present value costs in the range of $100 billion to $870 billion. Military resources devoted to postwar occupation account for more than half the total costs except in optimistic scenarios that envision a short occupation, little postwar conflict and a smooth reconstruction effort.

The high cost of the Iraq intervention is sometimes seen as a compelling argument against the decision to forcibly overthrow the ruling order and install a new regime. This argument is deficient because it ignores the costs of alternative responses to the national security and humanitarian concerns presented by the prewar Iraqi regime. A well-founded verdict on the Iraq intervention requires, at a minimum, an evaluation of what these alternatives would cost. We tackle this issue by assessing the costs of sticking with the prewar containment policy.

Containment required the continuous engagement of a potent U.S. military force in southern Turkey, the Middle East, and the Persian Gulf. The United States devoted roughly 28,000 troops, 30 naval vessels, 200 military aircraft, and other equipment to Iraqi containment efforts prior to the prewar build-up. We estimate the economic cost of these military resources to be about $14.5 billion per year. Based on our assessment of the likely duration of a dangerous regime in Iraq, absent external intervention, this annual flow translates into an expected present value of nearly $300 billion. Hence, containment was also a costly option for the United States, even under the favorable assumption that it would be completely effective in achieving its national security goals.

Advocates for forcible regime change in Iraq expressed several concerns about the prewar containment policy. Some stressed an erosion of political support for the containment policy that threatened to undermine its effectiveness and lead to a much costlier conflict with Iraq in the future. Others stressed the difficulty of compelling Iraqi compliance with a rigorous process of weapons inspections and disarmament, widely seen as a critical element of containment. And others stressed the potential for Iraqi collaboration with international terrorist groups. To evaluate these concerns, we model the possibility that an effective containment policy might require the mounting of costly threats and might lead to a limited war or a full-scale regime-changing war against Iraq at a later date. We also consider the possibility that the survival of a hostile Iraqi regime raises the probability of a major terrorist attack on the United States. We draw on our empirical analysis to assess the potential costs of these contingencies, but their probabilities are especially difficult to assess with confidence.

We show that any one of these contingencies can sharply raise the expected cost of the containment policy. We also develop an integrated analysis that simultaneously captures several possible contingencies under a policy of containment. The integrated analysis focuses on three scenarios chosen to capture a range of views about the likelihood and cost of the contingencies. Factoring the contingencies into the analysis yields present value costs for the containment policy in the range of roughly $350 billion to $700 billion. These large sums are in the same ballpark as the likely costs of the Iraq intervention seen from the vantage point of early 2006. Thus, even with the benefit of partial hindsight, it is difficult to gauge whether the Iraq intervention is more costly than containment.

We also consider the consequences of the war-versus-containment choice in two other respects: the economic well-being of Iraqis and the loss of Iraqi lives. Based on our analysis, we conclude that the war will lead to large improvements in the economic well-being of most Iraqis relative to their prospects under the policy of containment. This conclusion follows from some basic observations. First, the Iraqi economy was in terrible condition before the war and would have remained so under the policy of containment. Second, the regime of Saddam

Hussein was an economic failure of tremendous proportions. The available evidence suggests that real income per capita fell by roughly 75 percent as a consequence of Saddam's misrule. In addition, much of Iraq's greatly diminished output was diverted to an oversized military, terror and repression, and the glorification of Saddam. Third, the removal of sanctions, the expansion of petroleum exports, large-scale reconstruction aid, and the reintegration of Iraq's economy into the world economy provide a strong basis for economic gains, even in a society with serious institutional weaknesses. If Iraqis regain even half of the economic losses that occurred under Saddam Hussein, they will be substantially better off in material terms as a consequence of forcible regime change.

The economic failures of the Saddam Hussein regime were not its greatest crimes. The regime brought torture, repression, displacement, and death to huge numbers of Iraqis and others. We review some of the evidence in this regard, drawing heavily on work by others. All told, the regime killed or caused the deaths of more than 500,000 Iraqis. Under the policy of containment after the 1991 Gulf War, a reasonable estimate is that at least 200,000 Iraqis died prematurely at the hands of the regime or as a direct consequence of its policies, including its refusal to comply with resolutions of the UN Security Council and its diversion of oil revenues and other resources to palaces and monuments. Had containment remained in effect, the historical record suggests that premature Iraqi deaths would have continued indefinitely at the rate of 10,000 to 30,000 per year. There is, of course, a great deal of uncertainty about the number of premature Iraqi deaths under either war or containment, but we think the weight of evidence points to a greater Iraqi death toll from a continuation of the prewar containment policy. A reason to question this assessment is the possibility, which cannot be ruled out, that a postwar Iraq could experience an extended and large-scale civil war. However, in light of the evidence, we can rule out the notion that the leading alternative to war involved little loss of Iraqi lives.

The question of how to deal with "tyrants, rogue states and terrorists who threaten not only their own people but also others" is a profoundly difficult one. The stakes, human and economic, are enormous. The policy options are complex and fraught with uncertainty. And sound decision-making requires a daunting range of inputs and analysis. Yet, precisely because the stakes are so high and the decisions are so difficult, it is essential to systematically evaluate alternatives as an input to decision making and the formulation of national security policy. Our study is an effort to apply a systematic approach to the evaluation of the two leading policy options prior to the Iraq war.

8.8   Afterword

Shortly before the March 2003 invasion of Iraq, we circulated an essay titled "War in Iraq versus Containment: Weighing the Costs" (Davis, Murphy, and Topel 2003). As the title suggests, the essay sought to analyze and compare the chief U.S. policy options regarding Iraq at the time. We wrote and circulated the essay for three reasons: first, to help structure our thinking about the wisdom of a looming war; second, to show how basic economic principles and a quantitative approach can inform analysis of national security issues; and third, because of our dissatisfaction with the shallow nature of much public and private discourse about U.S. policy toward Iraq.

In 2005 we revised and substantially expanded the essay into a larger study. We replaced off-the-shelf government war cost projections with our own projections. We considered a broader range of possible scenarios under the war and containment policy options, and we deepened the analysis in other respects. As in the earlier essay, we retained a focus on the choice between major policy options facing the United States as of 2002 and early 2003. The previous sections of this chapter present the larger study.

At this writing, in March 2008, the ultimate cost and outcome of the Iraq intervention remain uncertain. Violent sectarian conflict, terrorism, resistance to U.S. military occupation, and widespread criminality have caused a large loss of life, displaced many Iraqis from their homes, and escalated U.S. military costs. Violence, sabotage, and corruption have impeded reconstruction and economic development. The security situation inside Iraq deteriorated markedly during 2006 before improving dramatically in 2007. According to the Brookings Institution's Iraq Index, Iraqi deaths by violent means rose from about 1,450 per month in October–December 2005 to more than 3,300 per month in the second half of 2006. Violent deaths fell over the course of 2007 and reached postinvasion lows of about 700 per month in the period from October 2007 to January 2008.[61] U.S. troop fatalities in the Iraq conflict show a similar pattern, falling sharply after May 2007, as

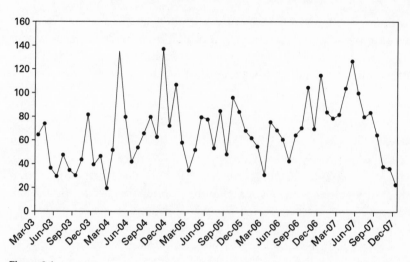

Figure 8.4
U.S. troop fatalities in Operation Iraqi Freedom, March 2003–December 2007. From Saban Center for Middle East Policy, Brookings Institution, *Iraq Index*, March 3, 2008.

shown in figure 8.4. Whether progress in restoring internal security and order to Iraq can survive a gradual or rapid withdrawal of U.S. troops remains to be seen.

The Iraq intervention has proved to be much costlier for the United States than our baseline estimate for the cost of containment (roughly $300 billion in 2003 dollars) and at least as costly as the most pessimistic containment scenario we considered in table 8.11. Experience to date with respect to U.S. casualties and reconstruction costs is in line with war scenarios 5 and 6 (table 8.8). However, none of our scenarios fully anticipated the extended duration of a large-scale U.S. occupation force in Iraq. Scenario 5 projected a U.S. force in theater of 200,000 through October 2006 and a draw-down to zero by October 2008. Scenario 6 envisioned a force of 200,000 through September 2007 and a draw-down to zero by 2013.

Figure 8.5 shows actual U.S. forces inside Iraq through December 2007. The "surge" brought U.S. forces to their highest levels since the occupation began. The troop numbers in figure 8.5 do not include support personnel stationed outside Iraq but directly engaged in Operation Iraqi Freedom. We are unaware of publicly available data on total U.S. military forces in the Iraq theater or directly engaged in Operation Iraqi Freedom, but we believe that these force levels have been greater than 200,000 during the surge period and perhaps earlier.[62]

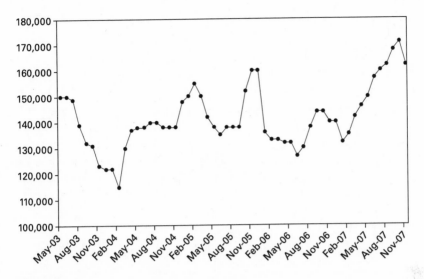

Figure 8.5
U.S. Troops in Iraq, May 2003–November 2007. From Saban Center for Middle East Policy, Brookings Institution, *Iraq Index*, March 3, 2008.

Higher troop levels imply larger personnel and support costs, larger capital costs for the equipment and facilities used by extra troops, and additional costs for transport and redeployment. The extended duration of a large-scale U.S. occupation force has substantially increased the cost of the Iraq intervention above the levels we projected for scenarios 5 and 6. In addition, the value we applied for labor costs per troop/year under occupation may be too low. Whether realized user costs for capital goods exceed the rates we applied (table 8.1) is unclear to us, although the large run-up in fuel prices pushes in the direction of higher costs to operate equipment and transport troops.

Developments since the invasion of Iraq also raise questions about our analysis of containment costs. The intensity and duration of sectarian conflict since 2004 suggest that violent civil conflict might have erupted following the eventual death of Saddam, a possibility we did not consider in our containment scenarios. The apparent success of the containment policy in degrading Iraq's military capabilities suggests that it had less capacity to threaten its neighbors than some national security analysts had feared. Whether the United States and its allies would have sustained the political will to maintain indefinitely an effective containment policy seems as uncertain now as it was in 2002.

Our study and the earlier essay elicited a wide range of responses, many quite passionate, some dismissive, some laudatory, and some constructive. Many critics, including sympathetic ones, expressed the view that it is important to consider a broader range of costs and benefits implicated by the choice between war and containment. We agree, and we hope that social scientists will not hesitate to apply their tools and skills to the Iraq conflict and other critical matters of national security and humanitarian concern. We believe there is considerable value in spelling out assumptions, grounding analysis and conclusions in data where possible, articulating explicit counterfactuals, and weighing policy options in a systematic manner. We also think that U.S. national security decision making, planning, and implementation are ill served by an aversion to the systematic application of analytical tools from economics and other social sciences.

Notes

This chapter is a revised version of an analytical essay circulated by the authors shortly before the March 2003 invasion of Iraq (Davis, Murphy, and Topel 2003). For many thoughtful comments on the earlier essay, we especially wish to thank, without implicating, Ricardo Caballero, Charles Himmelberg, Eric Rasmussen, Roberto Rigobon, Christopher Sims, and Andy Torok. We also thank seminar participants at the University of Chicago, the NBER Working Group on the Economics of National Security, and the CESifo conference. We thank Chris Foote for assistance with data on Iraqi employment and oil production. Sophie Castro-Davis provided research assistance.

1. Davis, Murphy, and Topel (2003).

2. Broader studies of the economic costs of military conflict include those by Hess (2003), who investigates the empirical relation between consumption growth and military conflict throughout the world in recent decades; and Collier et al. (2003), who document the highly detrimental effects of civil war on economic development.

3. Seventeen countries participated in or provided logistical support to the maritime interdiction force (Garamone 2000). France initially participated in the enforcement of Iraqi no-fly zones along with the United States and Britain. France ceased participation in the Northern no-fly zone in 1996 and in the Southern no-fly zone in December 1998.

4. U.S. Senate Committee on Armed Services (2000).

5. U.S. Department of Defense (2001).

6. U.S. Congressional Budget Office (2002).

7. This figure does not include the cost of heavy reconstruction after a prospective war in Iraq. See CBO (2002, 5, tables 3, 4).

8. See, for example, CBO (2002, 2).

9. To arrive at this estimate, we divide Army personnel costs in FY 2001 by the estimated number of full-time equivalent Army personnel as of September 2000. As of September

30, 2000, the Army had 482,170 active-duty personnel (U.S. Department of Defense 2002b, table 1.1). The ready reserve component of the U.S. armed forces numbered about 1.2 million persons in 2000 and 2001 (U.S. Bureau of the Census 2005, table 508). In 2000 and 2001 the annual number of active-duty days per ready reserve member was about 14 (CBO 2005a, fig. 6). Army reserve units accounted for the vast majority of all active-duty days by reserve personnel (CBO 2005a, 3). On that basis, we attribute all active-duty days by reserve personnel to the Army, which implies 14 days times 1.2 million active-duty days by Army reserve units. Assuming that regular Army personnel work 220 days per year, the full-time equivalent Army military force as of September 2000 amounts to $(14/220)(1.2$ million$) + 0.482$ million $= 566,000$. According to U.S. Department of Defense (2005a, table 6-22), Army outlays for FY 2001 included $28.11 billion in personnel costs. We ignore any special pay for hazardous duty in this figure because few U.S. military forces were actively engaged in combat operations or other hazardous duty in 2000 and 2001. Dividing $28.11 billion by the number of full-time equivalent Army personnel in September 2000 yields an annual per person figure of $49,670, or $51,223 in 2003 dollars. If the CBO uses an 80-20 mix of regular and reserve personnel in its cost projections, then the omitted personnel costs amount to $(.80)(\$51,223) = \$40,978$.

10. See the discussion of troop rotation ratios in CBO (2003a, app. C). An analogous point clearly applies to military equipment—naval vessels, for example—that rotates through the theater of operations over time.

11. U.S. Congressional Budget Office (2000).

12. U.S. Congressional Budget Office (2002, tables 4, 5).

13. We carry out all price-level adjustments using the GDP implicit price deflator for all goods and services.

14. Military equipment per Army personnel deployed in Iraq, Kuwait, and Afghanistan is about $189,000 according to data in CBO (2005b). We apply this figure to the number of Army troops and Marines devoted to the containment policy and half this amount to the number of Air Force personnel. The result is about $1.5 billion in 2003 dollars.

15. The two assumptions underlying the entries in table 8.1, line 2, are strong ones, and we would prefer to relax them by exploiting detailed data on normal O&M spending for military equipment. Unfortunately, as noted in CBO (2001, 2), the Department of Defense does not produce detailed breakouts for its equipment-related spending on fuel, spare parts, other consumables, and depot maintenance. This lack of data precludes a more direct estimate of normal O&M costs for military equipment.

16. We regard the $0.2 billion figure for munitions as a low-end guess. According to Center for Defense Information (1998), cruise missiles and other smart munitions expended by U.S. forces during the four-day December 1998 Desert Fox operation cost $478 million to produce. Desert Fox was one of the largest operations conducted by allied forces during the containment of Iraq.

17. U.S. Department of Defense (2000b, tables 6.18–6.20).

18. This calculation may also lead to a substantial understatement of containment costs. First, it does not include the costs of compensating, supporting, and training the additional troops who rotate through the theater of operations over time. Second, it does not include the additional costs of constructing and maintaining naval vessels and other equipment that rotate through the theater over time. Third, the calculation rests on an implicit assumption that depreciation, maintenance, and operating costs for military equipment is the same whether or not the equipment is in theater. Fourth, the calculation

includes no adjustment for higher munitions expenditures in theater. Nevertheless, this calculation may also lead to an overstatement of containment costs if the naval vessels devoted to the containment policy are less costly to build or operate than the average U.S. naval vessel. The calculation may also lead to an overstatement if containment operations facilitate the training, readiness, and development of U.S. military forces because these benefits are not netted out of the estimated costs.

19. See, for example, Higgs (2004).

20. During a press briefing shortly after the end of Desert Fox, General Anthony Zinni, Commander in Chief of U.S. Central Command (CENTCOM) stated, "The operation involved over 30,000 troops, and 10,000 more outside our area of responsibility who supported and alerted from bases virtually around the world.... Over 300 aircraft were involved in strike and support roles.... Over 40 ships performed strike and support roles.... Thousands of ground troops deployed to protect Kuwait and to respond to any counteraction. Hundreds of our Special Operations Forces troops also deployed to carry out their assigned missions." A transcript of the press briefing is available at ⟨http://www.defenselink.mil/transcripts/1998/t12211998_t1221fox.html⟩.

21. See, for example, the testimony of General Tommy R. Franks before the U.S. Senate Committee on Armed Services on September 19, 2000: "Iraq's WMD capabilities remain a key concern. It has been more than a year and a half since UN weapons inspections last occurred in Iraq, and Saddam Hussein has thus far refused new inspections." UN weapons inspectors did not return to Iraq until November 2002.

22. In his December 1998 address to the American people, shortly after U.S. and British forces commenced Operation Desert Fox, President Bill Clinton described the importance of the weapons inspection program this way: "First, without a strong inspection system, Iraq would be free to retain and begin to rebuild its chemical, biological and nuclear weapons programs in months, not years. Second, if Saddam can cripple the weapons inspection system and get away with it, he would conclude that the international community—led by the United States—has simply lost its will. He will surmise that he has free rein to rebuild his arsenal of destruction, and someday—make no mistake—he will use it again as he has in the past. Third,... If we turn our backs on his defiance, the credibility of U.S. power as a check against Saddam will be destroyed. We will not only have allowed Saddam to shatter the inspection system that controls his weapons of mass destruction program; we also will have fatally undercut the fear of force that stops Saddam from acting to gain domination in the region." A transcript of President Clinton's full address is available at ⟨http://www.cnn.com/ALLPOLITICS/stories/1998/12/16/transcripts/clinton.html⟩.

23. See, for example, "U.N. Withdraws U-2 Planes," New York Times, March 12, 2003.

24. Another argument is that U.S. forces engaged in containment activities can and will continue to carry out some of the same general training and readiness preparation that they would undertake in any event.

25. See U.S. General Accounting Office (1991) for an overview of U.S. military activities in the Middle East during the 1980s and their costs. While the U.S. had few grounds in the Middle East prior to Iraq's invasion of Kuwait in 1990, developments in the broader Southwest Asia region provided much of the motivation for the creation of a U.S.-based Rapid Deployment Force in the early 1980s.

26. See Bueno de Mesquita et al. (2003) for a detailed analysis of the factors that influence the survival of political leaders and regimes. In their chapter 7, they estimate survival functions and hazard rates for individual political leaders. The issue at hand for our anal-

ysis, however, is the duration of a dangerous regime in Iraq, not the survival of a particular leader. We are unaware of econometric studies that speak directly to the regime survival question.

27. See U.S. Congressional Research Service (2003).

28. The Iraqi Baath party took power by way of a military coup in 1968. General Ahmed Hassan al-Bakr became president and, shortly thereafter, prime minister and commander in chief of Iraqi military forces. At the time, Bakr was also secretary-general of the Baath party and chairman of its powerful Revolutionary Command Council. Saddam Hussein played a significant role in the coup and held considerable sway over Baath party, and later Iraqi, security forces. The early stages of Saddam's rise to power owe much to the support he received from Bakr. Saddam accumulated power and influence throughout the 1970s, eventually eliminating or overshadowing all rivals, including Bakr. In August 1979 he persuaded Bakr to step aside and to designate Saddam as his successor. See Coughlin (2005), especially chapters 3 to 5, for an account of these developments. Although Saddam's ruthlessness, propensity for violence, and fascination with military force were evident long before he achieved the presidency and undisputed power within Iraq, the nightmarish quality of the regime was not easily foretold. For most ordinary Iraqis who did not directly challenge the regime or the Baath party, the 1970s were a decade of rising prosperity. Some outside observers saw the early Baathist government as one of the most progressive regimes in the Middle East.

29. As of March 2003, there were 37,000 U.S. military personnel stationed in South Korea and another 45,000 in nearby Japan (Burns 2003). The United States also relies on additional military resources to contain and deter North Korea. For example, Burns writes, "In response to recent North Korean moves to reactivate its nuclear weapons program, the Pentagon this week is sending 12 B-52 bombers and 12 B-1 bombers from U.S. bases to Guam, within striking distance of the Korean peninsula."

30. A more sophisticated treatment of regime change would allow the hazard rate to be nonstationary and to depend on the precise character of the containment policy. We would welcome such an analysis, but it is beyond the scope of this study.

31. See HBC (2002) and CBO (2002). The HBC and CBO have issued several additional reports on the costs of the Iraq war since September 2002.

32. See Executive Office of the President (2003). It was widely understood at the time that additional requests for spending authority related to the Iraq war would be forthcoming (see, e.g., Firestone 2003).

33. See the cover letter from the CBO director to the ranking members of the House and Senate Budget Committees that accompanies CBO (2002). The report states, "CBO's estimates represent the incremental costs that DoD [Department of Defense] could incur above the budgeted costs of routine operations. As a result, the estimate excludes items such as the basic pay of active-duty military personnel but includes the monthly pay for reservists recalled to full-time duty. Similarly, the estimates reflect only the costs of aircraft flying hours and ship steaming days above those normally provided in DoD's regular appropriations" (2).

34. HBC (2002, 28).

35. CBO (2002, 2).

36. This view is consistent with news reports that U.S. Army and Marine forces have been stretched thin by an extended engagement of ground forces in the Iraq theater.

Concerns about the ability of the U.S. Army to meet the force requirements of an extended occupation of Iraq also arose prior to the March 2003 invasion. For example, CBO (2002, 5) states, "Army forces would be unable to support [normal] rotations for a prolonged 200,000-person occupation."

37. Despite these adjustments, the figures in table 8.6 are lower than the costs implied by the methods of section 1, "Baseline Case." To see this point, consider the heavy air option with two months of major combat. The sum of "personnel and personnel support" costs, "operations support including munitions," and "transport to and from theater" is $34.3 billion in this scenario, according to table 8.6. Applying the method 1 cost per person/year of $226,000—which covers personnel and their support, some operations support, and the rotation of personnel into and out of theater—yields a cost of $38.1 billion for an eight-month engagement (initial deployment, major combat, redeployment). The reasons for this discrepancy are unclear to us. Perhaps large engagements involve significant scale economies not present under containment. Or perhaps we have overstated the costs of containment relative to those of initial deployment, major combat, and redeployment. If so, and because we rely on method 1 to compute the costs of occupation, we also overstate the cost of postwar occupation relative to the initial war phase.

38. Table 8.7, panel B, shows projected occupation costs based on method 2 and using the "all-in costs per person/year" reported in table 8.2. Method 2 yields much larger costs than method 1, as before.

39. Relative to the projection in CBO (2002), our per person cost figure during occupation is 39 percent greater at a high operations tempo and 26 percent greater at a low tempo.

40. Relative to containment, the ratio of ground troops to naval personnel is more than 70 times higher in an occupation, according to our calculations and projections. The ratio of ground troops to Air Force personnel is about 19 times higher in an occupation.

41. U.S. Department of State (2005).

42. See Packer (2005), especially chapter 4, for an account of influential preinvasion views about the likely course of a postwar occupation in Iraq.

43. Sack and Elsasser (2004) provide evidence on the yields implied by inflation-indexed U.S. Treasury securities. It is clear from their study that the difference between yields on nominal U.S. Treasury securities and survey measures of inflationary expectations implies a lower real cost of funds and hence a lower discount rate than 2 percent.

44. The recent economics literature develops several rationales for declining discount rate schedules. See Groom et al. (2005) for a review.

45. Table 8.10 is based on the heavy air option in CBO (2002). The heavy ground option involves an extra $11 billion–$16 billion in present value costs, depending on the length of the major combat phase.

46. See, for example, Coughlin (2005, ch. 7).

47. This assessment has not gone unchallenged. For instance, see Lopez and Cortright (2004).

48. Pollack reiterated this argument shortly before the invasion of Iraq: "The choice we have before us is we either go to war now or we will never go to war with Saddam until he chooses to use a nuclear weapon and he chooses the time and place. The question for me is not war or no war. It's a question of war now, when the costs may be significant, or war later when they may be unimaginable" (Zernike 2003).

49. Campaign Against Sanctions on Iraq, www.casi.org.uk/info/scriraq.html#1998.

50. Press briefing by General Anthony Zinni (see note 20).

51. The time line and quotations in this paragraph are drawn from Infoplease, ⟨http://www.infoplease.com/spot/iraqtimeline2.html⟩.

52. See Pollack (2002, ch. 3) for brief accounts of these episodes.

53. The sum of costs for initial deployment, major combat and redeployment plus the cost for 500 U.S. fatalities and about 3,600 U.S. injuries.

54. Peaceful regime change under a policy of containment and forcible regime change as a consequence of war need not have the same impact on the probability of a terrorist attack. Hence, to quantify the present value cost of terrorist attacks under both policy options, it is necessary to specify five parameters: the discount rate, the cost of a terrorist attack, the attack probabilities under containment, peaceful regime change, and forcible regime change. One of the probabilities can be normalized to zero when calculating the net impact of the war-versus-containment choice on the present value cost of terrorist attacks.

55. Data on Iraqi oil production are available at ⟨http://www.eia.doe.gov/emeu/international/contents.html⟩.

56. Data on the number of persons in security organizations and military units are drawn from Pollack (2002, 116–117). Chris Foote supplied us with an unpublished table from Iraq's Ministry of Planning with employment data. The table shows total employment of 4.6 million based on a 1997 census of Iraq and projected total employment of 5.2 million in 2000.

57. Donnelly (2004, 4).

58. Pollack (2002, 131, 135).

59. See Garfield (1999a; 1999b) for two of his original studies.

60. Pollack (2002, 139).

61. Iraq Index, March 3, 2008. ⟨http://www.brookings.edu/saban/iraq-index.aspx⟩.

62. The war cost estimates in our study are based on projected military forces in the Iraq theater of operations, which includes forces in Kuwait, Qatar, and other countries in the region as well as naval vessels.

References

Bilmes, L., and J. E. Stiglitz. 2006. The economic cost of the Iraq War: An appraisal three years after the beginning of the conflict. NBER Working Paper 12054. Cambridge, Mass.: National Bureau of Economic Research.

Bram, J., J. Orr, and C. Rapaport. 2002. Measuring the effects of the September 11 attack on New York City. *Economic Policy Review* 8 (2): 5–20.

Bueno de Mesquita, B., A. Smith, R. M. Siverson, and J. D. Morrow. 2003. *The Logic of Political Survival*. Cambridge, Mass.: MIT Press.

Burns, R. 2003. Rumsfeld: Move U.S. troops from Korea DMZ. Associated Press. March 6. ⟨http://nucnews.net/nucnews/2003nn/0303nn/030306nn.htm#032⟩.

CBO. *See* U.S. Congressional Budget Office.

Center for Defense Information. 1998. Cost of U.S. military action against Iraq. Fact Sheet. December 22. ⟨http://www.cdi.org/issues/iraq/costs_Dec1998.html⟩.

Collier, P., V. L. Elliott, H. Hegre, A. Hoeffler, M. Reynal-Querol, and N. Sambanis. 2003. *Breaking the Conflict Trap: Civil War and Development Policy*. Policy Research Report. Washington, D.C.: World Bank.

Coughlin, C. 2005. *Saddam Hussein: His Rise and Fall*. New York: Harper.

Davis, S. J., K. M. Murphy, and R. H. Topel. 2003. War in Iraq versus containment: Weighing the costs. ⟨http://faculty.chicagogsb.edu/steven.davis/research/⟩.

Donnelly, T. 2004. *Operation Iraqi Freedom: A Strategic Assessment*. Washington, D.C.: AEI Press.

Executive Office of the President. Office of Management and Budget. 2003. Request for FY 2003 supplemental appropriations. March 25. ⟨http://www.cfo.doe.gov/budget/billrept/fy03/presbud_supp.pdf⟩.

Firestone, D. 2003. What price war? It's too soon to tell, but expect the final tab to be high. *New York Times*, April 7.

Foote, C., W. Block, K. Crane, and S. Gray. 2004. Economic policy and prospects in Iraq. *Journal of Economic Perspectives* 18 (3): 47–70.

Garamone, J. 2000. Embargo chief says Iran in cahoots with Iraq oil smugglers. Armed Forces Press Service. ⟨http://www.defenselink.mil/news/newsarticle.aspx?id=45074⟩.

Garfield, R. 1999a. Morbidity and mortality among Iraqi children from 1990 through 1998: Assessing the impact of the Gulf War and economic sanctions. ⟨http://www.fourthfreedom.org/Applications/cms.php?page_id=7⟩.

———. 1999b. Health and wellbeing in Iraq: Sanctions and the Oil for Food Program. *Transnational Law and Contemporary Problems* 11 (2): 278–297.

Groom, B., C. Hepburn, P. Koundouri, and D. Pearce. 2005. Declining discount rates: The long and short of it. *Environmental and Resource Economics* 32: 445–493.

HBC. *See* U.S. Congress. House. Committee on the Budget.

Hess, G. D. 2003. The economic welfare cost of conflict: An empirical assessment. CESifo Working Paper 852. Munich: CESifo Group.

Higgs, R. 2004. Billions more for defense—and we may not even know it. *San Francisco Chronicle*, January 18, D3. ⟨http://www.sfgate.com/cgi-bin/article.cgi?file=/c/a/2004/01/18/INGSM4A8JB1.DTL⟩.

Lopez, G. A., and D. Cortright. 2004. Containing Iraq: Sanctions worked. *Foreign Affairs* 83 (4): 90–103.

McKibbin, W. J., and A. Stoeckel. 2003. The economic costs of a war in Iraq. ⟨http://www.brookings.edu/views/papers/mckibbin/20030307.pdf⟩.

Moseley, T. M. 2003. *Operation Iraqi Freedom: By the Numbers*. U.S. Air Forces Central (USCENTAF). Assessment and Analysis Division. April 30. ⟨http://www.globalsecurity.org/military/library/report/2003/uscentaf_oif_report_30apr2003.pdf⟩.

Murphy, K. M., and R. H. Topel. 2005. The value of health and longevity. NBER Working Paper 11405. Cambridge, Mass.: National Bureau of Economic Research.

Nordhaus, W. 2002. The economic consequences of a war with Iraq. In *War with Iraq: Costs, Consequences and Alternatives*, by C. Kaysen, S. E. Miller, M. B. Malin, W. D. Nordhaus, and J. D. Steinbruner. Cambridge, Mass.: American Academy of Arts and Sciences.

O'Hanlon, M. 2002a. Counting casualties: How many people would die in an Iraqi war? *Slate*, September 25. ⟨http://www.slate.com/?id=2071530⟩.

———. 2002b. Overthrowing Saddam: Calculating the costs and casualties. ⟨http://www.brookings.edu/papers/2002/1009iraq_ohanlon.aspx⟩.

———. 2002c. Saddam's bomb: How close is Iraq to having a nuclear weapon? *Slate*, September 18. ⟨http://www.slate.com/id/2071135/⟩.

Packer, G. 2005. *The Assassins' Gate: America in Iraq*. New York: Farrar, Straus and Giroux.

Pollack, K. M. 2002. *The Threatening Storm: The Case for Invading Iraq*. New York: Random House.

Sack, B., and R. Elsasser. 2004. Treasury inflation-indexed debt: A review of the U.S. experience. *Economic Policy Review* 10 (1): 47–63.

Shawcross, W. 2004. *Allies: Why the West Had to Remove Saddam*. New York: Public Affairs.

U.S. Bureau of the Census. 2005. *Statistical Abstract of the United States*. Washington, D.C.: Government Printing Office.

U.S. Central Intelligence Agency. 2003. Statement by David Kay on the Interim Progress Report on the Activities of the Iraq Survey Group (ISG) before the House Permanent Select Committee on Intelligence, the House Committee on Appropriations, Subcommittee on Defense, and the Senate Select Committee on Intelligence. October 2. [Kay report] ⟨http://www.fas.org/irp/cia/product/dkay100203.html⟩.

———. 2004. *Comprehensive Report of the Special Advisor to the DCI on Iraq's WMD (Weapons of Mass Destruction)*. September 30. [Duelfer report] ⟨http://news.findlaw.com/nytimes/docs/iraq/cia93004wmdrpt.html⟩.

U.S. Congress. House. Committee on the Budget. Democratic Staff. 2002. *Assessing the Cost of Military Action Against Iraq: Using Desert Shield/Desert Storm as Basis for Estimates*. September 23.

———. 2003. *The Cost of War and Reconstruction in Iraq: An Update*. September 23.

U.S. Congress. Senate. Committee on Armed Services. 2000. Statement of General Tommy R. Franks. September 19. ⟨http://www.fas.org/news/iraq/2000/09/iraq-000919a.htm⟩.

———. 2002. Prepared Testimony of Secretary of Defense Donald H. Rumsfeld. February 5. ⟨http://www.defenselink.mil/speeches/2002/s20020205-secdef4.html⟩.

U.S. Congressional Budget Office. 2000. *Budgeting for Naval Forces: Structuring Tomorrow's Navy at Today's Funding Level*. ⟨http://www.cbo.gov/showdoc.cfm?index=2603&sequence=3⟩.

———. 2001. *The Effects of Aging on the Costs of Operating and Maintaining Military Equipment*. ⟨http://www.cbo.gov/doc.cfm?index=2982⟩.

————. 2002. *Estimated Costs of a Potential Conflict with Iraq.* ⟨http://www.cbo.gov/doc
.cfm?index=3822⟩.

————. 2003a. *An Analysis of the U.S. Military's Ability to Sustain an Occupation of Iraq.*
⟨http://www.cbo.gov/doc.cfm?index=6682⟩.

————. 2003b. Letter from the CBO Director to Congressman John M. Spratt, Jr., Ranking
Member of the Committee on the Budget, U.S. House of Representatives. October 28.
⟨http://www.cbo.gov/doc.cfm?index=4683&type=1⟩.

————. 2005a. *The Effects of Reserve Call-Ups on Civilian Employers.* ⟨http://www.cbo.gov/
ftpdocs/63xx/doc6351/05-11-Reserves.pdf⟩.

————. 2005b. The Potential Costs Resulting from Increased Usage of Military Equipment in Ongoing Operations. Statement of Douglas Holtz-Eakin, CBO Director, before
the Subcommittee on Readiness Committee on Armed Services, U.S. House of Representatives. April 6. ⟨http://www.globalsecurity.org/military/library/congress/2005_hr/
050406-holtz-eakin.pdf⟩.

U.S. Congressional Research Service. 2003. *North Korea's Nuclear Weapons Program.*
Updated August 27. ⟨http://fas.org/spp/starwars/crs/IB91141.pdf⟩.

U.S. Department of Defense. 2000a. *National Defense Budget Estimates for FY 2001.* ⟨http://
www.dod.mil/comptroller/defbudget/fy2001/fy2001_greenbook.pdf⟩.

————. 2000b. *Selected Manpower Statistics, Fiscal Year 2000.* ⟨http://siadapp.dmdc.osd
.mil/personnel/M01/Fy00/m01fy00.pdf⟩.

————. 2001. Overseas Contingency Operations Transfer Fund. FY 2001 President's
Budget   Submission.   ⟨http://www.dod.mil/comptroller/defbudget/fy2001/budget
_justification/pdfs/overseas/fy01pb_overseas.pdf⟩.

U.S. Department of the Navy. Office of the Budget. 2001. *Highlights of the Department
of the Navy FY 2002 Budget.* ⟨http://www.globalsecurity.org/military/library/budget/
fy2002/navy/index.html⟩.

U.S. Department of State. Bureau of Near Eastern Affairs. 2005. *Section 2207 Report on Iraq
Relief and Reconstruction: Status of Funds.* July. ⟨http://www.state.gov/p/nea/rls/rpt/
2207/jul2005/html/48779.htm⟩.

U.S. General Accounting Office. 1991. *Southwest Asia: Cost of Protecting U.S. Interests.* Report NSIAD-91-250. August. ⟨http://archive.gao.gov/d19t9/144832.pdf⟩.

Viscusi, W. K., and J. E. Aldy. 2003. The value of statistical life: A critical review of market estimates throughout the world. *Journal of Risk and Uncertainty* 27 (1): 5–76.

Wallsten, S., and K. Kosec. 2005. The economic costs of the war in Iraq. Working Paper
05-19. AEI-Brookings Joint Center for Regulatory Studies.

Weitzman, M. L. 2001. Gamma discounting. *American Economic Review* 91 (1): 260–271.

Welch, M. 2002. The politics of dead children: Have sanctions against Iraq murdered mil-
lions? *ReasonOnline.* ⟨http://www.reason.com/news/show/28346.html⟩.

Zernike, K. 2003. Some of intellectual left's longtime doves taking the role of hawks. *New
York Times,* March 14.

9 Using Household Data to Study the Economic Consequences of Violent Conflict: The Case of Rwanda

Marijke Verpoorten

Violent conflict entails a cost for the parties involved. Human lives are lost, both in combat and because of the hardships of wartime, such as lack of food, drinking water, and medical care. Additional welfare costs may stem from the destruction of physical assets, the disruption of economic activities, the collapse of public services, and increased uncertainty in institutions such as property rights and the rule of law.

Quantifying the war-related costs and identifying their underlying mechanisms can serve three distinct policy goals. First, it allows policymakers to take into account the cost of violent conflict while deciding whether to seize arms or intervene in order to put an end to the conflict. Second, upon the outbreak of a war, a thorough understanding of the mechanisms through which war affects human welfare may help international institutions and aid organizations in designing relief and rescue operations. Finally, well-developed insights into the consequences of violent conflict may lead to better targeting of reconstruction efforts in the postwar years.

However, measuring the welfare cost of violent conflict is cumbersome. For example, there is no uniform way to measure the psychological burden of war. The measurement remains difficult even when focusing only on material welfare losses. For example, although the loss of human lives is countable, it is not a priori clear how to translate these losses into material welfare losses. One option is to use the income that the person who died would have earned if he or she had lived (Lewbel 2003).

At the macroeconomic level, there are some comprehensive indicators that can be used to evaluate the cost of violent conflict. Among these are gross domestic product (GDP) per capita, GDP growth, and the fiscal balance. Several scholars have studied the effect of war on these indicators (Easterly and Levine 1997; Collier 1999). There are often some human development indicators available that may provide insight into the welfare consequences of violent conflict, such as education enrollment, malnutrition, and mortality. The evolution of these indicators in war and postwar years has also been the topic of research (Ichino and Winter-Ebmer 2004; Ghobarah, Huth, and Russet 2003; De Walque 2004; Baez 2008).

Although the study of these aggregate indicators can provide some insights into the extent of war-induced welfare losses, many questions remain. Which households or groups in society face the largest welfare losses? Do households have access to effective strategies to cope with war-related shocks? How fast do the affected households recover from war-related shocks? In order to answer these questions, household data on war-related shocks are needed. The scarcity of this type of data has limited microeconomic research on the consequences of violent conflict to a handful of studies (Deininger 2003; Brück 2004; Bellows and Miguel 2006).

This chapter aims to illustrate the use of household data for the analysis of the economic consequences of violent conflict. The data set used is unique. It was collected in 2002, eight years after the Rwandan genocide, and includes recall information on 258 households for the period 1990–2002. For 188 of these households, panel data are available because they were part of a survey in 1990. The illustration entails three parts. First, I briefly discuss descriptive statistics of self-reported wartime and peacetime shocks at the household level. Second, I study a typical household response to negative income shocks, namely, the depletion of livestock. The main question is whether the use of this coping strategy differs in peacetime and wartime. Third, using the information from the household panel, I analyze the long-term effect of war-related shocks on household material welfare. These three different items are interlinked as follows. Coping strategies serve to smooth consumption upon the occurrence of negative income shocks. When these strategies fail, consumption may drop to dangerously low levels, jeopardizing long-term human capital and welfare outcomes. Even when these strategies succeed, long-term welfare outcomes may be at risk, for example, if the coping strategies included the depletion of productive assets.

The remainder of the chapter is organized as follows. Section 9.1 presents some facts about the Rwandan genocide, and section 9.2 elaborates on the collection of the household data. Section 9.3 gives an overview of the wartime and peacetime shocks that affected the households in the sample, and section 9.4 focuses on household responses to these shocks, in particular one specific coping strategy, the use of cattle as a buffer stock. Section 9.5 studies the long-term effect of war-related shocks by analyzing whether the shocks of the genocide still affected household welfare in 2002.

9.1   The Rwandan Genocide and Its Aftermath

Unrest broke out in Rwanda at the end of 1990, when the RPF (Rwandan Patriotic Front) started launching attacks from Uganda. Intermittent hostilities and negotiations resulted in a power-sharing agreement between the government and the RPF. But on April 6, 1994, the plane carrying President Habyarimana was shot down. Thereafter, Rwanda sank into chaos. Within hours, the military, administrators, the Interahamwe militia,[1] and ordinary people started to kill Tutsi, moderate Hutu, and Hutu leaders from political parties that rivaled the president's party, the MRDN (Mouvement Révolutionnaire pour le Développement Nationale). Simultaneously the war between the Rwandan army and the RPF was restarted. An important fraction of the population took refuge in neighboring countries. Late in June 1994 the killing and the war came to an end.[2]

The balance made up was shocking: an estimated 800,000 Tutsi were killed, or about 70 percent of the total Tutsi population. In addition, tens of thousands of Hutu were killed or died from deprivation in refugee camps, 2 million people were displaced, and more than 100,000 persons suspected of participation in the genocide were imprisoned (Des Forges 1999). Many of these figures, not the least the death toll among Tutsi, remain debated (Des Forges 1999; Prunier 1998; Verpoorten 2005).

Before generalizing the lessons drawn from the study of this conflict situation, some features have to be taken into account. Violent conflicts differ by intensity, spread, duration, and initial vulnerability of the affected population. The longer the period of violence, the more likely it becomes that households liquidate their productive assets or abandon them to take refuge. However, a short war can also have long-lasting effects on household welfare, especially if the violence is intense and widespread, and if households were already vulnerable at the outset of the conflict (Stewart and Fitzgerald 2001).

The genocide in Rwanda was concentrated in a relatively short time period (April 1994–June 1994), but its impact was huge because the ethnic violence was intense and affected all regions in the country. In addition, the Rwandan population was already vulnerable at the outbreak of the genocide, living on the edge of food security.[3] Therefore, any disruption of economic activities could easily push Rwandan households below subsistence. The month in which the violence broke out (April 1994) fell between planting (February/March) and harvesting (June/July). During the genocide, households thus needed to rely on the stocks of the previous harvest (January/February). These stocks were hardly supplemented with emergency food aid because insecurity in Rwanda was so severe that only a handful of relief agencies delivered (sporadic) assistance.[4]

Even when relative peace was established late in June, food insecurity remained high, and many people were still dependent on food aid, among them the 2 million people who were internally displaced or sought exile in neighboring countries, leaving their fields unattended. Apart from the virtual standstill in food production, livestock was decimated, coffee and tea production dropped to unprecedented low levels, the processing infrastructure was rendered nonfunctional, and the forest subsector incurred massive losses.

In the years following the genocide, several regions faced structural socioeconomic problems such as lack of labor (many people were killed, imprisoned, or in refugee camps) and lack of manure (due to the huge losses of livestock). Up to two years after the genocide, 1.7 million Rwandans continued to live in refugee camps outside their country. They returned massively between June 1996 and June 1997, putting a heavy strain on the country's limited food resources (Prunier 1998; FAO 1997).[5]

9.2   The Household Data

In the remainder of this chapter, I work with two different though overlapping data sets. For the analysis of shocks and household responses to these shocks (sections 9.3 and 9.4), I use data on 258 rural Rwandan households. This data set was collected in 2002, eight years after the genocide. Besides detailed socioeconomic information for 2002, it includes recall information on shocks, assets, and household composition for all 11 years within the time span 1991–2001. The sample of 258 households is not random. Since Tutsi represented only a small minority of the population, especially after 1994, it was decided to oversample Tutsi-headed households, lifting their share from below 10 percent to 22.5 percent.

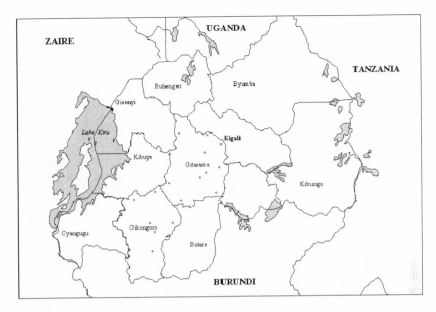

Figure 9.1
Location of the 16 administrative sectors in Gikongoro and Gitarama provinces at the time of the Rwandan genocide, 1994. During the administrative reform of the Rwandan territory in December 2000, the borders of some provinces were modified, and Umutare was added as the twelfth prefecture.

The 258 households are clustered in 16 communes, ten of which are located in Gitarama province and six in Gikongoro province (see figure 9.1). Both in Gitarama and Gikongoro, unrest was very high in 1994. These provinces had a relatively high proportion of Tutsi among their populations, respectively, 9.2 and 12.5 percent, compared to a national average of 8.3 percent.[6] It is estimated that only 20–25 percent of Tutsi in Gikongoro survived the genocide, whereas the survival rate in Gitarama is believed to have been much higher (Des Forges 1999; Verwimp 2003; Verpoorten 2005).

For the analysis of the long-term effect of shocks (section 9.5), I use panel data on 188 households located in Gikongoro and Gitarama, with two waves, one prior to the genocide, in 1990, and one after the genocide, in 2002.[7] The collection of the panel data proceeded in three steps. First, in 1990, the Division of Agricultural Statistics (DSA) of Rwanda's Ministry of Agriculture and Livestock (MINAGRI) included 256 households of Gitarama and Gikongoro in their nationwide random sample of 1,248 farm households. This survey provided information on several socioeconomic topics. Second, in 1999 and 2000, an attempt was made to trace the same households of the 1990 survey (for details on the tracing, see Verwimp 2003). In this second stage, only demographic and criminological data were collected. Third, data on socioeconomic variables were collected in February and March of 2002 as part of a study for the Belgian Department for Development Cooperation (DGOS) under the Policy Research Program. The questions asked in the 2002 survey were comparable to those of the 1990 survey. Additionally, we were interested in finding out what happened to the households between 1990 and 2002. Therefore, we asked for recall information about war-related shocks, other adverse income shocks, household consumption shortfalls, changes in physical capital (land ownership and cattle stock), and changes in household composition for the period 1991–2001.

However, not all the 256 households initially interviewed in 1990 could be located. Of the 256 households, 44 had dropped out by 2002. "Dropped out" means that the household was no longer living in its initial location and could not be found in the same or in neighboring administrative sectors. Of the 212 remaining households, 13 could not be considered the same households because all former household members had been replaced by distant family or even by neighbors. Overall, attrition in the sample amounts to 23.3 percent (57/256), but for Tutsi-headed households it is as high as 45.5 percent (10/22). In addition, for 11 of the remaining 199 households, some crucial information was missing in the 1990 data set. The panel data set I use for the analysis of the long-term effect of shocks has complete data on 188 households that could be identified in both years.

These 188 households are also part of the cross-sectional data on 258 households that I use in sections 9.3 and 9.4. The cross-sectional data set actually stems from the panel data set but is larger because of the inclusion of the 13 households that could not be considered the same as in 1990 and 2002, the inclusion of the 11 households for which there were missing data in 1990, and the inclusion of 46 newly sampled Tutsi-headed households. Table 9.1 presents the ethnic composition of the two data sets used.

9.3 War-Related and Other Adverse Income Shocks at the Household Level

It is well known that rural households in developing countries regularly face adverse income shocks such as illness, drought, crop diseases, insect plagues, and, in some cases, war-related shocks. The data

Table 9.1
Ethnic Composition of Household Data

	Cross-Sectional Data, 2002 (sections 3 and 4)	Panel Data, 1990 and 2002 (section 6)
Hutu-headed households	193	172
Tutsi-headed households	59	12
Twa-headed households	5	4
Unknown	1	–
Total	258	188

Note: These samples are not random. In 2002, Tutsi-headed households were over-sampled. The panel data were subject to attrition and are therefore not representative for the population that suffered from the genocide.

set contains retrospective information on all these types of household-level shocks for the 11 years between 1990 and 2002.

Table 9.2 gives the proportion of households affected by each type of shock within the 11-year period. The results show that approximately 40 percent of the households had crop damage because of political insecurity (mostly because they left their fields unattended). Almost one out of three households lost at least one member to violence, but this proportion amounts to more than 80 percent for the Tutsi-headed households. The Tutsi-headed households in the sample were also more affected by cattle raiding (40.7%) and the destruction of their houses (44.1%) because of violence. Two shocks were more common among the Hutu-headed households: seeking refuge abroad (18.8%) and imprisonment of a household member (13.2%).

Looking at the peacetime shocks, the usual shocks threatening the livelihoods of a farm household prevail: crop shocks due to rainfall (95.0%) and temperature fluctuations (41.9%) as well as insect plagues and crop diseases (46.9%). There is no noteworthy ethnic difference for these shocks. However, we notice a difference for the peacetime shock "natural death of household member," with 47.7 percent of Hutu- and Twa-headed households affected compared to 27.1 percent of Tutsi-headed households. An explanation for this difference could be that the weakest and oldest members of Tutsi-headed households died prematurely under war conditions.

Figure 9.2 gives the evolution over time of the proportion of households suffering from war-related shocks. As expected, the figure shows a peak in 1994. Some households were also affected in the postwar years, mainly because one of their members was still imprisoned or

278 Marijke Verpoorten

Table 9.2
Typology of Reported Shocks, by Ethnic Group, 1991–2001 (Recall Data, Collected 2002)

	Hutu- and Twa- Headed Households (N = 198)	Tutsi- Headed Households (N = 59)	All Households (N = 258)
War-related shocks			
Crop shock due to political insecurity	38.1%	49.2%	40.3%
Violent death of household member(s)	15.2%	84.7%	31.0%
House destroyed by violence	5.6%	44.1%	14.3%
Cattle killed or stolen	15.7%	40.7%	21.3%
Household seeking refuge	18.8%	3.4%	15.1%
Household member imprisoned	13.2%	3.4%	10.9%
Other shocks			
Crop shock: rainfall	93.9%	98.3%	95.0%
Crop shock: insects or diseases	46.7%	47.5%	46.9%
Crop shock: high temperature, frost	40.6%	47.5%	41.9%
Crop shock: animal trampling, theft of crops	12.2%	13.6%	12.4%
Crop shock: labor shortage due to illness	23.9%	22.0%	23.3%
Natural death of household member	47.7%	27.1%	42.6%
House destroyed by heavy rainfall	11.2%	13.6%	11.6%
Cattle lost to disease or natural death	16.2%	27.1%	18.6%

Note: The sample of 258 households is not random. Tutsi-headed households were oversampled.

because they spent several years in a refugee camp. To gain insight into the immediate effect of shocks at the household level, households were asked to indicate on a time line in which years they did not have enough food to eat. Figure 9.2 shows that the proportion of households reporting a food shortage peaks in 1994. As mentioned, this indicates that the adverse income shocks occurring in 1994 were difficult to cope with. In addition, food shortages were rather frequently mentioned in the most recent years under study, which is owing to the retrospective nature of the data.

9.4 Coping Strategies of Rwandan Households during Wartime: Cattle Sales

Despite the prevalence of civil war in many parts of the developing world, little is known about household responses to adverse income

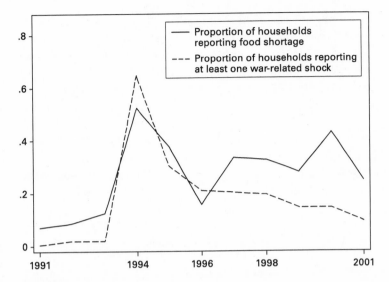

Figure 9.2
Proportion of households reporting war-related shocks and food shortages from 1991 to 2001 (recall data for 258 households, collected in 2002).

shocks stemming from violent conflict. In contrast, household re-sponses to other sources of income shortfall, such as rainfall irregu-larities and illness, have been extensively examined.[8] According to this literature, households have developed several coping strategies for smoothing their consumption in the face of adverse income shocks, such as informal insurance through social networks, temporary migra-tion, and the depletion of assets to purchase food. To a large extent, this literature can be applied to the analysis of household responses in wartime, because political unrest may lead to increased food inse-curity, prompting households to use one or several of their coping strategies.

On the other hand, household strategies in wartime may differ from those in peacetime depending, for example, on the length of the war and the degree of danger created by killing and looting soldiers or rebel groups. This lack of safety often restricts the movement of people and the distribution of food aid, making households dependent on their own coping strategies. In addition, markets as a whole may not function properly during wartime, reducing the effectiveness of market-based household coping strategies. Similarly, the scope for in-formal insurance may be limited because violent conflict often affects whole communities at the same time.

To what extent can households keep up with food consumption during wartime? Which coping strategies fail and which are effective? Answering these questions not only sheds light on the ability of households to cope with crises when aid is absent but also leads to a better understanding of the kind of aid and targeting that are required to allow households to use their own coping strategies, both during and after times of political unrest.

Ideally, all household coping strategies should be studied simultaneously, but because of data limitations, I focus on a single strategy, the use of cattle as a buffer stock. I study whether households used cattle sales to compensate for an income shortfall following political unrest. This section discusses the buffer stock hypothesis for livestock, presents summary statistics on cattle ownership transactions during 1990–2002, and tests for the use of cattle as a buffer stock in both wartime and peacetime.

The Buffer Stock Hypothesis for Livestock
According to the buffer stock hypothesis, households save assets in good times, when income is relatively high, and deplete the accumulated assets in bad times, when income is relatively low (for a formal model see Deaton 1991). Empirical work has confirmed that rural households in developing countries save and deplete in order to smooth consumption over time (Morduch 1992; Paxson 1993; Udry 1995; Deaton 1997). However, there remains much to be said about which assets are saved and depleted for this purpose. In developing countries, financial savings are often an unattractive option because of high inflation and the scarcity of banks in rural areas. Grain stocks are very useful for smoothing consumption over a short time horizon, but the longer the horizon, the higher the storage losses. In contrast, livestock may have a positive return in the form of animal traction, manure, offspring, and milk. Therefore, livestock seems to be an appropriate asset to use as a buffer.

So far, several empirical studies have found evidence for the use of livestock as a buffer in developing countries, either as part of a common strategy to deal with recurrent shocks or in response to unusual stress (Kinsey, Burger, and Gunning 1998; McPeak 2004; Rozensweig and Wolpin 1993). However, an equally large number of studies report contradictory results (Fafchamps, Udry, and Czukas 1998; Lim and Townsend 1998; Udry 1995). These latter studies point to the difficulties of using livestock as a buffer, such as the lumpiness of livestock, its risky return, its terms-of-trade risk, the importance of livestock for agricultural production, and the cost associated with livestock ownership (e.g., the time needed for watering and feeding). For an extensive discussion on the effectiveness of livestock as a buffer stock, see Dercon (2004).

In wartime there may also be difficulties in using livestock for consumption smoothing. First, since a violent conflict often affects whole regions or countries, many households may simultaneously want to sell livestock in exchange for food, driving down the prices of livestock compared to food prices (terms-of-trade risk). In addition, soldiers or rebel groups at roadblocks may restrict the movement of people and livestock and thus livestock sales. On the other hand, if the movement of people is still possible, households may decide to quickly deplete their livestock in anticipation of an increased risk of livestock raiding or the need to take refuge (risky return).

In sum, both in peacetime and wartime, the decision to use livestock as a buffer stock is characterized by a series of trade-offs. Therefore, it is not *a priori* clear whether livestock is among the assets used for buffering by Rwandan rural households. Because of land scarcity in Rwanda, the cost of feeding and watering cattle rapidly increases with herd size. Households in Rwanda may therefore prefer less costly alternatives for insurance, such as informal insurance or temporary off-farm work. In wartime, it is also not *a priori* clear whether Rwandan households used livestock for buffering. Households faced a huge covariant income shock in 1994, and full sails had to be employed to make ends meet. It is not unthinkable that households tried to quickly deplete their cattle stock in exchange for food, certainly because emergency food aid was hardly available, and many alternative coping strategies, such as informal insurance and temporary off-farm work, were undoubtedly under stress. On the other hand, the more households decided to do so, the lower the price of cattle compared to food and the less effective this strategy. Moreover, lack of safety on the roads may have prevented sellers and buyers of cattle from meeting.

Microlevel Evidence: Cattle Ownership, Prices, and Transactions, 1990–2002

Table 9.3 shows information on cattle ownership and cattle transactions over time. The first column gives the proportion of households owning cattle. The mean proportion over the period 1991–2001 is 32.4 percent, with a peak of 38.0 percent in 1993 and a low of 27.5 percent

Table 9.3
Cattle Ownership and Cattle Transactions over Time (Recall Data for 258 Households, Collected 2002)

	Proportion of Households Owning Cattle	Head of Cattle (Total of Sample)						
		Owned	Lost	Sold	Bought	Born	Received	Given
1991	36.4%	267	0	5	8	1	2	3
1992	36.0%	262	17	7	13	11	3	1
1993	38.0%	296	8	15	13	20	2	1
1994	33.3%	257	135	27	8	9	5	2
1995	27.5%	163	22	14	12	6	10	2
1996	27.9%	175	4	15	20	11	6	3
1997	29.1%	184	8	8	16	9	5	3
1998	30.6%	194	8	18	7	9	10	6
1999	31.4%	180	10	27	9	11	5	6
2000	30.6%	181	16	10	18	13	8	8
2001	35.7%	197	10	21	22	19	5	9

in 1995.[9] Cattle ownership is concentrated among the more wealthy households. Probably the lumpiness of cattle combined with low purchasing power prevented many poor households from accumulating cattle.

Column 2 in table 9.3 provides information on the total number of heads of cattle in the sample over time. The subsequent columns show the total number of heads of cattle lost, sold, bought, born, received, and given in each year. According to the data, approximately half of the cattle stock was lost in 1994. During the genocide, looting soldiers, militia, and ordinary civilians killed cattle for immediate consumption or to spread terror. In addition, cattle were also lost because of indirect effects of warfare, namely, the lack of pasture, fodder, and veterinary attention.

The data show some evidence of restocking of cattle in the first couple of years after the genocide. Both in 1996 and 1997 a relatively large number of animals were bought. In addition, the number of cattle received as a gift or transfer was quite high in the postwar years. This stems from the fact that in the sample several Tutsi widows received cattle from IBUKA, a Rwandan association for the survivors of the genocide.

In general, few cattle in the sample were sold, on average 15.2 head per year (7.5 percent of the cattle stock). In 1994, 27 head of cattle were

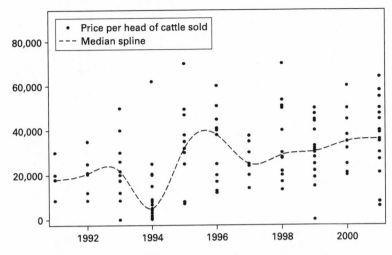

Figure 9.3
Evolution of cattle prices from 1991 to 2001 (recall data for 258 households, collected in 2002).

sold, approximately twice as many as the average number sold in other years. The average price received for a head of cattle during 1991–2001 was almost 30,000 RWF, more than half of the annual expenditure per rural inhabitant for this period.[10] In 1994 the cattle price plummeted to only 11,500 RWF per animal sold. The price observations are set out in figure 9.3. A cubic spline is fit to (the medians of) the observation points. The line plot clearly shows a low in cattle prices in 1994 and a peak shortly after.

Besides the number of cattle sold and the price received, the reasons for selling cattle differ between wartime and peacetime. For each animal sold, households were asked to give the main reason for selling. Table 9.4 shows the results. During 1991–2001, the need to purchase food was the main reason for selling (17.3%). In most cases, the household sold cattle in order to make another investment, be it in physical (23.1%) or human capital (32.7%). For 1994 the picture looks very different: more than eight out of ten animals were sold either because of the need to buy food (44.4%) or because of insecurity (40.7%). By "insecurity" I mean the fear of cattle raiding or the need to seek refuge. For example, one peasant answered that there was no pasture land in the refugee camps, and he was therefore obliged to sell his cattle at a very low price.

Table 9.4
Reported Reasons for Cattle Sales (Recall Data for 258 Households, Collected 2002)

	Number		Percent of Total Sales	
	All Years	1994	All Years	1994
Purchase of food	27	12	17.3%	44.4%
Insecurity	12	11	7.7%	40.7%
Investment in physical capital and farm expenditures			23.1%	3.7%
Construction of house or purchase of bike	20	0		
Purchase of agricultural inputs	16	1		
Investment in human capital and wedding expenses			32.7%	7.4%
Health care fee	26	2		
School fee	17	0		
Wedding expenses	8	0		
Need for cash to pay others			4.5%	0%
Pay wife upon divorce	3	0		
Divide inheritance upon father's death	1	0		
Pay bribe or fine	3	0		
Cattle stock adjustment			14.7%	3.7%
Animal is ill, wild, old, or useless	19	1		
Cannot take care of (more than 1) animal	4	0		

Testing for the Use of Cattle as a Buffer Stock: A Comparison between Peacetime and Wartime

In this section I test whether households sold cattle upon the occurrence of an adverse income shock. To ascertain that these cattle sales were not just reflecting shifts in the household asset portfolio, I repeat the test with cattle sold for the purpose of purchasing food as explanatory variable.

The dependent variable, z_{it}, is a binary variable taking the value 1 when household i sold cattle in year t, and 0 otherwise. The explanatory variable of interest is the shock index, s_{it}, a measure of the shocks faced by household i in year t. This measure was defined in section 9.3.[11] The shock index is interacted with a dummy, d_t, indicating cattle ownership at the start of period t. This yields more precise estimates because only cattle-owning households can sell cattle upon the occurrence of a shock. The model can be formulated in terms of the following underlying latent model:

$$z_{it}^* = s_{it}d_{it}\gamma + x_{it}\beta + \alpha_i + \varepsilon_{it},$$ (9.1)

$$z_{it} = \begin{cases} 1 & \text{if } z_{it}^* > 0, \\ 0 & \text{if } z_{it}^* \leq 0, \end{cases}$$

where z_{it}^* is the latent dependent variable; x_{it} are a series of control variables;[12] α_i are N household-specific unknown parameters; and ε_{it} is the error term.

The parameters α_i in model (9.1) can be treated as random unknown parameters or as fixed unknown parameters. In the first case, the model can be estimated using the random effects probit approach. The crucial assumption behind this approach is that the household-specific effects α_i are independent of s_{it} and x_{it} (Maddala 1987). If this assumption is violated, a fixed effects treatment is more appropriate. Since both the Hausman and the Mundlak tests reject that α_i and s_{it} are orthogonal, I use the fixed effects approach and fit a conditional fixed effects logit model to the data set (Hausman and Taylor 1981; Mundlak 1978). It can be shown that under weak regularity conditions, the conditional maximum likelihood estimator is consistent and asymptotically normal (Maddala 1987). The conditional fixed effects logit model has, however, the disadvantage that the observations of households that do not change status over time drop out. As a result, the hypothesis test is limited to households that sold cattle at least once during the period 1991–2001. This considerably reduces our household-year observations from 2,580 to 830 and to 220, respectively, for the binary dependent variables "cattle sold" and "cattle sold in exchange for food".[13]

Table 9.5 describes all variables used in the regression analysis. Tables 9.6 and 9.7 show the fixed effects logit estimates, respectively, for all cattle sales and cattle sales in exchange for food. I first test the basic hypothesis, whether households sold cattle in a year in which one or more adverse income shocks occurred (column 1 of table 9.6). The estimate for γ is clearly positive and significantly different from zero. Its value (2.20) implies that an increase of the shock index from 0 to 1 results in a 2.20 unit increase in the log of the odds of selling cattle. Put in another way, the odds of selling cattle when the shock index equals 1 is 9.03 (exp(2.20)) greater than when the shock index equals zero. Alternatively, one can compute the marginal effect of a change in the shock index, evaluated at the sample median for the other explanatory variables. Doing so, I find that the probability of a household

Table 9.5
Explanatory Variables Used in Regressions I–VI (Definition and Descriptive Statistics, 1991–2001)

Definition	Description[a]	N = 830 Mean	N = 830 Variance
Shock index (t)	Sum of shocks listed in table 9.1	0.23	0.21
Shock index 1994 (t)	Part of shock index attributable to 1994	0.33[b]	0.24[b]
Shock index other years (t)	Remaining part	0.18[c]	0.20[c]
Highly violent component of shock index 1994 (t)	Part of shock index due to violent death of household member and destruction of house	0.17[b]	0.31[b]
Other components of shock index 1994 (t)	Remaining part	0.47[b]	0.17[b]
Cattle lost to violence (t)	No. of head lost to war or theft	0.06	0.4283489
Cattle lost to other cause (t)	No. of head lost to disease or natural death	0.053012	0.2814478
Cattle born (t)	No. of head born	0.0915663	0.3277311
Cattle received (t)	No. of head received as gift/transfer	0.0445783	0.2065005
Cattle given (t)	No. of head given as gift or transfer	0.0373494	0.1897308
Cattle stock (t − 1)	No. of head owned	1.83494	2.234283
Cattle lost (t − 1)	No. of head lost	0.1120482	0.5087646
Cattle born (t − 1)	No. of head born	0.0783133	0.3026016
Cattle received (t − 1)	No. of head received as gift/transfer	0.0433735	0.2038192
Cattle given (t − 1)	No. of head given as gift/transfer	0.0325301	0.1775102
Land size (t − 1)	Hectares of land owned	1.110951	1.11
Children (t − 1)	No. of individuals < 15 years	2.826506	1.811709
Women (t − 1)	No. of women 15–65 years	1.572289	1.035651
Men (t − 1)	No. of men 15–65 years	1.291566	1.084734
Elders (t − 1)	No. of individuals > 65 years	0.1795181	0.3963826

Notes:
a. All shock indexes are normalized to fit the interval [0,1].
b. Mean and variance, 1994.
c. Mean and variance, 1991–2002 as well as 1994.

Table 9.6
Fixed Effects Logit Estimates of the Determinants of Cattle Sales

Dependent Variable	Cattle Sale (yes $= 1$, no $= 0$)		
	I	II	III
Shock index (t)	2.20 (0.000)		
Shock index 1994 (t)		1.20 (0.223)	
Shock index other years (t)		2.66 (0.000)	2.92 (0.000)
Violent component of shock index 1994 (t)			−0.85 (0.506)
Other components of shock index 1994 (t)			1.69 (0.017)
Chi-squared statistic	137.87 (0.000)	139.84 (0.000)	144.02 (0.000)
No. of observations	830	830	830

Note: p-value in parentheses. Shock variables are interacted with a dummy of cattle ownership at the start of period t; control variables included but not reported are cattle lost to violence (t), cattle lost to other cause (t), cattle born (t), cattle received (t), cattle given (t), cattle stock $(t-1)$, squared cattle stock $(t-1)$, cattle born $(t$ and $t-1)$, cattle received $(t$ and $t-1)$, cattle given $(t$ and $t-1)$, land size $(t-1)$, no. of children $(t-1)$, no. of women $(t-1)$, no. of men $(t-1)$, and no. of elders $(t-1)$.

Table 9.7
Fixed Effects Logit Estimates of the Determinants of Cattle Sales in Exchange for Food

Dependent Variable	Cattle Sale in Exchange for Food (yes $= 1$, no $= 0$)		
	IV	V	VI
Shock index (t)	3.31 (0.052)		
Shock index 1994 (t)		4.73 (0.030)	
Shock index other years (t)		2.56 (0.176)	3.96 (0.056)
Violent component of shock index 1994 (t)			−76.96 (1.000)
Other components of shock index 1994 (t)			4.11 (0.005)
Chi-squared statistic	41.52 (0.000)	42.53 (0.000)	47.42 (0.000)
No. of observations	220	220	220

Note: p-value in parentheses. Shock variables are interacted with a dummy of cattle ownership at the start of period t; control variables included but not reported are cattle lost to violence (t), cattle lost to other cause (t), cattle born (t), cattle received (t), cattle given (t), cattle stock $(t-1)$, squared cattle stock $(t-1)$, cattle born $(t$ and $t-1)$, cattle received $(t$ and $t-1)$, cattle given $(t$ and $t-1)$, land size $(t-1)$, no. of children $(t-1)$, no. of women $(t-1)$, no. of men $(t-1)$, and no. of elders $(t-1)$.

selling cattle increases with 0.55 percentage points for a marginal increase in the shock index. The results in table 9.7, with cattle sales in
exchange for food as the dependent variable, are qualitatively similar,
indicating that we are not merely picking up the effect of shifts in the
household's asset combination upon an adverse income shock.

The main question of interest here is whether buffer stock behavior
differs between wartime and peacetime. To test for this, I decompose
the shock index into shocks that occurred in 1994 and shocks that
occurred in other years. The results of regression II (table 9.6) show
that cattle sales were less responsive to shocks in 1994 than to shocks
in other years. However, the results of regression V (table 9.7) show
the opposite, indicating that in contrast with the peacetime years, in
1994 cattle sales were primarily used to smooth consumption.[14] This
result for 1994 is obtained despite the bad terms of trade (see figure
9.3) and the high risk of cattle raiding (see table 9.3). However, not all
households were equally targeted in the violence. To test whether a
high exposure to violence prevented the war-affected households from
selling cattle, I disaggregated the shock index of 1994 into two components. The first component includes the two most violent shocks
(household members killed and house destroyed), and the second captures all other shocks that occurred in 1994. The results of regressions
III (table 9.6) and VI (table 9.7) indicate that cattle sales were not significantly responsive to the most violent shocks of 1994, whereas other
less violent 1994 shocks did trigger cattle sales. In this respect, it is also
noteworthy that none of the Tutsi-headed households in the sample
sold cattle in response to war-related shocks in 1994.[15]

Summary

The question addressed in this section was whether rural Rwandan
households used cattle sales to smooth consumption in the period
1991–2001. Special attention was devoted to cattle sale behavior in
1994, a year of extreme violence in Rwanda. The empirical analysis
used data on 258 rural Rwandan households. These households faced
multiple adverse income shocks during the period 1991–2001, and
many of them were severely affected by war-related shocks.

The regression analysis showed that upon the occurrence of a covariant adverse income shock, the probability of selling cattle increases.
This probability is stronger in peacetime than in wartime. However,
the peacetime sales are largely motivated by shifts in asset composition. When looking only at cattle sales in exchange for food, the war-

time response is stronger than the peacetime response, indicating that Rwandan rural households used cattle sales as a buffer in response to the unusual and severe covariant shocks of 1994. However, this form of wartime self-insurance is unlikely to have been effective for smoothing consumption because the cattle price was extremely low in 1994 while food prices soared. Moreover, the regression analysis demonstrated that households that were targeted in the violence and most severely hit by war-related shocks did not respond with cattle sales. I argue that the lack of safety on the roads prevented these households from selling cattle.

These results demonstrate that households may react differently to food insecurity stemming from peacetime and from wartime shocks. To improve the design of war and postwar rescue and relief operations, further research on household responses during violent conflict is needed. It is likely that other coping strategies, such as temporary off-farm work, the reorganization of household units, and informal insurance also fail to effectively smooth consumption in wartime. Two policy conclusions emerge. First, there is a great need for food aid during wartime because the households' own coping strategies are likely to be severely constrained. Second, because households may lose or deplete their productive assets in wartime, they are at a risk of becoming extremely vulnerable to postwar shocks. The recapitalization of assets after a conflict is crucial to reestablish coping strategies as well as to ensure economic productivity and diminish the dependence on food aid in postwar societies.

9.5   Long-Term Effects of the Genocide at the Household Level

The less effective household coping strategies are during wartime, the higher will be the household's immediate welfare loss. Moreover, the welfare losses may die out slowly. For example, malnutrition may have a long-lasting negative effect through persistent lower productivity (Behrman 1996), households may need time to make up for losses in physical capital, and rebuilding solid institutions may proceed slowly.

About six years after the genocide, in 2000–2001, a nationwide socioeconomic survey was organized, allowing scholars to compare the prewar with the postwar situation in Rwanda. Rwanda's per capita GDP rebounded much in the postwar period, but Lopez and Wodon (2005) calculate that in 2001 it was 25 to 30 percent lower than it would have been without the genocide. The same authors find a rapid recovery of child mortality and malnutrition in the postwar years and a complete return of primary education enrollment to its pregenocide trend line. The studies of Piron and McKay (2004) and McKay and Loveridge (2005) also suggest considerable recovery in the postwar period, using information on agricultural production, household income, and child malnutrition.

However, despite this postwar recovery, the proportion of people below the poverty line increased, from two out of five in the early 1990s to three out of five in 2001 (Government of Rwanda 2002a). This increase in poverty goes hand-in-hand with a trend of increasing inequality. From two nationwide surveys, it can be calculated that the Gini coefficient of inequality rose from 0.29 in 1984–1986 to 0.45 in 2000–2001 (Government of Rwanda 2002b).

The nationwide 2000–2001 survey did not include questions on the shocks suffered during war and genocide, and therefore it does not allow a study of the effect of these shocks on long-term household welfare. The panel data of 188 households can be used for this purpose. The following sections explain how I measure household material welfare, compare household welfare between 1990 and 2002, and use regression analysis to analyze the longterm welfare effect of the shocks of the war and the genocide. Finally, I elaborate on possible attrition bias in the analysis.

Measuring Material Welfare: Income per Adult Equivalent and an Asset Index

Material welfare can be measured by income or expenditures. Expenditures are the preferred measure of material welfare, but because of lack of data, I used income as a measure of household welfare. To measure income, I used information on five income sources: subsistence agriculture, crop sales, beer brewing, livestock production and off-farm earnings. Gross income was calculated by taking the sum over the monetary values[16] of these different income sources, using data of both seasons A and B for subsistence agriculture and for crop sales, and taking data of season A on an annual basis for the other three income sources. To obtain net income, I subtracted the cost of hiring in casual labor and of the inputs needed for beer brewing. Satisfactory data on other agricultural inputs are missing. However, the net income measured is likely to be a good approximation because farming in Rwanda is still overwhelmingly traditional, relying almost exclusively on manure for fertilizing the soil and on small hand implements (hoes and machetes) for most tasks.

Income may be measured with substantial error, for example, because of the difficulty of accounting correctly for the value of subsistence production. In addition, especially in an agricultural setting, income may vary greatly from year to year. Therefore, I used an alternative proxy for material welfare, the physical assets owned by the household. In general, physical assets are measured with little error and are indicators of the long-run economic status of households. The two most important assets for Rwandan rural household are livestock (cattle, goats, sheep, and pigs) and land. Information on these assets is available for both 1990 and 2002. Principal component analysis was used to assign weights to these different assets. Basically, the data of 1990 and 2002 were pooled, and a linear combination that transforms the five assets into one index was determined (the first principal component). This index accounts for as much of the variability in the five assets as possible.[17] For a discussion and an illustration of this method, see Filmer and Pritchett (2001).

Comparison of Material Welfare and Other Household Characteristics, 1990–2002

As mentioned, studies comparing the Rwandan economic situation in 1990 and 2000 showed that Rwanda's economic welfare reached its pregenocide level by 2001 (McKay and Loveridge 2005; Lopez and Wodon 2005). A similar result is found in the household panel data set. Table 9.8 shows that the average net income per adult equivalent was not significantly different between 1990 and 2002. However, this result has to be taken with care because the sample is small and the income measure is highly susceptible to weather conditions. For example, for one administrative sector in the sample (Kigoma) 1990 was a poor crop year, but the sector profited from an extraordinary banana harvest in 2002.[18] Leaving out this commune, income per adult equivalent decreases from 26,354 RWF in 1990 to 23,256 RWF in 2002. When studying the effect of war-related shocks on income in 2002, I controlled for regional weather conditions. For now, I conclude that in the panel data set there is no indication of a significantly lower or higher income in 2002 than in 1990.

Similar to income, the other measure of material welfare, the ownership of physical assets, does not differ significantly between 1990 and 2002. The average farm size owned per household decreased from 0.96

Table 9.8
Summary Statistics for the 188 Households of Gitarama and Gikongoro Provinces (Panel
Data Set, 1990/2002)

	1990		2002	
	Mean	St. error	Mean	St. error
Material welfare: income				
Annual household net income /ae (RWF, in 2002 prices)	25.855	1486	27.300	2344
Material welfare: assets				
Land size (hectares)	0.960	0.063	0.866	0.073
TLU[a]	0.954	0.099	0.907	0.111
Cattle	0.711	0.089	0.686	0.102
Goats	0.775	0.102	0.793	0.100
Sheep	0.319	0.070	0.181	0.043
Pigs	0.262	0.077	0.234	0.038
Household composition				
Household size	5.410	0.167	4.963	0.172
Adult equivalent[b]	4.822	0.155	4.593	0.165
Dependency ratio[c]	107.0	6.339	127.8	7.685
Female headed (% of households)	17.6%	0.028	42.6%	0.036
Household member imprisoned[d]			7.4%	0.019
Inequality				
Gini of net income /ae	0.39	0.020	0.5	0.026
Gini of land size	0.439	0.018	0.518	0.024
Gini of TLU	0.480	0.022	0.535	0.025

Notes:
a. One TLU (tropical livestock unit) is 175 kg of life mass. Cattle = 1 TLU, pig = 0.25
TLU, sheep = goat = 0.15 TLU.
b. The adult equivalent is based on the calorie needs of household members, depending
on their age and sex. The reference is an adult, aged 20–39 years, engaging in moderate
activities. We took the same values as those used in the IHLCS (Government of Rwanda
2002b).
c. The dependency ratio is calculated as the ratio of dependent over active household
members (*100).
d. By 2002 one-third of household members in the sample, who were imprisoned after the
genocide, had been released.

ha in 1990 to 0.87 ha in 2002, but this decrease was not statistically significant. Moreover, land ownership per adult equivalent remained approximately constant at about 0.22 ha. The total livestock, expressed in TLU (tropical livestock units), was also similar in both years. Looking at the different types of livestock, one notes that there are no significant differences between 1990 and 2000, except for a significant decline in the number of sheep. This information on asset ownership provides again some evidence that in the panel data set material welfare in 2002 was close to its prewar level.

In table 9.8, I also list some information on household composition in 1990 and 2002. This information indicates a considerable increase in the dependency ratio (from 107 to 128) and the proportion of female-headed households (from 18 percent to 43 percent). These increases stem from the large number of male casualties and male prisoners. In 2002 about three out of four households who lost a member to violence or who had a member in prison were female-headed. By 2002, 7 percent of the households included in the sample had a member who was still in prison.

Finally, the Gini coefficient for inequality suggests that the income distribution has become more skewed.[19] Concurrently the inequality of land and livestock ownership increased over the period under consideration. This finding of an increasingly unequal land and income distribution corresponds with the results of several studies (Clay, Kampayana, and Kayitsinga 1997; André and Platteau 1998; Government of Rwanda 2002b).

Shocks as Determinants of Long-Term Material Welfare: Regression Analysis

In this section, I use regression analysis to study the effect of shocks on household material welfare in 2002. The dependent variables are the logarithm of income per adult equivalent in 2002 and the asset index in 2002. The explanatory variables of interest are the war-related shocks (see table 9.2). In addition, I include three indices of non-war-related shocks, corresponding to the time periods 1994–1996, 1997–1999, and 2000–2001, to distinguish between shocks that happened at the time of the genocide, in the aftermath of the genocide, and most recently.[20] I test for time dependence in material welfare by including material welfare in 1990. Additional information on initial conditions, such as household composition in 1990, is also included These may capture household strategies and life cycle factors. Finally, commune dummies control for changes in material welfare at the commune level, including regional weather variability.

Table 9.9 shows the results. The estimated coefficients on the war-related shocks are not significantly different from zero, except for the coefficient on having a household member in prison until 2002. In regression VII this coefficient is estimated to be -0.45, indicating that households of which a member was still in prison in 2002 had an average income approximately 45 percent lower compared to other households. In contrast, households with a member imprisoned in the past but released by 2002 did not have a significantly lower income level in 2002. None of the war-related shocks is found to have a significant effect on the asset index in 2002.

A reason for the income loss of households with a member in prison might be that prisoners become dependent members of the household. From interviews we learned that households bring food and other basic necessities (e.g., soap) to the prisoner on a weekly or twice-daily basis. For the prisoner's household this implies a cost not only in terms of expenditure but also in terms of time, especially when the prison is far from the household's residence.[21]

Because several of the war-related shocks included are correlated, I repeated regressions VII and VIII, entering each of these shocks separately. The results hardly changed, and all qualitative conclusions remained the same. This analysis suggests that by 2002 the households included in the panel data set had recovered from the war-related shocks that did not persist over time, such as the number of members lost to violence and the destruction of a household's house. Whether this result holds for the complete set of households initially interviewed in 1990 is the topic of the following section.

Attrition and Endogeneity

As already stated, of the 256 households initially surveyed in 1990, 57 could not be traced. The attrition was especially high among Tutsi-headed households. The panel data used are therefore not representative for the households that suffered from the shocks of the genocide. They may also not be representative for the households that survived the genocide, if the surviving households that could not be traced differed systematically from the households included in the panel. In addition, the omission of these households may cause attrition bias in the analysis of the long-term effects of shocks on material welfare. Such bias occurs if the selection rule is nonignorable, that is, if selection into

Table 9.9
Least-Squares Estimates of the Determinants of Material Welfare, 2002

	Log Income/ae 2002 VII	Asset Index 2002 VIII
Initial conditions (1990)		
Log income/ae	0.044 (0.134)	
Asset index		0.294*** (0.090)
Income/ae rank		
Asset rank		
Household size	0.028 (0.039)	0.108** (0.044)
Dependency ratio	−0.024 (0.079)	−0.037 (0.107)
Age household head	0.005 (0.005)	−0.009 (0.007)
Years of education household head	0.018 (0.034)	0.067 (0.056)
Female-headed household	−0.062 (0.161)	0.135 (0.210)
Land size owned	0.075 (0.112)	
Cattle owned	0.030 (0.065)	
War-related shocks		
Crop shock due to political insecurity	0.260 (0.167)	0.213 (0.214)
No. of household members killed	−0.094 (0.108)	−0.106 (0.123)
House destroyed by violence	−0.018 (0.299)	−0.019 (0.259)
Cattle killed or stolen	−0.059 (0.225)	−0.115 (0.392)
Number of months household took refuge abroad	0.004 (0.004)	−0.004 (0.005)
Household member imprisoned, still in prison in 2002	−0.454** (0.226)	0.059 (0.367)
Household member imprisoned but released by 2002	−0.186 (0.237)	−0.024 (0.599)
Other shocks		
Shocks 1994–1996	0.987 (1.067)	−0.936 (1.140)
Shocks 1997–1999	0.172 (0.528)	−0.021 (0.788)
Shocks 2000–2002	−1.405* (0.788)	−1.053 (1.200)
Constant	8.478*** (1.596)	0.927 (1.080)
Commune dummies	Yes	Yes
R^2	35.3%	28.7%

Note: Standard errors in parentheses. Significant at *** (1%), ** (5%), and * (10%) levels. All inferences are based on Hubert/White standard errors because of heterogeneity with respect to destruction of a household's house, and on a commune dummy.

the sample depends upon the variable of interest (material welfare in 2002), even when allowing the selection probability to depend upon the exogenous variables.

A number of econometric techniques exist to test and control for sample selection bias.[22] I report the results of a two-step estimation of the Tobit II model (Heckman 1979).[23] The results are presented in table 9.10. The first-stage results stem from the probit maximum likelihood estimation of the selection equation. The variables included in this equation are the initial conditions in 1990, variables indicating civil strife at the commune level, and ethnicity of the household head in 1990.[24] The results show that the probability of selection is significantly lower for Tutsi-headed households, households with a relatively old head, and households living in a commune that was characterized by a high proportion of Hutu perpetrators of the genocide. The selection probability increases with income per adult equivalent and household size in 1990.

The second-stage results are approximately the same as for the least-squares estimation. The inverted Mill's ratio (or Heckman's lambda) is not significantly different from zero.[25] According to these results, the hypothesis of no sample selection bias in the least-squares estimations IX and X cannot be rejected. However, we cannot claim to have dealt with attrition in a completely satisfactory way because the presence of nonrandom selection induces a fundamental identification problem. The validity of the Heckman model depends on the (nontestable) exclusion restrictions and on the assumptions of the structural form of the selection equation.

Besides attrition, another caveat for the panel data set concerns the breakup of households. Household members might leave the households between the two survey rounds. Examples are individuals migrating to the city, members leaving for marriage, and in the case of conflict, refugees. Nonrandom household division might cause similar bias as attrition. For an extensive discussion and illustration of nonrandom household division, refer to Foster and Rosenzweig (2002) and Rosenzweig (2003). One way to prevent problems arising from attrition and nonrandom household division is to trace as many households and individuals as possible during the field and survey work. A second-best option consists in gathering information of the missing households and individuals via neighbors and relatives (Rosenzweig 2003).

Table 9.10
Two-Step Estimation of the Determinants of Material Welfare, 2002 (Tobit II Model)

	Log Income/ae 2002 IX	Asset Index 2002 X
Second Stage		
Initial conditions (1990)		
Log income/ae	−0.012 (0.140)	
Asset index		0.354*** (0.099)
Income/ae rank		
Asset rank		
Household size	−0.001 (0.050)	0.152** (0.062)
Dependency ratio	0.007 (0.083)	−0.094 (0.129)
Age household head	0.009 (0.006)	−0.017* (0.010)
Years of education household head	0.029 (0.031)	0.062 (0.046)
Female-headed household	−0.062 (0.179)	0.123 (0.268)
Land size owned	0.035 (0.107)	
Cattle owned	0.014 (0.065)	
War-related shocks		
Crop shock due to political insecurity	0.306* (0.159)	0.177 (0.230)
No. of household members killed	−0.079 (0.103)	−0.143 (0.151)
House destroyed by violence	0.056 (0.225)	−0.156 (0.322)
Cattle killed or stolen	0.051 (0.237)	−0.208 (0.331)
Number of months household took refuge abroad	0.004 (0.004)	−0.003 (0.005)
Household member imprisoned and still in prison in 2002	−0.444* (0.229)	0.107 (0.327)
Household member imprisoned but released by 2002	−0.027 (0.376)	0.026 (0.501)
Other shocks		
Shocks 1994–1996	0.927 (0.894)	−0.956 (1.282)
Shocks 1997–1999	0.160 (0.479)	−0.032 (0.679)
Shocks 2000–2002	−1.392** (0.670)	−1.079 (0.968)
Constant	9.402*** (1.867)	0.463 (1.270)
Commune dummies	Yes	Yes
First Stage		
Household-level variables		
Log income/ae 1990	0.302* (0.163)	
Asset index 1990		0.127 (0.092)
Income rank 1990		
Asset rank 1990		
Household size 1990	0.126** (0.053)	0.087* (0.047)
Dependency ratio 1990	−0.042 (0.119)	−0.097 (0.114)

Table 9.10
(continued)

	Log Income/ae 2002 IX	Asset Index 2002 X
Age household head 1990	−0.010 (0.007)	−0.013* (0.007)
Education head 1990	−0.020 (0.048)	−0.003 (0.045)
Female-headed 1990	0.089 (0.263)	0.034 (0.256)
Land size owned 1990 (ha)	0.115 (0.174)	
Cattle owned 1990	−0.053 (0.111)	
Tutsi-headed 1990	−0.762** (0.323)	−0.709** (0.319)
Commune level variables		
Tutsi in commune 1990 (%)	0.424 (1.005)	0.072 (0.426)
Tutsi killed 1990 (%)	0.028 (0.429)	4.119 (3.387)
Hutu killed 1990 (%)	4.084 (3.457)	−2.163 (1.021)
Hutu perpetrators 1990 (%)	−2.210** (1.056)	0.262** (0.597)
Persons taken refuge abroad (%)	0.070 (0.627)	1.293 (0.460)
Constant	−2.052 (1.740)	1.293*** (0.460)
Heckman's lambda	−0.648 (0.663)	1.317 (1.128)

Note: Standard errors in parentheses. Significant at *** (1%), ** (5%), and * (10%) levels. The estimated coefficient on Heckman's lambda gives the estimated covariance between the error terms of the first-stage and second-stage equations. Estimating the Tobit II model with maximum likelihood yields similar results.

Finally, the analysis of the effects of war-related shocks is hampered by the possible endogeneity of the occurrence of such shocks. This was also noted by Bellows and Miguel (2006), who argue that the location of war violence may not be randomly assigned. In the framework of this study, it can be argued that some of the war-related shocks included may be endogenous. For example, whether a member is still in prison by 2002 may depend on the welfare position of the household. Relatively wealthy households may have a high social status or be able to pay bribes, increasing the probability of its member's liberation from prison. Furthermore, both perpetrators and victims of the genocide may have had a distinct economic profile. As such, there is suggestive evidence that both the poorest (with nothing to lose and often immediately rewarded upon participation in the killings) and the richest Hutu (close to power, lots to lose in case of a Tutsi victory in the civil war) actively participated in the genocide (Verwimp 2005). Furthermore, envy may have driven assailants to attack households that experienced upward economic mobility before the violence broke out. This is in line with evidence presented by André and Platteau (1998) on the profile of victims of the 1994 events in one cellule (the lowest administrative unit) in northwestern Rwanda.

Instrumental analysis can be used to mitigate endogeneity bias. Doing so, I find that the hypothesis "the coefficient on number of members killed equals zero" is rejected (these results are not reported). This finding suggests the presence of some endogeneity bias in line with what was described: households who experienced upward economic mobility were especially targeted in the violence. An extensive discussion of the instrumental strategy and results can be found in Verpoorten and Berlage (2007).

9.6   Conclusion

So far, few studies have used household (panel) data to study the economic causes and consequences of violent conflict. Furthermore, there exists no empirical analysis of household responses to adverse income shocks during wartime. Nonetheless, the study of household-level data can provide valuable insights about war-related shocks, household responses to these shocks, and their effect on long-term household welfare. Such insights can be useful for informing the decision-making process about starting or ending a war, for the design of relief and rescue operations during a war, and for focusing construction efforts in postwar years.

Using a small household data set for Rwanda, I showed that the war and the genocide had a devastating impact on Rwandan rural households. Evidence was found for the massive killing of Tutsi, for the large-scale destruction of houses and loss of cattle, and for a large number of refugees and prisoners. Besides these direct effects of the war and the genocide, households had to deal with the indirect effects of warfare. For example, because of widespread insecurity, many households left their fields unattended, leading to a standstill in food production. As a result of both direct and indirect effects of the violent conflict, about half the households included in the sample reported food shortages in 1994.

In peacetime, households may mitigate the effect of negative income shocks on consumption using several coping strategies. It was shown that at least one common coping strategy in peacetime, the use of cattle as a buffer, was not an effective response to shocks in 1994. It is very likely that other coping strategies, such as informal insurance and temporary off-farm work, are also constrained in wartime. The failure of household coping strategies during violent conflict may contribute considerably to the immediate negative effect of war-related shocks on household material welfare. If such immediate welfare effects translate into lower human and physical capital, long-term material welfare may be at risk.

With respect to longer-term material welfare, the study of a small panel data set suggests that with the exception of the number of members killed (according to the instrumental variable analysis) and the imprisonment of a household member until 2002 (according to the least-squares estimation), there is no relation between income mobility and the violent shocks linked to the war, the genocide, and their aftermath.

These findings should be qualified because the use of household-level (panel) data is not without problems. The caveats are threefold. First, information on war-related shocks and household responses to these shocks is generally based on recall. Even though severe war-related shocks may not easily slip one's mind, other shocks and household responses to these shocks might be more difficult to recall. For example, thanks to the social and economic importance of cattle in rural Rwanda, recall information for cattle ownership and transactions was easily gathered, but this information would be much more difficult to obtain for small livestock. A second caveat concerns attrition in panel data, which may be especially high in war-torn societies where an important part of the population was killed or took refuge. Therefore, econometric techniques to test and correct for sample selection bias should be employed. However, these techniques are only a partial solution because sample selection poses a fundamental identification problem, and any technique relies on a set of nontestable assumptions. Ideally, when using panel data, as many as possible of households and individuals included in the first wave should be traced in subsequent waves. Finally, the war-related shocks affecting households may not be randomly assigned. Therefore, endogeneity bias cannot be entirely ruled out.

Notes

I'm grateful for comments from Brock Blomberg and other participants at the 2005 CESifo conference. I also benefited from discussions with Romain Houssa, Daniel Ali, Pablo Rovira Kaltwasser, Geert Dhaene, Jo Swinnen, and Lode Berlage. I owe thanks to MINAGRI (Rwandan Ministry of Agriculture and Livestock) and USAID (United States Agency for International Development) for the use of the prewar data set, and to Philip

Verwimp for the tracing of the households in 1999–2000. Field research for the postwar data set was made possible by funding from DGOS (Belgian Directorate General for Development Cooperation) and VLIR (Flemish Interuniversity Council). All errors and opinions expressed remain my own.

1. Interahamwe literally means "those who stand together" or "those who attack together." This militia was formed by Habyarimana's political party in 1992, when the party started giving military training to its youth.

2. For a discussion of the causes of war and genocide in Rwanda, see Mamdani (2001), Prunier (1998), Newbury (1998), Uvin (1998), and Baines (2003).

3. In 1990, Rwanda was among the ten countries with the lowest Human Development Index (UNDP 2005), and about half of its population was living below the national poverty line (Government of Rwanda 2002a).

4. The relief agencies operated from Bujumbura (Burundi) or Bukavu (the Congo) and undertook extremely hazardous missions to provide food and medical care to displaced persons within Rwanda. In general, persons in need were difficult to reach, and the amount of food aid distributed was very limited (Borton et al. 1996).

5. Although returnees were eligible for emergency assistance, including up to six monthly food rations, food prices soared. Between June 1996 and June 1997 prices of pulses tripled, cassava prices doubled, prices of sweet potatoes more than doubled, and sorghum and potato prices increased 45–65 percent. In addition, many returnees found their homesteads, which they had fled in 1994, occupied by those who remained behind or by newcomers who had been in exile until 1994. This sometimes led to land disputes between residents and returnees, which impeded cultivation (FAO 1997).

6. These percentages stem from the 1991 population census. However, the Habyarimana regime is said to have deliberately underreported the number of Tutsi to keep their school and public employment quotas low. Using data from the local administration of Gikongoro, Verpoorten (2005) provides evidence that the proportion of Tutsi in Gikongoro was close to 18 percent, much higher than the 12.5 percent reported in the census.

7. The 1990 survey collected socioeconomic data during season 1989 B (April 1989–September 1989) and season 1990 A (October 1989–March 1990). In 2002 we collected similar data during season 2002 A (October 2001–March 2002) and recall data for season 2001 B (April 2001–September 2001). More details on the collection of the panel data can be found in Verpoorten and Berlage (2004).

8. See, for example, Paxson (1993), Morduch (1992), Rozensweig (1988), Townsend (1994), and Udry (1995).

9. These figures may give the impression that only 30–35 percent of households owned cattle in the period 1991–2001. However, the households that own cattle change over time. Actually, more than half of the households (57.8%) were cattle owners in one or more years of the period studied. For a study on economic mobility in Rwanda, refer to Verpoorten and Berlage (2004).

10. In 2000 the annual expenditure per rural inhabitant (adult equivalent) amounted to 61,433 RWF, and in 1990 it was 8,125 RWF. The inflation for this period was 664% (Government of Rwanda 2002b; McKay and Loveridge 2005).

11. The shock index accords an equal weight to the shocks listed in table 9.1. An alternative way is to construct a weighted index to reflect the shocks' negative impact on

household income. Lacking income data, I set the weights equal to the estimated coefficients of a logistic regression that calculates the probability of a food shortage for household i given the shocks that hit the household in year t. The weighted index gives a high (low) weight to a shock that considerably (only slightly) increases the probability of a consumption shortfall. Qualitatively, the results of the regression analysis are comparable across both measures (these results are not reported but can be obtained from the author on request).

12. Besides buffering motives, cattle stock adjustment may play an important role in livestock sale behavior, so I include the cattle stock in year $t - 1$, its square, and changes in the cattle stock in year $t - 1$ as control variables. For the same reason, I include the heads of cattle born, received, and given in year t. In addition, the number of cattle stolen or killed and the heads of cattle that died from a disease in year t are included. Finally, I control for household land and labor, which determine the costs of cattle herding but may also capture household preferences and the availability of other coping strategies. For example, as an alternative to selling assets in periods of distress, active adults may look for temporary off-farm employment, or the presence of small children may induce households to hold on to cattle for their milk.

13. The observations for 1991 are dropped because of the inclusion of lagged variables. Therefore, the maximum possible number of observations is 2,580 (258 · 10).

14. These results persist even when the shock indices for 1994 and for other years are further decomposed into common and idiosyncratic parts (as in column 2 of table 9.6) or into temporary and persistent parts (as in column 3 of table 9.6). These additional regressions are not reported but can be obtained from the author on request.

15. For the other years between 1991 and 2001, the cattle sale behavior of Hutu- and Tutsi-headed households is not significantly different.

16. Between 1990 and 2002 the general price level rose by a factor of 3 (McKay and Loveridge 2005; Government of Rwanda 2005). Therefore, to obtain income in prices of 2002, the income of 1990 was multiplied by 3.

17. The results of the analysis are similar when using implicit prices to weight the assets or when determining the principal components separately for the samples of 1990 and 2002.

18. During a visit to Kigoma in 2002, our interviewer found many of the inhabitants drunk in daytime. This was not a one-day event; our interviewer complained of night noise during her three-week stay in Kigoma. Drinking banana and sorghum beer is a popular activity in Rwanda, and people were spending their occasional surplus in feasting and drinking.

19. Part of the increased income inequality is due to the outstanding harvest of the Kigoma commune in 2002. If data for Kigoma are omitted, the Gini coefficient of income per adult equivalent increases from 0.39 to only 0.46 instead of to 0.50.

20. The weights for these indices were obtained from a logistic regression of the occurrence of household food shortages in year t on the shocks in year t. The weights correspond to the calculated probability of a shock leading to a household food shortage.

21. When we control for the change in the dependency ratio between 1990 and 2002, the effect of having a member in prison is no longer significant. The same is true when controlling for the change from a male household head in 1990 to a female household head in 2002. These changes in household composition, which are strongly related to the im-

prisonment of a household member, appear to be highly significant determinants of income mobility.

22. For an overview, see Little and Rubin (2002).

23. Maximum likelihood estimation of the model yields similar results.

24. Information on war-related and other adverse income shocks at the household level is missing for the 57 households that dropped out. Instead, some war-related shocks at the commune level are used. These are described in Verwimp (2003). In addition, the ethnicity of the household head may be a good indication of the selection probability because many individuals from Tutsi-headed households were killed (Verwimp 2003). This variable is not significant in the second-stage equation and therefore may be excluded from this stage to facilitate identification.

25. The estimated coefficient on Heckman's lambda gives the estimated covariance between the error terms of the first-stage and the second-stage equations. A negative covariance indicates that there is unobserved heterogeneity that affects material welfare and the probability of selection in the opposite direction.

References

André, C., and J. P. Platteau. 1998. Land relations under unbearable stress: Rwanda caught in the Malthusian trap. *Journal of Economic Behavior and Organization* 34 (1): 1–47.

Baez, J. E. 2008. Civil wars beyond their borders: The human capital and health consequences of hosting refugees. IZA Working Paper 3468. Bonn, Germany: Institute for the Study of Labor.

Baines, E. K. 2003. Body politics and the Rwandan crisis. *Third World Quarterly* 24 (3): 479–493.

Behrman, J. 1996. The impact of health and nutrition on education. *World Bank Research Observer* 11 (1): 23–37.

Bellows, J., and E. Miguel. 2006. War and institutions: New evidence from Sierra Leone. *American Economic Review* 96 (2): 394–399.

Borton, J., E. Brusset, A. Hallam et al. 1996. *The International Response to Conflict and Genocide: Lessons from the Rwanda Experience*. Study 3: *Humanitarian Aid and Effects*. Copenhagen: Steering Committee of the Joint Evaluation of Emergency Assistance to Rwanda.

Brück, T. 2004. Coping strategies in post-war rural Mozambique. HiCN Working Paper 02. Brighton, UK: Households in Conflict Network.

Clay, D. C., T. Kampayana, and J. Kayitsinga. 1997. Inequality and the emergence of nonfarm employment in Rwanda. In *Changing Rural Social Systems: Adaptation and Survival*, ed. N. E. Johnson and C. Wang. East Lansing: Michigan State University Press.

Collier, P. 1999. The economic consequences of civil war. *Oxford Economic Papers* 51: 168–183.

De Walque, D. 2004. The long-term legacy of the Khmer Rouge period in Cambodia. Policy Research Working Paper 3446. Washington, D.C.: World Bank.

Deaton, A. 1991. Saving and liquidity constraints. *Econometrica* 59 (5): 1221–1248.

———. 1997. *The Analysis of Household Surveys: A Microeconometric Approach to Development Policy*. Baltimore: Johns Hopkins University Press.

Deininger, K. 2003. Causes and consequences of civil strife: Microlevel evidence from Uganda. *Oxford Economic Papers* 55: 579–606.

Dercon, S. 2004. *Insurance against Poverty*. New York: Oxford University Press.

Des Forges, A. 1999. *Leave None to Tell the Story: Genocide in Rwanda*. New York: Human Rights Watch.

Easterly, W., and R. Levine. 1997. Africa's growth tragedy: Policies and ethnic divisions. *Quarterly Journal of Economics* 112 (4): 1203–1250.

Fafchamps, M., C. Udry, and K. Czukas. 1998. Drought and savings in West Africa: Are livestock a buffer stock? *Journal of Development Economics* 55: 273–305.

FAO. 1997. Crop and food supply assessment mission to Rwanda. Special Reports and Alerts. July. Rome: United Nations Food and Agriculture Organization.

Filmer, D., and L. Pritchett. 2001. Estimating wealth effects without expenditure data—or tears: An application to educational enrollments in the states of India. *Demography* 38 (1): 115–132.

Foster, A. D., and M. Rosenzweig. 2002. Household division and rural economic growth. *Review of Economic Studies* 69: 869–870.

Ghobarah, H. A., P. Huth, and B. Russet. 2003. Civil wars kill and maim people long after the shooting stops. *American Political Science Review* 97: 189–202.

Government of Rwanda. 2002a. Poverty reduction strategy paper. Kigali: Ministry of Finance and Economic Planning.

———. 2002b. Integrated household living conditions survey, 2000–2001. Kigali: Ministry of Finance and Economic Planning.

———. 2005. Consumer price index. Kigali: Ministry of Finance and Economic Planning.

Hausman, J., and W. Taylor. 1981. Panel data and unobservable individual effects. *Econometrica* 49 (6): 1377–1398.

Heckman, J. 1979. Sample selection bias as a specification error. *Econometrica* 47 (1): 153–161.

Hirano, K., G. Imbens, G. Ridder, and D. Rubin. 2001. Combining panel data sets with attrition and refreshment samples. *Econometrica* 69: 1645–1659.

Ichino, A., and R. Winter-Ebmer. 2004. The long-run educational cost of World War II. *Journal of Labor Economics* 22 (1): 57–86.

Kangasniemi, J. 1998. People and bananas on steep slopes: Agricultural intensification and food security under demographic pressure and environmental degradation in Rwanda. Ph.D. diss., Michigan State University.

Kinsey, B., K. Burger, and J. W. Gunning. 1998. Coping with drought in Zimbabwe: Survey evidence on responses of rural households to risk. *World Development* 26 (1): 89–110.

Lewbel, A. 2003. Calculating compensation in cases of wrongful death. *Journal of Econometrics* 113: 115–128.

Lim, Y., and R. Townsend. 1998. General equilibrium models of financial systems: Theory and measurement in village economies. *Review of Economic Dynamics* 1: 59–118.

Little, R. J. A., and D. B. Rubin. 2002. *Statistical Analysis with Missing Data.* New York: Wiley.

Lopez, H., and Q. Wodon. 2005. The economic impact of armed conflict in Rwanda. *Journal of African Economies* 14 (4): 586–602.

Maddala, G. S. 1987. Limited dependent variable models using panel data. *Journal of Human Resources* 22 (3): 305–338.

Mamdani, M. 2001. *When Victims Become Killers: Colonialism, Nativism, and the Genocide in Rwanda.* Princeton, N.J.: Princeton University Press.

McKay, A., and S. Loveridge. 2005. Exploring the paradox of Rwandan agricultural household income and nutritional outcomes in 1990 and 2000. Working Paper Rw-FSRP-RR-14. Department of Agricultural Economics, Michigan State University.

McPeak, J. 2004. Contrasting income shocks with asset shocks: Livestock sales in northern Kenya. *Oxford Economic Papers* 56: 263–284.

Morduch, J. 1992. Risk, production, and saving: Theory and evidence from Indian households. Ph.D. diss., Harvard University.

Mundlak, Y. 1978. On the pooling of time series and cross-section data. *Econometrica* 46 (1): 69–85.

Nevo, A. 2001. Using weights to adjust for sample selection when auxiliary information is available. NBER Technical Working Paper 0275. Cambridge, Mass.: National Bureau of Economic Research.

Newbury, D. 1998. Understanding genocide. *African Studies Review* 41 (1): 73–97.

Paxson, C. H. 1993. Using weather variability to estimate the response of savings to transitory income in Thailand. *Journal of Political Economy* 101 (1): 39–72.

Piron, L. H., and A. McKay. 2004. Aid in difficult environments: Rwanda case study. ODI Background Paper 4. London: Overseas Development Institute.

Prunier, G. 1998. *The Rwanda Crisis: History of a Genocide.* London: Hurst.

Rozensweig, M. R. 1988. Risk, implicit contracts, and the family in rural areas of low-income countries. *Economic Journal* 98: 1148–1170.

———. 2003. Payoffs from panels in low-income countries: Economic development and economic mobility. *American Economic Review* 93: 112–117.

Rosenzweig, M. R., and K. I. Wolpin. 1993. Credit market constraints, consumption smoothing, and the accumulation of durable production assets in low-income countries: Investments in bullocks in India. *Journal of Political Economy* 101 (2): 223–244.

Rubin, D. B. 1976. Inference and missing data. *Biometrika* 63: 581–592.

Stewart, F., and V. Fitzgerald. 2001. *War and Underdevelopment.* Vol. 1: *The Economic and Social Consequences of Conflict.* Oxford: Oxford University Press.

Townsend, R. 1994. Risk and insurance in village India. *Econometrica* 62 (3): 539–591.

Udry, C. 1995. Risk and saving in Northern Nigeria. *American Economic Review* 85 (5): 1287–1300.

UNDP. 2005. *International Cooperation at a Crossroads: Aid, Trade, and Security in an Unequal World*. Human Development Report. New York: United Nations Development Programme.

Uvin, P. 1998. *Aiding Violence: The Development Enterprise in Rwanda*. West Hartford, Conn.: Kumarian Press.

Vella, F. 1998. Estimating models with sample selection bias: A survey. *Journal of Human Resources* 33 (1): 127–172.

Verpoorten, M. 2005. The death toll of the Rwandan genocide: A detailed study for Gikongoro Province. *Population* 60 (4): 331–368.

Verpoorten, M., and L. Berlage. 2004. Genocide and land scarcity: Can Rwandan rural households manage? CSAE Discussion Paper WPS/2004-15. Oxford: Centre for the Study of African Economies.

———. 2007. Economic mobility in rural Rwanda: A study of the effects of war and genocide at the household level. *Journal of African Economies* 16 (3): 1–44.

Verwimp, P. 2003. Development and genocide in Rwanda: A political economy analysis of peasants and power under the Habyarimana regime. Ph.D. diss., Catholic University of Leuven.

———. 2005. An economic profile of peasant perpetrators of genocide: Microlevel evidence from Rwanda. *Journal of Development Economics* 77: 297–323.

Index